P9-CRB-061

Resumes

8th Edition

by Laura DeCarlo

for
dummies®
A Wiley Brand

Resumes For Dummies®, 8th Edition

Published by: **John Wiley & Sons, Inc.**, 111 River Street, Hoboken, NJ 07030-5774, www.wiley.com

Copyright © 2019 by John Wiley & Sons, Inc., Hoboken, New Jersey

Published simultaneously in Canada

For general information on our other products and services, please contact our Customer Care Department within the U.S. at 877-762-2974, outside the U.S. at 317-572-3993, or fax 317-572-4002. For technical support, please visit https://hub.wiley.com/community/support/dummies.

Wiley publishes in a variety of print and electronic formats and by print-on-demand. Some material included with standard print versions of this book may not be included in e-books or in print-on-demand. If this book refers to media such as a CD or DVD that is not included in the version you purchased, you may download this material at http://booksupport.wiley.com. For more information about Wiley products, visit www.wiley.com.

Library of Congress Control Number: 2019930237

ISBN 978-1-119-53928-5 (pbk); ISBN 978-1-119-53931-5 (ebk); ISBN 978-1-119-53929-2 (ebk)

Manufactured in the United States of America

V10010284_051419

Contents at a Glance

Contents at a Glance

Table of Contents

Introduction

Let's be clear — this is not your father's resume! In our think-fast, technology-driven world of 24/7 communication, things change virtually overnight — including resume writing. The eighth edition of *Resumes For Dummies* includes extensive updated information on the newest trends and changes with a one-two punch of creative elements that the tech savvy will excitedly embrace.

Get ready for an innovative ride as I take you through fresh digital ideas — from social networking profiles to resume-capable mobile devices — and new techniques. I present a fresh but still user-friendly approach to making sure your resume stands up out of a virtual stack of applicants and screams, "Read me!"

Much of what worked before in resume writing still applies but is rarely sufficient now. Just as you have to keep up with the changes in your professional field, you have to keep up with changes in presenting yourself in writing, and this book helps you do exactly that. Prepare to embrace the next chapter in personal marketing!

Ready to win that interview for your dream job? Okay, let's getting going to update your resume and find the job you want.

About This Book

Resumes For Dummies, 8th Edition, is the playbook showing you how to write powerful, targeted, and creative resumes. Just as importantly, I show you how to use them with important ideas and strategies in your search for the right job. The first five chapters spotlight the latest resume technology and innovations; the remainder of the book covers timeless resume success factors and includes samples of winning resumes. In this edition, I've upped the game by providing you with the new and the next in creative marketing resumes — *for those who dare.*

I hope you spend some time studying the sample resumes in the book, and maybe even model your own resume on one of the dozens I've included. Please note that all resume samples, except those in the creative resume chapter (Chapter 18), have the word *dates* as a placeholder for actual dates so you can focus your attention on key resume concepts.

You may note that some web addresses break across two lines of text. If you're reading this book in print and want to visit one of these web pages, simply key in the web address exactly as it's noted in the text, pretending as though the line break doesn't exist. If you're reading this as an e-book, you have it easy — just click the web address to be taken directly to the web page.

Foolish Assumptions

I assume you picked up this book for one of the following reasons:

» You've never written a resume and want an expert, yet friendly, hand on your shoulder.

» You've written a resume — it got you where you are today — and you want to do better next time.

» You like where you are today but want more from life than blooming where you're planted. To move to the next level, your experience tells you that it's time for a resume makeover.

» You need a new resume for that great job you heard about but worry that too many competitors will submit virtually the same cookie-cutter document pirated from somewhere. To stop looking like a human copy machine, you want to understand resume writing from the ground up.

» You've heard about sweeping technology-based changes in the way people and jobs find each other. A realist, you know that technology can't be uninvented. You want to be sure your resume is in sync with the latest updates.

» You understand that today, job searches (and resume writing) are all about self-marketing, and you want a competitive edge so you can stand out and compete in a world where resumes can look as glossy and polished as the finest advertising.

I further assume that you're someone who likes information that cuts to the chase, sometimes with a smile. You find all that and more in the following pages.

Icons Used in This Book

For Dummies signature icons are the little round pictures you see in the margins of the book. I use them to guide your attention to key bits of information. Here's a list of the icons and what they mean.

REMEMBER

Some points in these pages are so useful that I hope you keep them in mind as you read. I make a big deal out of these ideas with this icon.

TIP

Advice and information that can spark a difference in the outcome of your resume-led job search are flagged with this icon.

WARNING

You don't want to go wrong when presenting yourself and your achievements on paper. This icon signals that trouble may be ahead if you don't make a good decision.

Beyond the Book

In addition to all the great info you can find in the book you're reading right now, this product also comes with some access-anywhere goodies on the web. Check out the cheat sheet at www.dummies.com/cheatsheet/resumes for details on how to make your resume the best it can be, how to protect your personal information, and what to leave off of your resume.

Where to Go from Here

Most *For Dummies* books are set up so you can flip to the section of the book that meets your present needs. You can do that in this book, too. I tell you where to find the information you might need when I refer to a concept, and I define terms as they arise to enable you to feel at home no matter where you open the book.

But this book breaks new ground in resume creation and distribution. To get ahead and stay ahead, start by reading Chapters 1 through 5. In this era of tweeting and texting, they help you say hello to new ideas that offer more reach for your time investment.

1

Getting Started with Resumes

Find out why resumes remain relevant and get an overview of how technology plays a role in your job search.

Mine the wide world of social media for job leads, networking opportunities, and self-marketing.

Discover the ins and outs of using smartphones and tablets in your job search.

Check out how employers gather information from your resume and see how formatting can affect this process.

Understand why it's so important to be aware of your online reputation and know how to keep it in top-notch condition.

Recognize when you have to go the extra mile to network your way to job opportunities.

Chapter **1**

Getting a Job in the Digital Age

Are resumes outdated? Every few years an employment expert excitedly announces a so-called new discovery: Resumes are old hat and unnecessary. The expert advises job seekers to forgo resumes and talk their way into an interview. This advice rarely works in real life. Very few people are eloquent enough to carry the entire weight of an employment marketing presentation without a resume. Plus, employers expect some type of resume as a form of researchable and documentable proof.

One resume strategy depends not on verbal talent but on technology. In some situations, recruiting professionals encourage employers who've grown weary of hiking over mountains of resumes to decide who gets offered a job interview to replace them with rigid application forms on the web — complete with screening questions and tests.

Another scenario — also technology dependent — reflects the view that online profiles on social networking sites are pinch-hitting for resumes as self-marketing documents. As I point out in Chapter 2, online profiles are equivalent to generic resumes. Because prospective employers are likely to hunt down your LinkedIn profile, the ideal strategy is to make it as targeted as possible to your current job target.

Most recently, recruiters and employers are adopting artificial intelligence (AI) systems such as Mya and HigherVue to perform resume and interview screening. This development is yet another reason for having a strong and effective resume.

This book combines the details of creating a marvelous resume with various technological delivery options. In this chapter, you preview what's ahead in this comprehensive guide to resumes and how to use resumes and other career-marketing communications to reach your goal in the great job chase.

Resumes Are Here to Stay

At some point in a hunt for better employment, everyone needs effective career-marketing communications. That is, everyone needs a resume — or something very much like a resume — that tells the employer why

>> You're an excellent match for a specific job

>> The value you bring matters

>> Your skills are essential to the bottom line

>> You're worth the money you hope to earn

>> You're qualified to solve the employer's problems

>> Your accomplishment claims can be believed (and verified)

Resumes that deliver on these decision points remain at the heart of the job search ecosystem.

Keeping Up with Resume Times

The ongoing need for terrific resumes doesn't mean the job chase is frozen in time. Far from it. In this digital age — when 66 percent of young people (ages 18–24) are checking their social media updates when they first wake up, even before they go to the bathroom or brush their teeth — every job seeker needs to embrace the entire package of tools and strategies for getting a new job. The package contains new and traditional components:

>> Digital tools that are rapidly altering the nature of how jobs are found and filled in America and across the globe

>> Timeless know-how and savvy developed by the best employment giants over decades

TIP

Don't think the digital age is just for the young. In fact, the number of people in the 55- to 64-year-old age bracket using social media has grown by 79 percent in the past few years with sites such as Twitter. Further, the 45–54 age group is currently the fastest growing demographic user of sites such as Facebook.

REMEMBER

New technological ideas enhanced with historically proven smarts are a winning combination. Technology changes in a decade; human nature doesn't.

Reset your concept of what you must know about resumes in the job chase. Writing great resumes is no longer enough. You must know how to distribute those resumes to people who can hire you or at least move you along in the process.

Targeted resume rules

Job seekers, brace yourselves: Navigating the job market is getting ever trickier and requires considerably more effort than the last time you baited your resume hook — even a short five years ago. The *generic resume*, which I refer to as a *core resume* throughout this book, is at the top of the list of job search tools on the way out. (Read all about it in Chapter 8.)

WARNING

You probably have an all-purpose resume lying around in a desk drawer somewhere. What legions of job seekers everywhere like about the all-purpose resume is that it casts a wide net to snag the attention of many employers — and it saves time for those of us who are too busy getting through the day to keep writing different resumes for different jobs. I appreciate that. But your one-size-fits-all work of art is obsolete, and it's getting lost in more and more recruiting black holes.

The core resume has been replaced by the *targeted resume* (which I refer to in this book as OnTarget), a customized resume tailor-made for a specific employment opportunity.

REMEMBER

An *OnTarget resume* is a valuable marketing tool to convince the reader your work can benefit a specific employer and that you should make the cut of candidates invited in for a closer look. An OnTarget resume

>> Addresses a given opportunity, showing clearly how your qualifications are a close match to a job's requirements

>> Uses powerful words to persuade and clean design to attract interest

>> Plays up strengths and downplays any factor that undermines your bid for an interview

Unfit resumes are zapped

The word got out, slowly at first. And then — *whoosh!* — millions of job seekers found out how easy it was to instantly put an online resume in the hands of employers across town as well as across the country.

Post and pray became the job seeker's mantra as everyone figured out how to manipulate online resumes and upload them into the online world with the click of a mouse.

Resume overload began in the first phase of the World Wide Web, a time frame of about 1994 to 2005. It became exponentially larger and more frustrating as commercial resume–blasting services appeared on the scene. Almost overnight, it seemed, anyone willing to pay the price could splatter resume confetti everywhere an online address could be found.

The consequences of resume spamming for employers were staggering: Despite their use of the era's best recruiting selection software (and now use of AI), employers were overrun with unsolicited, disorganized generic resumes containing everything but the kitchen sink.

And what about the job seekers who sent all those generic, unstructured resumes? They were left to wonder in disappointment why they never heard a peep from the recipient employer.

The answer's in the numbers: A job advertised online by a major company creates a feeding frenzy of many thousands of resumes. Employment databases are hammered with such mismatches as sales clerks and sports trainers applying for jobs as scientists and senior managers, and vice versa.

WARNING

Even when you use your OnTarget resume to apply to opportunities you find posted online, don't hold your breath. Popular job boards can have as many as 40,000 new resumes uploaded every day. With that kind of volume, an employer finding your resume among all the applicants for a job is like someone finding a needle in a haystack.

Tried-and-true techniques remain

A resume that doesn't show off the great goods you're selling isn't worth much. Show off your assets in effective style by making sure you follow the suggestions in this book. I show you how to

>> **Choose the resume format that fits your goals and situation.** What goes where in a resume isn't a one-size-fits-all consideration. Chapter 6 tells you about formatting your resume and provides outlines for popular resume designs.

>> **Get your points across in powerful language.** Make your strengths stronger by describing results in vibrant language that stands tall. I give you examples in Chapter 10.

>> **Use design techniques effectively.** Big chunks of text cause eye strain (and boredom). Present your information in a way that enables readers instead of inhibiting them. Chapter 11 shows you how.

>> **Overcome hurdles.** Getting attention from potential employers is harder in certain situations. Chapter 14 gives you suggestions for easing your transition into a new phase of life by overcoming challenges in your background.

>> **Exercise your creative muscle and think outside the box with unique formatting options for a marketing-savvy, standout resume.** Chapter 12 walks you through steps on how to leverage these new layout techniques.

TIP

See your resume as a reverse funnel that pulls the prospective employer into it (see Figure 1-1). Your resume starts narrow to match the job you're targeting. Next, it expands with your summary to show how you stand out from the competition (which excites prospective employers and pulls them in further). Then your resume further expands to encompass all the requisite skills you possess to fit the position. Finally, your resume ends with the large base of the funnel showing your relevant employment experience using those skills and producing those results.

Use this easy system to create your resume funnel:

1. **Objective Header Statement:** Begin with the position you are targeting.

2. **Summary of Qualifications:** Add an overview of the strengths that make you a perfect fit for the job.

3. **Keywords/Areas of Expertise:** List the key skills you have for the position.

4. **Professional Experience/Employment History:** Your employment history section provides proof that supports the objective, summary, and keyword sections.

This simple strategy encourages employers to read your entire resume.

RESUME FUNNEL

Objective Header Statement:

Clarifies exact job you are targeting. (Should be specific)

Summary of Qualifications:

Shows how you stand out from the competition, what makes

you unique. (Narrow, unique, and specific to you)

Keywords/Areas of Expertise:

Provides quick checklist that you meet the requirements to do the job.

(Broad and comprehensive)

Professional Experience/Employment History:

Supplies tangible proof through experience, challenges faced, actions taken, and

results attained that back up your summary, keywords, and targeted position.

FIGURE 1-1:
Use the reverse funnel method to write your resume and strategically present yourself and your qualifications.

Technologies Facilitate Job Searching

After the Internet caught job-search fire in the mid-1990s — instantly whisking resumes to and fro — little new technology changed the picture until the social web groundswell burst upon us in the mid-2000s. Now job seekers have the tools to

>> Use social networks to dramatically enlarge personal networks

>> Tap their networks to identify jobs and for recommendations

>> Go directly to hiring authorities

>> Market accomplishments in professional profiles

>> Pinpoint employment targets with position mapping

REMEMBER

Continue to apply for jobs with an OnTarget resume and cover letter. Classic job-search methods still pay off, but they're not enough in an economy where jobs have gone missing.

Work every day on a well-rounded approach that emphasizes face-to-face networking, social networking, web tools, online identity building, and professional associations while still briefly touching on less viable elements such as job boards and print ads.

Social networking scoops jobs

Enormously popular social networking sites and social media are poised to gain even more fans in the employment process. Chapter 2 reports on the state of the industry and suggests how you can "go social."

Expect a never-ending stream of new technical bells and whistles in social media, which you can see in the constantly emerging (and disappearing) features on such biggies as LinkedIn and Facebook.

Tools such as location awareness will help you identify companies with opportunities in your area on Facebook. LinkedIn's Search for Jobs feature and the ability to make contacts with just about anyone also let you identify and nail down opportunities as they are listed.

It's all about the new and the now, which means watching trends. For breaking news about social networking, become acquainted with the following websites:

» **Mashable** (www.mashable.com) is a top guide to social media and a hub for those looking to make sense of the online realm.

» **Social Media Today** (www.socialmediatoday.com/) provides the latest tools, tips, and trends in social media.

Chapter 5 discusses ways to keep your online reputation in good shape for the job search.

Mobile's on the move

Smartphones came on fast. Tablet computers are all the rage. Mobile communication is here to stay. Even when you're not rooted to a desktop computer, you can send and receive emails, network online, and download apps. Chapter 3 examines the latest in mobile job chasing.

WARNING

Despite the move to mobile and Google's penalties for sites that aren't mobile adapted, many companies and job sites are still unable to accept applications from a phone or tablet. When you find yourself clicking an Apply Now link that just won't click, that's your tip that you need to migrate to a desktop to apply.

Quick-change process customizes content

In this employers' market, you need to become 100 times more strategic and savvy in writing OnTarget resumes and getting them to key decision makers. The generic resume has become a nonstarter, and successful seekers are writing customized resumes.

But have no fear: In Chapter 9, I take you through how to turn a one-size-fits-all core resume into OnTarget resumes with ease.

Bios gain new importance as profiles

The short professional bio is making a comeback as a social profile (see Chapter 2). The short bio helps when you want to apply for a job, network, post on a guest blog, and so on. It tells people quickly who you are, what you do, and why they should care.

TIP

Plan on writing a bio in three lengths — a micro bio, a short bio, and a longer bio. A micro bio is a sentence you can use on your Twitter profile (280 characters). A short bio is a paragraph (about 100 words). A long bio can be up to a page.

YourName.com becomes vital

More people are living their lives on the Internet, and episodes of name highjacking are rising. Realization is mushrooming that controlling the exclusive online rights to your own name makes sense, even if you're not a business owner.

You can protect your identity in its purest web form by buying a domain for your name — YourName.com. You can also purchase a URL (web address) for your resume — YourNameresume.com. See Chapters 2 and 5 to find out why owning your name has gained red-alert status in the digital age. Claim your name!

Chapter **2**

Enlisting Social Media

The familiar adage claiming that the secret to landing a good job "is not what you know but who you know" is hereby officially stamped incomplete in this era of online social connectivity. Consider this revised version: The secret to landing a good job is what you know, who you know, who knows you, and who your friends know.

All this knowing is exploding on the web's *social networking sites*, a big part of *social media*. The terms overlap in popular usage and definitions vary widely. Here's my take:

» **Social networking sites** are web venues with huge online databases of information that individuals have uploaded about themselves. They do it to mingle with other people in the site's database — to put themselves "out there." Their autobiographical information is public or semi-public and usually includes a description of who they are (a *profile*) or a short biography (a *bio*) or both.

Many social networkers just want to hang around with each other. Others aim to grow their circle of acquaintances and their influence. Still others are interested in a specific subject (such as dating or business). Social networking sites typically have a personal focus, but a growing number, such as LinkedIn, operate with a professional purpose.

» **Social media** is a set of technologies and channels that enable a virtual community to interact in the same space. Social media includes a wide variety of forums, ranging from social sharing sites, such as YouTube, Instagram, Pinterest, and Flickr, to social networking sites, such as LinkedIn and Facebook.

There's little question that two-way communication on the interactive web is dramatically changing the game for job seekers and recruiters alike. If you're scratching your head about how social networking actually works and are unsure how to use it to find a job and promote your career, you won't want to miss this chapter.

The Sweeping Reach of Social Networking

Reflecting the shape of job search now and job search to come, social networking dominates Internet use. With over two billion users, Facebook alone claims over 70 percent of the world's Internet population as visitors. Bigger than most countries, Facebook has more users than the United States has citizens.

To give you some context, when this book was last updated just three years ago, there were only half a billion Facebook users. The growth rate of social networking is startling: The number of people visiting social media sites keeps rising in all age brackets. Social networking is not a fad but an honest-to-goodness paradigm shift in the way people do business around the globe, including the business of finding employment.

Think about how to harness this power, which offers a double rainbow of job-search help — from direct access to hiring managers and quick identification of potential allies at prospective employers, to easy look-ups on company profiles and obtaining posted endorsements from your network. Just to keep it interesting, different services offer different features. (Similarly, some charge fees, and others are free.)

But, at root, the many benefits of using social networking services for career management and job-hunting fall into two basic categories. In signing on with one or more social networking services, you are

>> **Showing the world how hirable you are.** By filling out profiles and listing your credentials, you advertise your potential or immediate availability on an e-billboard that helps recruiters and employers find you.

>> **Gathering supporters to hold open doors.** When you collect, connect, and network with friendly contacts, you gain a potential source of referrals, get updates on their employers' hiring modes, receive insider fill-ins on company culture, and uncover other useful information.

Eyeing the Big Three of Social Networking Job Searches

Of the countless social networking services available to you, three services top the charts in career-management and job-search potential: LinkedIn, Facebook, and Twitter.

REMEMBER

Because the music plays on but the lyrics keep changing in online networking tools, jump on the website of each social network to obtain the service's latest operating guides and opportunities. Here's a starting peek at each of these industry leaders.

LinkedIn focuses on professionals

Regardless of your profession, LinkedIn (www.linkedin.com) is the big-league social site you want with its 575 million worldwide members. Totally business focused? LinkedIn (LI) is your online chance to put a home run up on the board.

Unsurprisingly, case histories of LinkedIn members using the professional social network to find jobs keep rolling out. Here are the LI experiences of two people:

>> A laid-off engineer landed a promising new post paying more money at a financial services website. This happened shortly after a headhunter found the engineer's job status on LI had been changed from current to past.

>> A radio station marketing manager lost his job and decided to post a forthright status note: "I'm up for grabs, who wants me?" Someone in his network saw it and referred him as a candidate for the position of programs and events manager at a city's chamber of commerce organization. The former radio man cinched the job offer a week later.

REMEMBER

These are simply examples. Most job searches, even using your social media network, require a lot more footwork. But how nice is it to have this encyclopedic-size database at your fingertips showcasing contacts, companies, recruiters, colleagues and even employment positions?

Sampling the LinkedIn benefits buffet

LinkedIn keeps new features coming at a brisk pace while extending its global reach around the world. Already LinkedIn overflows with free ways that job seekers can work the job market scene. The following options are the tip of the iceberg:

>> **Post a profile.** An LI profile contains similar information to your core resume. (See Chapter 6 to find out more about this overall resume format.) You include your work history, education, competencies, and skills. *Open to opportunities* means you're unemployed or about to be, trying to move from part-time to full-time work, or just seeking greener pastures.

>> **Expand your network.** By "working social," you can continue to add voices to your chorus of colleagues, creating a strong source of referrals and endorsements. You want to stand out, but you don't have to stand alone when you need professional helping hands.

>> **Join groups.** Much like participating in traditional professional associations and trade groups, LI groups offer camaraderie according to a particular occupation, career field, or industry. Getting involved in groups also helps to greatly increase your visibility and stand out with recruiters. If no existing group zeroes in on your requirements, start your own.

Each group maintains a job-posting area where recruiting and hiring managers post their openings before word gets out; as a group member, you see all the posted job openings while they're fresh. Each LI member can join up to 100 groups.

>> **Periscope your future.** When you're puzzling over how next to position yourself to reach career goals, LinkedIn Jobs can help. You can use it to identify job opportunity matches and companies of interest. You should also take advantage of powerful LinkedIn tools such as Salary Insights, Open Candidates (recruiter notification), and LinkedIn Learning. To use Open Candidates, sign in to your account and click Jobs. At the top you'll see a section called Next Steps in Your Job Search, where you can select whether or not you're currently applying for jobs.

>> **Allow employers to find you.** It's easy to personalize your profile with a custom URL. Instead of setting up and maintaining your own website, direct viewers to your LI profile with a vanity address that includes your name, like this: www.linkedin.com/in/*FirstLast*.

>> **Use premium search tools.** If you want to rev up your search, choose a LinkedIn premium plan by paying between $30 and $120 a month for benefits like these:

- Top billing for your profile (comparable to a sponsored link on Google's first page)

- The ability to communicate with hiring managers, even those outside your network

- Access to full profiles of hiring decision makers

LinkedIn upshot

If you feel you can devote serious job-search and career-management time to only one social network, make it LinkedIn, the recruiters' favorite. According to a recent social recruiting survey, 95 percent of recruiters use LinkedIn in their recruiting process. (Surveys report 55 percent of recruiting responders use Facebook, and 54 percent use Twitter. See later sections for more on these social sites.)

The orientation time to sharpen your skills on LinkedIn may cost you a few nights out on the town. However, after you get the hang of it, you'll be glad you're linked in with other people who are as willing to help you as you are to help them.

Facebook hands adults important search tools

What's with Facebook? Unlike LinkedIn, Facebook seems like a fun place. But surprisingly, recruiters are told in surveys that this represents the greatest membership worldwide and the greatest social media use of the big three. So while Facebook isn't set up as clearly for job search as LinkedIn, it's worth taking a look.

From preteens to super seniors, the age curve of the world's Facebook users is no longer perceptible. This change in Facebook users has heralded more focus on professional-networking and job-finding opportunities.

Facebook is wonderful for chat, status updates, or wall posts to keep your friends and family wired into your life. The social site is also a convenient way to remind your contacts to keep you in mind if they get wind of a job that could blow in your direction, as indicated by the story of a young woman in the American capital:

> I used Facebook to get my current job, and I couldn't be happier. Last year I posted several status updates about my job. A friend of a friend saw the posts and emailed me about an opportunity at [the federal agency where she worked]. I went in for an interview and three days later (light speed in the federal government), I had a job offer.

Sampling the Facebook benefits buffet

Facebook is a runaway success offering a heavy slice of opportunities to move forward with your plans for the future. Here are a handful of those opportunities:

>> **Network to useful faces.** Many of your colleagues and the professionals in your field are on Facebook. Remember to update your status with your current job situation and what you're looking for. When you're in full job-hunt mode,

keep your network in the loop with regular progress reports — you don't want them to forget to help you.

TIP

The interactive Facebook crowd includes prospective employers (solo operators, recruiters, hiring managers, and human resource specialists). Because Facebook isn't a professional network (like LinkedIn; see the preceding section), contacting employers through FB can help you get noticed because there's less competition from other job seekers.

>> **Look at job listings.** For the best source of job opportunities, use the Groups function or simply search for jobs and companies of interest. Performing a quick FB search of the words *job search* will bring up job opportunities.

>> **Milk groups.** Groups on Facebook are virtually the same as groups on LinkedIn — a place to share breaking news and developments of collective interest. Join up or start groups for a topic, an industry, or an interest. By hanging out with people who care about the same things you do, you can be noticed and in a good spot to hear about unadvertised jobs in the hidden job market as well as advertised jobs you might otherwise overlook.

>> **Cruise relevant pages.** Stay abreast of what's up on Facebook's job-site pages and company pages. When you spot a company you'd like to work for, click that you like its page and get company news that may aid your job search.

>> **Create a web presence.** Even when you don't operate your own website (most people don't), you can be on digital deck with a profile on Facebook. Direct viewers to your profile with a vanity address that reflects your name, like this: www.facebook.com/FirstLast.

Facebook upshot

Facebook has won the hearts of a big slice of users for finding friends, classmates, staying in touch, gossiping, and more. Users age 35 and up find Facebook useful as a communications bonanza for job searching and promoting their personal brands.

Twitter opens quick, slick paths to employers

Free, personal, and highly mobile, Twitter is a web-based message-distribution system for posting messages. Before 2017, the character limit was a concise 140 characters. Twitter increased the character count to 280 but the increase has yet to catch on.

Twitter talk describes your activities for *followers* — people who want to keep track of what you're up to. You can include links to other content in your messages, including a resume you've stashed on the web. A Twitter message is known as a *tweet*; the verb is *to tweet*; the forwarding of other people's tweets is *retweeting*.

Until recently, Twitter was commonly seen as the social site for trivial pursuits — specializing in the "I'm having a veggie sandwich for lunch" kind of thing. But current traffic counts changed that perception, giving Twitter new respect.

Statistics suggest that about 336 million or so visitors worldwide now use Twitter, generating about 500 million tweets a day. A recent study for marketing and advertising firms reveals Twitter's power in spreading messages far and wide: "The majority of Twitter users never post anything . . . but they are definitely reading and clicking."

Twitter offers a stable of techniques to make a successful job search materialize for you, including bumping up your visibility and connecting with employment targets.

One of the techniques — inspiring a friend to tweet for you — is illustrated by the case of a young Chicago woman who told a pal she hoped to find an internship in public relations but was having zero luck. Her friend tweeted a marketing pitch: "Anyone hiring for a PR internship? I know a well-qualified candidate on the hunt." A follower of the tweeter immediately responded with an opportunity. An internship was born at a start-up PR firm in Chicago that, after graduation, morphed into a full-time job.

Direct pitching for yourself on Twitter is another way to go. When a woman was laid off from an Idaho-based computer company, she packed up her desk and on the way out tweeted: "Just been laid off from XYZ computer company." By the time the newly minted employment seeker left the parking lot, she had a job offer from a friend who ran a local web-development company.

Sampling the Twitter benefits buffet

"Short is sweet" describes Twitter's capability to communicate big ideas in a few words, a feature increasingly appreciated by job searchers and those who advise them. Here's a taste of Twitter:

>> **Speed toward jobs.** In a job market where every opening attracts unbelievable numbers of resumes and often closes application within the first 24 to 48 hours, speed counts. Through Twitter, you can get new openings sent to you before most recruiters get them by following the right tweeters.

>> **Get tweets from job boards.** Monster reaches out to job seekers in its database to encourage them to apply on Monster for jobs matching their qualifications. Other job boards that tweet jobs announce the collaboration on their websites.

>> **Follow recruiters and hiring managers.** You can seek out and follow recruiters and get early dibs on breaking job opportunities.

>> **Follow influencers.** Do a quick search for *Twitter job search* on the Internet and you'll quickly come up with a list of the top Twitter accounts to follow for job search help.

>> **Tweet for help.** Here are examples of tweets you can send to kick-start a job search:

- I'm looking for a sales job. Not retail. Here's my resume link. Can anyone push it around?

- I'm trying to get hired in accounting by XYZ Corp. Know anyone inside who could walk my resume to HR or acct. mgr?

- Will you set up meeting, or can I call using your recommendation?

- Have you seen any great job postings for insurance claims adjusters? Pls advise.

- Hey, 300 pals: Who'll rehearse me for big job interview?

>> **Research with hashtags.** A *hashtag* is any word in Twitter immediately preceded by the pound symbol (#), such as #marketing, #healthcare, and #engineering. Twitter corrals all tweets that contain the same hashtag, letting you easily track down a topic.

>> **Create a search.** Use the advanced search functions to search for the jobs you want. After you've tweaked your search to get what you want, tap Follow Search in the top right. You won't get alerts from Twitter, but you can find them through your search bar.

Twitter upshot

Twitter is a great channel for quickly sharing news, asking questions, and connecting. At a basic level, it's simple to use. You can find helpful insider employment news by following the right people. Unlike LinkedIn and Facebook, you need not ask for anyone's acceptance — you just click Follow on a Twitter user's name and you're in the game.

Making Sure Online Profiles Capture Your Best Side

Social networking is an A-team option in today's job market because job seekers want to be where recruiters and hiring managers can find them. But the truth is that online profiles on networking sites can help or harm your job search. I discuss the upside and downside to online profiles in this section, and suggest tips to gain the best of all possible outcomes. (For more on representing yourself professionally online, see Chapter 5.)

Let's hear it for profiles!

In the social networking job world, visibility is the name of the game, and that's why online professional profiles have become favorite self-marketing instruments. Consider the profile's virtues:

>> **Get discovered.** Job finding is a numbers game. The more prudent information you include in your public profile about your marketable qualifications — and the more social networking sites where you post it — the more employers who can find you and the more they learn about you to incite their interest. The more employers who become interested in what you have to offer, the higher the bidding is likely to be for your services.

>> **Advance references.** A public profile equips your networking supporters to recommend you as a candidate when they come across a job you may want.

>> **Broadcast your branding.** By creating a potent online presence that sells your competencies, skills, and talents, you boost your personal brand. Your brand is the buzz about you, what you are known for, your personal reputation — how you are distinguished by accomplishments and characteristics. (For more information about branding, read *Personal Branding For Dummies* by Susan Chritton [Wiley].)

Similar to going to a party and standing in the corner, if you don't use your social profiles, you basically stay invisible. Be active, use the tools, post, update, and share relevant news within your groups and with those whom you are connected.

Sometimes you've done nothing to create a negative online identity for yourself, but someone with your exact name has. Or your name is so common that a search for it brings up pages and pages of results. How can you overcome these negatives and stand out? Consider using your full name instead of just first and last name for all your online profiles. For example, if your name is Fred Smith, use Fred

Lincoln Smith to build your online identity. Then be sure to use that name on resumes, online job applications, and other employment documentation. Problem solved!

Not all profiles should be cheered

Wait. Not so fast. Even the best online profiling moves aren't immune from built-in problems that can leave craters in your search. As you craft a carefully written profile, be aware of potential troublemakers.

A public profile on a social networking site is a kind of generic, or core, one-size-fits-all resume. Because an online profile is static in the presentation of a job seeker's qualifications, you don't change and customize it to match a specific job. (I discuss the vast advantages of customizing resumes in Chapter 9.)

The all-purpose profile works fine when you anticipate staying in the same field or career cluster. A *career cluster* is a grouping of occupations and broad industries based on commonalities, such as medicine, criminal justice, or construction.

But a public online profile can cause you to be passed over by recruiters when you're trying to change careers — when you're an editor who wants to become a chef, for instance. A static public online profile can leave you out of consideration for jobs that your abilities and background qualify you for.

WARNING

Employers perennially rank good communication as a must-have skill in candidates. Nothing shrieks poor communication skills and sloppy work louder than poor grammar and faulty spelling in online profiles. And even though it's popular and fun to use acronyms and abbreviations, remember that the eyes of the world are upon you.

A further risk in posting a public online professional profile is being *pigeonholed* — perceived as being a good fit for only one kind of professional role. When you're pigeonholed, boundaries are put up around you, limiting the directions in which you're free to move.

WARNING

Even after you initially gain an employer's attention, an interested employer can be motivated to turn over many online stones to confirm his or her original judgment. An inappropriate focus or stray fact on a static profile can cause reconsideration of your value — your customized resume says you're a marketing specialist, but your profile emphasizes your hotel management experience. Whoops! Do your best to stay consistent in how you present yourself across mediums.

Great tips for great profiles

Ensure that your social networking profiles produce big rewards and don't spoil your chances of landing the new job you want by following these suggestions:

» **Focus on workplace relevance.** A social networking profile can be much longer than a resume, but a profile is neither a life history nor an employment application. The trick is the right selection of content. Chapter 7 tells you more about the subject matter employers expect to see when reviewing your qualifications for employment.

» **Plan your profile photo.** The way you look can draw viewers to — or away from — you. Aim for including a professional headshot in which you are smiling, professional, well-groomed, and dressed in today's styles.

» **Stay current with profile pages.** Technology changes with the season, and the flow of new products never stops. You can stay current by periodically checking SocialMediaToday (www.socialmediatoday.com).

» **Display your profile widely.** After you've sweated through the crafting of your perfect profile, link it with LinkedIn, Facebook, Twitter, and other social networking sites.

» **Load up on keywords.** After completing your profile (never leave it unfinished or you look like a quitter), review it for a healthy helping of search-engine friendly keywords that describe your qualifications and will help hiring honchos find you, maybe even before they post a job ad.

» **Use the headline box to focus on your expertise instead of your current position.** For example, focus on your most important keywords in a phrase like the following: Marketing Manager with 10 years of branding, advertising, and promotions expertise.

» **Evaluate the bells and whistles offered with the profile.** Are you able to upload presentations you've written or professional video presentation you've made? If so, take advantage of these features to further demonstrate your value.

» **Entice with endorsements.** Include recommendations from former managers, colleagues, customers, and vendors. Shy about asking? Start by offering to write recommendations for them — maybe they'll return the favor.

» **Strike a balance.** If you're vulnerable to the pigeonholing trap — you're changing careers or you qualify for multiple roles — watch what you say in your social networking documents. And take care not to look like a liar by allowing your profile to unmask a history that contradicts the one you present in a customized resume.

Your best strategy: Selectively show the breadth of your capabilities without coming across as a jack-of-all-trades but master of none. Except for small companies, employers prefer to hire a specialist for many of the best jobs. Balancing the appeal of your profile can be tricky, which is why you may want to consult an experienced professional resume writer for help with it. Chapter 21 contains guidelines for choosing writers and career coaches.

TIP

After you make sure your profile looks good, it's time to make it live and visible. But don't stop there. The next step is reaching out to your contacts to connect, seeing what groups they belong to, and joining them when they're a fit for your job search. After you're connected, give endorsements and recommendations (as relevant to the social site). Recipients will be more inclined to do the same for you when you start the process.

Writing Your Social Profile

Trying to write an online profile for your job search but can't seem to come up with anything you think is good enough to post? Debating whether your profile should be compact or comprehensive? Here are some strategies and examples to get you started.

Summary section

Think of the summary section of your online profile as an elevator pitch. Emphasize your unique selling propositions or branding in short paragraphs or bullets or both. The summary is typically limited to 2,000 characters, so be concise and choose your words carefully. I recommend writing the summary section in first person ("I implemented. . .").

Check out these summary section examples.

> **Example 1: Retail Executive – VP/Director, Furniture & Design Industry** (courtesy of Barb Poole, Hire Imaging, LLC)
>
> As an intuitive retail executive with a progressive 10-year rise leading start-up and emerging business units in the modern furniture and design industry, I have amplified sales and bottom-line profits for retail brick-and-mortar, catalog, and online business.
>
> I created order out of chaos and found solutions in uncertain and distressed times, paving the way for business strength and market dominance.

During the past decade, I have influenced and co-piloted a new venture's growth from start-up to IPO, navigating manageable growth from launch, to international retailer, to a publicly traded $725 million business.

Example 2: Patient & Provider Support Professional, Medical Center Specialization
(courtesy of Barb Pool, Hire Imaging, LLC)

Bridging connections through compassionate patient advocacy and professional support for healthcare teams is my expertise.

I've earned a reputation as a calming, welcoming presence for those dealing with scary unknowns. Time and again, I've been praised for facilitating best practices without compromising patients' needs or trust.

In a seven-year career as provider-patient communication link, I have served as information "gatekeeper" and "disseminator" for patients and their families, physicians, nurses, support and partner teams, and the general public.

Chosen for mentorship and leadership roles, including Performance Improvement Council Co-Chair, Interpreter Committee, and the Patient Workflow Committee, I also led the Center's migration from IDX to leading-edge EPIC Cadence technology.

Example 3: Sales & Operations Executive (courtesy of Erin Kennedy, Professional Resume Services)

- Top-producing, forward-thinking leader consistently successful in driving operational profitability in close collaboration with sales and business development.

- Rapidly seizes new opportunities and implements business changes while driving desired results in sales and profits.

- Effective in breaking business needs into detailed tactical plans and processes for maximizing market growth.

- Successful in coaching, mentoring, and building high-performance sales teams to aggressively market and promote products across large market territories.

- Well-versed conceptualizing and implementing best-in-class sales and customer-training programs and strategies to identify and capture new market channels and revenue opportunities.

Example 4: Sales & Marketing Management, National and Regional (courtesy of Darlene Dassy, Dynamic Résumé Solutions)

My background spans a 15-year career encompassing various positions in sales, marketing, and operations management. As a natural leader who consistently meets and exceeds sales targets, I am known for my strong leadership, interpersonal, and creative-thinking skills.

I am passionate about embracing new challenges, championing organizational change, and routinely seeking new ways to restructure systems and implement continuous process improvements. For the last three years, I have been Sales & Marketing Manager (Regional and National) for a $12 million firm where I'm accountable for business and market analysis, media planning, staff training, and strategic development initiatives.

In my current position, I have spearheaded company growth through driving sales from zero base to $250,000 in one year, producing 100 percent of plan in gross sales for fiscal year (2014–2015), remaining in Top 10 (out of 47) in national rankings, and establishing local marketing support while educating the management team on ways to incorporate a sales and marketing mind set.

In my previous nine-year position as Sales & Marketing Director, I directed and designed various marketing campaigns for a $1.3 million company, which led to increased gross sales, reduced COS, and improved market share.

I am recognized as a highly energetic and positive role model who takes calculated risks in order to achieve goals and objectives. My goal is to make a difference by sharing my expertise with a sales team through instilling in them the skills necessary for becoming successful in any sales endeavor!

Specialties section

It's important to view the specialties section of your profile as your keywords or key skills section. For example, for a Director of Operations, this section may look something like:

Example: Core Competencies

- Strategic planning & execution
- Business reengineering
- Continuous process improvement
- Sales growth & management
- Start-ups & turnarounds
- Team leadership & collaboration
- Staff training & development
- Budget accountability
- Project & program management

TIP

If your profile doesn't feature a specialties section, you can include your specialties in your summary section.

Experience section

The experience section of a social profile isn't meant to be a rehash of everything in the resume. The best way to approach each section is as an overview. Think of your top achievements, and consider providing value-added CAR (challenges, actions, and results) stories. You want to keep descriptions brief — typically one or two paragraphs each. Consider these examples.

Example 1: Retail Executive – VP/Director, Furniture & Design Industry (courtesy of Barb Poole, Hire Imaging, LLC)

Vice President, Merchandising – ABC Company: Shaped first private-label program and forged manufacturer relationships, creating niche product line brought to market. Launched an unprecedented four new product categories.

Vice President, New Business Development & Real Estate – ABC Company: Orchestrated and executed development of four regions. Launched first international store in Belgium. Spearheaded a new Contract Sales Strategy Division that pulled in $1.5 million revenue its first quarter.

Vice President, Real Estate & Construction – ABC Company: Headed finance and operations of new store rollouts. Opened 40 stores four months ahead of schedule and 17 percent under budget. Surpassed annual retail unit growth by 39 percent.

Director, Retail Operations – ABC Company: Led development of retail brick-and-mortar rollout strategy, positioning business for a successful IPO. Opened 32 studios throughout the U.S. in three years — six months early and 24 percent under budget.

Example 2: Patient & Provider Support Professional, Medical Center (courtesy of Barb Poole, Hire Imaging, LLC)

Patient Services Coordinator, Medical Scheduling – XYZ Health Company: Handpicked as point-of-contact with patients, providers, and visitors in a specialized chemo treatment unit. Mentored team of 14 through growth of seven to 32 chemo infusion suites. Ranked 98 percent or more in all peer/supervisor reviews, four years consecutively.

Patient Services Assistant, Scheduling – XYZ Health Company: Promoted to full-time role with increased accountability for managing patient, visitor, and provider relationships. Created Excel spreadsheet tracking wait-time studies for 34 monitored patients each quarter (15 benchmark points addressed).

Switchboard Operator/Scheduler – XYZ Health Company: Assumed part-time position answering multiline phone system; assisted patients, outside physicians, and other callers with scheduling, inquiries, and troubleshooting resources.

Example #3 – Sales & Operations Executive (courtesy of Erin Kennedy, Professional Resume Services)

Group Vice President, Western U.S.

1-2-3 Pharma, 2013 to Present

Privately held; Pharmaceuticals industry

Enterprise Impact:

- Created sales analysis tool that systematized all pricing proposals and product-level profitability modeling enterprise-wide, accelerated customer response, and eliminated inconsistency and time/cost of manual process.

- Achieved group sales rate of nearly double the company's growth rate.

- Improved annual operating expense 5 percent.

- Led cultural introduction programs to rebrand business with both internal and external customers.

Vice President of U.S. Pharmacy Operations

A3 Bio Pharma, 2009 to 2012

Public Company; BTX; Medical Devices industry

Enterprise Impact:

- Vital to sale of A3's distribution network of 32 pharmacies by presenting potential buyers with its advantages, including its ability to reach in excess of 65 percent of a $1 billion market, 3 million patient-specific doses annually, low turnover, potential to expand offerings, and skilled leadership and staffing.

- Successfully led inter-company team of more than 45 people and completed 52 separate Skills & Endorsements section projects to transition ownership and operations of radiopharmacy business from A3 to 1-2-3 Pharma.

- Grew sales 5 percent, volume 4 percent, and EBIT $30 million, while reducing expenses 2 percent.

Regional Operations Manager

A3 Bio Pharma, 2007 to 2009

Public Company; BTX; Medical Devices industry

Enterprise Impact:

- Secured multiyear service agreement for key 1,500 hospital network worth $100 million in annual sales by leading the Premier Service Improvement (PSI) initiative, which equipped sales and operations team with the most successful best practices tools from the field and improved customer's perception of our services.

- Rolled out PSI initiative across the network, attaining similar results in service and satisfaction.

- Reduced errors in order taking and delivery 26 percent and order dispensing and processing 92 percent by facilitating the creation, development, and implementation of a "Back to Basics" Standard Operation Procedures program.

- Streamlined customer-related Internal communications, increased business profitability, and enhanced public image by originating Sales/ Operations Alignment Programs.

Fine-tuning your profile

Regardless of what section of your profile you're working on, write it as if you're speaking to a professional employer in the interview. A few key tips follow:

>> Make sure your profile is 100 percent complete with keywords to ensure you rank high in Internet searches.

>> Avoid disclosing any confidential company information about your past employers.

>> Use lively, professional language (for suggestions on how to do this, see Chapter 10).

>> Always use the suggested skills in the Skills & Endorsements section instead of making up your own.

>> Check your profile carefully for errors, even in third-party recommendations.

>> Regularly update your profile to ensure it's accurate at all times.

>> Write your profile in first person.

Putting Your Best Face Forward

A problem with some social networking online profiles is the tendency to share stuff that seems okay when you're speaking to friends but may not be perceived favorably by potential employers. One job seeker wrote that she rides a motorcycle with her husband, which can raise questions about risk taking and health insurance costs. Her revelation would have been positive had she been applying for a job as a stunt double, but, alas, she wants to be a court reporter.

Another job seeker led off his profile with the good news that he is a cancer survivor. Health insurance costs? Reliable attendance? Longevity on the job? Avoid these red flags that can certainly hurt your chances down the road.

Even if you're not the original author, be mindful of sharing what someone else has written or posted. It might seem funny or powerful, but someone else may deem it offensive or rude. Your best bet is to chuckle in private and move on. A simple share on your timeline can indicate your feelings and beliefs to a prospective employer.

TIP

The litmus test for revealing personal data in a professional online profile is the same as that for a resume: Does including this information enhance my perceived qualifications for the type of job I seek? Put yourself in the shoes of the employer before you put it on your profile or write a post.

If you feel you must share personal information on certain kinds of profiles, such as Facebook, make sure you've taken steps to control your privacy regarding who can see what. This step is relatively easy to set up on Facebook and can ensure that only what you want to be seen can be seen or shared. Remember that other users can print data or make a screenshot on mobile devices, so keeping it professional is truly a good policy! Reserve your fun photos and risky statements for your face-to-face communications.

To start appearing like an authority to your target employers and influencers, begin with a few easy steps:

» **Curate content.** Share what you know by seeking out articles, reports, updates, surveys, and trends in your area of expertise and posting them. Produce keywords that match your topic and show where your interests and expertise lie.

» **Share blog posts.** If you're already generating content in a blog on your topic, be sure to repurpose it and share it on social media. Summarize your topic and ask a specific question so you can get participation in comments and discussions.

» **Ask thought-provoking questions.** One of the best ways to get traction and participation on social media is to ask an easy-to-answer question. Make it relevant for the best value-add to your job search.

» **Post powerful tips.** Think about your expertise and break one specific topic down into bites. Then share one bite a day to demonstrate authority and topic knowledge.

Visit Chapter 4 for more strategies on blogging and content curation.

Chapter **3**

Going Mobile

The world is mobilizing (pun intended). Nearly five billion mobile phones are in use across the globe, and 95 percent of people in America are mobile phone subscribers, 77 percent of whom use smartphones. That's a bunch. Tablets aren't far behind with nearly 50 percent of Internet users in the U.S. having one. More than 1.2 billion tablets are in use worldwide. In a nutshell, numbers of mobile devices and their users are heading in one direction — straight up!

This historical mobile effect is obvious in everyday life: When the majority of mobilized people now leave their houses, they pack along these three things: keys, wallet or purse, and a mobile phone or tablet. How different is that from ten years ago?

A sizable and growing proportion of people — including resume-writing job seekers — get their daily information fix via their mobile devices. The mobile job search is quickly claiming star status because more of today's working adults grew up with the Internet and accept technological change. However, if you're uncomfortable with the idea of searching for a job using your smartphone or tablet, don't be. This chapter is here to guide the way.

Earning New Rewards with Mobile Search

Looking for a few reasons to add mobile to your job search mix — or not? This section shares the potential benefits for taking your job search with you wherever you roam:

» You're not tied down waiting to send or receive a resume or job message. You can job search while you're on the bus, waiting for a friend in a restaurant, or sitting in a dentist or doctor's office.

» If you set up job alerts, you can respond quickly to opportunities even when you're out and about. Response time is a big factor in crowded job markets because there are so many people looking for jobs that the recruiter has plenty of candidates to consider within a day or two.

» You can seize unexpected opportunities to market yourself. Suppose you're on a commuter train or a plane, chatting with a seatmate who shows a legitimate interest in your resume. You can instantly display your resume on your mobile device, as well as immediately send it to your seatmate's email address.

» You can invest more effort into your search because you don't have to wait until you're home to use your desktop computer. Mobile search bridges the gap between online and offline.

» Mobile devices are helpful for short-notice interview invitations. Suppose your resume was strong enough to attract a recruiter's interest, and the recruiter phones to ask if you can meet the same day. You say yes, but realize you're short on information about the employer. Pull out your smartphone or tablet to research quickly.

WARNING

Perish the thought of going on a mobile job search using a work phone provided by your employer. Your employer owns what's on it and can check the content at any time. For your personal phone, make sure all security patches are installed to keep your business *your* business. Be sure you have all the new bells and whistles that enhance your mobility.

TIP

Always check to see whether the site you're using for a job search has an app for your smartphone or tablet. An out-of-date app can create problems in your ability to see and apply for new opportunities, so be sure to either have apps update automatically or check regularly for updates.

Knowing When and Where to Stick to Home Computer Searches

In the previous edition of this book, I talked about professions that weren't a good fit for a mobile job search. This no longer holds true because the world has gone into the palm of our hands with the virtual and portable tools that most of us carry.

However, as I mention in Chapter 1, sometimes you can see a job on your mobile device but the Apply button simply won't work. This simply means that the site lacks mobile functionality or doesn't work with your device's browser. Hightailing it to a desktop computer is the only way to apply online.

TIP

When you're using a smartphone to identify job leads but remain uncertain about applying for those jobs mobile-style — or perhaps you just want time to think over your response — choose the half-and-half solution: Email the job link to yourself and use your desktop or laptop computer to apply when you get home. Proceed as you would if you had found the job on your computer instead of on your smartphone.

Powering a Mobile Search

Embarking on any endeavor in which you are a novice carries a certain amount of uncertainty and frustration. To increase your productivity and save you time chasing dead ends, consider the following basic advice.

Choose job search apps wisely

Cheerleaders for employment-related apps explain that they are super-convenient, offer intuitive and user-friendly interfaces, and are plentiful. That's true, but your best bet is researching the apps for your own preferences. Here's a mere snippet of what's available in the apposphere:

>> Many popular job-search web services have created apps that search their own sites, such as Monster (www.monster.com), CareerBuilder (www.careerbuilder.com), Indeed (www.indeed.com), and SimplyHired (www.simplyhired.com).

>> Staffing companies are fielding such creations as Adecco Jobs, produced by employment service Adecco USA.

>> Not to be left behind, employers are joining the app crowd, as illustrated by Hyatt Job Search for Hyatt Hotels.

Most job apps enable you to apply for a job on the spot, but some ask you to email the job's link to yourself. (Check your options on how to respond.)

Beyond personal experimentation, seek referrals from fellow job seekers and media experts. Analysts for *PC Magazine* and website Mashable (https://mashable.com) regularly comment on the quality of specific apps, as well as report what's coming up next in the app business.

Watch type size and font

Readability is the password to your resume. In typefaces, serifs are the small elements at the end of strokes. Typefaces come with or without serifs.

TIP

You can never go wrong when using a clean sans serif text for the resume body, whether using it online or for print. Select sans serif typefaces such as Verdana, Helvetica, and Arial.

Formatting can be a concern as well. If you're sending a resume attached to an email, your formatting should remain intact, but when you're writing an introduction or cover letter on a website, remember that your formatting may go out the window. Keep it simple and direct. This is a good reason to send the opportunity to yourself so you can respond later when you're at your computer.

Empower RSS to send job news

Before you launch a mobile search, download a free Really Simple Syndication (RSS) reader (which I describe in Chapter 4) to your smartphone or tablet. Subscribing to a reader means you get immediate notice of new jobs in your industry or career field.

The free Google suite for mobile phones works on all smartphones and gives you an RSS reader, Gmail access, Google Docs, and more. For additional information, use your mobile phone or tablet to visit www.m.google.com/search. Or just go to the app store to download the Google app.

SEARCH MANAGEMENT SAVES SANITY

Other than road warriors, job seekers using mobile search moves often combine them with home-based search. Imagine frantically hunting for a critical but missing little slip of paper last remembered as being in your pocket, or trying to make sense of a bunch of online tidbits that now appear to be orphans.

Ward off the headache of disorder by managing your job search with JibberJobber, a free service that enables you to track where you've sent resumes and the jobs you've applied for, as well as to record your progress as you pass through the hiring process. You can also keep a nose count of your networking contacts and comment on how they have provided assistance.

JibberJobber remains available online for desktop Internet job search, but use your smartphone to check out its mobile address at www.m.JibberJobber.com.

CEO Jason Alba confirms the free service at entry level is "forever," but moderately priced upgrades are available if you choose.

As long as you are tracking, you can't go wrong. Whether it's paper, computer, app, or online service, make sure you track every activity you take in your job search, from networking contacts and when, what, and how you communicated to jobs applied for and every step of follow-up, interviews, and communication.

TIP

You can sign up for free job alerts offered by job boards and job search engines (using RSS or email), but less may be more. Unless you are selective in choosing to hear about jobs that meet your criteria, you may suffer from too much information. If you find yourself oversubscribed, cancel some of them. Choose the best and lose the rest.

Stay in the running with a rehearsed salary strategy

Using the correct salary strategy is critical when filling out online applications. Being overpriced or underpriced screens you out of consideration for a job that's already been priced in a company's budget — computer software will see to it. But you can have an effective plan for handling online application salary questions.

When including requested salary data, use an option that gives you the most flexibility possible, if the website allows it. You can choose from several options:

» **Do your homework.** Sites such as Payscale (www.payscale.com), Glassdoor (www.glassdoor.com), and Salary (www.salary.com) can tell you what your qualifications are worth. Be sure to factor geographical cost of living into that number.

» **Go with negotiable whenever possible.** You will always face factors you can't know about the job until you have the interview. So, when possible, type *negotiable* or *competitive*.

» **Use a range when you can.** Sometimes you want to be more specific; this is when using a range is best. For instance, if you know this position ranges from $65,000 to $85,000 and this is the range in which you are also seeking, then list that as your range.

» **Shoot for the middle.** When you can only enter a number and not text or a range, use the research you did to shoot for around the 50-70 percent of the salaries you identified. If this number seems low to you, be sure you're targeting the right level of job opportunities for your experience.

Choose your work site with GPS

When you live in the north end of a city and have zero interest in commuting to work in the south end — or when you want to work in a specific geographically desirable area — use a location-finding app equipped with GPS (global positioning system) technology, such as CareerBuilder's free Jobs (www.careerbuilder.com/browse). This tool tracks down jobs in your target area by keywords. Location-finding apps are increasingly available for mobile job search apps.

Score with proven keywords

As with all your employment documents, anything you send via a mobile device needs to be keyword enhanced. When sending your *resume note* (a synopsis or summary with fewer than 500 characters that includes a link to your full-design resume on a web hosting site), be sure that your note is keyword rich for the position. With a limit of 500 characters, your note won't have the space to say much, so what it does say had better be choice, or your note will be deleted as spam.

TIP

When you know the specific keywords that target a job you want, use them. If not, do your homework by looking at job descriptions for your target positions to identify the necessary keywords that represent the qualifications you possess. Chapters 8 and 10 give you the lowdown on effective keywords.

Avoiding Mobile Job Search Mistakes

Experience is the name everyone gives to his or her mistakes, but here are three you can easily sidestep in your mobile job search.

Thinking technology overcomes poor resume quality

No matter how impressive the technology that puts it into a hiring manager's hands, your resume speaks loudly about who you are and what you offer. Expecting anything other than that document to do your talking is a mistake. This caveat applies to all age groups, but has special relevance for seasoned job searchers.

Older workers know they can illustrate they work on today-time, not yesterday-time, by job hunting with the latest technology and techniques. But eye-popping technology won't cover weak resumes that fail to address a job's requirements, lack accomplishments, and are missing other persuasive qualities revealed in these pages.

WARNING

If you fail to create a first-rate, customized resume before you master technology, you'll have wasted your time on a mobile job search. Don't worry. I show you how to create a custom resume in upcoming chapters.

Going on too long when going mobile

Because the screens of smartphones are between 3 and 5 inches, consider sending in plain text a *resume note* (synopsis or summary with fewer than 500 characters) that links to your full-design resume stored on a web hosting site.

The screens of tablets and readers can handle total resumes, but hold the size to one or two pages. Consider using a 12-point font and sending the document as a PDF. Size counts. If the resume reader doesn't have 20-year-old eyes and literally can't read your resume, you're out of luck. Chapter 20 gives you the complete scoop on how to send your resume in which situations.

Looking naive in following up

Because the process of sending resumes through mobile platforms isn't always perfect, if you don't hear a peep back after sending yours, you may wonder whether your resume was lost in the weeds of the mobile web. Should you call the recipient company to ask? Not immediately. Most resume-intake specialists view such calls as flat-out nuisances.

There's a better way to deal with the question of whether your mobile resume arrived at its destination: When you don't receive even a computer-generated acknowledgment within a few days, resend your resume on a desktop or laptop computer to the employer's email address.

Still no response? Okay, call. But make yourself appear more knowledgeable by asking: "Has my resume arrived and has it been routed? To whom? Is there any other information you'd like me to provide?"

Chapter **4**

Leveraging Familiar Search Tools

Although not all web technology tools have held up under the rigors of time and progress, some are still favored job finders in the 21st century. Job boards and company websites, for instance, retain star status in determining where to send your resumes. The handsome full-design resume is another tool that remains on job seekers' hit parade. (Chapter 11 gives you the scoop on resume design.)

Also, if you take me up on creative marketing resume strategies in Chapter 12, you'll need to know how to prepare a more simplified resume. Why? You'll need a version of your resume that can be read by applicant tracking systems (ATS) and other scanning systems used by human resources and recruiters.

REMEMBER

In this chapter, I describe a carousel of familiar job search tools with a broad brush because technology changes rapidly. Technology experts estimate the average lifespan of current technology is about 24 months. Whatever the time frame of change, its warp speed quickly renders many details in a book obsolete. Not only does technology move forward, but companies marketing and using it also come and go.

Whether you're a job seeker with a streak of ambition a mile wide or a person who just wants to go with the flow but keep an escape hatch handy if your job starts to sink, now's the time to bone up on the rudiments of how technology can serve you in the job market. Technology is not going away, so keep reading to get the lowdown on what you need to know.

Plain-Text Resumes Are Still on the Scene

The *plain-text resume* (also known as an ASCII resume) is an online document constructed without formatting in plain-text file format. The main characteristic about this resume is its looks (or lack of same). Figure 4-1 shows a plain-text resume. The creature's so ugly only a computer could love it. But for the foreseeable future, the job market is stuck with plain-text resumes. As Jim Lemke, a human resources executive, says:

> "A plain-text resume is still good to have to use when you need it. Some lower-end applicant tracking systems require that you paste a resume in a text window. A pasted formatted text resume will come out much better than a pasted MS Word resume. A formatted text resume also comes in handy to send to handheld devices."

These days, few companies require that you submit a plain-text resume, but it's still important to have one just in case. Create your resume in your favorite word-processing program, save it, and then convert it to plain text (ASCII) by following these steps:

1. **Open the original document in your word-processing program.**

2. **Choose File ⇨ Save As, and then choose Plain Text (.txt) from the Format drop-down menu.**

3. **Save and close the document.**

4. **Open the document again.**

   Now it's in plain text.

```
┌─────────────────────┐
│ Plain Text Resume   │
└─────────────────────┘

        Della Hutchings
        890 Spruce Ave.
        Las Vegas, NV 22222
        945-804-9999
           E-mail: dellah@aol.com
        Admin Assist, 4 yrs exp, 6 software pgms, time mgt skills

        SUMMARY
        ====================================================================
        Word. WordPerfect. Lotus. Excel. PageMaker. QuickBooks
        Bilingual: Spanish. Time management. Budgeting. Organizational
        skills.

        EMPLOYMENT
        ====================================================================
        University of Upper Carolina                            [dates]
        Church Knoll, NC


        ASSISTANT TO DIRECTOR OF ACADEMIC TECHNOLOGY
        Use and support a wide variety of computer applications
        Work with both Macs and Dell computers
        Communicate with clients in South America
        Apply troubleshooting and problem solving skills
        Maintain complex scheduling for employer, staff, self
        Responsible for dept. budget administration; 100% balanced

        Mothers for Wildlife Inc.                               [dates]
        ADMINISTRATIVE ASSISTANT

        Edited/wrote newsletter
        Organized rallies and letter-writing campaigns
        Maintained mailing lists
        Saved organization $5,000 changing equipment

        EDUCATION
        ====================================================================
        University of Upper Carolina at Chapel Hill, NC         [dates]
        BA with honors in International Studies

        Won Gil award for best honors thesis on Latin America
        GPA in Major: 3.8/4.0

        AFFILIATIONS
        ====================================================================
        Carolina Hispanic Students Association
        Amnesty International
        Concept of Colors (Multicultural modeling group)

        HOBBIES
        ====================================================================
        Like details: Writing and Web design

        AWARDS
        ====================================================================
        On present job: Administrative Assistant of month four times  [dates]
        Recognized for productivity, organization, attention to detail
        and interpersonal skills
```

FIGURE 4-1:
This sample
resume is
included solely
to illustrate the
appearance
of a plain-text
resume. It is
not intended
to convey
strong content.

5. **Alter the margins to 1 inch on the top, left, and bottom, and 2.5 inches on the right.**

6. **Scan through the document looking for odd characters or strange line breaks and fix them.**

   For instance, bullets may have become question marks. You can make them greater than signs (>) or asterisks (*). Also, items you had in columns will need to be made into a paragraph list with commas placed between each item.

7. **After you have cleaned up the file, save it again.**

Not all versions of .txt software (Notepad, TextEdit) have a spell-check feature, so be sure to spell-check *before* you save your resume as an ASCII file.

Because your resume now has ASCII for brains, it won't recognize the formatting commands that your word-processing program uses. Don't use any characters that aren't on your keyboard, such as smart quotes (those tasteful, curly quotation marks that you see in this book) or mathematical symbols. They don't convert correctly.

You know that you're off in the wrong direction if you have to change the preferences setting in your word processor or otherwise go to a lot of trouble to get a certain character to print. Remember that you can use dashes and asterisks (they're on the keyboard), but you can't use bullets (they're *not* on the keyboard). In addition, don't use any fonts you've added to your computer. Keep it simple!

ATTACHMENT ETIQUETTE

Ed Struzik knows what recruiters want. Struzik, former president of BEKS Data Services, Inc. (www.beksdata.com), speaks from the vantage point of years' experience in providing outsourced resume-processing services and consulting to many major companies. Here are a few pitfalls Struzik says to avoid when emailing attachments:

- *Do not* **attach EXE files.** An executable file can contain a virus, and no one will chance having his or her hard drive or network infected.

- *Do not* **attach ZIP files.** Who's to say the ZIP file doesn't contain an infected executable. And besides, can your resume be so large that you have to ZIP it?

- *Do not* **attach password-protected documents.** How would you expect someone or something to open it without the password?

Although you can't use bullets, bold, or underlined text in a plain-text document, you can use standard characters (+, >>, ~, *) at the beginning of a line to draw attention to part of your document. You can also use a series of dashes to separate sections and capital letters to substitute for boldface. When you don't know what else to use to sharpen your ASCII effort, you can always turn to Old Reliable — white space.

Although you'll clean up the formatting when you convert to ASCII, it's still a good idea to be aware of these other common ASCII landmines:

>> **Typeface and fonts:** You can't control the typeface or font size in your ASCII resume. The text appears in the typeface and size set in the recipient's computer. This means that boldface, italics, or different font sizes don't appear in the online plain text version. Use all caps for words that need special emphasis.

>> **Tabs:** Don't use tabs; they get wiped out in the conversion to ASCII. Use your spacebar instead.

>> **Alignment:** Your ASCII resume is automatically left-justified. If you need to indent a line or center a heading, use the spacebar.

>> **Page numbers:** Omit page numbers. You can't be certain where the page breaks will fall, and your name and page number can end up halfway on a page.

When you send your ASCII resume, paste it with a cover note (a very brief cover letter) into the body of your email.

Creating an ATS-Friendly Resume

As technology has grown, so has the capability to read — and understand — text-based resumes. Enter ATS (applicant tracking system), a sophisticated system that does more than just look for keywords in your resume to determine your qualifications. While the keywords are still relevant, ATS looks for the connection of when, where, and how you used that skill. It also has the capability to view fully formatted resumes.

Listing your keywords in a section is not enough. Instead, you need to provide proof of using those skills in the body of your resume.

Robin Schlinger of Robin's Resumes, considered a pioneer resume writer in understanding and translating the needs of ATS-friendly resumes, shares the following tips:

>> If you are not a match for the job, don't try to trick the system. Apply only for jobs for which you are qualified.

>> Be sure to include all relevant information for the target position.

>> Include relevant keywords and phrases found in the job description in your experience description and throughout the resume.

>> Emphasize any technology listed in the job description.

>> Spell out acronyms the first time you use them, and put the acronym in parentheses after the full words.

>> Modify your resume for each job to match what the employer is seeking.

>> Keep formatting simple. Fancy characters, graphics, and tables can negatively affect the readability of your resume.

>> Ensure that your both humans and computers can read your resume.

>> Use your word-processing software (preferably Word) to create your resume.

THE SUBJECT LINE ONLINE

When you're sending an online resume in any form, the subject line of your email can bring you front and center to a recruiter's attention:

- In responding to an advertised job, use the job title. If none is listed, use the reference number.

- When you send an unsolicited resume, write a short sales headline. For example: *Bilingual teacher, soc studies/6 yrs' exp.* Or: *Programmer, experienced, top skills: Java, C++.* Never write just *Bilingual teacher* or *Programmer.* Sell yourself! Keep rewriting until you've crammed as many sales points as possible into your marquee.

If you're emailing a hiring manager (such as the accounting manager), copy the human resources department manager; that saves the hiring manager from having to forward your resume to human resources and is more likely to result in your landing in the company's resume database to be considered for any number of jobs.

TIP

Although you should never use more length than is necessary, ATS resumes can run longer than a standard one- to two-page resume.

In regard to naming your resume sections, Schlinger also recommends using standard recognizable resume section headers, such as those in Figure 4-2. (Visit Chapter 7 for common resume sections.)

This is not the time to be creative! Specific headers to consider include the following:

>> **Contact Information:** At a minimum, include your name (including your preferred nickname), phone number, and email. I recommend also including at least your city and state for geographic job matching.

>> **Summary:** Provide an overview of your top-selling qualifications for the target position, referred to as unique selling propositions.

>> **Professional Experience:** Use formal titles for each position held, including duties and accomplishments with keywords and phrases from the announcement. Repeat keywords and phrases from position to position to score higher and show more experience.

>> **Education:** Type the full name and abbreviation for the degree, major, school name, and school location. Optional information you may want to include are the degree date and GPA. Definitely enter any honors.

>> **Training:** Consider this as an optional section if you have extensive professional training related to your job target.

>> **Certifications:** Make relevant certifications stand out by putting them in a section by themselves.

>> **Skills:** Include related skills or keywords because ATSs factor them in heavily when searching for job matches.

TIP

Schlinger adds, "When you don't have a particular keyword in your background, include the following in your summary":

Capable of learning/performing the following functions: <list the keywords and phrases you do not have in your background>.

FIRST LAST
Address | City, ST Zip | Phone | name@isp.com

Summary
TITLE OF POSITION APPLYING FOR
Modifier 1 | Modifier 2

Enter your profile here – describe your background either in bullet style or using a paragraph. Use keywords.

Skill | Skill | Skill | Skill | Skill
Skill | Skill | Skill | Skill | Skill
Skill | Skill | Skill | Skill | Skill

- **<Accomplished what>** by <describe what was done> through using <list technology>.
- **<Accomplished what>** by <describe what was done> through using <list technology>.
- **<Accomplished what>** by <describe what was done> through using <list technology>.

Capable of doing <keywords not in other parts of the resume>.

PROFESSIONAL EXPERIENCE

Job Title 1, Company 1 Company, City, ST   mm/yyyy – mm/yyyy
Describe company
Type a paragraph or more of job duties, include keywords.
CATEGORY 1
- **<Accomplished what>** by <describe what was done> through using <list technology>.
- **<Accomplished what>** by <describe what was done> through using <list technology>.
- **<Accomplished what>** by <describe what was done> through using <list technology>.
- **<Accomplished what>** by <describe what was done> through using <list technology>.
CATEGORY 2
- **<Accomplished what>** by <describe what was done> through using <list technology>.
- **<Accomplished what>** by <describe what was done> through using <list technology>.
- **<Accomplished what>** by <describe what was done> through using <list technology>.
- **<Accomplished what>** by <describe what was done> through using <list technology>.

Job Title 2, Company 2 Company, City, ST   mm/yyyy – mm/yyyy
Describe company
Type a paragraph or more of job duties, include keywords.
- **<Accomplished what>** by <describe what was done> through using <list technology>.
- **<Accomplished what>** by <describe what was done> through using <list technology>.
- **<Accomplished what>** by <describe what was done> through using <list technology>.
- **<Accomplished what>** by <describe what was done> through using <list technology>.

Job Title 3, Company 3 Company, City, ST   mm/yyyy – mm/yyyy
Describe company
Type a paragraph or more of job duties, include keywords
- **<Accomplished what>** by <describe what was done> through using <list technology>.
- **<Accomplished what>** by <describe what was done> through using <list technology>.
- **<Accomplished what>** by <describe what was done> through using <list technology>.
- **<Accomplished what>** by <describe what was done> through using <list technology>.

Previous experience: **Job Title 4,** Company 4; **Job Title 5,** Company 5

EDUCATION

Degree in Major, University Name, City, ST, mm/yyyy, GPA 3.xx/4.0, Graduation Honors

TRAINING

List training here

CERTIFICATIONS

List certifications here

SKILLS

List skills here

FIGURE 4-2:
This ATS resume template illustrates the basic sections and layout of an ATS resume.

Courtesy of Robin Schlinger of Robin's Resumes

E-Forms: Fill in the Blankety-Blanks

The *e-form* is just a shorter version of the plain-text resume, and you usually find it on company websites if the company doesn't accept full-design resumes. The company encourages you to apply by setting your plain text into designated fields of the forms on the site.

The e-form is almost like an application form, except that it lacks the legal document status an application form acquires when you sign it, certifying that all facts are true.

Follow the on-screen instructions given by each employer to cut and paste the requested information into the site's template. You're basically just filling in the blanks with your contact information, supplemented by data lifted from your plain-text resume.

TIP

Remember that e-forms can't spell-check, so cutting and pasting your resume into the e-form body, instead of typing it in manually, is your best bet. Because you spell-checked your resume before converting it to ASCII (of course, you did!), at least you know that everything is likely to be spelled correctly.

WARNING

E-forms work well for job seekers in high-demand occupations, such as nursing, but they don't work so well for job seekers who need to document motivation, good attitude, and other personal characteristics and accomplishments that computers don't search for. When you rely on an e-form to get an employer's attention, you're playing 100 percent on the employer's turf.

STOP AND ASK DIRECTIONS

You can never be 100 percent sure what technology is being used where you want to send your resume. The solution is to ask — by telephone or by email — the company human resources department or the company receptionist the following questions:

> *I want to be sure I'm using your preferred technology to submit my resume. Can I send it as an attachment, say in MS Word or Adobe PDF? Are you using ATS to screen your resumes?*

Alternatively, if you don't have a clue, you can send your resume in the body of your email as plain text and also attach it as a word-processed document.

Online Screening Guards the Employment Door

Your OnTarget resume may never be read if an employer's online screening program decides in advance that you aren't qualified for the position's stated — or unstated — requirements. In essence, screening software has the first word about who is admitted for a closer look and who isn't.

Online screening is an automated process of creating a blueprint of known requirements for a given job and then collecting information from each applicant in a standardized manner to see whether the applicant matches the blueprint. The outcomes are sent to recruiters and hiring managers.

Online screening is known by various terms — *prescreening* and *pre-employment screening*, to mention two. By any name, the purpose of online screening is to verify that you are, in fact, a good candidate for the position and that you haven't lied about your background. Employers use online screening tools (tests, assessment instruments, questionnaires, and so on) to reduce and sort applicants against criteria and competencies that are important to their organizations.

If you apply online through major job sites or many company website career portals, you may be asked to respond yes or no to job-related questions, such as:

» Do you have the required college degree?

» Do you have experience with (specific job requirement)?

» Are you willing to relocate?

» Do you have two or more years' experience managing a corporate communications department?

» Is your salary requirement between $55,000–$60,000/year?

Answering "no" to any of these kinds of questions disqualifies you for the listed position, an automated decision that helps the recruiters thin the herd of resumes more quickly, but that may be a distinct disadvantage to you, the job searcher. (Without human interaction, you may not show enough of the stated qualifications, but you may have compensatory qualifications that a machine won't allow you to communicate.)

On the other hand, professionals in high-demand categories, such as nursing, benefit by a quick response. Example: *Are you an RN?* If the answer is "yes," the immediate response, according to a recruiter's joke, is "When can you start?"

In the following sections, I go into greater detail about online screening and how it affects your job search.

Sample components of online screening

The following examples of online screening aren't exhaustive, but they are illustrations of the most commonly encountered upfront filtering techniques:

» **Basic evaluation:** Evaluates the match between a resume's content (job seeker's qualifications) and a job's requirement and ranks the most qualified resumes at the top.

» **Skills and knowledge testing:** Uses tests that require applicants to prove their knowledge and skills in a specific area of expertise. Online skills and knowledge testing is especially prevalent in information technology jobs where dealing with given computer programs is basic to job performance. Like the old-time typing tests in an HR office, nothing is subjective about this type of quiz: You know the answers or you don't.

» **Personality assessment:** Attempts to measure work-related personality traits to predict job success are one of the more controversial types of online testing. Dr. Wendell Williams, a leading testing expert based in the Atlanta area, says that personality tests expressly designed for hiring are in a different league than tests designed to measure things such as communication style or personality type.

"Job-related personality testing is highly job specific and tends to change with both task and job," he says. "If you are taking a generic personality test, a good rule is to either pick answers that fall in the middle of the scale or ones you think best fit the job description. This is not deception. Employers rarely conduct studies of personality test scores versus job performance and so it really does not make much difference."

» **Behavioral assessment:** Asks questions aimed at uncovering your past experience applying core competencies the organization requires (such as fostering teamwork, managing change) and position-specific competencies (such as persuasion for sales, attention to detail for accountants). I further describe competencies in Chapter 8.

» **Managerial assessments:** Presents applicants with typical managerial scenarios and asks them to react. Proponents say that managerial assessments are effective for predicting performance on competencies such as interpersonal skills, business acumen, and decision making. Dr. Williams identifies the many forms these assessments can take:

- **In-basket exercises:** The applicant is given an in-basket full of problems and told to solve them.

- **Analysis case studies:** The applicant is asked to read a problem and recommend a solution.

- **Planning case studies:** The applicant is asked to read about a problem and recommend a step-by-step solution.

- **Interaction simulations:** The applicant is asked to work out a problem with a skilled role player.

- **Presentation exercises:** The applicant is asked to prepare, deliver, and defend a presentation.

- **Integrity tests:** The applicant's honesty is measured with a series of questions. You can probably spot the best answers without too much trouble.

Pros and cons of online screening

Here's a snapshot of the advantages and disadvantages of online screening, from the job seeker's perspective:

>> **Advantages:** In theory, a perfect online screening is totally job based and fair to all people with equal skills. Your resume would survive the first cut based only on your ability to do well in the job. You are screened out of consideration for any job you may not be able to do, saving yourself stress and keeping your track record free of false starts.

>> **Disadvantages:** The creation of an online process is vulnerable to human misjudgment; I'm still looking for an example of the perfect online screening system. Moreover, you have no chance to make up for missing competencies or skills. (An analogy: You can read music, but you don't know how to play a specific song. You can learn it quickly, but there's no space to write "quick learner.")

REMEMBER

As I mention in Chapter 1, artificial intelligence (AI) has been brought on the scene to perform screening functions in resumes and in virtual interviews. You likely won't have a clue you aren't interacting with a human, but you'll actually have a better chance of follow-through and responsiveness because AI systems don't have to contend with human limitations such as time, illness, and exhaustion.

Can your resume be turned away?

If you get low grades on the screening questions, can the employer's system tell you to take your resume and get lost? No, not legally. Anyone can leave a resume, but if a person doesn't pass the screening, the resume is ranked at the bottom of the list in the database.

The bottom line is that if you don't score well in screening questions, your resume is exiled to a no-hire zone. If you're lucky, you'll receive an email letting you know you that didn't meet the qualifications. But more likely, you'll hear nothing. Don't let the rejection phase you; just start again using the strategies in this book to straighten your aim.

Blogs Give a Global Brand

Career experts recommend blogging as a *branding tool,* an extraordinary opportunity to become better known in a profession or career field. You can headline your own blog or write entries for someone else's blog. Millions of blogs operate around the globe, with new ones launching every day.

Keeping a blog running requires a fair amount of work. Because most blogs are maintained by an unpaid individual with regular entries of commentary, one-person blogs come and go. Sometimes the bloggers become guest commentators on blogs maintained by others.

REMEMBER

Blogs are the ultimate web insider's clubhouse. They attract loyal readers who hold an avid interest in a blog's topic. Recruiters understand that to hire the right people, you should go where the right people hang out. That's why recruiters cruise career-field-related blogs, looking for top talent in a specific occupation — or for experts who can steer them to top talent.

Finding blogs for role models takes a bit of shopping around. Try these suggestions to kick off your hunt:

1. **Browse for a topic and add *blogs* to the search term.**

   For example, *employment blogs* brings up a zillion possibilities, such as The Job Blog (www.blog.job.com/). You can also turn to a blog search engine, such as BlogSearchEngine (www.blogsearchengine.org) or Blogger (www.blogger.com).

2. **When you find a blog you like, check to see whether it includes a *blog roll* (list of hyperlinks to other blogs or websites).**

   You can use a feed reader such as Feedly (www.feedly.com) and select the More Like This feature to find more blogs like your topic. You can also perform a related search in Google to find blogs similar to the one you like. A sample search would be *related: https://careerdirectors.com/blog/.* When you search for that phrase and URL, Google will return a list of blogs similar to the one you listed.

TIP

To establish your own blog, find a host site that offers free services for beginning bloggers — such as WordPress (www.wordpress.com) — and start writing. You can also harness the power of blogging but without as much original writing by performing content curating. For instance, Scoop.it (www.scoop.it) lets you curate existing content on your favorite topic directly from the Internet. You gather the content, display it, and comment on it as well. You show your expertise by creating a repository of the best and most relevant information on the Internet, becoming a source that employers can turn to as well. Other examples of content curation sites include Pinterest (www.pinterest.com) and Feedly (www.feedly.com).

RSS Delivers Job Alerts on Your Time

The evolution of *really simple syndication* (RSS), the technology designed to give you a heads-up when a job you want becomes available, reminds me of the difference between all-news cable television and up-to-the-moment news on the Internet. Instead of having to wait for it to come up on your television (or TV app), you can view breaking news on your timetable 24/7.

Familiar free online job search agents at major job boards periodically send you email alerts about jobs that meet your specific search criteria. But the modern and also free RSS technology whisks *live feeds* to your computer or mobile devices around the clock with the latest jobs from thousands of employers and job sites. RSS is a rapidly growing service for the immediate distribution of online content, in this case, job postings.

How does RSS beat the older email job agents? Three ways: efficiency, relevance, and timeliness. Sending RSS job feeds to your RSS reader prevents email job alerts from clogging your inbox.

Moreover, RSS feeds more closely match your stated requirements. Like an advanced search, you get a closer match to what you want. For example, if you're an accountant and you want a job in Milwaukee, an email search agent might return everything with the term *accountant* or its variations, such as *accounting for lost automobiles in Milwaukee*. RSS job feeds are programmed to mirror what you specifically want.

RSS job feeds are a wonderful way to get the first word when a new job is posted. And you can program the feeds to include breaking news in industry concerns, information that can put you at the head of the line in job interviews. Jobs are filled quickly these days and you know the old saying about early birds.

You can receive RSS feeds in a few ways. You can download a free RSS reader, or you can use the RSS reader built into websites you want to follow. For example, the job search engines I describe in Chapter 20 give simple instructions on how to add their live job feeds to your computer or mobile devices.

Resume Blasting: A Really Bad Idea

WARNING

Resume blasting services (also jokingly known as resume spamming services) advertise their willingness to save you time and trouble by "blasting" your resume to thousands of recruiters and hiring managers all over the Internet — for a fee, of course. The pitches are tempting, but should you avail yourself of this miraculous service? Just say no!

As you discover in the following sections, resume blasting can bring you big trouble, from making identity theft easier for crooks, to irritating your boss, to making you an untouchable for recruiters. Moreover, as I explain in Chapter 9, customized OnTarget resumes are a shortcut to job interviews.

Privacy and identity theft problems

Concerning identity theft issues, privacy expert Pam Dixon advises being cautious with your resume's information. Read about it on her nonprofit World Privacy Forum (www.worldprivacyforum.org), where Dixon has posted a must-read report titled "Job Seeker's Guide to Resumes: Twelve Resume Posting Truths."

Admittedly, merely being careful about releasing your resume information online won't keep you safe from identity theft in these days when the guardrails on privacy are coming down in so many ways in so many places. But do be stingy with your private information — in particular, omit your home address and just use city, state, and zip code.

GET YOUR RESUME PAST SPAM GATEKEEPERS

You may not know whether your resume becomes cyber-litter because a spam or virus filter deletes it unread. Susan Joyce, who operates Job-Hunt.org (www.job–hunt.org), offers good tips for getting your resume where you want it to go:

- **Do** send email to only one employer at a time. Do not send email to more than five people at that employer's address at the same time. (It's okay to send to a single person, with copies to others at the same employer, but don't send the same message to a large group of people at the same employer.) The employer's spam filter may see all the messages from one source and conclude that you are sending spam.

- **Do** send your resume to yourself and a few friends using different Internet service providers, such as AOL, Outlook, Gmail, and Yahoo!, to see whether your message arrives with your resume still usable.

- **Don't** use junk-mail-type subject lines, for example, as exclamation points, all capitals, or spam buzzwords such as *free, trial, cash,* or *great offer.* Even appropriate phrases like "increased sales $10,000 a month" can trigger spam filters, thanks to junk pitches such as "Make $10,000 a month from home working part time." When you're in doubt, try spelling out dollar amounts.

- **Don't** use too many numbers in your email address, such as jobseeker12635@yahoo.com. Filter software may think the numbers are a spammer's tracking code.

Identity theft may be the worst-case scenario, but it isn't the only life-altering problem that can arise when you put your business online. Use a resume-blasting service while you're employed, and you may lose your current job. Experts say that employers search for their employees' resumes in job site resume databases. "When employees' resumes are found grazing in someone else's pasture before noon," says CareerXroads' Mark Mehler, who consults with countless company managers, "they may be on the street by the end of that same day."

Overexposure to recruiters

One more reason not to spread your resume all over the map: When you're targeting the fast track to the best jobs, nothing beats being brought to an employer's notice by an important third person — and an independent recruiter qualifies as an important third person.

Employers are becoming resistant to paying independent recruiters big fees to search the web when they theoretically can save money by hiring in-house corporate recruiters to do it. That's why recruiting agencies need fresh inventory that employers can't find elsewhere. If you want a third-party recruiter to represent you, think carefully before pinning cyber-wings on your resume.

WARNING

In addition to losing control of your resume, its wide availability can cause squabbles among contingency recruiters over who should be paid for finding you. An employer caught in the conflict of receiving a resume from multiple sources, including internal resume databases, will often pass over a potential employee rather than become involved in deciding which source, if any, should be paid.

Going directly makes all the difference

With all this great low-hanging fruit of online job postings and social media networking, why would you need anything else? Let me be crystal clear: Taking advantage of all online options is a great way to start, but it's not all you should do.

When you embark on an online job search, remember that everyone can easily apply that way in this land of push-button application technology. You lose an opportunity to stand out and can get lost in an overwhelming sea of job applicants.

Use the Internet as a springboard: Find the jobs that interest you, apply for them, but then take the extra step to find the right contact who can walk your resume in for you, live and in person. You need to get that resume in front of the right person, not hidden in a pile of other applicants!

And don't ignore the power of the telephone. The squeaky wheel very often does get the grease, so don't be afraid to take all the right steps and then follow up, human to human.

Making recruiters work for you

I've nixed the idea of blasting your resume off to recruiters, but I want to also describe the importance if reaching them.

The two types of recruiters are contingency and retained. _Contingency recruiters_ work for employers but are paid only if the employer hires one of their candidates. _Retained recruiters_ are paid (retained) by the employer to find the right candidate.

To find recruiters, you can perform online searches, check with your professional association career center, peruse journals and magazines, and buy lists. My favorite resource for purchasing targeted lists is Custom Databanks (www.customdata banks.com). This paid service might save you significant time in putting together a list of targeted recruiters.

Don't forget to use LinkedIn.com as a free and easy place to find recruiters at their targeted companies.

Remember that recruiters

>> Prefer to work with candidates who are currently employed.

>> Work for the employer and not for you, but because they benefit if you get hired, they will work with you.

>> Tend to be opinionated about resumes. Make whatever changes to your resume that they suggest. Opinions may vary from recruiter to recruiter and will likely not match anything you have been told.

>> Need to know the salary you expect to make, so include it in your cover letter.

>> Rarely if ever work with career changers or those who aren't a perfect fit.

TIP

Recruiters and resumes make for strange bedfellows. My company, Career Directors International, has hosted several global resume surveys of recruiters. Time and time again, what stands true time is that no two recruiters can agree on what they like or require. For example, some like resume summaries and others detests them. Some want a one-page resume while others insist on a two-page resume. Write your best resume according to this book but be prepared to change it upon request for each recruiter's preference. Don't put up a fight — if you want them in your corner do what is asked but remember to use your OnTarget resume wherever else you apply.

Chapter **5**

Checking Your Online Image

A 40-something job seeker in the Northeast felt as though life was kicking him to the curb after four weary months of chasing job after job and never being called to interview. Eventually he discovered he was being mistaken for another man with the same name who had serious digital dirt: His namesake was involved in a Supreme Court obscenity case.

A 30-something single mother in the Midwest was fired from her job at a non-profit organization — for something she did on her own time — the day after her boss Googled employees and discovered the mom was writing a sex blog.

A 20-something banking employee in the South was disappointed to learn that his good friend, who was interviewing for a job in the bank, lost out to another applicant because the interviewer checked the friend's Facebook page and was turned off by photos of the candidate drinking and cavorting with buddies.

REMEMBER

These three incidents reflect today's reality: Your online image is as important to your career as your customized resumes and carefully managed references.

This chapter examines — in understandable, low-tech terms — how your digital footprint can make you or break you.

Your Online Life Is an Open Book

The digital boom has given social media recruiting a prominent seat at the meet-up table where employers and job seekers connect. Recruiters who chase data on social networks now have the tools to add their own insight to the formality of information fed to them by candidates. As they click through the pages of Facebook, Twitter, LinkedIn, Pinterest, Instagram, Snapchat, and other sites, hiring authorities discover areas of people's lives, and the outcome of social media searches isn't always to a job seeker's advantage.

The numbers of employers using social media searches keep heading higher. As much as 70 percent of employers admit to using online information to screen job candidates.

A look at the dark side

A whopping one in three job candidates (up from one in ten just a few years ago) don't get hired because of what a potential employer finds on his or her social media profiles. According to studies by CareerBuilder and the Society for Human Resource Management (SHRM), the following social media findings created reasons employers cited for not hiring a candidate:

>> Posting provocative, vulgar, or inappropriate photographs or information (including cute but rude memes)

>> Posting content about drinking, using drugs, or criminal behavior

>> Bad-mouthing previous employers, coworkers, or clients

>> Showing poor communication skills

>> Making discriminatory comments

>> Not keeping your social media account up to date

>> Being too private (blocking content publicly to the point where you appear to have something to hide)

>> Conversely, posting too often leads some employers to believe there just isn't any time for work

>> Lying about qualifications or reasons for work absences

>> Having an unprofessional screen name

>> Being too focused on selfies, all the time

>> Sharing confidential information from a previous employer

>> Having followers who don't appear to be real

SOCIAL MEDIA ABSENTEEISM ALSO RISKY

"There was a time when you went full bore on a job search where you mainly concentrated on proofing your resume and cover letter for typos, checking out your interviewing wardrobe and performance, and giving your references a heads-up," says Scott Swimley, former sales vice president for Alumwire, a San Francisco-based company that provides a social media platform created for interaction by individuals, schools, and corporations.

"Change happens," Swimley adds. "Not only can Internet information about you hurt your reputation, employers may not hire you — especially if you're a young adult working in marketing or communications — if you entirely lack a social networking presence."

As a job seeker, you have a real chance of being prejudged or eliminated if digital dirt stains your reputation. Why take that chance?

A look at the bright side

In the same CareerBuilder survey mentioned in the preceding section, 38 percent of responding employers reported that they found content on social networking sites that caused them to hire a candidate. From most common to least common, those reasons include the following

>> A profile that provided a good idea of the candidate's personality and fit

>> A profile that supported the candidate's professional qualifications

>> Content that showed creativity

>> Content that highlighted solid communication skills

>> Content that indicated a well-rounded candidate

>> Content that provided good references

>> Content that included awards and accolades that the candidate received

Cleaning Up Your Act

Perhaps you've heard the joke about young people having to change their names on reaching adulthood to disown youthful hijinks stored on their friends' social media sites. It's a gag, but an important gag because we live in an age where your posted past can haunt your real-life future.

I asked Susan Estrada, a preeminent Internet pioneer and authority, this question: "What happens to all the data that floats in cyberspace? Is it possible to totally erase information that you or others have posted about you on the web?"

Estrada's candid answer: "Nope. So much of the stuff, once in the cloud, is out of control. You should figure it will live forever. I have stuff out there from the '80s and '90s that I can't touch."

Former Google CEO Eric Schmidt agrees; he once told pundit Stephen Colbert: ". . . just remember that when you post something (online), the computers remember it forever."

WARNING

Moreover, here's a wild card: What eventually happens to your posted information on a social media site remains legally unclear when, by its rules, the site claims ownership of your personal data and everything you share on its space. Reading a site's privacy rules is a good idea.

Moving to other places on the web and starting all over again as a virgin may be difficult, but do the best you can to shape up your hirable image before you head out to search for a job.

Also, straight-out websites are no better. You may have a blog and abolish all those posts that could get you disfavored. But savvy employers only need to go to the Wayback Machine (https://archive.org/web/) to find archived copies of your site.

Restoring Your Online Reputation

A Pew Research Center Internet report cements the general belief that search engines and social media sites now play a central role in building a person's identity online. The majority of adult Internet users (57 percent) say they have used a search engine to look up their name and see what information is available about them online.

Many users in the Pew study refine their online reputation as they go by changing privacy settings on profiles, customizing who can see certain updates, and deleting unwanted information about them that appears online.

What's the Internet buzz about you? If you discover your reputation is crippling your job search efforts, I offer suggestions to help kick those skeletons out of your online closet.

Your first move requires research to uncover exactly what, if any, reputation problems are holding you back. Google your name and see what turns up. Check Bing and Yahoo!, too. And don't forget Pipl (www.pipl.com), a people-search engine where you may discover forgotten clues to your behavior on sites you no longer use.

Other tools you can use to search for information about yourself include Twazzup (http://new.twazzup.com/) and Social Mention (http://socialmention.com/).

When the news is bad, first try simple remedies. When you find something you don't like, email the person responsible and ask that it be taken down.

Sometimes asking nicely is all you need to make negative news about you disappear. If that doesn't work, here are additional steps to consider, whether your online distress is self-inflicted or someone else is out to get you:

1. **Vacuum any crime scene.**

   Remove photos, content, and links you control that can torpedo you in an employer's eyes. If you don't control the posting site, ask the individual who does control it to ditch it. When in doubt, take it out.

2. **Overwhelm the bad stuff.**

   Smother indiscretions you've committed with a lot of new and favorable photos, content, video, blog posts, links, and endorsements from upstanding people (teachers, clergypersons, employers, and coworkers, for example). Google searchers normally read only the first few pages of results, not page 38. When you can't convince a site owner to make harmful content go away, your best bet is to entomb the hurtful data six feet under on page 10 or deeper.

TIP

The best books I've seen about rebuilding your brand is *Ditch, Dare, Do* by Deb Dib and William Arruda (Trades Mark Press) and *Wild West 2.0: How to Protect and Restore Your Online Reputation on the Untamed Social Frontier* (AMACOM) by Michael Fertik and David Thompson.

Keeping Watch on Your Online Reputation

Your digital good name comes from everything you do online that can be viewed by others — anything and everything. Your online activity includes content on social media such as Twitter, LinkedIn, and Facebook as well as blogs, forums, and websites where you leave comments. It even includes the kinds of products and services that interest you.

Don't fool yourself with wishful thinking — "Oh well, my online reputation isn't the real me." Real or not, it *is* you, and your digital presence indicates how employers are likely to perceive you. Perception rules. As inconvenient as it is, in the online world, perception is reality. In the following sections, I provide some tips for keeping tabs on your online rep.

Staying out of trouble online

Think down the road, and think twice before engaging in a flame war or lighting one up with firecrackers that carry your nametag. How do employers and recruiters ferret out your faults? They search for your name on various websites and search engines. The following recommendations help you put your best digital footprint forward.

Set up a free Google Alert on your name

The alerts you receive offer early warnings about identity mix-ups — those evil twins who have your same name and are out there online ruining it. Go to `www.google.com/alerts` and type your name (surrounded by quotation marks) in the Search terms box. For Type, select Everything.

To be doubly sure you're free, clear, and clean, perform a daily search for your name on Google or a search engine of your choice. Even if an employer doesn't check social networks or blogs, you can bet a basic Google search is part of how you're researched. Pages from social media and blogs may appear at the top of such a search.

Beware the overshare

Don't post trash you don't want everyone to know — no one needs to see you surrounded by beer cans at a party. Don't post anything about your dating life. Don't post your birthdate. Don't post anything that may embarrass you five years down the road. Unless you're posing with the president of a nation or the Dalai Lama, don't tag or post your name on party photos. Don't mix business and personal details online.

Most of all, if you're employed, don't post news of your job search in tweets or status updates, which is as dangerous as the boss finding your resume in the office copy machine.

Select Facebook friends with caution

To friend or not to friend bosses and coworkers? The jury's still out on that question but remember this: No matter whom you allow past the velvet rope and into your Facebook life, lock down privacy filters to create different levels of friends, such as professional and personal, and to select how much information each group can see.

All the security settings under the sun won't protect you if one friend decides to share your content with the rest of the world. Ignoring friend requests isn't rude, and gathering friends competitively opens you up to privacy problems. But it is a myth that you can see who has viewed your profile — that's technically impossible.

Keep an eye on comments

Remember that you're not the only writer on your account. Any of your friends can comment on your Facebook wall or your LinkedIn posts. Daggers have been known to slip in among the diamonds.

Network building is a worthy pursuit, but a huge number of pseudo friends doesn't count for much in your career world and creates needless risk. Moreover, becoming online pals with celebrities and politicians isn't always a hot idea: It may cause employers to wonder whether you're too full of yourself and will be overly demanding.

Don't go naked on Twitter

Letting it all hang out on the tweet line invites everyone to follow and see what you're up to. That's not only unsafe, it's uncool. Instead, open multiple free accounts (no limit) and make sure the one with your real name on it is as pure as a falling snowflake. If you feel you must pass on frisky questionable links, use an alias account.

List respected groups on LinkedIn

Give thought to which interest groups and associations claim you as a member, and give deeper thought as to whether all of them do you proud on your professional profile.

In the United States, civic groups such as Kiwanis and Rotary contribute to your good name, but Vampire Cretins of America cause pause because . . . well, it may lead some people to perceive you as a weirdo. Further, keep in mind that even seemingly innocent groups, such as ones that are politically motivated, can cause angst in your job search. (Chapter 7 tells you more about the kinds of organizations that look good on your profile.) Unlike data that search engines dig up about you, information in your profile is under your control.

Bird-dog your blog tracks

If you're blogging on your own site and as a guest on other blogs, be mindful of what you're saying (and have said) as it relates to your job life. Maybe you ranted something you regret, like a previous depression or law case, and would like a rematch. Perform a search to see what's up and what you'd like to take down. If the search engines aren't indexing your personal blog, look into registering it with the likes of Google, Yahoo!, and Bing.

Keep mum on grievances

Bellyache elsewhere when you please, but not in the land of cyber-please. Stay positive. And don't overlook specific accomplishments that boost your brand. (See Chapter 2 for more about branding.)

Remember that turnabout is fair play

Don't sabotage others by indiscreetly spilling unsavory beans or playing jokes that can provoke injury to a friend. For example, don't comment online to someone starting a new job, "Congrats! Hope you break your record and last three months!" Blabbing state secrets invites reciprocal action.

Join the right armies

Participate on forums, discussion threads, groups, and so on that create positive content and jibe with your career plans. Comment on websites and blog postings with high traffic. For example, adding your profile to LinkedIn, which has a high rank with search engines, pushes your profile higher in Google search results. You can also publish your profile on VisualCV (`www.visualcv.com`) and About.me (`www.about.me`). Check possible cross-reference links on each website where you post a profile.

Not only does being seen in the right places give you online credibility, but these mentions also help crowd out dirt and relocate it to the back of the line.

Looking like a champ online

If the Internet is one giant resume, as comedian Stephen Colbert says it is, use online reputation management to boost your appeal as an ideal job candidate. The rise of social media and advances in technology can make favorable words about you sound like confidence, not bragging. The following tips deal with your routine behavior when you open doors to the way you think and what others think about you.

Make cheerful comments

Even when you're down and out and suffering a bad case of the blues, don't make those feelings part of your online persona. Employers aren't looking to hire Gloomy Gus or his sister, Dora Dour. Instead, employers look for new hires who radiate a positive attitude. To paraphrase your mother's admonition: "If you can't say something nice, say nothing at all on the Internet." (Or use a screen name.)

Mention popular traits

Although they may be clichés, certain keywords for personal attributes and abilities have not outlived their usefulness. Major job search engine Indeed analyzed millions of job ads on its site over a six-month period. The object of the analysis was to find out which popular traits employers ask for again and again.

In descending order, expressed in keywords, the top 15 professional attributes or abilities employers want in the people they hire are

» Leadership

» Interpersonal skills

» Problem-solving

» Motivation

» Efficiency

» Attention to detail

» Ability to prioritize

» Teamwork

» Reliability

» Ability to multitask

» Time management

» Passion

» Listening skills

» Outgoingness

» Honesty

TIP

Look for ways to incorporate these wanted traits into your comments. You may say, for example, "My boss was highly complimentary about my last report, saying it showed leadership and solved key problems in holding the line on material cost."

Post kudos on social media

Have you won an award? Has someone praised you? Don't hold back. Just post the facts on your page — "I was excited to get these good words from Carl Case, the head official of the Little League where I coach: 'We're proud of Jake's great 9–1 win record this year. The kids think he's Superman.'"

Announce your promotions

Let friends know when you move up a notch. Don't forget to add how much you appreciate working for such a fine employer. You look successful and loyal.

Relate growth experiences

Relate on your page or blog the life or professional experiences that are helping you to mature into a better person or more competent worker. Education is an obvious topic. But think about other positive shaping experiences as well. Perhaps you worked in a soup kitchen or helped build housing for the poor. Maybe you read a book on time-management skills or a guide to managing the friction between generations in the workplace. You're painting a picture of who you are and what you can do.

Give 'em an image that sticks

Whenever you can, use photos along with your words — showing you receiving the award, making the speech, volunteering at the soup kitchen. Images are sticky, and the search engines love them!

Create your own group

A powerful technique for creating a positive impression about who you are and what you have to offer is to create your own group. You have to be able to attract members, monitor comments, and incite lively conversation, but creating a group can be a great way to demonstrate the positive you.

Look Who's Talking . . . about You

It seems that the younger you are, the quicker you're getting the memo about the career-risky behavior of living out loud and having bad news about you infest the web. People 18 to 29 are more apt to vigorously scrub unwanted posts and limit information about themselves than are older adults, according to surveys. Why is that? My guess is that older adults come later to social media, have already established their careers, and spend little time thinking about digital dirt.

That characterization certainly described me until the day a friend called my attention to a well-known website that reviews products and services. It included a ridiculous, anonymous, and blistering attack on an award-winning colleague, whom I have partnered with and known professionally for years. The post questioned her credibility, skills, expertise, and credentials and basically smeared her reputation for all to read. Speaking to her, I learned that she had an Internet troll intent on ruining her reputation after she had decided that she was not the best fit to assist him in his career transition.

To repair this type of damage, my colleague needed many positive reviews to that same site as well as a focused effort to build up positive parts of her online identity. Browsers such as Chrome tend to promote postings to sites like this very high in their search engine rankings.

That was the day I moved from passively understanding that there's a real threat of accidental damage and malicious attacks on the Internet to actively advocating the care and feeding of online reputation management.

2

Pulling Together a Winning Resume

IN THIS PART . . .

Choose which resume format works best for your background and experience.

Meet the various sections that make up a resume.

Know where to find the information that goes into your resume and see how to put together a core resume.

Find out why an OnTarget resume is the way to go and get details on creating one.

Chapter 6

Selecting the Best Resume Format

How much are you worth to employers? Are you a top pick, a maybe pick, or . . . gulp, a no-hire pick? Your resume inspires their first best guess, so you want to ensure that it's a compelling portrait of how your strengths and skills benefit the enterprise that you're hoping will write your next paycheck.

One key element that comes into play is how you present information in your resume. You don't have to limit yourself to presenting your experience using the traditional reverse-chronological resume. In fact, unless you've had a traditional career history of rising through the ranks, this standard resume could hurt your chances of getting an interview. However, nontraditional formats can go awry if not mastered, so pay close attention to this chapter to understand the nuances of the different resume formats.

Resume Formats Make a Difference

Resume format refers not to the design or look of your resume but to how you organize and emphasize your information. Different format styles flatter different histories.

At root, formats come in three styles:

» The *reverse-chronological format* (or traditional format), which lists employment beginning with the most recent and working backward

» The *chrono-functional format*, which most frequently emphasizes skills and accomplishments first and chronology timeline second

» The *hybrid format*, which lets you customize how you emphasize both the functional skills and the chronology depending on your unique needs

WARNING

Yes, there is such a thing as a functional resume that focuses primarily on skills and leaves out company names and dates where the work was performed. However, this format presents a big red flag for prospective employers, so don't be tempted to use it under any circumstances.

Table 6-1 gives you a breakdown of which of the three formats enhances your personal curb appeal.

TABLE 6-1 **Your Best Resume Formats at a Glance**

Your Situation	Suggested Formats
Perfect career progression	Reverse chronological
New graduate	Chrono-functional
Seasoned ace	Reverse chronological; hybrid when old jobs are most relevant
Military transition	Reverse chronological or chrono-functional
Job history gaps	Chrono-functional or hybrid
Career change	Hybrid; sometimes reverse chronological
Special issues	Hybrid or chrono-functional
Multitrack job history	Chrono-functional
Demotions	Any

REMEMBER

The big question to ask yourself when you're considering different formats is: "Does this format maximize my qualifications for the job I want?" The format you choose should promote your top qualifications, so make sure to select a format that helps you present your top-pick value.

The following sections explore each type of resume format so you can choose the style best for you and your skills.

Reverse-Chronological Format

The *reverse-chronological* (RC) format, shown in Figure 6-1, is straightforward: It cites your employment history from the most recent back, showing dates as well as employers. You accent a steady work history with a clear pattern of upward or lateral mobility. In the remaining sections, I go into more detail about when and why to use the reverse-chronological format.

Understanding the RC format's strengths and weaknesses

Check to see whether the reverse-chronological resume's strengths work for you:

>> This upfront format is by far the most popular with employers and recruiters because it puts the emphasis on what you've been doing most recently in your career and lets your career progression easily be seen.

>> RC links employment dates, underscoring continuity. The weight of your experience confirms that you're a specialist in a specific career field.

>> RC positions you for the next upward career step.

>> As the most traditional of formats, RC is a good fit for traditional industries but is the resume of choice for all industries when you can demonstrate solid progression in your career.

Take the weaknesses of the reverse-chronological format into account:

>> When your previous job titles are substantially different from your target position, this format doesn't support your objective. Without careful management, the RC reveals everything, including inconsequential jobs and negative factors.

YOUR NAME

City, State   Phone Number   Email Address

─────────────── **JOB YOU ARE TARGETING** ───────────────

Paragraph or bulleted list that explains why you are the best candidate for the job – typically emphasizes elements that reflect on contributing bottom-line value to the company (how you make money, save money, optimize, improve, and grow for the company).

Also include other high-value items such as languages spoken, awards, relevant certifications or degrees. Ask yourself, "What makes me stand out from the competition?"

Add pizzazz by including a value-added quote from a former employer.

─────────────── **KEY COMPETENCIES** ───────────────

2-3 column list of 12-21 items that position you for the job. These are hard skills and technical competencies required to perform the job. Look closely at target job descriptions to identify these words.

- • • •
- • • •
- • • •

─────────────── **PROFESSIONAL EXPERIENCE** ───────────────

Covers your work history in reverse chronological order. The most recent position is typically the most detailed.

COMPANY NAME – City, ST   [Date – Date]

Job Title
Brief paragraph provides the 'hook' or overview data that sets the stage with the challenge, goal, and responsibility of the position.

- Provide supportive bullets that emphasize challenges, actions, and results you took to meet the goal.
- Use specifics such as dollar amounts, rankings, and percentages.
- Emphasize other accomplishments such as awards and promotions attained.

COMPANY NAME – City, ST   [Date – Date]
Detailed as above

COMPANY NAME – City, ST   [Date – Date]
Brief; likely has paragraph only and no bullets.

─────────────── **EDUCATION & TRAINING** ───────────────

List Degree – School Name, City, ST – GPA (if at least 3.5); other relevant honors
Include relevant certifications, certificates, credentials, licenses, continuing education

─────────────── **OTHER SECTIONS** ───────────────

Include additional sections such as Awards, Publications, or Affiliations/Volunteer only as relevant to job target.

FIGURE 6-1:
The tried-and-true, reverse-chronological format.

>> RC can spotlight periods of unemployment or brief job tenure.

>> Without careful management, RC reveals your age.

>> If you aren't careful, RC may suggest that you hit a plateau and stayed in a job too long.

Deciding whether you should use the RC format

Use the reverse–chronological if you fall into any of these categories:

>> You have a steady work record reflecting constant growth or lateral movement.

>> Your most recent employer is a respected name in the industry, and the name may ease your entry into a new position.

>> Your most recent job titles are impressive stepping-stones.

>> You're a savvy writer who knows how to manage potential negative factors, such as inconsequential jobs, too few jobs, too many temporary jobs, too many years at the same job, or too many years of age.

Think twice about using the RC under these circumstances:

>> You're a new graduate with limited experience in your target profession.

>> You have work history or employability problems such as gaps, demotions, stagnation in a single position, job hopping (four jobs in three years, for example), or re-entering the workforce after a break to raise a family.

>> You're trying to change careers.

>> You're trying to re-enter a profession you worked in many years ago that isn't showing up front and center with an RC.

Creating a reverse-chronological resume

To create an RC resume, remember to focus on areas of specific relevance to your target position. For your work history section, you typically want to concentrate on your last four jobs or your last 10 to 15 years of employment.

Be sure to include for each the name of the employer and the city in which you worked, the years you were there, your title, your key responsibilities, and your measurable accomplishments.

To handle problems such as unrelated experience or early experience that could date you but is too relevant to leave off, you can group unrelated jobs in a second work history section under a heading of *Additional Experience*, *Previous Experience*, or *Related Experience*. I tell you more about handling a variety of special circumstances in Chapter 14.

TIP

When it comes to including dates on your resume, you have multiple options:

>> If your jobs were extremely fluid, meaning you left one company and immediately started with the next, you can use months and years. However, if you had gaps of several months between one job stopping and one starting, it is perfectly acceptable to just list the years employed.

>> When you have held multiple progressive positions with an employer, you don't have to list the employer all over again. Instead, create an umbrella for the positions, listing the employer only once and the total dates, and then show your reverse chronology below. Figure 6-2 shows how to present multiple progressive positions with the same employer.

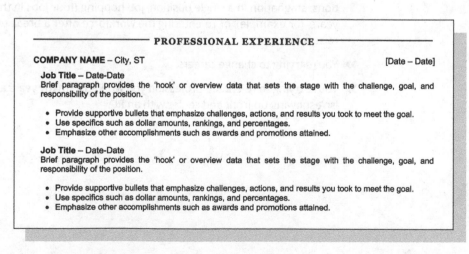

FIGURE 6-2:
Listing multiple progressive positions with one employer.

PROFESSIONAL EXPERIENCE

COMPANY NAME – City, ST   [Date – Date]

Job Title – Date-Date
Brief paragraph provides the 'hook' or overview data that sets the stage with the challenge, goal, and responsibility of the position.

- Provide supportive bullets that emphasize challenges, actions, and results you took to meet the goal.
- Use specifics such as dollar amounts, rankings, and percentages.
- Emphasize other accomplishments such as awards and promotions attained.

Job Title – Date-Date
Brief paragraph provides the 'hook' or overview data that sets the stage with the challenge, goal, and responsibility of the position.

- Provide supportive bullets that emphasize challenges, actions, and results you took to meet the goal.
- Use specifics such as dollar amounts, rankings, and percentages.
- Emphasize other accomplishments such as awards and promotions attained.

>> If your positions were similar and varied little, or you had the same job with a different title, it's okay to group them versus describing them twice. Figure 6-3 shows an individual who had progressive positions with the same employer, but some of the jobs were similar enough to group instead of listing redundant information in two places.

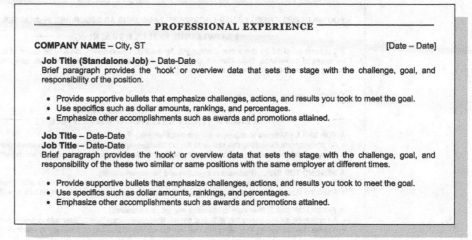

FIGURE 6-3:
Grouping similar positions held at the same employer.

Chrono-Functional Format

The *chrono-functional* (CF) format, shown in Figure 6-4, is a resume of ability-focused topics — portable skills or functional areas that position you best for your new job target (or to overcome some challenge in your timeline). It ignores chronological order or even whether a particular skill came from employment. However, the chrono-functional format backs up all listed skills with a chronology that might come from employment, courses or education, volunteer work, and paid or unpaid internships. Read more about the chrono-functional format in the following sections.

FIGURE 6-4:
A chrono-
functional
resume format,
which is used to
overcome
timeline
challenges in
your work
history.

YOUR NAME

City, State   Phone Number   Email Address

──────────────── **JOB YOU ARE TARGETING** ────────────────

Paragraph or bulleted list that explains why you are the best candidate for the job – typically emphasizes elements that reflect on contributing bottom-line value to the company (how you make money, save money, optimize, improve, and grow for the company).

Also include other high-value items such as languages, awards, relevant certifications or degrees. Ask yourself, "What makes me stand out from the competition?" Add pizzazz by including a value-added testimonial.

YOU WILL LIKELY NEED TO USE CROSSOVER LANGUAGE AS DESCRIBED IN CHAPTER 9.

──────────── **KNOWLEDGE, SKILLS & TRAINING** ────────────

2-3 column list of 12-21 items that position you for the job. These do not have to be areas of expertise but can be areas of knowledge, skills learned, or hands-on/classroom training that you have completed. Look at job descriptions to understand key skill requirements.

- · · ·
- · · ·
- · · ·

──────────── **RELEVANT EXPERIENCE & EMPLOYMENT** ────────────

A TOP SKILL (Pertinent to objective and job requirements).
- An achievement illustrating this skill, and the job title/class/company/volunteer role in which performed.
- A second achievement illustrating this skill and the job title of position or company in which performed.

A SECOND TOP SKILL (Pertinent to objective and job requirements).
- An achievement illustrating this skill, and the job title/class/company/volunteer role in which performed.
- A second achievement illustrating this skill and the job title of position or company in which performed.

A THIRD TOP SKILL (Pertinent to objective and job requirements).
- An achievement illustrating this skill, and the job title/class/company/volunteer role in which performed.
- A second achievement illustrating this skill and the job title of position or company in which performed.

A FOURTH TOP SKILL (Pertinent to objective and job requirements).
- An achievement illustrating this skill, and the job title/class/company/volunteer role in which performed.
- A second achievement illustrating this skill and the job title of position or company in which performed.

A UNIQUE AREA OF PROFICIENCY (Pertinent to objective and job requirements).
- An achievement testifying to proficiency, including job title/class/company/volunteer role in which performed.

──────────────── **EXPERIENCE TIMELINE** ────────────────

Don't be afraid to mix volunteer roles, school, internship, and paid jobs in this section. This is 'experience' and not just jobs.

Job Title – Company Name, City, ST   [Date – Date]
Subject, Full-Time Student – University Name, City, ST   [Date – Date]
Volunteer Title – Company Name, City, ST   [Date – Date]

──────────────── **EDUCATION & TRAINING** ────────────────

List Degree – School Name, City, ST – GPA (if at least 3.5); other relevant honors
Include relevant certifications, certificates, credentials, licenses, continuing education

──────────────── **OTHER SECTIONS** ────────────────

Include additional sections such as Awards, Publications, or Affiliations/Volunteer only as relevant to job target.

Understanding the CF format's strengths and weaknesses

The following are the strengths of the chrono-functional format:

>> A CF resume directs a reader's eyes to what you want him or her to notice. It helps a reader visualize what you can do instead of locking you into when and where you learned to do it. CF resumes salute the future rather than embalm the past.

>> The CF format — written after researching the target company — serves up the precise functions or skills that the employer wants. It's like saying, "You want budget control and turnaround skills –– here's where I offer budget control and turnaround skills." The skills sell is a magnet to reader eyes!

>> It uses unpaid and nonwork experience to your best advantage.

>> The CF format allows you to eliminate or subordinate work history that doesn't support your current objective.

The weaknesses of the chrono-functional format include the following:

>> Recruiters and employers are more accustomed to reverse-chronological formats than other types. Departing from the norm may raise suspicion that you're not the cream of the crop of applicants. Readers may assume that you're trying to hide inadequate experience, educational deficits, or who knows what.

>> Functional styles may leave unclear which skills grew from which jobs or experiences.

>> This format doesn't clearly describe your career progression.

Deciding whether you should use the CF format

The chrono-functional resume is heaven-sent for career changers, contract workers, new graduates, ex-military personnel, and individuals with multitrack job histories, work history gaps, or special issues.

Job seekers with perfect backgrounds (no gaps, career changes, or the like) and managers and professionals who are often tapped by executive recruiters should avoid this format.

Creating a chrono-functional resume

Choose areas of expertise acquired during the course of your career, including education and unpaid activities. These areas become skill, competency, and functional headings, which vary by the target position or career field. Note accomplishments below each heading. A few examples of headings are: *Operations Management, Sales, Budget Control, Cost Cutting, Project Implementation, Growth,* and *Turnaround Successes.*

List the headings in the order of importance and follow each heading with a series of short statements of your skills. Turn your statements into power hitters with measurable achievements. The easiest way to do this is to always write CAR statements — the challenge you faced, actions you took, and results you obtained.

WARNING

It's important to note two key elements that allow a chrono-functional resume to work:

>> Your resume has a work history listed either above or below the experience and accomplishments section.

>> Each top skill lists the role in which it was attained.

If you do not make these key connections in your resume, prospective employers will question the validity of your skills and become confused about where or when they were used. By providing this small bit of connective data, you make a chrono-functional a safe choice when navigating career challenges on your resume.

Hybrid Format

The hybrid resume format may likely be something you haven't encountered before. While it has been in use by a handful of professional resume writers for over a decade with great success and employer acceptance, it has rarely been shared with job seekers before now.

A *hybrid resume format* takes elements from different resume types so you can maintain an employment chronology as well as use creative functional characteristics to overcome your career challenge without raising any red flags. This strategy works great if

>> You want to highlight jobs from earlier in your career that might otherwise not be seen.

>> Your most recent job was not as strong or as close a fit to your target.

>> You have a gap in employment.

Essentially, with the hybrid format, you're addressing employment circumstances in which there are challenges but a full chrono-functional adaptation would be overkill. Such challenges might include

>> You held the target experience or industry experience previously in your career.

>> The position experience or industry experience most relevant to your target is earlier in your career and will be hidden on page 2 of the resume.

>> You were demoted with your current employer and wish to make that less obvious.

>> Your recent employment is lower level, irrelevant, or covering a gap but your prior history is right on target.

Understanding the hybrid format's strengths and weaknesses

Check out some of the strengths of the hybrid format to decide whether it's for you:

>> It quickly points prospective employers to early experience you have that matches your target, and it makes it seem more relevant.

>> It can cleverly mask a gap in your employment history.

>> It allows you the flexibility to put your best foot forward even if your most recent employment was not in line with your current target.

When crafted correctly for job seekers with these kinds of challenges, there aren't any weaknesses to using a hybrid format.

Deciding whether you should use the hybrid format

A hybrid resume helps you position your relevant experience and work history more effectively when you have gaps, demotions, career changes, career backtracking, or haven't worked in the target industry for many years.

Although the hybrid resume looks neat and is highly efficient at what it does, those with strong career progressions in their chosen industry should steer clear. You don't need to get fancy when you're already on track.

Creating a hybrid resume

Some employment challenges require the lightest of tweaking to make them blend in, and others require more of a major renovation. You can decide on a case-by-case basis how much work your resume needs when you look at the job target and compare it to your work history.

If your career progression is all lined up for the job you want but the industry experience is hiding on page 2, all you need is a light tweak to help draw the eyes of prospective employer to relevant career information. You can stick with your reverse chronology and all the other elements that make an RC successful, but add a little summary line at the top of your professional experience section that connects your prior positions or industries with the target, as shown in Figure 6-5.

But what if you're facing one of those challenges that make it more crucial for you to play up a job from earlier in your career but going to a chrono-functional resume would be overkill? That's when you go heavy with the hybrid!

You have room to be creative here as long as you adhere to two simple rules:

>> Always include a timeline, either before the professional experience section or after it.

>> List jobs in the order they best serve you, but without the dates (since those appear elsewhere in the chronology). Feel free to leave out descriptions that don't serve you.

Figure 6-6 shows you how you might present the timeline and job list on a resume.

For more on tackling resume challenges, see Chapters 12 and 13.

YOUR NAME

City, State   Phone Number   Email Address

—————— JOB YOU ARE TARGETING ——————

Paragraph or bulleted list that explains why you are the best candidate for the job – typically emphasizes elements that reflect on contributing bottom-line value to the company (how you make money, save money, optimize, improve, and grow for the company).

Also include other high-value items such as languages spoken, awards, relevant certifications or degrees. Ask yourself, "What makes me stand out from the competition?"

Add pizzazz by including a value-added quote from a former employer.

—————————— KEY COMPETENCIES ——————————

2-3 column list of 12-21 items that position you for the job. These are hard skills and technical competencies required to perform the job. Look closely at target job descriptions to identify these words.

- · · ·   · · ·   · · ·

—————— PROFESSIONAL EXPERIENCE ——————

Covers your work history in reverse chronological order. The most recent position is typically the most detailed. However, because you are wanting to showcase earlier jobs that might not appear on page one it adds a little sentence here at the top that looks like this:

Offering key expertise in <Target Job> through positions as Job Title at Company A, Job Title at Company B, Job Title at Company C, and Job Title at Company.

COMPANY NAME – City, ST   [Date – Date]

Job Title
Brief paragraph provides the 'hook' or overview data that sets the stage with the challenge, goal, and responsibility of the position.

- Provide supportive bullets that emphasize challenges, actions, and results you took to meet the goal.
- Use specifics such as dollar amounts, rankings, and percentages.
- Emphasize other accomplishments such as awards and promotions attained.

COMPANY NAME – City, ST   [Date – Date]
Detailed as above

COMPANY NAME – City, ST   [Date – Date]
Brief; likely has paragraph only and no bullets.

———————— EDUCATION & TRAINING ————————

List Degree – School Name, City, ST – GPA (if at least 3.5); other relevant honors
Include relevant certifications, certificates, credentials, licenses, continuing education

———————————— OTHER SECTIONS ————————————

Include additional sections such as Awards, Publications, or Affiliations/Volunteer only as relevant to job target.

FIGURE 6-5: Use the light hybrid when your reverse-chronology resume is on track but some key relevance is getting hidden in your resume layout.

YOUR NAME

City, State   Phone Number   Email Address

JOB YOU ARE TARGETING

Paragraph or bulleted list that explains why you are the best candidate for the job – typically emphasizes elements that reflect on contributing bottom-line value to the company (how you make money, save money, optimize, improve, and grow for the company).

Also include other high-value items such as languages, awards, relevant certifications or degrees. Ask yourself, "What makes me stand out from the competition?" Add pizzazz by including a value-added testimonial.

YOU WILL LIKELY NEED TO USE CROSSOVER LANGUAGE AS DESCRIBED IN CHAPTER 9.

KNOWLEDGE, SKILLS & TRAINING

2-3 column list of 12-21 items that position you for the job. These do not have to be areas of expertise but can be areas of knowledge, skills learned, or hands-on/classroom training that you have completed. Look at job descriptions to understand key skill requirements.

-
-
-

PROFESSIONAL EXPERIENCE

LIST JOBS IN THIS SECTION BY RELEVANCE TO YOUR TARGET, NOT BY CHRONOLOGY.

REGIONAL VICE PRESIDENT – Company Name, City, ST – 4 years
Brief paragraph provides the 'hook' or overview data that sets the stage with the challenge, goal, and responsibility of the position.

- Provide supportive bullets that emphasize challenges, actions, and results you took to meet the goal.
- Use specifics such as dollar amounts, rankings, and percentages.
- Emphasize other accomplishments such as awards and promotions attained.

BRANCH MANAGER – Company Name, City, ST – 7 years
Brief paragraph provides the 'hook' or overview data that sets the stage with the challenge, goal, and responsibility of the position.

- Provide supportive bullets that emphasize challenges, actions, and results you took to meet the goal.
- Use specifics such as dollar amounts, rankings, and percentages.
- Emphasize other accomplishments such as awards and promotions attained.

DIRECTOR OF OPERATIONS – Company Name, City, ST – 3 years
Brief paragraph provides the 'hook' or overview data that sets the stage with the challenge, goal, and responsibility of the position.

EMPLOYMENT TIMELINE

Operational Consultant – Company Name, City, ST   [Date – Date]
Sabbatical (Publishing Industry book) – City, ST   [Date – Date]
Director of Operations – Company Name, City, ST   [Date – Date]
Regional Vice President – Company Name, City, ST   [Date – Date]
Branch Manager – Company Name, City, ST   [Date – Date]

FIGURE 6-6:
The heavy hybrid format comes into play when you have had solid jobs but they just aren't presenting in the best order to qualify you for the position.

Other Resume Presentations

A few adventuresome job seekers are using innovative resume formats. Here's a quick look at two possibilities that can't be classified as mainstream methods but may be just the vehicle you need to find the job that seems beyond your grasp.

Resume letters

In a targeted postal mailing campaign, a resume letter attracts attention because it reads more like a story than a document. The resume letter is a combination of cover letter and resume; often it is two pages. It typically opens with a variation of the question: "Are you looking for a professional who can leap high buildings in a single bound?" A resume letter opening might look a little something like this:

> *Should you be in the market for an accomplished, congenial senior human resources specialist who has earned an excellent reputation for successful HR technology acquisition analysis and management, this letter will be of interest to you.*

The resume letter continues to give a basic overview of a job seeker's strengths, including previous employers, achievements, skills, and competencies, as they would apply to the recipient company.

TIP

Take extra care to discover the key qualifications most often required for the position you seek. Targeting is a no-lose strategy even for cold mailings.

Your strengths message may be in paragraph form or in bulleted statements. The resume letter format can be especially useful for a professional with an abundance of experience. But never substitute a resume letter when you're responding to a job advertisement that asks for a resume. The employers call the shots, and you need to show that you can follow their directions.

One of the most amazing placements I've ever heard about was the case of the chemist who at age 50 left the profession to take a stint dealing cards at a casino. Five years later, at age 55, he wanted to return to the chemistry workplace. A cold mailing of a well-written resume letter to owners of small chemical companies turned up a caretaker CEO job while the owner took an extended two-year trip out of the country. Would the resume letter and broadcast mailing approach work as well with email? I have no data on this question. The trick would be to do research and target key decision makers.

TIP

Resume letters are best used when sending an inquiring employment campaign letter — whether electronically or by regular mail. If you have the name of a specific hiring authority or an influential person at a company, you can send a general resume letter with some hooks about your background as they specifically pertain to the employer's business. You can ask to be referred to a department head or manager, you can use it to ask for a meeting over lunch or coffee to learn more about the company, or you may directly ask about current opportunities. The key is to make sure the reader gets a clear perspective of your skills and abilities as they apply to the company without pressuring them or asking directly for a job. You're trying to create interest and a reason they should want to speak with you.

Portfolios

Hard-copy samples of your work, gathered in a portfolio, have long been valuable to fields such as design, graphics, photography, architecture, advertising, public relations, marketing, education, and contracting.

Often, you deliver your portfolio as part of the job interview. Some highly motivated job seekers include a brief version of a career portfolio when sending their resumes, although recruiters say that they want fewer, not more, resume parts to deal with. If you must include work samples to back up your claims, send only a few of your very best. Better yet, create a website where you display these items and include the URL on your resume.

The portfolio is a showcase for documenting a far more complete picture of what you offer employers than is possible with a resume of one or two pages. Getting recruiters to read it is the problem. When you determine that a portfolio is your best bet, take it to job interviews. Put your portfolio in a three-ring binder with a table of contents and tabs separating its various parts. Mix and match the following categories:

» **Career goals** (if you're a new graduate or career changer): A brief statement of less than one page is plenty.

» **Your resume:** Use a fully formatted version.

» **Samples of your work:** Include easily understandable examples of problem solving and competencies.

» **Proof of performance:** Insert awards, honors, testimonials and letters of commendation, and flattering performance reviews. Don't forget to add praise from employers, people who reported to you, and customers.

>> **Proof of recognition:** Here's where you attach certifications, transcripts, degrees, licenses, and printed material listing you as the leader of seminars and workshops. Omit those that you merely attended unless the attendance proves something.

>> **Military connections:** The U.S. military provides exceptionally good training, and many employers know it. List military records, awards, and badges.

TIP

Make at least two copies of your hard-copy portfolio in case potential employers decide to hold on to your samples or fail to return them.

Your portfolio should document only the skills and accomplishments that you want to apply on a job. Begin by identifying those skills and accomplishments, and then determine which materials prove your claims of competency.

WARNING

A portfolio should be relevant! Don't look at your accomplishments based on what you're proud of. Some of my greatest accomplishments came in my early career in a role that is nothing like what I would work in today. Be selective in telling something like that as a problem-solving story in an interview. For instance, if you're an engineer, it's not pertinent to include an all-state music winner certificate from high school, although it may have been a proud moment for you.

Chapter **7**

Understanding the Parts of a Resume

prospective employer makes a leap of faith investing money in you as a new and untried employee. Are you really a good match for the position and the company? A resume's content can make or break the initial impression that determines how that question gets answered (and if you get the interview).

How important is content? In comparing a position's requirements to your qualifications (see Chapter 9), what your resume says is critical. This chapter outlines the sections you include on your Core resume. Chapters 9 to 11 explain how to sell, not tell, your worth.

REMEMBER

As you work on crafting your resume, don't rush it. If you build it correctly, the interviews will come.

Breaking Down the Parts of Your Resume

To make your content easy to access, organize the facts into various recognizable categories. These sections make reviewing your resume much easier for prospective employers who have historical knowledge of where to find certain information that's critical to them.

REMEMBER

Here are the essential parts that make up a resume:

» Contact Information

» Objective Header Statement

» Summary

» Key Skills

» Education and Training

» Experience

» Activities and Affiliations

» Honors and Awards

You may also include:

» Certifications and Licenses (also frequently grouped with Education)

» Endorsements

» Work Samples (not actually included, but listed as available)

To increase the likelihood that your resume positions you for an interview, take the time to understand the purpose of the different resume parts, which I explain in the following sections.

REMEMBER

No more than you want to carry around 30 pounds of extra weight do you want fat in your resume — family, early education, favorite things, and so forth. Trim it! The rule for including data on a resume is simple: If the data doesn't support your objective to be invited for an interview, then it's not OnTarget — leave it out. See Chapter 9 for more on targeting your resume.

Leading with Contact Information

No matter which format (see Chapter 6) your experience requires you to choose, place your name first on your resume. If your name isn't first, a computer may mistake Excellent Sales Representative for your name and file you away as Ms. Representative.

Use boldface to display your name in a size range of 14- to 26-point typeface, depending on your preference. The rest of your contact information can appear in 10- to 12-point typeface. Keep adjusting type sizes until you get the visual effect you prefer.

Here's a shocker: Except for specific and overriding reasons, limit contact information to your

WARNING

>> **Email address.** This is your single most important contact data point because that's how the majority of employers will initially contact you.

Don't use a work email address on your resume; use a personal email address instead. If you use your work address, a prospective employer will see this as taking advantage of your employer and wonder what you would do if you were to work for them.

Additionally, if you have a personal email address that isn't professional sounding (rockinralph@gmail.com or mommalovespugs@gmail.com), please sign up for a simple, professional-sounding address. jillk123@gmail.com is much better! Also, avoid creating email addresses with your birth year in them. You don't want to give away your age before the prospective employer even sees you!

If you have them, you can add your website or blog, web portfolio, and social media page URLs. (Caveat: Don't go overboard with social media extras or readers may wonder whether you're too busy being social to work hard. Consider listing just one professional site, such as LinkedIn.)

>> **Phone number.** Some employers prefer to pick up the phone and give you a call. Select the phone number where you can most easily be reached.

>> **City and state of residence.** This information shows you have roots. Employers understandably resist springing for relocation costs unless the talent they seek isn't available locally.

TIP

If you live in a large metro area, a commute might be an hour or more from your suburb to the prospective workplace. Therefore, you may be better off not listing your city and state at all. Watch for these positions and leave off your location; go with just your phone number and email address.

Why has there been a reduction in the recommended amount of contact information? Long answer short: technology and crime. The need for a home street address has passed into history because employers are now far more likely to communicate by Internet than by postal mail. What's more, rising concerns about identity theft and privacy loss argue against listing a home street address unless there is an overriding reason to do so.

REMEMBER

The first page of your resume is valuable real estate: Ditching unnecessary text such as your street address is akin to clearing weeds out of your lawn. Why not leave blank any unused white space to make your resume more open and readable, or use it for key information that markets you?

Placing Your Job Target in the Objective Header

An *objective header statement* clearly defines the position you're targeting. It gives immediate focus to your resume and is the hub around which all the other information in your document relates.

You may have noticed I'm not using the term *objective* but instead *objective header* here. The important difference is that an objective makes you think of a long-winded statement about what you want, such as

Seeking a management position with opportunity for growth and achievement.

Blah, blah, blah. It's fatty and bloated with words that do nothing to sell you and are too focused on what you want. Instead, you want to edit this down ruthlessly to an objective header, which is nothing more than a succinct title of the position you are targeting with your resume. For example, a retail manager may simply include one of the following phrases:

RETAIL MANAGEMENT PROFESSIONAL

or

RESULTS-DRIVEN RETAIL MANAGER

It really draws the eye as a header versus a lengthy all-about-me sentence.

Most studies show that employers prefer a targeted header objective for quick identification purposes. They like to see the name of their job openings at the top of a resume. Because you cite those qualifying accomplishments that support your objective header and leave out random experiences, the finished product shows that you and the desired job appear to be a well-matched pair.

TIP

If you're responding to an advertised job, match the basic qualifications it requires in the body of your resume, even if the job seeks a "window pane technician" and your objective says "window pane technician." An objective header that echoes the job title in the job ad is merely a first step toward showing that you're a great match.

Ideally, write a customized resume for each position (or career field) for which you apply. You should even write a different customized resume for each position for which you apply at the *same* company. (For more about targeting your resume, flip to Chapter 9.) The downside to a narrow job objective header is that the same employer may not consider you for other open positions that you didn't know about. But if the objective header is too broadly focused, your objective header statement becomes meaningless. Stay OnTarget!

WARNING

Is this objective header necessary? Absolutely. Think of your resume as a maze — it has to have a visible entrance or no one would ever get started. Without an objective header, the prospective employer won't know for which position you are applying. Don't assume they'll scan it or read it anyway. Instead, your resume will likely fall into the black hole of job seekers who don't know what the company needs or what they want. Make each resume OnTarget with an objective header.

Grabbing the Reader with the Summary Section

Your OnTarget resume needs to provide an overview of your strengths and key talents to show that you have what it takes to excel in that position. This is known as your summary section.

A *summary* typically contains the three to five skills and competencies — sometimes more — that best support your job aspiration. The data in your statement need not be proven with examples in this brief section. In effect, you're saying, "Here's who I am and how I stand out from the equally qualified competition." The summary is your teaser commercial, encouraging the reader to hang in there for proof of what the opening claims.

Part 4 contains sample resumes that illustrate a variety of effective summaries. But Figure 7-1 gives you a quick peek at a strategic summary. I've also included the objective header statement and key skills section so you can get the entire picture. You'll quickly see that an effective summary is a results-teaser that makes prospective employers both see that you're qualified and excited to learn more about you.

FIGURE 7-1:
A strong summary section supports your objective header statement and leads into your key skills section.

YOUR NAME

City, ST Zip   Email Address   Phone Number

SENIOR TECHNOLOGY OPERATIONS MANAGER

Cited by XYZ manager for, "leverages unparalleled technical expertise in information technology (IT) to guide cost savings and responsibly manage resources."

Talented Sr. Technology Manager with proven expertise in directing multi-million dollar technology programs. Talent for leveraging emerging technologies to position employer for market dominance – three time winner of the industry *IT Bleeding Edge Innovator Award* (out of 100 companies). Lauded for emphasis on "innovation with cautious cost control" to attain effective product and service solutions with a positive bottom line. Possess a Top Secret Clearance.

Information Technology
- IT Acquisition
- Communications Security
- Intranets, LANs & WANs
- Workstations
- Software Upgrades

- Multilevel Security Systems
- Trouble Desk Management
- Troubleshooting
- End User Support & Training
- System Administration

- Life Cycle Management
- Web Services / HTML
- Windows NT Servers
- System Upgrades
- Technology Transfer

Management
- Multi-Site Operations
- Budget Administration

- Training & Development
- Resource Allocation

- Policy & Procedure
- Customer Relations

REMEMBER

A summary is known by many names. Among the most popular are areas of expertise, skills summary, highlights summary, asset statement, power summary, career highlights, career summary, career profile, career focus, summary of qualifications, unique selling proposition, and accomplishments profile.

In the following sections, I show how to make your summary section work for you.

Maximizing the summary section

Only initially, when you create your Core, one-size-fits-all resume, does this section have all your strengths. However, when you go OnTarget to impress an employer that you are a job match, it will be critical to make this section tight and dynamic toward the job for which you're applying.

This brief section, which is typically one or two short paragraphs, a list of bullets, or a combination of the two, provides your 30-second commercial to a prospective employer on why you are a match worth pursuing. This section builds trust and excitement that you not only have the skills required but will also be a return on investment for the company that hires you.

REMEMBER

Summaries offer an easy way to identify the qualifications you have that match a particular job's requirements. This section may also identify qualifications that position you for related positions you don't know about in a given career field.

WARNING

The only disadvantage to using a summary can come from user error. Specifically, if you try to oversell yourself with irrelevant data that you think makes you look better, you instead appear to be overqualified or confused, neither of which lands your resume a second look.

Selling yourself in your summary

When you attempt to meet the employer's position needs in your summary with generic words and phrases such as "good communicator" or "works well with others," all you do is group yourself in the huge pool of applicants who have the basic skills for the position. Your summary needs to sell what is called your *unique selling proposition*, or USP.

To identify your USP, look at two areas:

>> **Your CAR stories during your career:** *CAR* stands for challenges you've faced, actions taken to resolve them, and results attained. Consider your own CAR stories. Do they demonstrate an ability to turn around failing operations, to identify and institute cost savings, and/or to create processes that save time (and thus money)? Look for these bottom-line strengths and then translate them into your summary with your unique value stated such as in the following two examples:

- *Visionary Operations Manager with a proven reputation for lowering expenses, turning around operations, and creating positive culture that consistently results in multimillion-dollar revenue gain.*

- *High-energy Administrative Assistant who excels at meeting the needs of a team of busy executives and technical engineers. Talent for identifying opportunities to create tracking and data management processes, which result in up to 30 percent time savings.*

>> **Your key selling features:** These include degrees, certifications, licenses, awards, and even publications that make you stand out for your target job. For instance, if you are a marketing professional who made the Twitter

Top 50 Pros to Follow list, or you published a book on a key topic, highlight these accomplishments in your summary. For example:

- *Recognized authority on web development. Authored* The Authoritative Guide to WordPress *(XYZ publisher); book has been called "If you can read only one, this is it" in press reviews.*

- *Attained <Certification Name> credential — a qualification held by only 30 professionals worldwide.*

REMEMBER

An accomplishment is a key selling feature only if it makes you stand out from the competition. That's why it's called a *unique* selling proposition. So if a certification is listed as a prerequisite for the position or it positions you as uniquely qualified, include it in your summary section. But, on the other hand, if you have an MBA that's not requested or that's too common a qualification to take up valuable summary space, mention it only in your education section.

Matching the Job Target with Key Skills

Skills are the keywords of your resume. They are a critical component of surviving much of the initial resume scanning that takes place, both by humans and computers, to determine whether you make it to the decision maker and the interview.

TIP

Although there are specific competencies and skills for each type of job (think plumber, sales person, administrative assistant, CEO), the way they are specifically worded can vary from company to company, and when you are making an industry change, from industry to industry. For instance, an entry-level job in shipping and receiving could have Logistics, Shipping and Receiving, Material Handling, or even Kitting in the title. So it's critical to carefully study job advertisements and use the wording that the company has used to be a perfect match and to survive applicant tracking systems (ATS). For more on ATS, check out Chapter 4.

In the following sections, I define two categories of skills and explain how to incorporate the different types into your resume.

Hard skills

Hard skills are the technical qualifications you possess that your profession and target position require. For instance, there is a specific set of unique skills required of a retail manager, administrative assistant, veterinary technician, sales person, or an aerospace engineer. An example of a veterinary technician might include

Animal restraint techniques, treatment administration (oral/injectable), medication dosage calculation, IV catheter placement, X-rays, blood draws, laboratory testing, diagnostic equipment operation

These technical competencies become the cornerstone of your keyword section, which is placed directly under the summary. This section is typically best expressed in a two- to three-column list that includes short, to-the-point key skills and a few competencies. You typically need to include 9 to 21 key skills and competencies. (Flip to Chapter 8 for details on how to identify your skills.)

Soft skills

Soft skills are important but can be secondary in how much stress you place on them in this section. *Soft skills* are interpersonal talents such as the ability to work as part of a team or to communicate effectively with customers. You're required to have them for the position, but because of how generic the skills can be, they aren't always listed in the key skills section. Instead, roll them into the summary (see earlier section) when you are describing how you excel and add to the bottom line. It can become clear that you are a strong communicator when you mention "selected to give keynote speech for the industry's leading national conference."

The Proof Is in the Experience

Experience — for the traditional professional — includes your professional experience or work history presented in reverse chronological order (also known as RC). This section is critical because it's where you provide the proof to support your objective header, summary, and keyword sections. This is where the employer looks for these details, but this is also where you can easily lose that attention.

Each position will have at minimum your specific job title, employer company name, location (city, state), and dates of employment. Account for each position in a way that shows progression and promotion within an organization whenever possible. I go into more detail about shaping your experience in the following sections.

TIP

For new graduates or those professionals making a serious transition, this section could encompass experience gained from volunteer work, internships, school projects and papers, personal studies, and a variety of nonpaid areas. Check out Chapters 13 and 14 for strategies.

Defining the parts of your experience

A job description is made up of two key parts, which include

» **The position overview or hook.** This part is typically presented as a brief paragraph that sets the stage for the position by laying out the goal or challenge of the position.

» **Proof-of-experience statements.** This is typically presented as a series of bullets that follow the hook paragraph. The goal of these statements is to show that your experience matches that of your job target.

WARNING

Do not make the mistake of thinking of the parts of your experience from the point of view of "responsible for." This phrase should never appear on your resume. Further, when you write about your responsibilities, position them to show you stand out from your similarly qualified competition by telling very brief stories that explain the challenges you faced, actions you took to deal with those challenges, and the results you attained (also called CAR stories). By using this CAR method, you direct prospective employers to the value you would bring to their companies.

Playing up target expertise

Your Core, one-size-fits-all resume that you will develop first, before beginning to target positions with your OnTarget resumes, is going to cover all the competencies (experiences) and related accomplishments you have for the job you performed. Under each job listed, your Core resume will have a seemingly long list of bullets that you can use to pick and choose from as you later tailor your OnTarget resumes to specific positions.

When you write, always try to focus on the top accomplishments that lure most employers, because they emphasize the bottom-line value you represent to the company (make money, save money, and so on). The most valuable accomplishments include

» Increased revenues

» Saved money

» Increased efficiency

» Reduced overhead

» Increased sales

» Improved workplace safety

>> Attained purchasing accomplishments

>> Introduced new products/new lines

>> Improved record-keeping process

>> Increased productivity

>> Launched successful advertising campaign

>> Captured market share

>> Maximized budgets

As you write, turn continuously to how you affected these power areas, even if you weren't recognized for the contribution. If you made your life easier and your job more efficient, it counts!

The snapshot of the resume in Figure 7-2 depicts a job description from a one-size-fits-all resume. Notice how the first paragraph hooks the reader with the challenge and the bullets cover all areas of key responsibilities while emphasizing CAR stories (for more on CAR stories, see Chapter 8).

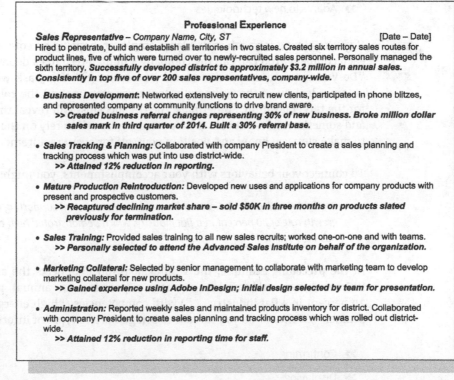

Professional Experience

Sales Representative – Company Name, City, ST   [Date – Date]
Hired to penetrate, build and establish all territories in two states. Created six territory sales routes for product lines, five of which were turned over to newly-recruited sales personnel. Personally managed the sixth territory. ***Successfully developed district to approximately $3.2 million in annual sales. Consistently in top five of over 200 sales representatives, company-wide.***

- *Business Development:* Networked extensively to recruit new clients, participated in phone blitzes, and represented company at community functions to drive brand aware.
  >> ***Created business referral changes representing 30% of new business. Broke million dollar sales mark in third quarter of 2014. Built a 30% referral base.***

- *Sales Tracking & Planning:* Collaborated with company President to create a sales planning and tracking process which was put into use district-wide.
  >> ***Attained 12% reduction in reporting.***

- *Mature Production Reintroduction:* Developed new uses and applications for company products with present and prospective customers.
  >> ***Recaptured declining market share – sold $50K in three months on products slated previously for termination.***

- *Sales Training:* Provided sales training to all new sales recruits; worked one-on-one and with teams.
  >> ***Personally selected to attend the Advanced Sales Institute on behalf of the organization.***

- *Marketing Collateral:* Selected by senior management to collaborate with marketing team to develop marketing collateral for new products.
  >> ***Gained experience using Adobe InDesign; initial design selected by team for presentation.***

- *Administration:* Reported weekly sales and maintained products inventory for district. Collaborated with company President to create sales planning and tracking process which was rolled out district-wide.
  >> ***Attained 12% reduction in reporting time for staff.***

FIGURE 7-2:
A succinct yet powerful listing of an applicant's professional experience.

When competencies come into play

Competencies are the behaviors required to do the work and are often hinted at more than listed. They don't come in a handy-dandy, one-size-fits-all package. To meet the needs of applicant tracking systems (ATS), which seek to connect that you have all the right skills and competencies, you need to go a step further in your job bullets to show how your accomplishments confirm your competencies. Or to turn it around, you must show how your competencies enabled you to rack up home runs.

Here are a few examples of competencies:

>> Displays knowledge of products

>> Prioritizes and plans work activities

>> Uses time efficiently

>> Achieves sales goals

>> Maintains customer satisfaction

>> Troubleshoots technological problems

>> Adapts to new technologies

TIP

If you're aiming for a job with a large employer, bone up on competency policy at each company. You can call the company's human resources department and ask, "Do you use a competencies model in recruiting?" If so, ask whether you can obtain a lexicon of the company's core competencies and the role competencies for the target position. Sometimes, the HR specialist will reveal the competencies and sometimes not. But ask. If they won't, you need to rely on the job description to make sure you know and position yourself for every requirement.

To connect your behaviors with your accomplishments, you might say

> **Product development:** *Created new mid-market segment supporting an annual growth rate of 20 percent in a flat industry, which demonstrated high energy and business acumen.*

In the preceding example, the verb *demonstrated* connects the accomplishment ("Created new mid-market segment supporting an annual growth rate of 20 percent in a flat industry. . .") with competencies ("high energy and business acumen"). Other verbs you can use to bridge the two types of information include:

>> Confirming

>> Displaying

- » Exhibiting
- » Illustrating
- » Manifesting
- » Proving
- » Revealing
- » Verifying

Education Makes the Grade

Education doesn't include only degrees you have earned. It should also include degrees you are currently pursuing and certificates required to perform your job. Sometimes the section is further expanded to cover certifications, licenses, and continuing education courses. In such cases, you can name the section

- » Education and Training
- » Education and Certifications
- » Training and Certification (use when you have no advanced degrees)
- » Education and Licensure

The rule of thumb is that if you have only one or two in each category, group them together. I flesh out how to present your education in the sections below.

Detailing your degree

Your Core resume lists everything in priority order from most relevant to least relevant, which allows you to pick and choose what to include for your OnTarget resumes. (For more on targeting your resume, see Chapter 9.)

The best order for the content is based on what matters most to the prospective employer. With most degrees, for example, the degree itself matters more than the school from which it was earned. So this listing might look like the following:

Degree in Specialty – *University Name, City, ST — honors attained*

If you are currently pursuing a degree or certificate, you can list it like this:

Currently pursuing **Degree in Specialty** — *University Name, City, ST*

You also could — and should — bold the degree so it stands out.

TIP

It's not a good idea to include the year of graduation (or completion) because it can either make you look too green or too dated. An employer will ask you for this information in an interview if it's needed.

Here are further tips for effectively highlighting your education:

>> New graduates shouldn't list courses taken in their education section. Instead, check out Chapter 13 for tips on making what you learned into keyword skills.

>> Do not list the high school you attended or accomplishments in high school.

>> Note continuing education, including seminars related to your work.

>> If you fall short of the mark on the job's educational requirements, try to compensate by expanding with continuing education. Give the list a name, such as *Professional Development Highlights,* and list every impressive (but, more importantly, relevant) course, seminar, workshop, and conference that you've attended.

WARNING

Sometimes an advanced degree can do more harm than help. This can be the case with doctorates and even master's degrees, especially if you are changing companies, industries, or careers. Apply this test to determine whether the degree is worth listing:

WHAT'S FIRST — EDUCATION OR EXPERIENCE?

Education and experience should always follow the objective header, summary, and keyword sections. But after you've cleared those sections, the best strategy regarding the order of education and experience is to lead with your most qualifying factor.

With certain exceptions (such as when you are using a CV for positions in science, medicine, or higher education), lead off with experience when you've been in the workforce for at least one year. When you're loaded with experience but low on credentials, list your education at the end — and perhaps even omit details that over- or under-qualify you.

>> Is it a similar level or type of degree as a requirement list for the job? If yes, then list it. If no, go on to the next question.

>> Do the people I report to typically have this level of degree? If no, then do not list it.

If the job doesn't request it or require it and your potential bosses don't have that level of education, chances are strong that including your advanced degree could be a killer. The prospective employer may see you as too expensive or assume you won't be challenged enough to stay, or may even be intimidated by your advanced credentials. Although I know you worked hard for this accomplishment, use extreme caution in deciding whether to list your advanced degree in this type of situation.

Featuring your certifications

List on your resume the relevant certifications you hold in your field because they add luster to your qualifications and help you stand out from the competition. Include your certifications either as a subsection of education or make it a stand-alone section if you have many relevant certifications.

Certification as a job search tool is gaining renewed respect because of the following points:

>> Certification is useful for resume triage by HR screeners who may not know the particulars of a given certification but nevertheless count it as a marker of extra knowledge and place resumes of cert holders in the coveted interview pile.

>> Certification is valued by outsourcing firms because the credentials add credibility to project proposals. Employees with certs in outsourced departments are thought to be (but not proven to be) more likely to keep their jobs than those without the credentials.

>> Certification is viewed as continuing education that indicates a job seeker has stayed up-to-date in a fast-moving field, is not stale, and is open to lifelong learning.

>> Certification for new college graduates shows they offer more than school-taught skills and are willing to make an extra effort to excel.

TIP

Certifications can be such a big, relevant deal to your job target that they may even be listed in your summary section. When you do this, still list them in the education section so you can add the granting entity and any particulars.

Listing your licenses

If you're in a field or function that requires a license to do your work — such as legal, certified accounting, engineering, teaching, real estate, or medicine — show your license prominently on your resume.

Licenses can be a subsection of education or you can use a heading of "Professional Licensing" (if only one license) or "Professional Licenses" (for more than one license).

TIP

Just as with certifications, holding a license can be so important to the position you're applying for that you may need to list it in your summary section as well. When you do this, list it in the education section as well so you can add the granting entity and any particulars.

Gaining Extra Points

You've covered the meat and potatoes of your resume content. What can you add that will strengthen your image? You could, for instance, draw from your activities to show that you've got the right stuff. John Gill of Carlsbad, California, paid his own expenses to spend his college spring break building houses for the poor in Mexico. That act of sacrifice shows Gill's character; he goes out of his way to do important things for others. That's good resume content.

What's in your history that may strengthen your image? Here are a few thoughts on buffing your image.

Activities

Activities can be anything from hobbies and sports to campus extracurricular participation. The trick is to analyze how each activity is relevant to the target job; discuss skills, knowledge, or other competencies developed; and list all accomplishments.

In addition, avoid potentially controversial activities: Stating that you're a moose hunter won't endear you to animal-loving employers. Stating you skydive in your spare time may make you appear a health risk. If you've been able to research the reader and have found that you two have a common interest, list it on your resume so it can become an icebreaker topic during an interview.

WARNING

It doesn't matter how proud of your activities and hobbies you might be. If they aren't relevant, don't include them because they'll just take up precious space that you could use to sell what really matters to the prospective employer.

Organizations and affiliations

Give yourself even more credentials with professional and civic affiliations. Mention all-important offices held. Relate these affiliations to your reader in terms of marketable skills, knowledge, and accomplishments. A high profile in the community (online or local) is particularly important for many professions.

Just as you should be careful about which activities you identify (see the preceding section), so too should you be sensitive to booby traps in organization memberships:

>> Listing too many organizations may make the reader wonder when you'd have time to do the job.

>> Noting that you belong to one minority group organization may work in your favor, but reporting your membership in five similar minority group organizations may raise red flags. The recruiter may worry that you're a trouble-making activist more focused on that than the job or target company.

>> And, of course, you know better than to list your membership in religious or political organizations (unless you're applying for a job that requires such membership). These affiliations don't apply to your ability to do the job, and some readers may use them to keep you out of the running.

Honors and awards

This part of your resume is tricky as a stand-alone section because it typically comes near the end of your resume and makes such valuable information easy to miss. Relevant awards can have greater punch if they appear higher in the resume, such as if you mention them in the summary or include them as an accomplishment under the job at which you earned them.

If the award is a major industry award, be sure to mention it in the summary section, even as "industry-award winner for . . ." If the award was for company performance, then tie it into that job and make it stand out with bolding and italics.

Smaller awards or lengthier listings can be in a separate section. Otherwise, don't hide your illustrious achievements. After all, someone saw fit to award you for them!

It's not necessary to list awards and recognitions that have nothing to do with work or that don't show you in a professional light, such as winning the Chili Cook-off if you aren't applying for a job as a chef.

However, some seemingly irrelevant awards can add value from a competencies standpoint. If there is a competency for a job you are targeting that you don't meet between work and school, an award could do the trick.

Consider new graduate, Tom Nichols. At 15, he was the youngest person to win a fishing tournament and his prize was a new boat. By itself, this accolade is meaningless to the resume, but the context makes it valuable toward his pursuit of a medical sales position. In order to keep the boat, he had to be able to pay for it. To pay for the boat, he started an informal charter business. His clients were local doctors and surgeons, because his dad is a doctor. Can you connect the dots? Tom has tons of transferable value to play up in his new graduate resume in areas such as physician relations, selling, drive, and enterprising spirit. (See Chapter 13 for more on new graduate resumes.)

Endorsements

After citing an accomplishment, add immediately beneath it a short, flattering quote from your boss or a client. (Alternative placement: Present an endorsement in an italic typeface in a left- or right-hand column by your summary, or at the bottom of your resume.) Here are a few examples of endorsements:

>> **For an information systems technician:** *Tom is a cost-cutting maven. He was the driving force behind an 80 percent cut in Internet access and telephone costs. — Bill Jones, CEO*

>> **For a sales rep at a toner and cartridge shop:** *Jennifer Robertson's resourcefulness in getting inside the SoapSuds account and expanding it by 15 percent after others had tried for months is truly impressive. — Kevin Bloch, General Manager*

>> **For an administrative support person:** *Sarah is a dynamo of energy and enthusiasm; she streamlined our project procedures, which saved hours of labor each week and made the office feel like a home. — Kathryn Smith, Business Owner*

Endorsements work, or advertisers wouldn't spend billions of dollars to use them. Be sure to check with your source before adding a quote to your resume.

Shaping Your Content on Application Forms

Application forms that you must sign aren't resumes. Once signed, an application form becomes a legal document. Lies can come back to bite and smite you. Stick to the facts by following these basic rules:

>> Verify all dates of employment and salaries.

>> Enter the full name and last known address of previous companies for which you worked. If these companies are out of business, write "N.A." or "defunct" in the address section.

>> If asked for salary history, list your base salary (or add commission and bonuses), omitting benefits.

>> Give a complete employment history in months and years, including trivial three-month jobs that you left off the resume. When you don't tell the whole story, you leave a loophole of withholding information that later can be used against you to deny unemployment benefits if you're let go.

>> Unless you have a condition directly affecting your ability to do the job for which you're applying, you need not elaborate on any disability.

>> Check your state laws because in some states having to disclose a former salary is discriminatory.

TIP

Become a fountain of knowledge about disability rights; start with such specialty websites as the National Organization on Disability (www.nod.org).

>> Divulge any criminal record (misdemeanor or felony) unless your records are sealed; consult a lawyer about the possibility of expungement before job hunting.

In certain instances, a job seeker can legally and ethically answer "no" on a question about a past offense; for information, visit Privacy Rights Clearinghouse (www.privacyrights.org).

When you have to divulge such information, always include an application addendum where you explain the situation in the most positive light possible and share how you have changed with employer references, employment tenure, and awards.

>> Be honest about having collected unemployment benefits (but remember that repeaters are frowned on). If you're caught lying about it later, practice your farewell speech.

>> State law regarding the criminal records you must divulge vary from state to state, so check the law in your state.

Notable Content to Leave Off Your Resume

Eager, inexperienced job seekers often want to include everything they think a prospective employer wants to see or could potentially ask about. In some of the earlier sections, I mention some insignificant details to leave off (such as high school info and political or religious affiliations).

However, there are two big categories of information that you should never, ever include on your resume: salary and references. I explain why these topics should be left off in the following sections.

Avoid addressing the salary question

Never mention salary on your resume. Period.

Sometimes a job ad asks for your salary history (past) or salary requirements (future). Realize that revealing dollar figures in advance puts you at a disadvantage. This is especially true if you've been working for low pay — or if you've been paid above market.

In addition to job ads, profile forms on job sites and online personal agent programs almost always ask for your salary information. If you decide to participate, state your expectations in a range and include the value of all benefits, bonuses, and perks in your salary history, not just cash.

TIP

Whenever possible, go with *negotiable*, *open*, or *flexible* instead of including dollar amounts.

REMEMBER

When you choose to disclose your salary history or requirements online, make a distinction between general information forms and formal signed applications (legal documents). Include benefits (total compensation) on general information forms, but omit benefits on formal signed applications that ask for salary history.

Before you reveal your salary requirements, research the market rate for someone with your skills and experience. Start with the websites Salary (www.salary.com), Salary Expert (www.salaryexpert.com), and PayScale (www.payscale.com).

Avoid being too quick to pipe up with hard figures on the money you've made and the money you want. When you reveal this information without already having a job offer, you might over-price yourself, be talked into taking a reduced salary, or not even get the interview. You always want to strive to get to the interview and the offer before talking dollars.

TIP

Exception to salary silence advice: As I mention in Chapter 4, tell recruiters with whom you have a serious interest in working how much you've earned and how much it will cost an employer to hire you. Otherwise, know that recruiters don't want to waste time playing games and are likely to fold up their interest and move on.

Hold off on providing your references

Employment references do not belong on a resume unless an employer specifically asks for them. In fact, the fastest way to date yourself (and your resume) is to include the words "References available upon request" at the bottom of your resume. This is a given that you will have those references available when they are requested.

TIP

Don't wait until an employer requests the contact information for your references to get in touch with people to ask if they'll put in a good word for you. If you haven't done so already, reach out to prior employers, customers, directors of organizations for which you volunteer, professors, teachers, and instructors. Get their permission to have potential employers contact them about you.

Be sure to send your references a copy of the resume you use to apply for a position, and when you give out your references contact list, provide courtesy notice to your references about the nature of the position and that they may be contacted.

Follow up repeatedly and thank everyone on your reference list when those individuals provide a reference. Be sure to let them know when you land your new job. After all, you need them to continue doing so for you throughout your career.

Chapter **8**

Making the Details Shine

Your ultimate goal is to customize your resume to be a specific OnTarget document for each job you seek. But getting there always starts with creating one master *Core* — or one-size-fits-all — resume document. That master document is a tool that, once created, you can pull from to ensure that you're OnTarget. But to get there, you have to cross the bridge from knowing you need a resume to figuring out what to put in it, and making sure that the content is powerful enough to make you stand out from all the other applicants for the job.

For most job seekers, this leads to what is called Blank Page Syndrome, where they end up sitting in front of a computer staring at a blank screen and not knowing where to get started or what is even important enough to include. After they sit long enough trying to fill in each of those resume sections, most people will end up just listing basic responsibilities held or skills performed.

WARNING

Although it's tempting to want to get the resume written quickly, settling for the basics in areas such as job descriptions and summary of qualifications won't allow you to stand out against the competition. You need to capture content for your resume that says more than what you can do and have done. When you follow the process outlined in this chapter, you'll sail past the stress of Blank Page Syndrome into concrete details and accomplishments that show an employer you're worth the interview.

Getting Started by Gathering Data

Making data gathering for your resume writing easy involves starting with the right information in front of you. That way you don't get stuck staring at a blank screen. Before you sit down to write, take the time to gather the following:

>> **Resumes:** Gather any resumes you have written in the past ten years.

>> **Employment records:** Collect any written evaluations, job descriptions, or other previous employment records.

>> **Training records:** Certificates or lists of training, continuing education, degrees, and licenses.

>> **Recommendations:** Letters of recommendations, thank-you letters, emails, or cards from bosses, customers, or other related persons.

>> **Projects:** Copies of any major projects or abstracts/details about them.

>> **Awards:** Copies of any awards received professionally or personally.

>> **Publications:** List of any publications written such as books or articles.

>> **Presentations:** List presentations made, topics, and where presented.

>> **Affiliations:** Create a list of all voluntary roles held (business, board level, social, civic, academic). Be sure to gather any details, such as recognitions or awards received, projects chaired and outcomes, hours contributed, and so on.

>> **For new graduates or those with a new major certification that is the job target:** Major course textbooks or material, course syllabi, and school's course descriptions (usually in the catalog).

Don't censor yourself when gathering data! Avoid judging what is relevant. It's better to include everything and whittle away later than to discount something that might have brought you value. You can always opt not to use something as you move forward with these steps.

Some of this data may require you to do a little thinking and a little free writing where you brainstorm on paper or directly into a document on your computer. That's okay. Get your lists and data together now so you can refer to them when you're ready to begin compiling your data into a single document of noteworthy information.

Although you can start manually on paper with the next steps of pulling out the data you need from the documents you have gathered or created, it will be much easier if you have access to a computer with word-processing software. Most employers accept and prefer Microsoft Word documents, so this is what you should build your document in.

TIP

You don't have to rely on trying to jump between multiple documents saved on your computer. Take the time to print all your documentation so you have it at your fingertips. Or if you can, copy and paste it into a single Word document. Either way will make getting the information you need much quicker and easier.

Compiling the Content for the Basis of Your Resume

After you've begun collecting your data (see the preceding section), start making lists that you can use later to write your resume. It's important to understand that this isn't the point at which your writing is polished, resume-worthy content for your final resume. Instead, you're going to be dumping information into your Word document (and saving it regularly to avoid losing it). So don't worry about grammar, impressive wording, formatting, or run-on sentences. Just follow the instructions in this section to get the information down.

Starting with your employment history and responsibilities lists

You're going to start with your employment history section (refer to Chapter 7 for details on the different sections of a resume), but don't worry if this isn't your area of strength or if your job target is different now. You'll have a chance to apply the same process to other areas, such as volunteer work, leadership, and courses or degrees completed next.

Start with your most recent job and begin by creating a bulleted list of your responsibilities. Get them all down, regardless of how trivial, because you may need them later when you put the resume together. Here's an example of how your list might look if you're a retail manager:

COMPANY: Weight Loss International (formerly Pacific Weight Loss)

TITLE: Center Manager

LOCATION: [City, ST]

DATES: [Start Date – End Date]

Responsibilities:

- Managed day-to-day business operations.

- Handled interviewing, hiring, training, and supervision of employees.

- Supervised a staff of two as well as an assistant manager.

- Trained staff in selling and customer-service techniques, and motivated them to meet up-selling goals.

- Sold memberships and products.

- Handled inventory management.

- Oversaw client account management and service.

- Maintained financial responsibility for payroll within budget as well as daily closeout, bank deposits, and balancing.

Repeat this process for any additional positions you held in the last ten years. If you are changing careers to return to a profession from your past, take this step on those older jobs as well.

REMEMBER

All your documentation is in front of you, so you should be able to whip this content together rather quickly. Again, don't worry about how you say it at this point. These are going to be your notes.

TIP

If you find you're struggling and don't have the data you need to create your job description, you can try the following:

>> Visit your former employer's web page to see whether it lists job descriptions in the hiring or job center section.

>> Contact Human Resources or a former colleague to see whether they can supply you with a description. If you haven't remained connected, LinkedIn can be a great resource for finding people by doing an advanced search that includes the company name.

>> Perform a Google search for your job title (such as retail manager in this example) to be reminded of responsibilities. Glassdoor (www.glassdoor.com) also has an impressive array of company-specific job information.

>> Visit industry professional associations to find job descriptions in their career center or regular resources.

Going down the rabbit hole to identify challenges

After you've compiled your past history and responsibilities, you need to go back and dig deep to get at what value you provided in each of those areas. This process is a little like going down the rabbit hole, where you continue to dig deeper and deeper until you get to your goal — in this case, the goal is listing specifics about the challenges you faced and what you accomplished.

In an OnTarget resume, not only do you need to emphasize matching yourself to the job you're targeting, but you also have to give the employer a reason to select you from all the other qualified applicants. To do that, you have to sell what you accomplished and not just tell what you did.

You do this by having concrete stories, which are commonly referred to as *CAR stories*. CAR stands for Challenge, Action, Result. In other words, in the overall job, as well as for any given responsibility, consider:

>> What challenge did you face?

>> What action did you take to overcome that challenge?

>> What result did you attain from your action?

So return to your most recent job description bulleted list. Think about your time in that position and ask yourself:

>> What did you step into with the new job? Did you face problems or challenges? Tell me about them. Dig deep or follow the rabbit.

>> Was this a newly created position? If so, what were the expectations? Follow the rabbit.

>> Were you filling a position that had been vacant for some time? What challenges did you step into? Follow that rabbit.

>> Were you recruited to the position? If so, what issues were the managers facing that they wanted you on board? Tell me about the issues. Follow that rabbit.

Brainstorm these answers into your notes. Do a brain dump of what you remember, and don't worry about how it reads or looks at this time. If you're drawing a blank, consider the following:

>> If the organization was already successful and it just wanted you to maintain the status quo, did you still find areas that needed improvement? Follow the rabbit.

>> Did you see ways you could make improvements after you were settled into the position? Tell me about it. Follow that rabbit!

For the retail manager example I've been using, here are some of the follow-the-rabbit elements that you can consider:

>> When you took over, did you have set goals for sales for your branch before you started? Were they being met? What was their percentage to goal per quarter/year? What did you identify as the problems? Talk about each of those.

>> What was the customer turnover/dissatisfaction level and why? What did you do about it? How quickly did numbers change? What were those new numbers?

>> Were branches ranked? If so, where did this branch rank when you started with them? Out of how many branches? Where do they rank now? What did you do to accomplish that? Follow that rabbit deeper as needed.

After considering these examples, the retail manager (from the previous section) might come up with something like this:

Overall Challenges:

The following needed to be restarted and targeted for massive turnaround: staff the center with customer-focused personnel, reclaim clients, overcome negative brand connotations, and meet aggressive revenue goals by increasing average dollars per sale on each transaction.

- Took over a poorly performing center. Many customers had abandoned their memberships and business was way down. How much? Almost 80 percent. This left the center ranked 23rd out of 27 centers.

- Quarterly sales goals were down by more than 40 percent.

- Their goal was an average sale of $580 but the center was only averaging $350.

- Customer satisfaction rating was only 66 percent. There were a lot of staff training issues to deal with.

- There was a lot of missing inventory. Approximately 20 percent monthly and that was costing the center about $1,200 in losses.

- Staff turnover was high. When I came in, there were only three staff members, and they had each been there less than six months. The center should have had five staffers. Obviously retention is a key to profitability and customer service.

You'll later use what you've just created to craft what is called a *hook* in your job description (more on this later in the chapter), which sets the stage for the potential employer by letting them know what you faced in the job.

After you've tackled the overall challenge(s) faced in the position, you want to turn to each of your responsibility bullets for that position. To get to the CAR statements, consider what the challenge, action, and result would be for each responsibility.

TIP

Don't forget to use *all* your documentation for putting together your CAR stories. Now is a great time to reread everything, especially letters of recommendation, award certifications, thank-you letters from bosses and clients, and evaluations. You should find lots of good accomplishments in those materials.

Showing how action and results overcame challenges

When you think about the challenges you faced in your jobs, your thoughts probably move naturally to what steps you took to overcome those challenges and what the outcomes of your actions were. After you've listed previous work-related challenges (see preceding section), it only makes sense to explain how you resolved them. Take your list of challenges for a particular position, and then build on it first with the actions and then the results.

REMEMBER

Don't worry about this Core resume document's page count at the end of this process — especially after you've done it for each of your positions. You will cut down these notes into final, succinct bullets for your final resume when you get to that step.

Using the retail manager example from the section "Starting with your employment history and responsibilities lists," consider the responsibility of selling memberships and products. You know that quarterly sales goals were down, average sale dollars were not being attained per customer, and customer service in the selling process was poor.

If you followed the rabbit into the story of the actions taken to overcome this along with the results, your notes may look like the following:

Challenges and Actions:

» Annual membership started at $350 but could be upgraded to a platinum maintenance plan of $580, which was the goal. To accomplish this, I directed staff in the following ways:

- Educated them on how to upsell the platinum level, giving them training materials and sessions to better understand the features and benefits of the upgrade, and educating them on how to present it to increase sales closures.

- Performed add-on sales demos and skits with staff to get them comfortable with all our supplemental products. Promoted them during weekly client meetings and ran mini incentive campaigns with staff to get them used to performing add-on sales.

» Called all former members and let them know that they were entitled to their membership, how many weeks they had left, and details on any product credits they still had pending. Made sure they were given excellent service and explained about the new leadership so they would perhaps come back.

» Held special customer open houses to reintroduce lost customers to the program and its services/products.

» Introduced referral bonus program for bringing someone in — if they joined and stayed at least four weeks, they received a $50 in-store credit.

» Sponsored specials to move excess inventory.

Results Achieved:

» Center averaged 50 percent close rate from call to walk through the door (against an expectation for this test center of 30 percent).

» Staff successfully upgraded 40 percent of clients from the standard one-year membership at $350 to the platinum maintenance program at $580.

» Increased up-front sales of nutritional bars by 20 percent by selling the benefits of bulk discount, which allowed facility to move more product and keep clients committed to the program.

» Moved ranking of center from 23rd to 13th in nine months. Ended first quarter in 2015 at 7th out of 27 and maintained status for four consecutive years.

» Began consistently meeting quarterly sales goals in second quarter of 2014 and continued to do so.

>> Positioned center to "Most Improved Center" for four consecutive years (2014, 2015, 2016, 2017).

Can you see that you are so much more than your responsibilities? After you take this step on each of your positions, you'll see you have rich stories to tell about your value!

Taking the Next Steps

It's now time to look at your other areas of experience and value. Because you may consider a variety of positions to target down the road, take these steps now, even if you don't see the relevance. The following sections give you some general ideas about what other information to round up and offer some specific statements you can use to point to your achievements.

REMEMBER

This document on your computer is going to be a hefty one, but don't let the length bother you. If you have pages and pages of notes, that's great! It means you have a lot of information to work with. If you don't have a long document, don't think it's the end of the world. In Chapter 13, I show you how to make your limited experience work best for you.

Considering other accomplishments

You're more than your work experience or career, even when it comes to your resume. To paint a complete picture of what you can offer an employer, consider your education, volunteer activities, and recognition given by previous employers. Think about some of the following areas of accomplishment:

>> **Academics:** Dig deep in this area only if you are entering a new career field based on a degree, training, program, or certification earned. Instead of looking at job responsibilities, however, look at courses you completed and then

- Make a list of relevant classes and pull the descriptions either from the textbook's table of contents, course description, or course syllabi into a bulleted list.

- Ask yourself about each class: What did I learn? What projects or papers or case studies did I complete? In those projects, papers, and/or case studies, what challenges, actions, and results did I attain?

>> **Awards:** If an award wasn't tied to a specific job and you haven't already considered it, dig into it here. What was it for? What does it mean in regard to my potential employment target(s)? What does it say about me from a strengths and value perspective?

>> **Publications and Presentations:** Again, do the same as with awards.

>> **Affiliations (Volunteer Work):** Delve into this area only if you need to emphasize a skill set not available in your current employment. After you list each organization and role held, consider your CAR stories (for more on this, see the earlier section "Going down the rabbit hole to identify challenges").

Brainstorming your way to success

TIP

When you hit a brick wall with your accomplishments, try the following plug-and-play strategy to help think of what value you bring. Just fill in the blanks and add these statements to your stories.

Saying it with numbers

A few numbers can reveal more about your experience and accomplishments than a thousand words can. Consider how you can apply these statements to your work history:

>> __ (#) years of extensive experience in _____ and _____.

>> Won ____ (#) awards for _____.

>> Trained/Supervised ____ (#) full-time and ____ (#) part-time employees.

>> Recommended by _____ (# of notable people) as a _____ (something good that they said about you) for excellent _____ (an accomplishment or skill).

>> Supervised a staff of ____ (#).

>> Recruited ____ (#) staff members in _____ (period of time), increasing overall production.

>> Sold ____ (# of products) in _____ (period of time), ranking ____ (1st, 2nd, 3rd) in sales in a company of ____ (#) employees.

>> Exceeded goals in __ (#) years/months/days, establishing my employer as ____ (1st, 2nd, 3rd, or whatever number) in industry.

>> Missed only ____ (#) days of work out of ____ (#) total.

>> Assisted ____ (#) _____ (executives, supervisors, technical directors, others).

Saying it with percentages

Percentages help you show how you ranked against your competition, how well you achieved a goal, or how much you cut costs. Percentages are often easier for a reader to make sense of than a number such as 600 hours, which may not have the necessary context to have an effect on the reader. Check out these statements:

>> Excellent _____ (your top proficiency) skills, which resulted in ___ (%) increase/decrease in _____ (sales, revenues, profits, clients, expenses, costs, charges).

>> Recognized as a leader in company, using strong skills in _____ (skills) to effect a/an ___ (%) increase in team/coworker production.

>> Streamlined _____ (industry procedure), decreasing hours spent on task by ___ (%).

>> Used extensive _____ (several skills) to increase customer/member base by ___ (%).

>> Financed ___ (%) of tuition/education/own business.

>> Graduated in the top ___ (%) of class.

>> Responsible for an estimated ___ (%) of employer's success in _____ (functional area/market).

>> Resolved customer-relations issues, increasing customer satisfaction by ___ (%).

>> Eliminated _____ (an industry problem), increasing productivity by ___ (%).

>> Upgraded _____ (an industry tool), resulting in ___ (%) increase in effectiveness.

>> Increased sales by ___ (%) by _____ (actions).

Saying it with dollar amounts

How often does corporate America talk about the bottom line? A *lot*. So your resume can be an acceptable place to talk about money and the savings you generated for an employer or the amount of revenue by which you increased the bottom line. Take a look at these statements:

>> Supervised entire _____ (a department) staff, decreasing middle-management costs by ___ ($).

» Purchased computer upgrade for office, saving the company ____ ($) in paid hours.

» Eliminated the need for _____ (one or several positions in company), decreasing payroll by ____ ($).

» Averaged ____ ($) in sales per month.

» Collected ____ ($) in memberships and donations.

» Supervised the opening/construction of new location, completing task at ____ ($) under projected budget.

» Designed entire _____ program, which earned ____ ($) in company revenues.

» Implemented new _____ system, saving ____ ($) daily/weekly/monthly/annually.

» Reduced cost of _____ (substantial service) by developing and implementing a new _____ system at the bargain price of ____ ($).

» Restructured _____ (organization/system/product) to result in a savings of ____ ($).

Click Save one last time, and . . . that's it! Pat yourself on the back because you just collected all the data you need to create your Core resume (and later the OnTarget resumes I discuss in Chapter 9).

Your Core Resume: Turning Your Data into Dynamite

Now that all your data is staring you in the face, it's time to make it work for you. With your Core resume, don't target a specific job advertisement, but rather focus on making all the skills, accomplishments, and experience you've accrued shine for you toward the type of job you desire (think "I am a chemical engineer" or "I am a receptionist"). That way you can pick and choose among the diamonds when you pull from your Core resume into your OnTarget one (see Chapter 9) to fit a specific job opening.

There's not really any other way around it. It's now you and your data with a lot of highlighting, copying, and pasting to go from a multipage road map to what will likely be a one- to three-page Core resume.

TIP

Don't worry so much about your first pass over this content. Feel free to write full sentences and even be verbose. Focus on writing it exactly as you would like it to read. Then, go back and ruthlessly edit, making sure your hook paragraph is only a few sentences covering three to five lines and that each bullet is no more than two lines.

The following sections show you how to best tackle the process.

Assembling the bones of the resume

You can rapidly create the bones of your resume with a few easy steps. (Chapter 7 walks you through specific content for each of these.)

1. **Save the file.**

Open a word processing program and save the document to make repeated saves easier. Include words such as the target role and date in the file name that allow you to easily identify the document.

2. **Set up your contact information.**

Lay out your brief contact information at the top of the page.

3. **Create section headers.**

Although these sections and their titles are subject to change as you format, you probably have a good idea of what your main sections are going to be for your resume. So you can put them in as placeholders: objective header statement, summary, key skills, experience, education, professional affiliations, and so on.

4. **Fill in the straightforward content.**

Sections such as education are going to be presented in black-and-white fashion. The most selling you do is to list an honor or GPA. Fill these out.

REMEMBER

The summary section doesn't get a title. It is set directly under your objective header and is meant to complement the job target with your requisite expertise and skill. Listing the word *summary* as a placeholder right now in your document will help you remember to go back and create it.

Another list-like section is the keyword skills, which is near the top of your resume (following your summary) in one to three columns of bullets. This list highlights the key skills you possess for your profession. You'll likely have anywhere from 9 to 21 bullets for your Core resume after you go through the content you've collected. Check out Chapter 10 for more on keywords.

Tackling your most recent professional or job-related experience

Whether it's your most recent employment position, volunteer role, internship, or project completed while pursuing your new degree that has the most value, start with your most recent professional experience.

REMEMBER

The rule is that if what's most recent is what's most relevant, play that up. Otherwise, dig around for what is most relevant and put your energy there. (For more on nontraditional resume situations, visit Chapters 13 and 14.)

For a traditional job seeker with a progressive career path, focus on the most recent employment position. Here is where you want to expend the most energy and time to get it just right. Your goal is to narrow your content down to:

>> A solid hook summary paragraph that sets the stage for the position, its goals, and the challenges you faced

>> Supplemental bullets or sub-areas (by function) that cover each of the core areas of responsibility for that employment position and that detail how you went above and beyond through challenges, actions, and results (CAR)

OMIT INTERVIEW-KILLER DATA

The best way to handle some land mines on your resume is to ignore them. Generally, revealing negative information on a resume is a mistake. Save troublesome information for the all-important job interview, where you have a fighting chance to explain your side of things.

Stay away from these topics when constructing a resume:

- Firings, demotions, forced resignations, and early termination of contracts
- Personal differences with coworkers or supervisors
- Bankruptcy, tax evasion, or credit problems
- Criminal convictions or lawsuits
- Homelessness
- Illnesses from which you have now recovered
- Disabilities that don't prevent you from performing the essential functions of the job, with or without some form of accommodation

To write your first paragraph, read through everything you've written down for this position and look for the story that brings it all together. As you go through, you can use a highlighter tool in the word-processing program to highlight items that stand out. These phrases likely sound like, "I was recruited to. . ." or "The company was facing. . ." or "I recognized this problem. . ." or even "I was able to. . ." or "It ended up saving. . . ."

The items that stand out in your work history and accomplishments come in handy when you're ready to identify your hook paragraph, but they can also be repurposed when you move on to the last step of resume assembly — crafting your summary section.

With the responsibility and accomplishment bullets, put like with like. If you have four to five areas about budgeting, first cut and paste them so they're all together and then look for what tells the best story of responsibility and CAR statements.

If you can't find a CAR statement, that's okay. Include the bullet on your Core resume anyway because you may need it when you start putting together your OnTarget resumes. Just describe your responsibilities and accomplishments as best you can, looking for ways to sound dynamic and value added. Chapter 10 gives you plenty of wording ideas.

REMEMBER

It's okay to have a lot of bullets for this job on your Core resume. You won't send this version out but will instead use it as a master document to pull from for your OnTarget versions.

Focusing on older positions

After you get through your main value position (see the preceding section), the others will be a breeze. Yes, you need to reread, highlight, and connect the dots in your content to understand the value of the position. But you don't have to go into one-tenth the detail you did in the position description you just finished writing.

The older or less relevant the job, the less detail it requires. Unless you're making a major career change that might require a nontraditional resume format, focus on creating a hook paragraph and only the top-line bullets for major accomplishments.

TIP

When you've covered four employment positions or the past 10 to 15 years (whatever comes first), your resume details can seem obsolete because the information is dated. Go ahead and stop listing and detailing positions. However, if a job feels relevant, you can add a new section to your resume called *Additional Employment* where you simply list job titles, company names, and locations (leave off the dates).

Playing up other experience

If your resume has other sections that are meaty but you haven't addressed them yet — such as volunteer work for a career changer — now is the time to do it. Remember that you want to put more time and detail into your most recent and relevant experiences. Visit Chapter 9 to learn about using crossover language in seemingly unrelated roles.

Building your brand in the summary section

Last, but certainly not least, address your summary section. I recommend doing this section last for a critical reason: You've combed over all your experience, responsibilities, skills, and accomplishments and can see a picture emerging about your unique selling proposition (USP).

As I describe in Chapter 7, your *USP* is where you provide your 30-second commercial on how you are not only qualified for the job but also the best candidate for the job. Here's how you do it: Tie together what makes you a return on investment for the employer. Do you have a reputation for making money or saving money? For turning things around? For optimizing processes? Have you won a major award or written a ground-breaking book in the industry? Have you earned a coveted credential for your profession?

The good news is that you have all these details already written down in the content you've been combing through to create the other sections of your resume. In fact, in your experience sections you probably highlighted the standout words, so you can easily find them now.

Gather all these ideas in one place. Look for standout items or consistent performance in a particular area. For example, if you're good at making money, your USP may include phrases that highlight you're a "rain-maker, focused on profit, able to exceed goals, or skilled at unprecedented financial wins." Conversely, you could have a reputation for finding ways to do things better in every job you've held, making one of your key USPs a "turnaround expert focused on improving processes, profits, and performance."

REMEMBER

Format isn't as key in the Core resume summary section, so get it all down into bullets or one or two paragraphs. State powerfully the three to six foundations in which you excel or have excelled that bring bottom-line value to an employer.

TIP

If you find yourself stumped about what really matters, review target job descriptions on the Internet. This exercise can give you a clear idea of what employers deem important in a candidate for the position and can guide you in your word choice and focus when crafting your summary and job descriptions.

Polishing Your Core Resume to Hand Out in Person

After you've mastered the Core resume as a resource from which to craft OnTarget resumes, you may need to spruce it up for possible distribution. You may realize that your Core resume is well suited to pass out at networking events and job fairs. At these open-ended events, you should be prepared to present the breadth and depth of your skills instead of targeting one opportunity. In such a case, you want your Core resume looking its best. Here are some tips to follow:

» Save your Core resume as a new document so as not to lose your master file.

» Pare content to two pages unless you're an executive. When in doubt, leave off secondary responsibilities and areas where you didn't have accomplishments.

» Proofread carefully to make sure you don't have typos, complex and confusing sentence structure, or run-on content.

» Make sure you've left adequate white space around the page so it's easy to read.

» Use a common font typeface such as Calibri 11 or Arial 10 or 11-point for body text, which is welcoming to older eyes.

» Take out skills you don't want to use. Just because you're good at it doesn't mean you have to market it.

» Look for ways to draw attention to the content with techniques such as bolding job titles, italicizing accomplishments, and including testimonial quotes from your bosses. Read more on this in Chapter 11.

» Avoid any negative information in your life and career that could derail your search.

Chapter 9

Using the OnTarget Approach

A Core, generic, or one-size-fits-all resume, when written well, tells and sells your whole career story. But if you actually use it as is to apply for open job opportunities, you will have a long, depressing wait. There are simply far too many job seekers contending for the same positions who will vie for the prospective employer's time and interest.

Instead, you need to tailor each resume and corresponding cover letter to the job you're targeting.

This chapter explains why your resumes aren't generating interviews and reveals time-saving techniques and strategies to increase your odds of making it to the interview.

Is Targeting Your Resume Really Necessary?

Sprinting ahead in today's candidate-cluttered job market gobbles up more research effort than the last time you baited your resume hooks. When there were plenty of jobs to go around, you may have needed to apply for, say, ten openings in a job search before meeting success. In today's job market, with technology what it has become, you will need to be more strategic in your thinking and possibly apply to many opportunities to find the position you truly desire.

What's more, when a job opening draws your attention, respond at first sight. In these tight times of global accessibility, employers have plenty of talent from which to choose, a reality that sometimes causes the application window to snap shut in as few as 48 hours.

So, yes: Customizing your resume really is necessary.

Consider the differing initial impressions a generic resume and a targeted resume make:

>> **A generic resume is candidate-centered.**

Translation: Here's my resume, Mr. or Ms. Employer. Hope you can find something you like about me. I'm too busy and I lack motivation to show you exactly why you want to hire me. You're on your own. Good luck. Signed: *No one you ever heard of.*

>> **A targeted resume is employer-centered.**

Translation: Glad to see you, Mr. or Ms. Employer. I'm so right for your job that I've gone the extra mile to make it easy for you to spot the fabulous match between my qualifications and your job's requirements. I promise it will be well worth your time to look me over more closely. Signed: *Someone you want to meet.*

With the exception of a handful of situations, the all-purpose resume does more harm to you and your job search than it's worth. Instead of wasting time and job opportunities, you need to be able to tailor your resume with the least fuss and muss. You can easily take your Core one-size-fits-all master resume and create customized OnTarget versions for each position.

If you're inclined to pooh-pooh the research required to effectively customize your resume, consider this sage insight from Winnie-the-Pooh's creator, A.A. Milne: "Organizing is what you do before you do something, so that when you do it, it's not all mixed up."

Why One-Size-Fits-All Never Works

Your resume is not a buffet at which a prospective employer will linger to happily select what he wants and leave the rest. Instead, if you are working with a one-size-fits-all resume, screening technology and human resources personnel will conspire to keep your potential boss from ever even seeing your resume.

Unless you are applying to a small mom-and-pop establishment, layers are probably in place for reviewing resumes and discarding applicants, from HR clerks to ATS systems and even artificial intelligence (AI). The reality is that only a few of the hundreds (and possibly thousands) of applicants get interviews. So it's critical to understand the path your resume could take on the way to the yes, no, and maybe piles.

First-line human resume screening

Understand that the first person to review your resume is likely not the person for whom you would work if hired. Envision instead that the initial screener is a busy secretary or human resources clerk. This individual is young, juggling multiple tasks, has never worked in your specific area before (and thus knows nothing about it), and has several hundred or thousand resumes sitting in her email inbox.

Her approach? Visually scan the resume in as little as 10 seconds, looking for keyword connections to the job description in front of her. If this lightning-fast scan reveals a strong enough match in keywords between the job opportunity and your resume, then into the "maybe" pile your resume goes.

Therefore, your resume must be quickly scannable for top-line content in under one minute, rich with keywords, error-free, and easy to read.

First-line computerized resume screening

Technology has put countless job opportunities at your fingertips, making it easy for you to apply with a click of the button. Because of the glut of unqualified (and untargeted) resumes that employers receive, they have had to find ways to cut down on man-hours in screening applicants. During the past decade, these systems have rapidly evolved, creating a potential black hole for job seekers who haven't targeted their resumes to the specific position.

It's all about applicant tracking systems (ATS) and electronic keyword scanning. These types of systems provide the first line of defense for screening out applicants who do not demonstrate an exact match to the target position. Plus, in recent years, artificial intelligence has been used to streamline and optimize some of these tasks, putting even more space between you and the human employer you want to reach.

Therefore, your resume must function with both content and appearance. It should be clean and uncluttered with a legible standard typeface with Arial, Calibri, or Times New Roman. You should approach keywords by first front-loading them in a special keyword section, typically presented in a 2- to 3-column list after your summary section, but then also making sure they are connected to examples of their application in the body of the resume. (For more on ATS, see Chapter 4.)

Final destination with decision-maker

Only if your resume survives the initial scans will it arrive in the hands of your prospective boss who understands the position and its needs, goals, and challenges. A one-size-fits-all resume might have snuck through to this point if it contained all the right data. However, this individual will take a deeper look and rapidly classify you as someone who isn't 100 percent committed to his department and the target role. No matter how qualified you may be, you will get screened out if you don't present a resume targeted to the needs of the prospective employer's position.

Therefore, your resume must target the position at each step of the way from your objective header statement through your summary of qualifications, keywords section, professional experience, and even in what education and training details you choose to include. The better the match you represent, the better the chance of landing an interview. See Chapter 7 for details on creating these sections.

TIP

Because your resume is now in a smaller stack of individuals who all seem qualified for the position, targeting allows you to laser in on not just what you know and can do for a targeted position, but how well you do it. By using *CAR stories* (challenges, actions, and results) to describe your responsibilities and accomplishments, you'll stand out from the other applicants. Visit Chapter 8 for details on incorporating CAR stories.

Taking a Custom Approach

In case you're wondering how the generic resume became the norm, national career expert Peter Weddle explains that way back when the typewriter was king, customizing resumes was almost impossible — like re-chiseling a statue. You typed up your one-size-fits-all resume, made photocopies, and off you went. Because the job market was so much more closed (think no Internet and no global information sharing), employers could spend more time really reading resumes because they received significantly fewer.

SPECIAL CASES WHEN GOING GENERIC IS OKAY

Although targeted resumes outperform generic resumes by a three-planet radius, a one-size-fits-all document can be effective in some circumstances.

- **Job fairs:** Customized resumes are impractical for wide distribution at dozens of employer booths. That's why I suggest you write the best all-purpose resume you can; when you get a nibble from a company you'd like to work for, quickly get back to the company recruiter with a targeted resume. Your willingness to go the extra mile makes you stand out from the competition.

- **Similar career pursuits:** When you have a single job goal — such as working only in the biotech industry developing new wonder drugs — you can work with one really good resume. But when posting your resume in online databases, you need a resume customized for each additional career field or job function you pursue.

- **Networking contacts:** If you hand out generic resumes to your inner circle of friends to help them help you in your search, mark them, "For Your Eyes Only." Ask them to contact you when they hear of job leads so you can respond with a targeted resume.

- **Reference refresher:** Send a generic resume or a bio to people who have agreed to serve as a reference in your job search.

- **Social media:** Profiles and bios are also typically in the one-size-fits-all family of information about you (but you should make every attempt to tweak your profile to your current target). When posted online, both bios and profiles defy customization. (Read about pigeonholing in Chapter 2.)

Today it is the exact opposite. Employers are inundated by resume submissions in a world where multitasking and information overload are already the norm. If you try to use that one-size-fits-all resume now, your resume will end up in a black hole.

Even though the computer age is upon us, fully customizing a resume remains a time-suck in busy lives — like preparing a five-course meal from scratch. That's why you want to check out the OnTarget approach to customization described in this section.

Here's how you can get started transforming your one-size-fits-all or Core resume:

1. **Read the job description to determine exactly what the employer needs.** Mirror back what you find in each section of the OnTarget resume. Specifically, tweak your objective header statement and the contents of your summary, keywords, and employment history sections.

2. **Cut out irrelevant content from each section of your Core resume.** Keeping this content won't make you look better; instead it makes you look like you're overqualified and not likely to stay — or uncommitted and likely to leave.

3. **Tweak wording to speak directly to the targeted position.** This step may require crossover language if you are going from working with physicians and surgeons as your clients in the healthcare industry to executives in the IT industry. Look at the language used in the job description and use it in your OnTarget resume.

WARNING

Staying OnTarget with your resume is a very simple process as long as you aren't making a major life change such as returning to work after a gap or entering the workplace for the first time as a new graduate. Visit Chapters 13 and 14 for additional strategies for these special needs.

TARGETING IS THE SECRET TO CAREER CHANGE

When changing careers is your goal, the OnTarget strategy is your secret weapon. The steps suggested in this chapter of reverse engineering job descriptions can help you identify necessary crossover language for wording your resume, show you what irrelevant skills and accomplishments to cut, and emphasize what key skills and experiences to play up. This powerful combination coupled with the right resume format for your situation (see Chapter 6) will make you ready to make that career change.

Drawing words from job descriptions

In order to spoon-feed a prospective employer directly what he is seeking in a position, take a look at the job description. If you find the description to be vague, perform an Internet search for that job title and look at other descriptions to get a deeper sense of what is desired.

For example, if you have a background in retail sales, retail management, and customer service, the Core one-size-fits-all resume you have developed positions you to use all these skills. But now you are targeting a job in outside sales. When you review the job description, you'll see no emphasis on retail or on management. From the description you can typically surmise:

» The objective header statement you need to use to show you are applying for this position.

» What the employer values in a candidate, which you can play up in your summary section and in your results-focused job descriptions.

» The key skills that you need to list and emphasize in your keyword section and then later connect with responsibilities and CAR stories in your professional experience section (job descriptions).

» The wording you need to adopt to make your experience feel as relevant as possible. This is crossover language where you speak in the new profession's language and not in your old profession's language. (For more, check out the later section on crossover language.)

Figure 9-1 shows a Core one-size-fits-all resume for a job seeker who is overqualified for her target position. In Figure 9-2, the same job seeker appears perfectly qualified for this job.

Using crossover language to be OnTarget

Imagine you need to cross a bridge to reach your prospective employer, have him open the door, and welcome you in. When you reach that door and he speaks the language of healthcare and you speak that of engineering, your interaction will be as if you are from two different countries. He'll close the door, unsure of why you came knocking, and you will go away feeling frustrated.

But it never has to be that way if you discover how to use crossover language when writing your OnTarget resume.

FIGURE 9-1:
This Core one-size-fits-all resume for a job seeker who last held a position in retail operations management makes her overqualified for targeting a sales position.

Luckily, crossover language is easy to apply when you have looked at the job description for your target position. Does the employer refer to clients as "patients"? Are their customers called "members" or "key decision-makers"? Do they "sell" or "consult"? Are their products "cardiothoracic medical devices" or "high-tech equipment"?

After you have a feel for this language, you can begin changing the wording in your Core resume to reflect the target for your new OnTarget resume.

YOUR NAME

City, State   Phone Number   Email Address

───────────────── **TOP PERFORMING SALES PROFESSIONAL** ─────────────────
Reputation for driving sales, sales margins, and customer retention levels

> ~ Established #1 out of 200 nationwide – Maintained 40% Profitability ~
> ~ Top individual performer: Awarded for highest growth in one fiscal year (#89 to #1) ~
> ~ First Director to Achieve $150K Per Month – Turned Around Struggling Center ~

Top-performing and high-energy Retail Operations Manager who draws upon proven experience and results to drive sales and revenue growth, boost client base, turn around struggling businesses, and start up profitable new ones. Recognized as a dynamic leader with proven success in turning individual performers into high-functioning teams which exceed all set goals. Vision for positioning company brands to stand out in the most flooded of markets. Awarded for personal sales performance.

───────────────────────── **KEY COMPETENCIES** ─────────────────────────

• Sales & Revenue Growth	• Promotional Programs	• Customer Needs Assessment
• Client Relationship Management	• Account Penetration	• Product / Service Up-Selling
• Client Motivation	• Prospecting & Cold Calling	• Account Troubleshooting
• New Product / Service Launch	• Sales Presentations	• Administration & Reporting

─────────────────────── **PROFESSIONAL EXPERIENCE** ───────────────────────

ABC COMPANY – City, ST   [Date – Date]

Key Sales Performer (Title: Operations Manager)
Leveraged hands-on sales and management skills to spearhead the turnaround performance in an operation where lowering sales, competition, and lack of market recognition had led to sales decline from #1 to #89 out of 200 centers nationwide.

- *Product Sales:* Attained sales closing rate of 75%+ (against prior center average of 22%) with average revenue per client increasing from $95 to $445. Positioned product upsells, which increased average total sale by 33%.

- *Revenue Growth & Ranking:* Helped overall center to move from #89 to #1 in sales performance in just eight months through aggressive sales efforts and cross-training of other staff. Personally contributed to 60% of all revenue growth, moving center from $30K to $150K per month.

- *Performance Awards:* Received prestigious award for top greatest sales growth in one fiscal year.

- *Customer Relations / Account Development:* Performed inside and outside sales, prospecting, product sales presentations, and product training. Helped shift company model from one-to-one consumer sales to calling on small businesses for group presentations and plans.

FIGURE 9-2:
This OnTarget resume is for the same job seeker, but the focus of the content has been changed based on the target job description to complement an opportunity in sales.

WARNING

When choosing crossover language for your OnTarget resume, don't use words that you don't have the knowledge to support in an interview. You must truly understand the language you're using in your resume. Be sure to dig deep, do your homework, and be able to talk in the language of your target industry. Otherwise, you may find yourself embarrassed in an interview.

Figure 9-3 shows a great example of using crossover language to target a new type of position. The job seeker's before language pigeonholed him to home cabinet projects; after he targeted his resume, the specific crossover language demonstrated his match for project management.

TIP

Job descriptions aren't the only place you can learn about language when targeting a position that may represent a change in industry or responsibility. Look at the *Occupational Outlook Handbook* (www.bls.gov/ooh/), perform general searches by job title, and visit the professional association for that industry. You can uncover a lot of key language, core responsibilities, and strengths a particular type of position and industry require to help you make your resume a strong OnTarget match.

TIP

Going OnTarget with your resume can seem time-consuming. However, you will rapidly find that if you are targeting the same type of position over and over again, you only have to change a few words after the first customization. So be sure to save a copy of each new target you create. That way, when the next sales position or operations manager position comes along that you want to target, you can open that file, perform any needed customization, and be ready to go in a matter of moments.

Before:

Cabinet Designer – Company Name, City, ST   [Date – Date]

Managed all aspects of home renovation projects such as kitchens, bathrooms, and closets from initial layout to completion. Created innovative cabinet designs. Sold renovation projects at 110%+ to quota. Helped trained less experienced cabinet designers.

After:

Project Management: Design/Build Installations - Company Name, City, ST   [Date – Date]

Provided strategic direction to both clients and staff in all aspects of design and build project lifecycles for projects valued at $15-150K. Facilitated entire process, which included project scope, initiation, planning, scheduling, budgeting, contractor selection, resource allocation, risk assessment, quality control, and cost control. Completed all projects under schedule, which encompassed all delivered, 99% customer satisfaction level, and high craftsmanship from concept to completion.

FIGURE 9-3:
An example of revising a job summary using crossover language.

TO CLONE OR NOT TO CLONE: MIRRORING AD LANGUAGE

Must you use the exact words you find in a job ad or position description? In a word, yes. Although sophisticated software may give you points for synonyms, the human recruiters who rule the second round of screening may not. Junior recruiters can't be counted on to recognize subtle differences in terminology. And high-volume recruiters racing through enough resumes to wear out a dozen pairs of eyes in eight hours may not take the time to carefully consider slight changes of expression. So, for now, you should stick with the ditto school of content and keywords.

Also, don't discount *applicant tracking systems*, or ATS. These software systems look for the specific words used in the ad but also look for correlation of how they were used by you as described in the resume. Think artificial intelligence, because ATS can make deductions based on whether you just list a keyword skill or go on to sell how you applied it in your career. (For more on ATS, check out Chapter 4.)

3 Resume Strategies to Wow Them

IN THIS PART . . .

Discover how to populate your resume with words that make employers sit up and take notice.

Make your resume stand out against the competition with a clean, well-designed format.

Understand how to revise your resume as you grow in your career.

Find out how to put together a resume that plays to your strengths and disguises less-than-ideal work histories.

Chapter 10

Working Wonders with Wow Words

Words: How powerful they are. It doesn't take many of them to change the world: Lincoln's Gettysburg address numbers just 286 words, and the U.S. Declaration of Independence contains but 1,322 words.

Winston Churchill needed only two words to bind Russia to the *Iron Curtain.* A brief four words memorialized Martin Luther King's vision: *I have a dream.* And in a single sentence, John F. Kennedy set the challenge for a generation: *Ask not what your country can do for you, but what you can do for your country.*

Words are powerful — big words such as *motherland* and *environmentalism* and small words such as *peace* and *war* or *dawn, family, hope, love,* and *home.* Words are pegs to hang your qualifications on. Words are the power that lifts you above the faceless crowd and sets you in good fortune's way. The right words can change your life.

Begin your hunt for the right words to build an OnTarget resume, from action verbs and keyword nouns to grammar and spelling tips.

TIP

Wow words are action verbs describing your strengths: *improve, upgrade, schedule.* Keywords are usually nouns demonstrating essential skills: *technology transfers, PhD organic chemistry, multinational marketing.* A smattering of both can make your resume stand up and sing. An absence of either can make your resume sit down and shut up.

When your words speak for you, you need to use words that everyone can understand and that relate to the job at hand. Value your words. As you can see in this chapter, each word is a tool to your future.

Bringing Good News with Wow Words

Use lively, energetic verbs to communicate your abilities and accomplishments. The important thing is to choose words of substance and power that zero in on what you're selling. Remember, little words never devalue a big idea.

REMEMBER

Try not to use the same Wow word twice on your resume — an online thesaurus, such as Thesaurus (www.thesaurus.com), can give you a range of possibilities.

Take a look at the Wow words that follow and check off those words that are authentic for you.

Wow words for administration and management

advised	initiated	prioritized
approved	inspired	processed
authorized	installed	promoted
chaired	instituted	recommended
consolidated	instructed	redirected
counseled	integrated	referred
delegated	launched	reorganized
determined	lectured	represented
developed	listened	responded
diagnosed	managed	reviewed

directed	mediated	revitalized
disseminated	mentored	routed
enforced	moderated	sponsored
ensured	monitored	streamlined
examined	motivated	strengthened
explained	negotiated	supervised
governed	originated	taught
guided	oversaw	trained
headed	pioneered	trimmed
influenced	presided	validated

Wow words for communications and creativity

acted	edited	proofread
addressed	enabled	publicized
arranged	facilitated	published
assessed	fashioned	realized
authored	formulated	reconciled
briefed	influenced	recruited
built	initiated	rectified
clarified	interpreted	remodeled
composed	interviewed	reported
conducted	introduced	revitalized
constructed	invented	scheduled
corresponded	launched	screened
costumed	lectured	shaped
created	modernized	stimulated
critiqued	performed	summarized

demonstrated	planned	taught
designed	presented	trained
developed	produced	translated
directed	projected	wrote

Wow words for sales and persuasion

advocated	judged	purchased
arbitrated	launched	realized
centralized	lectured	recruited
championed	led	reduced
consulted	liaised	reported
documented	maintained	repositioned
educated	manipulated	researched
established	marketed	resolved
expedited	mediated	restored
familiarized	moderated	reviewed
identified	negotiated	routed
implemented	obtained	saved
improved	ordered	served
increased	performed	sold
influenced	planned	solved
inspired	processed	spearheaded
installed	produced	stimulated
integrated	promoted	summarized
interpreted	proposed	surveyed
investigated	publicized	translated

Wow words for technical ability

analyzed	expedited	networked
broadened	fabricated	operated
charted	facilitated	packaged
classified	forecast	pioneered
communicated	formed	prepared
compiled	generated	processed
computed	improved	programmed
conceived	increased	published
conducted	inspected	reconstructed
coordinated	installed	reduced
designed	instituted	researched
detected	integrated	restored
developed	interfaced	revamped
devised	launched	streamlined
drafted	lectured	supplemented
edited	maintained	surveyed
educated	marketed	systematized
eliminated	mastered	trained
excelled	modified	upgraded
expanded	molded	wrote

Wow words for office support

adhered	distributed	managed
administered	documented	operated
allocated	drafted	ordered
applied	enacted	organized
appropriated	enlarged	packaged

assisted	evaluated	planned
assured	examined	prepared
attained	executed	prescribed
awarded	followed up	processed
balanced	formalized	provided
budgeted	formulated	recorded
built	hired	repaired
charted	identified	reshaped
completed	implemented	resolved
contributed	improved	scheduled
coordinated	installed	screened
cut	instituted	searched
defined	justified	secured
determined	liaised	solved
dispensed	maintained	started

Wow words for teaching

acquainted	designed	influenced
adapted	developed	informed
advised	directed	initiated
answered	dispensed	innovated
apprised	distributed	installed
augmented	educated	instituted
briefed	effected	instructed
built	empowered	integrated
certified	enabled	lectured
chaired	enacted	listened

charted	enlarged	originated
clarified	enticed	persuaded
coached	expanded	presented
collaborated	facilitated	responded
communicated	formulated	revolutionized
conducted	generated	set goals
coordinated	grouped	stimulated
delegated	guided	summarized
delivered	harmonized	trained
demonstrated	implemented	translated

Wow words for research and analysis

administered	detected	interviewed
amplified	determined	invented
analyzed	discovered	investigated
applied	documented	located
articulated	drafted	measured
assessed	edited	obtained
audited	evaluated	organized
augmented	examined	pinpointed
balanced	exhibited	planned
calculated	experimented	prepared
charted	explored	processed
collected	extracted	proofread
compared	focused	researched
compiled	forecast	reviewed
composed	found	riveted

concentrated	generated	screened
conducted	grouped	summarized
constructed	identified	surveyed
consulted	integrated	systematized
critiqued	interpreted	unearthed

Wow words for helping and caregiving

advanced	encouraged	reassured
advised	expedited	reclaimed
aided	facilitated	rectified
arbitrated	familiarized	redeemed
assisted	fostered	reeducated
attended	furthered	referred
augmented	guided	reformed
backed	helped	rehabilitated
balanced	instilled	repaired
boosted	liaised	represented
braced	mentored	served
clarified	ministered	settled
collaborated	negotiated	supplied
comforted	nourished	supported
consoled	nursed	stabilized
consulted	nurtured	streamlined
contributed	obliged	translated
counseled	optimized	treated
demonstrated	promoted	tutored
diagnosed	provided	unified

Wow words for financial management

adjusted	economized	reported
administered	eliminated	researched
allocated	exceeded	reshaped
analyzed	financed	retailed
appraised	forecast	returned
audited	funded	saved
balanced	gained	shopped
bought	generated	secured
budgeted	increased	sold
calculated	invested	solicited
computed	maintained	sourced
conciliated	managed	specified
cut	marketed	supplemented
decreased	merchandised	systematized
developed	planned	tested
disbursed	projected	tripled
dispensed	purchased	underwrote
distributed	quadrupled	upgraded
doubled	reconciled	upsized
downsized	reduced	vended

Wow words for many skills

accomplished	evaluated	overhauled
achieved	executed	performed
adapted	facilitated	prioritized
advocated	forecast	promoted
allocated	founded	proposed

appraised	governed	reconciled
arbitrated	guided	rectified
arranged	illustrated	remodeled
articulated	improved	repaired
assured	increased	reshaped
augmented	initiated	solved
championed	integrated	spearheaded
communicated	interpreted	stimulated
composed	invented	streamlined
conceptualized	launched	strengthened
conserved	led	trained
contributed	navigated	upgraded
coordinated	optimized	validated
demonstrated	organized	won
dispensed	originated	wrote

Helping Recruiters Find You

In the long-ago 1990s, recruiters and employers used keywords to search computer databases for qualified candidates. Today they type keywords into search engines to scour the entire Internet for the best people to select for a candidate pool. Employers allow powerful ATS systems to search the resumes they receive as well (for more on ATS, see Chapter 4).

That's why, when you're looking for a job, you can't afford to ignore search engines. Take pains to feed those wooly-mammoth software creatures with effective keywords that shoot your resume to the top of recruiting search results. (In techie talk, the concept is called search engine optimization, or SEO.)

So what are keywords as used in the job market? "Keywords are what employers search for when trying to fill a position: the essential hard skills and knowledge needed to do the job," explains employment technology expert James M. Lemke.

Keywords are chiefly nouns and short phrases. That's your take-home message. But once in a while, just to confuse everyone, keywords can be adjectives and action verbs.

Is there one comprehensive dictionary of keywords? No, Lemke explains, "Employers choose their own list of keywords — that's why no list is universal."

In computerized job searches, keywords describe not only your knowledge base and skills but also such things as well-known companies, big-name colleges and universities, degrees, licensure, and professional affiliations.

Keywords identify your experience and education in these categories:

>> Skills

>> Technical and professional areas of expertise

>> Accomplishments and achievements

>> Professional licenses and certifications

>> Other distinguishing features of your work history

>> Prestigious schools or former employers

Employers identify keywords, often including industry jargon, that they think represent essential qualifications necessary for high performance in a given position. They specify those keywords when they search for resumes.

Keywords are arbitrary and specific to the employer and each employer search. So the keywords (qualifications) — starting with the job title — in each job ad are the place to start as you customize your resume for the position. Make educated guesses when you're not responding to advertised jobs but are merely warehousing your resume online on a job search site. The following lists provide a few examples of keywords for selected career fields and industries.

Action verbs are a prelude for keywords in stating your accomplishments. You managed *what*? You organized *what*? You developed *what*? Applicant software looks for the *whats,* and the whats are usually nouns.

REMEMBER

Keywords are the magnets that draw junior screeners and nonhuman eyes to your talents.

TIP

The following lists are by no means comprehensive — make sure to turn to the "Where to Find Keywords" section later in this chapter to discover where to find your keywords.

Keywords for administration and management

administrative processes	facilities management
bachelor's degree	front office operations
back office operations	office management
benchmarking	operations management
budget administration	policy and procedure
change management	production schedule
crisis communications	project planning
data analysis	records management
document management	regulatory reporting

Keywords for banking

branch management	loan management
branch operations	loan recovery
commercial banking	portfolio management
construction loans	retail lending
credit guidelines	return on equity (ROE)
debt financing	return on investment (ROI)
financial management	trust services
first in, last out (FILO)	turnaround management
investment management	Uniform Commercial Code filing
investor relations	workout

Keywords for customer service

account management	help desk
call center	key account management
customer communications	order fulfillment

customer focus groups	order processing
customer loyalty	product response
customer needs assessment	records management
customer retention	sales administration
customer retention innovations	sales support
customer service management	service quality
customer surveys	telemarketing operations
field service operation	telemarketing

Keywords for information technology

application development	help desk
automated voice response (AVR)	information security
client/server architecture	multimedia technology
database development	network development
data center management	project life cycle
disaster recovery	systems configuration
end-user support	technology rightsizing or streamlining
global systems support	vendor partnerships

Keywords for manufacturing

asset management	manufacturing engineering
automated manufacturing	materials coordination
capacity planning	on-time delivery
cell manufacturing	outsourcing
cost reductions	production management
distribution management	shipping and receiving operation
environmental health and safety	spares and repairs management

inventory control	union negotiations
just in time (JIT)	warehousing operations
logistics management	workflow optimization

Keywords for human resources

compensation surveys	organizational development (OD)
cross-cultural communications	recruitment
diversity training	sourcing
grievance proceedings	staffing
interviewing	succession planning
job task analysis	team leadership
labor contract negotiations	training and development
leadership development	wage and salary administration

Finding Keywords

TIP

How can you find keywords for your occupation or career field? Use a highlighter to pluck keywords from these resources.

>> **Online job ads:** Highlight the job skills, competencies, experience, education, and other nouns that employers request.

>> **Job descriptions:** Read job descriptions for the job you want to apply for online. To find them online, just enter such terms as *job descriptions* or *job descriptions trainer* or *job descriptions electrical engineer* in a search engine.

>> **The *Occupational Outlook Handbook,*** published by the U.S. Department of Labor: Read free online at www.bls.gov/ooh/.

>> **Trade website career centers:** Professional associations for your occupation will be ripe with keywords.

>> **Social media sites and blogs:** Don't overlook tools such as industry-specific groups on social media and blogs written by industry and company insiders.

>> **Annual reports of companies in your field:** The company descriptions of key personnel and departmental achievements should offer strong keyword clues.

>> **Programs for industry conferences and events:** Speaker topics address current industry issues, a rich source of keywords.

>> **Internet search engine:** Plug in a targeted company's name and search the site that comes up. Look closely at the careers portal and read current press releases.

You can also use Internet search engines to scout industry-specific directories, glossaries, and dictionaries.

TIP

MINING FOR KEYWORDS IN JOB DESCRIPTIONS

You can easily find target keywords on the Internet. Take a look at the following two job descriptions where the keywords have been italicized.

Auto Dismantler:

- Knowledge of proper operation of *lifts, forklifts, torches, power wrenches,* and so on.

- Knowledge of *warehouse, core,* and *stack locations.*

- Skill to move *vehicles* without damaging vehicle, other vehicles, or personnel.

- Skill to remove *body* and *mechanical parts* without damage to part, self, or others.

- Ability to read a *Dismantler report* and assess *stock levels.*

- Ability to accurately assess condition of *parts* to be inventoried.

Budget Assistant:

- Reviews *monthly expense statements,* monitors *monthly expenditures,* and gathers supporting *documentation* for supervisor review and approval.

- Performs basic *arithmetic operations* to calculate and/or verify *expense totals* and *account balances.*

- Operates *computer* to enter data into *spreadsheet* and/or *database.* Types routine *correspondence* and *reports.*

- Operates older office equipment such as *photocopier, fax machine,* and *calculator.*

Using Keywords

Who reads the first pass of your resume? In many HR departments, resumes are screened by junior workers who lack the experience to read between the lines but work on a verbatim basis. That's why nearly matching word for word — rather than liberally paraphrasing — at least a portion of a job's requirements — is the way to go.

If the job requirements state:

> *Ability to lead the development of staffing strategies and implementation plans and programs that identify talent internally and externally through the effective use of external sources.*

You write:

> *Developed and implemented staffing strategies that identified talent internally and externally through the effective use of external sources.*

By incorporating some of the employer's language, you strongly increase your odds of surviving the first cut. Your resume lives to fight for you another round when senior screeners look you over.

WARNING

AVOID POISON WORDS

Recruiters advise staying away from the following words on your resume:

- **Responsibilities included:** Make your resume accomplishment-driven, not responsibilities-driven. Job-descriptions language tells, not sells, in a resume.

- **Salary:** Money talk doesn't belong on a resume, period. Spilling your financial beans limits your options because you may be priced too high or too low. If you absolutely must deal with salary history or salary requirements before the interview, discuss dollars in a cover letter.

- **Fired:** Don't let this word slip into your resume if you want it to escape being lost in a database. *Laid-off* or *reduction in force* generally aren't good terms either. There is no reason to list this data on your resume. Shorter jobs can be minimized (see Chapter 14) and discussed in the interview.

- **References available upon request:** References are assumed. Save the space for more important information.

- **Social Security number:** Never make yourself vulnerable in this era of identity theft. The exception to this rule is when you apply for a federal government position; in that case, you may be required to submit your SSN if the agency uses an older system, but the newer federal systems no longer ask for a SSN.

- **Also:** The word is unnecessary. (For example, Managed budget of $1 million. *Also* interfaced with consultants.) Write tightly. Eliminate *also, an, the,* and *and* wherever you can. Use the saved space to pack more punch, and the resume won't lose meaning.

- **Wimpy Words and Phrases:** Steer clear of words and phrases that cast doubt on your value. These can sound like: *think I did, helped with, believe I can, might, worked with, assisted with,* and many others. Think instead of powerful words that express have, do, and can, such as *performed, handled, completed, spearheaded.*

TIP

Don't neglect the opportunity to make this content stronger by looking for ways to tell your CAR story (challenge faced, action taken to resolve, and result attained). Then you can craft an even more powerful statement such as:

Recruited to develop and implement staffing strategies that identified talent internally and externally through the effective use of external sources. Completed process three months ahead of schedule with outcome of increasing new hire retention by 30 percent in first year.

Getting a Grip on Grammar

Resume language differs from normal speech in several ways. In general, keep the language tight and the tone professional, avoiding the following:

>> **First-person pronouns (I, we):** Your name is at the top of each resume page, so the recruiter knows it's about *you.* Eliminate first-person pronouns. Also, don't use third-person pronouns (he, she) when referring to yourself — the narrative technique makes you seem pompous. Simply start with a verb.

>> **Articles (the, a, an):** Articles crowd sentences and don't clarify meaning. Substitute *retrained staff* for *retrained the staff.*

>> **Helping verbs (have, had, may, might):** For professionals and managers, helping verbs weaken claims and credibility, implying that your time has passed and portraying you as a job-hunting weakling. Say *managed* instead of *have managed.*

>> **"Being" verbs (am, is, are, was, were):** Being verbs suggest a state of existence rather than a state of motion. Try *monitored requisitions* instead of *requisitions were monitored.* The active voice gives a stronger, more confident delivery.

>> **Shifts in tense:** Maintain consistent use of past tense in your job descriptions, even if you are still in the job. Using CAR stories (see previous section) to always talk about challenges you have faced and results you have completed allows you to maintain the same tense throughout the position and all throughout the experience section. Don't shift from present to past and back again — it's just awkward and reads like an error.

>> **Complex sentences:** Unless you keep your sentences lean and clean, readers won't take time to decipher them. Process this mind-stumper:

Reduced hospital costs by 67 percent by creating a patient-independence program, where they make their own beds, and as noted by hospital finance department, costs of nails and wood totaled $300 less per patient than work hours of maintenance staff.

>> Eliminate complex sentences by dividing ideas into sentences of their own and getting rid of extraneous details:

Reduced hospital costs by 67 percent. Originated patient independence program that decreased per-patient expense by $300 each.

>> **Overwriting:** Use your own voice; don't say *expeditious* when you want to say *swift.*

>> **Acronyms:** When an acronym is common to an industry or target position, spell it out the first time and follow it with the actual acronym in brackets after. Then you can simply use the acronym in the rest of the resume.

>> **Abbreviations:** Abbreviations are informal and not universal — even when they're career-specific. Use *Internet* instead of *Net.*

The exception is industry jargon — use it, especially in digital resumes. Knowledge and use of industry jargon adds to your credibility to be able to correctly and casually use terms common to the industry in which you're seeking employment.

Focusing on Spelling

What is the name of a resume self-defense manual for job seekers? The dictionary!

Of all the reasons causing recruiters and hiring managers to shoot down resumes, carelessness with spelling, grammar, and choice of words ranks close to the top. Even when the real reason for rejection is bias or something else entirely, the use of misspelled words is a convenient justification. Who can quarrel with the adage "Garbage in, garbage out"?

Employers especially recoil from impaired spelling when the job seeker botches the interviewer's name, organization's name, or the job title. (You can Google your way to the company's website to spell the organization's name; you can call to confirm the spelling of the interviewer's name. You can also use spell-check in MS Word to make sure you've spelled job titles correctly.)

Here's the take-away message: Know thy computer spell checker. Know thy online dictionary. And know a human being who can carefully proofread your resumes to pick up grammar mistakes or misused words. Don't just proofread once. Proofread three times, and consider even reading your resume backward — last word to first word, because it can be easier to spot errors in that manner.

WARNING

GOOFY SPELLING

You don't have to win a spelling bee, but if you're like me (someone who has been known to make some *humongus speling miztakes*), you need to be on Code Red alert when you're putting words down for the world to read. Here is a sampling of frequently misspelled words (some words seem easy, but accidentally leaving out one letter can dramatically change a word's meaning, such as manager becoming manger). Add your personal goofy spellings to the list.

accommodate	guarantee	personnel
address	immediate	public
assess/access	independent	recommend
bureau	its/it's	referred
calendar	judgment	relevant
category	manager	schedule
column	millennium	sergeant
committed	miscellaneous	their/they're/there
conscientious	misspell	truly
definitely	nuclear	until
experience	occasionally	your/you're
government	occurrence	weather/whether

Chapter **11**

Refining Your Design

Good design is about more than simply looking good. Good resume design means making your document appealing and accessible for prospective employers. Making it relevant for the job you seek. Making it appropriate for someone in your shoes.

In today's job market, content may be king, but getting a prospective employer to read it requires certain stylistic decisions that make it easy-to-read, attractive, eye-catching, and effective in drawing the prospective employer to the critical value that makes you stand out above the competition. You need to pay plenty of attention to your resume's appearance in presenting your targeted content. Well-chosen resume architecture and design are like a guided tour, leading a prospective employer's eyes to the factual tip-offs that answer these essential questions:

>> Why are you contacting me?

>> What can you do for me?

>> How do I know you can do this?

>> What makes you stand out from all the other applicants for this job?

REMEMBER

Modern recruiting software usually can handle fully formatted resumes in a word-processing attachment (typically MS Word). All the design tips I describe in this chapter work on paper and attached online resumes.

You may still need to convert your resume to an ASCII plain-text version for use on certain online submission sites, such as job boards or company career centers. To do that, you'll need to strip out all the formatting described in this chapter. Visit Chapter 4 for more on ASCII resumes.

Leaving Space

When writing your resume, the tendency can be to try to cram as much into a page as possible to ensure you don't leave out something critical. You then end up with what looks like a page out of a textbook or the dictionary — an overwhelming amount of text, likely a small font, and nothing that draws the eye. This type of over-packed and condensed resume typically gets tossed because no prospective employer needs to go to the trouble of reading it when so many other candidates are standing in line.

Instead, you need to create space, which might mean having to rewrite content to say it in a more concise manner, to switch from a serif to a sans serif font typeface to save a little room, or to tweak line spacing just a touch to fit more on the page but without content feeling thick.

In this section, you can explore the ways to provide necessary space in your document while keeping the eye's attention.

Measure your margins

Part of creating space involves leaving a sufficient white border around your content. You can do this easily by selecting to have your top and bottom margins never go below 0.5 to 0.6 inch and your left and right margins never below 0.7 to 0.8 inch. Conversely, don't go above a 1-inch margin all around the page. Anything larger than this begins to look like you have little to say to sell yourself.

WARNING

You may be tempted to show a clean right margin by using full justification (making your right margin flush with the right side of the page versus ragged). However, this decision can backfire, leaving what is termed as "rivers running through your text." If you can use full justification and not see channels running vertically down your page where spaces have been left to even out the lines, then go ahead and use it. However, if these pesky blank spaces are showing up and you can't make them go away by rewording your text, opt for left justification.

Balance blank space

It can feel very simple to left justify all content in each section, but sometimes that leaves you with just a lot of white space on the right-hand side of the page. Look for these large chunks of white space and make layout decisions that better balance the page. Look at Figure 11-1 to see a before example with white space that is unbalanced and Figure 11-2 for one that is balanced through the use of columns, bullets, centering, and indenting.

PROFESSIONAL EXPERIENCE

Job Title – Company Name, City, ST – [Date – Date]

Recruited to direct all aspects of corporate security for this distribution facility that was facing numerous logistical challenges, which included massive theft of assets from Asia Pacific markets, outdated security technology, and high levels of physical risk. Managed a $15M budget. *Turned around facility to attain all metric goals in first year.*

-
-
-

Job Title – Company Name, City, ST – [Date – Date]

Tasked with establishing technology and quality standards for this 6-building production plant, which ran three shifts and was slated to output $6M in product monthly (but was operating at 50% capacity). *Spearheaded improvements that optimized efficiency to meet high-volume production and fulfillment of daily quotas.*

-
-
-

EDUCATION & TRAINING

MS, Information Technology – University Name, City, ST

BS, Engineering – University Name, City, ST

Certification Name – Granting Organization

Continuing education: **Course Name, Course Name, Course Name, Course Name, Course Name, Course Name**

FIGURE 11-1: This snapshot shows a before resume with wasted white space.

PROFESSIONAL EXPERIENCE

Job Title – Company Name, City, ST   [Date – Date]

Recruited to direct all aspects of corporate security for this distribution facility that was facing numerous logistical challenges, which included massive theft of assets from Asia Pacific markets, outdated security technology, and high levels of physical risk. Managed a $15M budget. *Turned around facility to attain all metric goals in first year.*

- •
- •
- •

Job Title – Company Name, City, ST   [Date – Date]

Tasked with establishing technology and quality standards for this 6-building production plant, which ran three shifts and was slated to output $6M in product monthly (but was operating at 50% capacity). *Spearheaded improvements that optimized efficiency to meet high-volume production and fulfillment of daily quotas.*

- •
- •
- •

EDUCATION & TRAINING

MS, Information Technology – University Name, City, ST
BS, Engineering – University Name, City, ST
Certification Name – Granting Organization

Continuing education:

| • **Course Name** | • **Course Name** | • **Course Name** |
| • **Course Name** | • **Course Name** | • **Course Name** |

FIGURE 11-2:
This snapshot shows an after resume with balanced, attractive white space.

Employing Basic Design Elements for a Readable Resume

How often have you tried to read a solid block of text and given up because it makes you want to run for the eyedrops? Employers and recruiters reading resume after resume also zone out when reading dense text, especially in small type. The answer is to break it up, to segment your data points in related groups or by title, and to use font, typeface size, line spacing, and indent functions to your advantage. I provide more details on these options in the following sections.

Professional resume writers use many tricks of the trade to put more information in a resume without making it seem packed to the rafters. They condense type, use a smaller-size font, and manipulate vertical spacing. Most amateur resume writers don't want to get into this depth of detail. Doing so is a time-consuming learning experience and risks readability, something you can't afford to lose. So unless you have a background in design, stick to the easy suggestions in the following sections.

Come on, break it up! Avoid blocky text

Whether you are using a paragraph for your summary section or the opening hook paragraphs of your job descriptions, avoid long, blocky content. A good paragraph on a resume is two to four sentences and no more than approximately five lines of text. If you must say more, break it down into two paragraphs or a paragraph with supporting bullets.

Group content under a job description

After you've written your overview hook paragraph for a job description, it's time to include the supporting CAR story (**C**hallenge, **A**ction, and **R**esults) bullets. Too many bullets in a row leave the reader skipping and jumping, likely to miss what could be most important. To avoid this, break up your bullets. One way to do this is to insert a little space in between each bullet. However, you also want to draw the eye, which can be done either by putting titles in front of each of your bullets or by breaking the bullets down into categories. Compare the resume snapshots in Figure 11-3, Figure 11-4, and Figure 11-5 to get a feel for how you can break up a dense block of content so it's more reader-friendly.

FIGURE 11-3: This snapshot shows a before resume that is too blocky and dense.

> COMPANY NAME, City, State [Date – Date]
> **DIRECTOR OF BUSINESS DEVELOPMENT** – Arabian Peninsula, Southeast Asia
> Challenged to spearhead international and DOD business development and marketing in the areas of software development, system integration, and engineering services. *Key clients: Boeing and Sybase.*
>
> - Negotiated Crucial Teaming Agreements, partnering with Axyl, Cytograph, and Synex to pursue and capture contracts in excess of $1.2 billion.
> - Developed strategic international marketing and sales alliances with Macintosh, Oracle, and Microsoft. Established strong corporate and government ties in the Middle East and Japan.
> - Supervised engineers and managers in preparation of proposals, marketing strategy, site surveys, and costing for both international and DOD customers.
> - Performed strategic program planning and forecasting of long-term business development plans.

COMPANY NAME, City, State [Date – Date]

COMPANY NAME, City, State [Date – Date]

DIRECTOR OF BUSINESS DEVELOPMENT – *Arabian Peninsula, Southeast Asia*

Challenged to spearhead international and DOD business development and marketing in the areas of software development, system integration, and engineering services. *Key clients: Boeing and Sybase.*

- ***Contract Negotiations:*** Negotiated Crucial Teaming Agreements, partnering with XYZ Company, ABC Company, and 1-2-3 Company to pursue and capture contracts in excess of $1.2 billion.

- ***Strategic Alliances:*** Developed strategic international marketing and sales alliances with the big three technology firms (Name 1, Name 2, and Name 3). Established strong corporate and government ties in the Middle East and Japan.

- ***Business Proposals:*** Supervised engineers and managers in preparation of proposals, marketing strategy, site surveys, and costing for both international and DOD customers.

- ***Strategic Planning & Forecasting:*** Performed strategic program planning and forecasting of long-term business development plans.

FIGURE 11-4:
This snapshot shows an after resume that employs bullet titles to draw the eye.

COMPANY NAME, City, State [Date – Date]

DIRECTOR OF BUSINESS DEVELOPMENT – *Arabian Peninsula, Southeast Asia*

Challenged to spearhead international and DOD business development and marketing in the areas of software development, system integration, and engineering services. *Key clients: Boeing and Sybase.*

Contracts and Alliances
- Negotiated Crucial Teaming Agreements, partnering with XYZ Company, ABC Company, and 1-2-3 Company to pursue and capture contracts in excess of $1.2 billion.
- Developed strategic international marketing and sales alliances with the big three technology firms (Name 1, Name 2, and Name 3). Established strong corporate and government ties in the Middle East and Japan.

Planning & Operations
- Supervised engineers and managers in preparation of proposals, marketing strategy, site surveys, and costing for both international and DOD customers.
- Performed strategic program planning and forecasting of long-term business development plans.

FIGURE 11-5:
This snapshot shows an after resume that employs functional sections to draw the eye and break up content.

Draw attention with text boxes, charts, and graphs

You can use text boxes to draw the eye to something impressive such as an award, special accomplishment, or testimonial. They also work well if you want to set a snapshot or fact out to the right of your text. Figure 11-6 shows a variety of ways you can highlight information through the use of text boxes.

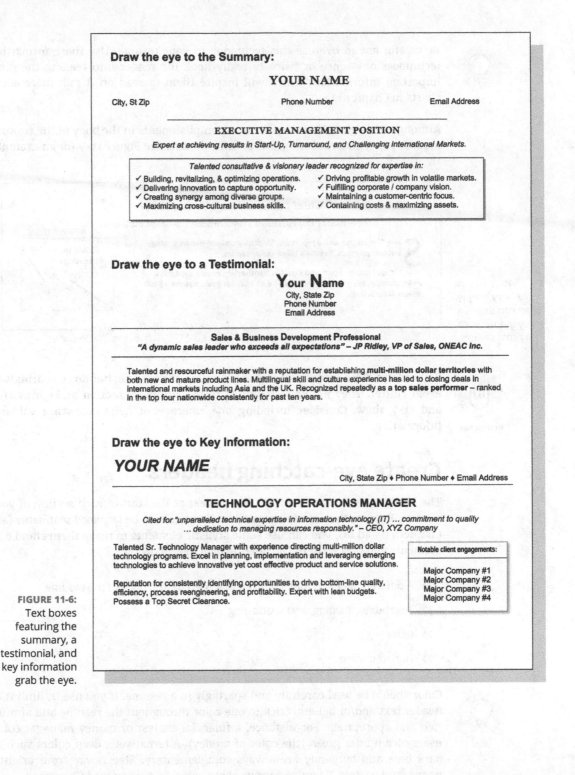

Draw the eye to the Summary:

YOUR NAME

City, St Zip   Phone Number   Email Address

EXECUTIVE MANAGEMENT POSITION
Expert at achieving results in Start-Up, Turnaround, and Challenging International Markets.

Talented consultative & visionary leader recognized for expertise in:
- ✓ Building, revitalizing, & optimizing operations.
- ✓ Delivering innovation to capture opportunity.
- ✓ Creating synergy among diverse groups.
- ✓ Maximizing cross-cultural business skills.
- ✓ Driving profitable growth in volatile markets.
- ✓ Fulfilling corporate / company vision.
- ✓ Maintaining a customer-centric focus.
- ✓ Containing costs & maximizing assets.

Draw the eye to a Testimonial:

Your Name
City, State Zip
Phone Number
Email Address

Sales & Business Development Professional
"A dynamic sales leader who exceeds all expectations" – JP Ridley, VP of Sales, ONEAC Inc.

Talented and resourceful rainmaker with a reputation for establishing **multi-million dollar territories** with both new and mature product lines. Multilingual skill and culture experience has led to closing deals in international markets including Asia and the UK. Recognized repeatedly as a **top sales performer** – ranked in the top four nationwide consistently for past ten years.

Draw the eye to Key Information:

YOUR NAME
City, State Zip ♦ Phone Number ♦ Email Address

TECHNOLOGY OPERATIONS MANAGER
Cited for "unparalleled technical expertise in information technology (IT) ... commitment to quality ... dedication to managing resources responsibly." – CEO, XYZ Company

Talented Sr. Technology Manager with experience directing multi-million dollar technology programs. Excel in planning, implementation and leveraging emerging technologies to achieve innovative yet cost effective product and service solutions.

Reputation for consistently identifying opportunities to drive bottom-line quality, efficiency, process reengineering, and profitability. Expert with lean budgets. Possess a Top Secret Clearance.

Notable client engagements:
Major Company #1
Major Company #2
Major Company #3
Major Company #4

FIGURE 11-6:
Text boxes featuring the summary, a testimonial, and key information grab the eye.

TIP

Be careful not to overuse this technique in your resume. Use these formatting techniques only once or twice to really hook the reader into reading the most important information, which will inspire them to read on. I talk more about charts in Chapter 12.

Although it's a good idea to spell out accomplishments in the body of the resume, make it pop with a chart or graph to draw the eye. See Figure 11-7 for an example.

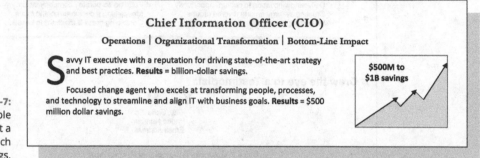

FIGURE 11-7:
A very simple chart can depict a key metric, such as cost savings.

Chief Information Officer (CIO)

Operations | Organizational Transformation | Bottom-Line Impact

Savvy IT executive with a reputation for driving state-of-the-art strategy and best practices. **Results** = billion-dollar savings.

Focused change agent who excels at transforming people, processes, and technology to streamline and align IT with business goals. **Results** = $500 million dollar savings.

$500M to $1B savings

REMEMBER

You can use these techniques anywhere within the resume, but do so sparingly to avoid clutter. They aren't just limited to the summary section as Figures 11-6 and 11-7 show. Consider including one wherever it helps showcase valuable information.

Create eye-catching headers

The headers are the section titles that appear at the start of each section of your resume. Because they rarely contain text that needs to be keyword scannable (see Chapters 9 and 10), you can use some stylistic elements to make them stand out. Elements you may want to consider include the following:

>> A different font and font size from that used for the body of the resume

>> Text boxes, shading, and shadowing

>> Color

>> Horizontal lines

TIP

Color should be used carefully and sparingly in a resume. If you use it, limit it to header text and/or bullets. Stick to one color throughout the resume and aim for rich and appropriate. For instance, a financial analyst or money manager could use a nice hunter green (the color of money). Alternatively, deep colors such as dark blue and burgundy are always complementary. Steer away from brights, neons, and pastels. If you're curious about color, be sure to read Chapter 12.

Take a look at Figure 11-8 to see the different header style options you can use in your resume.

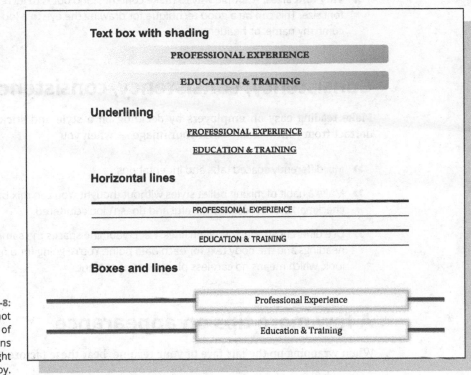

Have fun with fonts and font styles

One of the things I love to do is to make content stand out by making small changes to font sizes and bolding. For instance, if you look at Figure 11-7, you can see the use of a big letter S to start the summary paragraph word *savvy*. If you look at the middle example for testimonials in Figure 11-6, you can see that each letter of the objective header statement and the job seeker's name is slightly bigger than the other letters, making it look more stylistic and helping it stand out.

Although you don't have to get as fancy as these examples show, you can do a few things to draw the eye with your font choices:

>> **Use two different fonts in your resume.** This is typically using a serif font typeface for your headers (such as Times New Roman or Garamond) and a cleaner, simpler sans serif font for the body text (such as Arial, Calibri, Tahoma, or Verdana).

>> **Take advantage of bold and italic.** When used sparingly, bold and italic draw the eye to key information such as job titles and accomplishments.

>> **Vary font sizes.** A simple way to make content stand out is to increase the font size. This can be a good technique for drawing the eye to a job title, company name, or header title.

Consistency, consistency, consistency

Make reading easy on employers by deciding on a style and sticking to it. You detract from your words — and your image — when you

>> Mix differently spaced tabs and indentations.

>> Make a habit of mixing bullet styles without thought. You can mix bullets and checkmarks if the result is tasteful and doesn't look cluttered.

>> Use different spacing between lines. Keep your line spaces the same between headings and the body text for each data point. You're going for a finished look, which means no careless placement of content.

A few more tips on appearance

When wrapping up the fair face of your resume, bear these factors in mind:

>> Your name and contact information can be flush left, centered, or flush right.

>> Typos and spelling errors are attention killers and job opportunity killers. They come across as careless or unprofessional. Even when your resume is a customized point-by-point match for the available job, a spelling mistake or poor grammar blemishes its overall impression and may sink your chances.

Use your computer's spell-check feature, read your finished resume carefully, and ask a friend who is a good proofreader to read it a couple of times.

>> Watch out for widows and orphans in your text. Never leave just one or two short words on a line by themselves or one or two sentences from a job description on a page by itself. Spend time rewriting to get rid of these dangling, lonely words and sentences.

BEWARE WEBSITES OFFERING FREE RESUME TEMPLATES

Do a web search for "free resume templates" and you find a head-spinning 385 million sites. Even Microsoft Office offers scores of free resume templates. But I simply can't stress enough how important it is to avoid generic templates.

Although it can be tempting and easy just to fill in the blanks, you run the risk of looking like tens of thousands of other job seekers who used the same template. In fact, it's not uncommon for a recruiter at a job fair to collect as many as 50 resumes that look identical down to the font choice, font size, and resume section placement because the candidates all used a readily available generic template.

TIP

To minimize the risk of a page becoming an orphan, put a simple heading or footer atop each page after the first with your name and page number. In a multiple-page resume, you may want to indicate the total number of pages (for example, Page 1 of 2).

>> Avoid underlining text in the body of the resume because it can hinder scannability.

Because nothing is generic about you, your resume needs to act as your personal marketing piece, which requires a little more personalized care. Take it as far as you can, and if you stumble, get help from a desktop publisher or resume writer (see the appendix) to lay out the content and give it pizzazz and your individual stamp.

Tips for Printed Resumes

Although the job market has moved to digital resumes — and away from paper resumes — tree-and-ink products will be around for the foreseeable future. Paper resumes are the medium of choice in the following situations:

>> When you make the rounds of booths at career fairs, hand out your paper resumes. (Yes, some employers, for legal reasons, won't accept paper resumes at fairs, but they're in the minority.)

>> When you call on your personal network to assist your job search, circulate paper resumes. People are more likely to remember you and your search with a piece of paper to remind them than they are to recall that your resume is hanging out somewhere on the Internet.

>> When you meet an employer or recruiter in a job interview, bring along several copies of your paper resume. An attractive resume makes a good impression and can jump-start questions that you want to answer.

In a digital era, how good should your paper be? Although you're using paper only for hand-to-hand delivery, the standards haven't changed. The stock for a paper resume should be quality paper that contains rag content of perhaps 25 percent, as well as a watermark (a faint image ingrained in the paper). For lower-level positions, any decent-looking paper will do.

What color should you choose? Stick to white or off-white, eggshell, or the palest of gray. Print on only one side of the sheet.

What about theme papers — musical notes for musicians, tree leaves for environmental jobs, and the like? Although the use of theme paper for resumes has grown over the past decade, my preference is for plain stock unless you're in a highly creative field. Look to make what's in your resume visually pop as described earlier in this chapter as well as in the upcoming Chapter 12.

REMEMBER

Use a computer and a high-quality printer to produce your resume. Today's standard is a sharp-looking resume printed on a laser or inkjet printer.

Finally, don't staple together a two- or three-page resume or put it in a folder or plastic insert. The resume may be photocopied and distributed, or it may be — *gasp*, shades of ancient technology! — scanned into a database. Simply use a paperclip to attach the pages together, if desired.

IN THIS CHAPTER

» Learning when you should and
  shouldn't get creative

» Understanding additional creative
  principles

» Applying step-by-step strategies

Chapter 12

Opting for a Creative Resume

D o a quick online search for *creative resume,* and you'll see a wide array of plain to over-the-top resume formats. You might wonder whether full-color or graphic-filled resumes are what you need. I answer that question in this chapter, and provide step-by-step strategies for designing your own creative resume. For more ideas, see the award-winning graphic resumes in Chapter 18.

Understanding Why Creative Resumes Are Game Changers

The formatting, content, and presentation of a creative resume can give you an edge during a job search. Desktop publishing and design software, first made widespread in the 1980s, has enabled some people to elevate the marketing and advertising strategy in their resumes.

Anyone can use some creativity in a resume to help it stand out in a stack of plain resumes. As you read this chapter, you'll see examples of when to go all-out with design and when to be more restrained.

The key to this chapter is to learn new methods to stand out and to make certain you use them in an effective and winning way.

WARNING

Remember ATS from Chapter 4? It's important to recognize that the fancier your resume, the less chance it has of being ATS scannable. If resume content appears on a colored background or pertinent data is in a chart or box, computers can't read it. But don't discount these creative resumes — they don't replace your regular OnTarget resume. Instead, use your creative resume for targeted mailings, networking, job fairs, and any time you can put a resume directly into the hands of a decision maker.

I recommend that you submit both formats and include the following in your cover letter: "For your convenience, I have also included a plain, scannable copy of my resume." This approach solves the problem and gets your resume seen.

Defining creative resumes

So, you want to stand out from the crowd. What do I have to say about creative resumes?

Yes, please!

A creative resume can be as simple as a resume with a logo of your initials at the top or pops of color. It can also be a full-out design project. Here are some more extreme examples of creative resumes I've created:

>> A chef looking to land a position on a private yacht used a resume set up to look like an elegant, full-color, folding menu. I used fancy script fonts for headers and creative titles for sections, such as The Experience instead of Professional Experience. The chef currently sails the Mediterranean on a gorgeous sailing yacht.

>> A fine artist looking to break into advertising painted an original work, scanned it into the computer, overlaid it with sections of her resume, and then cut them into puzzle pieces under my guidance. Those were placed in a paint can with a custom marketing wrap branded to advertise her. The cans were delivered to agencies following a four-week postcard teaser campaign about solving your company's advertising puzzle. After interviews with many companies, she became a creative director with the then WB television network.

>> A tugboat captain wanted to land a position as a captain of a casino cruise ship. I created his resume with a line drawing of a cruise ship down one side of the page. He also used techniques from Chapters 13 and 14 to position his qualifications for the change. Despite his lack of direct experience, he applied for one job and landed it.

When you visit Chapter 18, you will see vivid examples of highly graphic yet more traditional 8.5-by-11 resumes created with the professional resume writers in MS Word. Some of these look like full-color brochures and others mix borders, graphics, and charts for the best of all creative worlds.

As long as you follow the strategies laid out for maintaining your OnTarget resume and keep in mind that what you've created is specifically a networking resume and must accompany at ATS-scannable resume, the sky is (almost) the limit.

The yes and no of creative resumes

It's critical to match your creative resume to the situation and make sure it is appropriate for the industry. Don't be creative just to be creative. Give the creativity a purpose. Think about the example resumes described in the preceding section.

For instance, I recently helped my husband through a job search in which he was opting to retarget from a high-paying, physically demanding position to one that would give him the quality of life he desired due to its slower pace and entry-level status. This would mean a pay cut and translating 26 years of over-qualified experience into appropriate credentials for entry-level jobs asking for 3-5 years in the logistics industry. The creativity in his resume was limited to putting the headers in soothing blue and including matching blue separating lines between sections. If he had been looking for a management position, we would have amped up the resume with a testimonial in a blue text box shaped like an arrow and added a chart next to his most recent position showing his accomplishments.

Lower-level, blue collar, or technical jobs can be appropriate for a creative resume. For example, I used gear-shaped text boxes across the top of an engineer's resume to highlight his strengths. Not a lot of design, but a thoughtful, applicable design. In Chapter 18, I present samples of technical resumes that use several stylistic techniques.

There really are no absolutes regarding the use of creative resume techniques as long as you pause and make sure that they won't oversell you for the position or industry or be seen as inappropriate. However, do consider the following few no-no's:

>> **Neon or bright colors that burn the corneas:** Instead, opt for soothing, professional shades or ones specific to the industry.

>> **Company logos:** You must have permission before using a former employer's company or product logo.

>> **Irrelevant, tasteless, or vulgar graphics or images:** Your graphics should be relevant, such as a custom logo of your name or initials, representative design elements (images, icons, or text boxes) for the industry, or charts and tables.

>> **Fancy, illegible fonts:** Creative resumes don't provide an excuse for using unreadable fonts. Choose an appropriate shape for non-relevant content such as headers; be elegant, bold, edgy, or fun. But make sure the font is readable and use a recommended font (see Chapter 11) for the body text of your experience, skills, and accomplishments.

>> **Busy layout:** It's fun to add creative elements to your resume, but don't make it crowded and overwhelming. Less is more, so plan carefully.

Don't be afraid to experiment and play. Remember, blank page syndrome is the biggest enemy in creating your resume. Just jump in and get started with ideas.

TIP

Professional resume writer Cheryl Lynch Simpson of Executive Resume Rescue is a pioneer of creative resumes. She advises that you look at print marketing for ideas. Keep your eye out for mailers you receive, brochures at companies, and magazine ads. Keep the ones that appeal to you and use them to drive your ideas when creating your resume.

Using Design Strategies That Pop

When approaching your creative resume, don't be afraid to play with layout, colors, and MS Office tools. With an open mind, and the Insert and Design menus, just about anything is possible when creating a visually distinctive resume. The process requires thought, practice, and play. Study the resumes in Chapter 18 to understand what others are doing.

This section provides examples of elements you might want to include in your creative resume.

Special thanks to resume writers Posey Salem of Radiant Resume Career Services and Marie Plett of Aspirations Career Services, Inc. for their ideas, strategies, and contributions, which are highlighted in the following examples and ideas.

TIP

Any instructions in the rest of the chapter for formatting in MS Word are subject to change depending on the version of the program you're using. I provide basic information. When you want to perform a task, such as insert text shading or insert page border, perform an online search, and include your version of MS Word. You'll find step-by-step instructions with screen shots and even videos.

Lines and shading

One of the easiest design techniques is to apply lines and shading to offset content in your resume. You can use lines and shading around or over section headings, your name, or other body text to make it stand out. Or do something as simple as changing your bullets from black to a color.

For an elegant look, use the page border function in MS Word to create a border around the entire resume. Experiment with single and double lines of different weights (widths) to create a custom look.

Check out Figure 12-1 for some examples of lines and shading.

Professional Experience

Professional Experience

PROFESSIONAL EXPERIENCE

Professional Experience

Philosophy & Reputation:
"Buckle down and get it done. Strive to be better and faster than the day before. Put quality, service and integrity first and you'll never suffer a sleepless night."

FIGURE 12-1:
Examples of lines
and shading.

Client Name   City, ST, ZIP • Phone • E□□□l • L□□□□□□□□□□L

Risk Management • Supply Chain Management • Strategic Sourcing

Courtesy of resume writer Posey Salem.

Text boxes

Text boxes are an easy way to draw the eye to content and make it stand out. You can add a text box in several ways. My favorite method is to choose the Insert menu, click Shapes, select the one shape I like, and insert it into the document. Hover your cursor over the shape and then right-click to display a menu with the option of adding text.

After you add text, experiment with adding color, shadows, and shading and changing the color of your font, as shown in Figure 12-2. A black font on a light background or a white font on a dark background can make a nice contrast and increase legibility.

> "Chris is a lead logistics supervisor with a proven history of strong operational and interpersonal skills. He consistently makes the best decisions which have cut outbound delivery route time by as much as 27% in an already lean environment."
>
> - Ron Jones, Senior Manager, XYZ Logistics

> "Chris is a lead logistics supervisor with a proven history of strong operational and interpersonal skills. He consistently makes the best decisions which have cut outbound delivery route time by as much as 27% in an already lean environment."
>
> - Ron Jones, Senior Manager, XYZ Logistics

Professional Experience

FIGURE 12-2:
Examples of text boxes.

WARNING

Be careful when selecting the content you include in a text box or other closed image, such as charts and graphs (described in the next section). This data can be rendered invisible by computer resume-scanning systems such as ATS. Always choose data that would help the reader but would not count specifically toward meeting the requirements of the position. My favorite choice for a text box is a testimonial from a former employer. Also, you can highlight top content in a text box as long as it is repeated in text elsewhere in the resume.

Charts and graphs

Charts and graphs make great additions to your resume when you have numerical data to display. By including the data visually, you draw the eye to the return on investment you can offer by demonstrating your ability to make money, save money, maximize resources, or maintain satisfied customers. Graphs and charts are a power-packed way to demonstrate this growth or savings over time, as shown in Figure 12-3.

The most commonly used charts and graphs are pie charts, column charts and graphs, and bar graphs and charts. But as you can see in Figure 12-3, many others are available. Which one you use in your resume depends on the type of data you want to convey. Experiment with MS Word's offerings by choosing the Insert menu and looking at the SmartArt and Chart options.

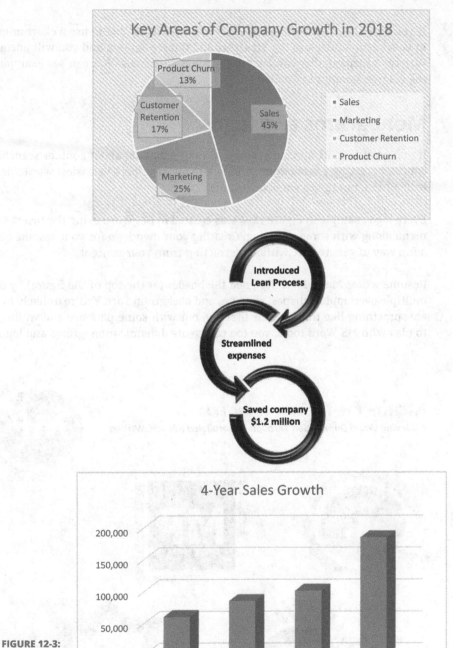

FIGURE 12-3:
Examples of
various charts
and graphs.

TIP

If you don't have concrete numbers, you may still be able to use a chart or graph in your resume. Explore the SmartArt and Charts options and you will uncover a variety of formats that can lead to unique data visuals. You can see examples in the resume samples in Chapter 18.

Monograms and logos

If you want to spiff up your resume without worrying about content scanability, consider creating a monogram or logo for your resume. The easiest way to do this is in a header at the top of your resume.

Every logo example in Figure 12-4 was created in MS Word using the Insert Shape menu along with some tweaking. Creating your own logo for your resume can be a fun way to get creative without detracting from your content.

Resume writer Marie Plett designed the header (at the top of the figure) by using multiple overlapping shapes, shading, and background art. You're unlikely to create something like this on your first try, but with some patience and willingness to play with MS Word tools, you too can create dynamic monograms and logos.

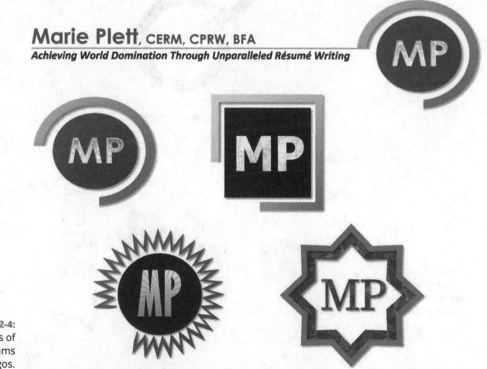

FIGURE 12-4: Examples of monograms and logos.

Courtesy of resume writer Marie Plett.

Graphics and icons

Have you earned an industry certification and been given permission by the granting organization to use the logo in your self-marketing? If so, including that logo would make a great addition to the header of your resume, as shown in Figure 12-5.

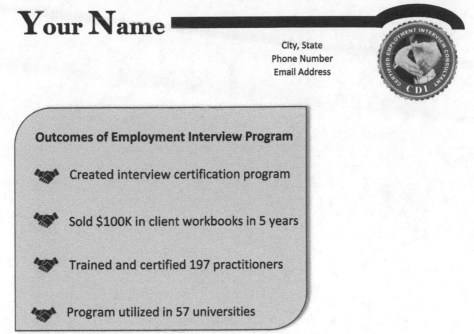

FIGURE 12-5:
Examples
of graphics
and icons.

Likewise, you might use icons in place of your bullets to represent an industry profession or a functional responsibility. These would be great in a key word list or the summary section at the top of a resume.

Although you can insert images in MS Word, you probably won't have to take that step. When you go to insert a new bullet into your resume, select Define New Bullet. Then look at the Symbols menu for various webdings and wingdings. Yes, those are funny names, but that's how MS Word refers to its symbol bullets. You have many choices that may be an appropriate match for your profession. For instance, pilots might select an airplane to represent bullets in the summary section of their resume. Or customer service representatives might select a phone for the bullets in their summary section.

Whatever you do with graphics and icons in your resume, keep it simple and choose to include strategies only if they further your positioning for the target job.

Chapter **13**

Dealing with a Major Life Change

Searching for a job is a stressful proposition, and navigating a life transition is stressful as well. When you put the two together, you may feel overwhelmed — and decide to play the lottery instead. However, you can move from one phase of your life to the next with the guidance offered in this chapter, especially if you find yourself in one of the following situations:

» Searching for your first job (new grads)

» Continuing your career (military transition, seasoned worker)

Sometimes you may have to figure out how to address a negative event — demotion, firing, too much or too little experience — on your resume. This chapter offers suggestions for how to present those situations so your resume doesn't automatically end up in the rejection pile.

Scoring Big with Your First Gig

When you've just walked the cap-and-gown line, you can sidestep "no experience" potholes by impressing employers with your vim and vigor, accomplishments, and up-to-date knowledge. Here's a primer on putting together a resume that can help you break into your desired field.

TIP

For effective examples of new graduate resumes, look at the new graduate resume samples in Chapter 16. Still stymied? Check out award-winning new graduate resumes created by professional resume writers at CareerDirectors (`https://careerdirectors.com`) under the Find a Career Pro navigation button. Here you can find a number of great examples for overcoming new graduate challenges. A few of these are also showcased in Chapter 18.

Promoting your strengths

As a recent graduate, you have four key selling points and various minor ones:

>> You're energetic and fired up to tackle assigned tasks and conquer the world.

>> Your job skills and knowledge are up-to-date, and you've likely gained a lot of hands-on experience you may take for granted.

>> You're available for the right price. You cost much less than an older, experienced person. Maybe half as much.

>> You belong to a global, networked era and aren't afraid of technology.

Throw in assertions that you're a fast learner, are untarnished by earlier workplace habits, and as a rookie, you're prime material to be developed in concert with a prospective employer's viewpoints. With these selling points, hiring managers will want to take a second look at how you may fit into their organization.

Recognizing your rookie soft spots

Your key weaknesses are internal and external, but luckily they can all be overcome with resume strategy. As a new professional, you risk

>> Being stereotyped by prospective employers as having book smarts but lacking practical experience.

>> Taking for granted the relevant value you have to offer and not selling all the knowledge and skills gained from projects, papers, class learning, volunteerism, internships, and seemingly unrelated employment.

These shortcomings are easy enough to put a positive spin on when you're putting together your resume. Keep reading for ways to turn these negatives into positives.

Demonstrating how recent graduates add value

Just as the times change, so do the strategies for putting together resumes. Your professors may recommend that you simply list your jobs and skills, but these days, that's not enough. You need to recognize that your resume isn't a list of everything you've done. It's about selling yourself for jobs in the field you're targeting. What is most important is including content on your resume that shows you're ready for that type of position.

Use the following key strategies to make your resume sell.

Data-mine your college experience

Need a job? Get experience! Need experience? Get a job! This predicament has frustrated new graduates since the Industrial Revolution.

It might seem like you have a difficult resume challenge when you have nothing but education to work with. But that's just not the case! Every core course you took and every volunteer role you held may offer juicy nuggets of value to your resume.

Consider the following factors to identify the experience and skills you garnered in college and match your information with the job you hope to land:

>> **Work:** Internships, summer jobs, part-time jobs, campus jobs, entrepreneurial jobs, temporary work, and volunteer work.

>> **Sports:** Proven ability to achieve goals in a team environment; strength in competition, which looks good for many types of positions such as sales.

>> **Awards and honors**

>> **Research papers and projects**

>> **Knowledge:** Skills and abilities gained from completing core courses.

>> **Campus leadership**

>> **Grade Point Average (GPA):** If it's 3.0 or above; otherwise, omit it (some advisers set the GPA floor at 3.5).

>> **Technical skills and software facility**

Clarify your aim

Always start by very briefly clarifying your job target with your objective header. Ditch the wordy (and lofty) job objectives because that's considered old school. Cut to the chase, like this:

Research position in urban planning field in Chicago area.

or

Qualified for positions in: Sales ~ Marketing ~ Public Relations

Summarize what makes you stand out

Include a summary to point out your strong points (I walk you through this process in Chapter 7). As a new grad, think about what professors told you were your strengths or what they wrote on your papers. Reread the recommendation letters you received from internships. Think about any recognitions or awards you were given for clubs, academics, or volunteer work.

Your goal is to state in two or three sentences what makes you stand out. For example:

Visionary and high-energy young professional recognized for savvy in targeting marketing projects and PR campaigns. Experience: worked on campaigns for the XYZ Company and the ABC Company. Creative: campaign selected out of 24 presented by fellow competitors. Quick-to-learn: attained 3.75 GPA in BS in Marketing.

And it's all true. Consider how it breaks down:

Statement: *Visionary and high-energy young professional recognized for savvy in targeting marketing projects and PR campaigns.*

Translation: I have been told by my professors, bosses, and internship managers that I have a lot of energy and vision for marketing and PR.

Statement: *Experience: worked on campaigns for the XYZ Company and the ABC Company.*

Translation: I completed case study projects in my marketing classes on these companies that led to mock campaigns being developed.

Statement: *Creative: campaign selected out of 24 presented by fellow competitors.*

Translation: One of my case studies was overseen by a real marketing agency. Of my 24 classmates, my campaign proposal was selected as the one they would pitch to the client.

Statement: *Quick-to-learn: attained a 3.75 GPA in BS in Marketing.*

Translation: It is always a good idea to showcase your GPA in your resume if you have attained at least a 3.0. Otherwise, leave it off.

Sell your skills, knowledge, and training

WARNING

You may feel compelled to follow the direction of your professors and friends, and limit what you have learned to the names of classes written under your new degree in the resume's education section. Don't do it! This is how employers get the idea you just have book smarts, and your resume fails to provide the necessary keywords for computer scans (more on this in Chapters 7 and 10).

Instead, this is where you turn your classroom learning, school papers, projects, transferrable work, and volunteer skills into resume gold. Under your summary, all you need to do is add a two- or three-column list with the title:

Knowledge, Skills, and Training

Fill this section with the key skills, knowledge, and training you have for your target job. A marketing grad might include:

Advertising, Marketing, Public Relations, Budgeting, Pricing, Graphic Design, Client Relations, Project Planning, Market Research, Branding, Writing & Editing, Social Media

Check out Figure 13-1 for an example of how this can look.

FIGURE 13-1:
List your knowledge, skills, and training with bullets.

Knowledge, Skills & Training		
· Advertising	· Public Relations	· Marketing
· Budgeting	· Graphic Design	· Pricing
· Branding	· Client Relations	· Social Media
· Project Planning	· Market Research	· Writing & Editing

Now your resume leads with some keyword meat that you will support later in the experience section.

REMEMBER

Most new grads make the mistake of skipping the keyword section because they feel they have little to offer. But that's just wrong and a disservice to all the knowledge and hands-on skills you gained while attaining your degree. Dig deep into course descriptions, course syllabi, and textbook tables of contents to find the keywords relevant to your job target.

TIP

If you aren't sure what to play up in the keyword section, take a look at descriptions of jobs you are targeting. This will give you a good indication of the skills employers are seeking and should help you shape what you include.

Experience isn't just about paid jobs

Thicken your work experience by including all unpaid positions, internships, special projects, and volunteer jobs/leadership roles (such as campus club president). List them just like you would employment in reverse chronological order under your experience section. For example:

Marketing Studies, FT – *ABC University, Orlando, FL*

Marketing Campaigns: Completed campaign design for XYZ company course project that was selected by Stark Advertising Agency as the best out of 24 entries. Met with customer and Stark staff on mock pitch.

Marketing Collateral: Designed numerous collateral pieces from press releases to emails, websites, and brochures using Photoshop, AI, and WordPress in design class.

President (Marketing Responsibility) – *123 Sorority, Orlando, FL*

Recruiting & Marketing Campaigns: Collaborated with volunteers to develop effective on-campus and off-campus recruiting campaigns that led to 30 percent increase in pledges over prior three years.

Communications & Promotions: Represented sorority to key influencers such as university administrative staff. Attained permission for unique on-campus fundraiser that led to raising $12,000 in one semester.

TIP

Highlight the experience most relevant to your intended future. If you have at least one year of full-time professional experience, place your education section after your experience section — unless your education is changing your career path.

Dump unhelpful information

Don't fatten your resume with irrelevant data such as hobbies, unless they are directly relevant to your job target or the employer. Include an activity only if it reveals skills, competencies, accomplishments, results, or other qualification to support your intended job. Omit high school data unless it adds a unique fact to the total impression that you're creating.

Also, if you're mailing your resume via the U.S. Postal Service, don't enclose it in a report cover or bulky package; just slip it and your cover letter in a standard envelope. And forget about including school transcripts or letters of recommendation. Those belong in a nice three-ring binder portfolio you carry with you to the interview.

Make unrelated work history relatable

It can feel easy to just write down what you did in your unrelated jobs and leave it at that. But what if your job was as a cashier and you're targeting marketing coordinator? Words just aren't going to mesh and sell you to the prospective employer.

This is where you have to do a little analysis of how what you have to offer can cross the bridge to what the employer needs.

First, break your job down into fragments and explain them. For example, with the cashier description, don't just say that your responsibility was "scanning products, making money transactions, and dealing with customers." Instead do this:

1. Look at job descriptions that match what you are targeting.

2. Consider how your skills can best be explained to fit those requirements.

3. Describe each function in terms of your accomplishments and their outcomes.

Avoiding gaffes common to new graduates

New graduates are more likely than experienced job seekers to make the following mistakes.

REMEMBER

>> **Falling short of image standards:** If you present an online resume blemished with the type of shorthand used for tweets and texting, or a paper resume flawed with typos, or a persona degraded with party pictures or a goofy profile on a social media site, you flunk.

>> **Omitting heavy-hitter points:** You fail to distinguish yourself by creating an opening summary that calls to mind an image of your brand, as I describe earlier in this chapter.

Keep your summary brief — three to four accomplishments is plenty.

>> **Overcompensating with gimmicky language:** Don't get cutesy in your resume to compensate for a lack of qualifications. Avoid using exotically original language, such as "eyelinered genius," a term used by a business graduate applying for an entry-level marketing position in the cosmetics industry. The term may be colorful, but charm communicates better in the interview.

>> **Making employers guess:** Employers hate being asked to decipher your intent. Merely presenting your declared major and transcript excerpts isn't enough to kick off a productive job search. Add a targeted objective header statement, summary, and keyword section directed at a specific career field and type of position.

>> **Leveling the experience field:** Your resume is no place to give every job equal billing. Do what you can to make each one relevant for the prospective employer, but don't be afraid to limit one to just a single line of job title, company name, location, and date in your reverse chronology for positions that just don't seem to offer any relevant value.

>> **Stopping with bare bones:** Some rookies look at a sheet of paper and then at their embarrassing, bedraggled collection of jobs in their paid-experience stew. Desperate to get *anything* written, they settle for employer, job title, and dates of employment.

The solution is to pull together *all* experience, including volunteer and part-time gigs. Sit, think, think some more, and add all your relevant competencies and skills pointing in the direction in which you wish to work. You can use Chapter 8 as a good guide for avoiding what I call this issue of blank page syndrome.

>> **Hiding hot information:** Data buried is data forgotten. Employers remember best the information you give first in a resume, not the data folded into the middle. The first one-third to one-half of the first page of your resume is prime real estate; determine your selling points and pack that punch up front.

>> **Ignoring employers' needs:** Even the smartest new graduates make this mistake: They forget to find out what employers want from new hires. At this moment in time, no one cares what you want — the only thing that matters is the value-pack you bring to the employer. Rigorously study numerous job descriptions for your targeted positions so you can gain gems of wisdom for where to put your focus.

>> **Writing boastfully:** Appearing too arrogant about your talents can cause employers to question your ability to learn and function as a junior team member. Even when you're just trying to compensate for your inexperience, avoid terminology that comes across as unnatural or blatantly self-important.

TIP

When you're not sure whether you sound too full of yourself, ask those who know you to read your resume and share feedback about what kind of person they think your resume represents. Then, go back and tweak wording if it needs to be toned down (or built up). An online thesaurus or crossword dictionary can be a great tool in coming up with similar words.

Moving Beyond "Too Old" to "In Demand"

If you're on the shady side of 50 (or even 40 in some occupations), don't bother wondering whether job-market age discrimination lives. It does. But it absolutely doesn't have to derail your career.

In this section, I show you how to do everything within your power to beat pesky bias and display your excellent qualifications for employment on your resume.

Selling your strengths as a seasoned worker

You have at least six main selling points and a slew of minor ones:

>> **Road-tested:** You have more knowledge and greater wisdom than you did when you were half your age. Your judgment is a valuable commodity. You can easily save an employer substantial "mistake dollars" because you've seen most situations play out in some form over the course of your learning lifetime. You have the common sense that comes with experiencing life. You won't rush into hasty decisions.

>> **Reliable:** You won't take off for frivolous reasons. Employers can count on you showing up and doing the job as expected. You're more grateful for a good job than younger workers and show your appreciation with a strong work ethic. Your work history shows that your word is your bond.

>> **Flexible:** You're motivated to be adaptable. You may value working less than a full-time schedule. You can adapt to the changing needs of a business.

>> **Financially viable:** You may be able to work for less money than your competition. Your kids are grown and your expenses are down.

>> **Collaborative:** You've perfected a talent for team playing because you've seen how all hands can work collectively for the good of a business.

>> **Big-picture vision:** You take a 360-degree view when dealing with people. You've had years to discover what makes them tick. You know from firsthand experience the quality of customer service consumers expect and appreciate. You've learned to look around corners before making decisions that may come back to bite an employer.

Your brain is better than ever between ages 40 and 65, say researchers. Older folks are better at all sorts of things than they were at age 20, including problem solving and making financial judgments. Middle-aged brains, according to studies, are primed to navigate the world better because they've been navigating the world better longer.

Busting myths about seasoned workers

The notion that older people have had their day and should make room for the next generation is deeply ingrained, say researchers. The stereotype is that you can't teach an old dog new tricks and that all mature workers are alike in their abilities to learn, perform, energize, remember, and deal with change in a new world.

Here is a selection of prevalent myths about workers of a certain age, followed by the defense realities to reflect in your resume:

>> **Older workers can't or won't learn new skills.**

A smart, well-executed resume proves this bit of conventional wisdom wrong: The over-50 crowd is the fastest growing group of Internet and social media users. Use technical terms on your resume if appropriate. Mention new skills recently acquired. Cite recent coursework, degrees, and certifications. Be sure to emphasize accomplishments.

>> **Training older workers is a lost investment because they won't be around for long.**

Older workers are just not retiring like they used to. Studies repeatedly report that workers are extending their careers, either by choice or because their retirement funding isn't where it needs to be. Find ways to tell employers that you

- Are committed to doing quality work

- Get along with coworkers and younger bosses

- Have strong skills in reading, writing, and math

- Are someone they can count on in a crisis

- Are cheerful about multiple hats and tasks

- Can work weekends if needed

>> **Benefit and accident costs are higher for older workers.**

Skyrocketing health insurance costs have become a third rail for hiring older workers. Employers pay a higher premium for employees between ages 50 and 65 (65 being the magic number when Medicare starts paying the medical bills).

Small employers in particular, pressing to keep their health insurance expense to a minimum and stay in business, may prefer to hire workers in a younger demographic — unless you change their minds.

Play your ace-in-the-hole: offsets. Certain characteristics even out generational cost differences. For example, a study by the AARP shows that older workers take fewer sick days per year than do other age groups because they have fewer acute illnesses and sporadic sick days. What's more, older workers take fewer risks in accident-prone situations and statistically have lower accident rates than other age groups.

Overall, employee benefit costs stay the same as a percentage of salary for all age groups. Handling this on a resume is tricky but, if true, you can say: "Robust health; physically active; no dependents other than spouse."

As new health insurance provisions roll out, generational differences in health insurance costs may become less important, and perhaps even moot. Be on the lookout for developments that level the playing field for older job-hunters and use them to your advantage.

Of course, if you don't need health insurance because you receive it from a spouse or other party, you can leverage that to your benefit.

TIP

As a seasoned worker, you're somewhat less likely to be clobbered by age bias in government (federal, state, local) work and more likely to be appreciated for your proven talents. Look for opportunities at USAJobs (www.usajobs.gov/).

Tips for the seasoned worker

To fight the age bias that can keep you out of job interviews, aim for a clean and contemporary resume design (see resume samples in Chapter 15) and stock it with accomplishments, skills, and experience that make you look sharp and professional by taking to heart the following tips.

Match your target job description

Find or write job descriptions of your target occupations. If you like your current field and are leaving involuntarily because it's disappearing from under your feet like the world's biggest sinkhole, start with job descriptions in closely related jobs. Compare requirements of related jobs with your transferable (crossover) skills profile. If you don't like your current field, forget I mentioned it.

TIP

To identify occupations closely related to your current field, check out the *Occupational Outlook Handbook* published by the U.S. Department of Labor. Read it online at www.bls.gov/ooh/.

Knowing what you have to offer gets you out of the past and into the future; it enables you to write a resume that readers respect, by, in effect, saying, "This is what I can do for you that will add to your productivity, efficiency, or effectiveness. And, of course, a little bump on the bottom line."

Shorten your resume

The general guideline is "Go back no more than 10 or 15 years." But if that doesn't work for the job you seek, one answer is to create a functional or hybrid resume (Chapter 6), in which you emphasize your relevant skills in detail toward the top of the resume and downplay overly impressive titles that might intimidate younger employers. For example, *Senior Vice President, Sales* becomes *Sales Executive*.

TIP

If you must list jobs prior to the 15-year mark, it's perfectly acceptable to list them in a section called *Other Relevant Experience, Additional Experience,* or *Prior Work History,* and leave off the dates. As long as you cover dates in the more recent positions, the older jobs can be talking points for the interview. This way you won't give away the actual number of years of work.

Focus your resume

For emphasis, I'll repeat that: Focus your resume. Concentrate on highlighting your two most recent or most relevant jobs. Don't attempt to give equal attention to each of your past jobs, especially if the experience is irrelevant to what you want to do now.

What can you do with all the experience that was great in your old job but means zero where you want to go? Lump it together at the end of your resume under *Other Relevant Experience, Additional Experience,* or *Prior Work History.* Shrink it to positions, titles, employers, and/or degrees and educational institutions. If extraneous experience is older than five years, boot it entirely.

When your job experience has been overly diverse, your resume probably looks like a job-hopping tale of unrelated job after unrelated job. (If that's your problem, see Chapter 14.)

Show that you're a tower of strength

Give examples of how you solved problems, recovered expenses, and learned to compensate for weaknesses in your working environment. Emphasize how quickly such adjustments occurred. Gray heads who've survived a few fallen skies are valuable assets in difficult times.

Demonstrate political correctness

Show that you're familiar with contemporary values by using politically correct terms wherever appropriate. Examples include *diversity, cross-cultural, mainstream, multiethnic,* and *people with disabilities* (never *handicapped*), and *women* (not *girls* or *gals*). Sensitivity is especially important for positions that have contact with the public.

Send your resume online

Doing so helps dispel any ideas that you're over the hill and haven't the vaguest idea that you live in a digital age. If you want to be seen as a hub of hip, tweet about your resume. See Part 1 for more on digital resumes and using social media.

Murder ancient education dates

Don't worry that the absence of dates will send a signal you're hiding something. When you earned your degree won't sell you at this point, but what you studied might. If a prospective employer really wants to know when you graduated, he/she will ask in the interview. In short: Leave dates off your education section.

TIP

Regardless of your age, if you have gone back to school to improve your odds or chart a different course, take a look at the new graduate strategies earlier in this chapter and don't be afraid to adopt the ones that will help you most.

Trim your resume to fighting weight

For very experienced professionals, sorting out the most powerful resume points can be difficult. It's like being a gifted child with so many choices, and you're good at all of them! Ask a couple of smart friends to help you decide what information stays and what information goes.

Employ appropriate headings

When you're relying on freelance or non-paid work — hobby or volunteer — as the substance for your timeline, use the heading *Professional Experience* so it covers both paid and unpaid roles.

But when you've changed your career focus through education, list *Education* before *Experience*. To refine the education heading, you can substitute target-job-related learning, such as *Accounting Education* or *Healthcare Education*. Your professional experience then follows.

Taking a lower-level job

When you're willing to step down from your previous level of work, don't try to do it solely with a resume. Go directly to the hiring manager in a personal meeting where you have a chance to color your positioning in the best hue. For instance, avoid the classic mistake of saying you no longer want to be the "point person."

Instead, here's your best positioning slant: You certainly are not a burned-out manager looking to bail by settling for a much less responsible job. You're a career changer exploring new fields:

> *In the past decade, I've put in very long hours and exceeded expectations in jobs in the same industry. I realized I'm a doer who needs new mountains to climb. I have too much to give to the business world to ride on autopilot the rest of my life. I want to check out other ways I can make a contribution in a different career field, hopefully at your company.*

Explain your reasoned willingness to accept lower compensation:

> *I have a great work attitude and excellent judgment. Show me a new task, and I get it right away. I understand, of course, that the trade-off in moving into your industry is less pay and responsibility.*

When you've opened the door, it's time to hand over your hybrid resume (described in Chapter 6). You need breathing room to shape your resume in a way that spotlights your crossover skills as they pertain to the job you seek, such as talent for working with numbers, reliability, and good attendance record, as well as fast learning ability. You can also cut out higher-level accomplishments that might make you appear committed to attaining that level in your next position.

When you're a major seeking a minor position, emphasize that sometimes the best workers need new chapters in their lives.

SHOW SKILLS AS THEY APPLY TO NEW POSITION

Making a career change? As you list your skills, competencies, education, and experience, lead with the information relevant to the new position and then list the other data. You have to quickly convince the employer that you have the ability to handle the position.

Assume an engineer wants to move into sales. The resume should mention things such as "client liaison," "preparing presentations for meetings," and "strong communications skills" — and accomplishments that back up the claims.

You may begin by writing: "Used a strong technical background and excellent communications skills in a sales role." Then continue to speak of your ability to provide good technical advice in a business relationship.

Writing that you "enjoy learning" is, in some cases, a coin with two sides: The employer may see you as admirable in your desire to further your education, or, conversely, make a negative judgment that you don't have the skills right now to hit the ground running.

Watching out for gaffes common to seasoned workers

When you have a long job history, you're more likely to need updates on the following issues.

>> **Choosing the wrong focus:** Choosing the wrong focus is a problem shared with new graduates who fail to elaborate on those jobs that best address the hoped-for next job. (See the "Gaffes common to new graduates" section earlier in this chapter.) Like the real estate adage that the operating principle is location, location, location, the operating principle for better jobs is target, target, target.

>> **Using old resume standards:** Many seasoned workers have an outdated concept of what a resume should be. An office neighbor recently expressed surprise when I told him to leave out his personal information, which once was standard fare on resumes. Busy employers and resume-processing computers don't care that you're a par golfer or play impressive tennis; this kind of personal information may come out at the interview. For more information on resume content, see Chapter 8.

>> **Lacking a summary:** Because of the extensiveness of your experience, your resume may be a grab bag without a summary. Suppose you're an auditor who yearns for the country life. You can write: *Internal Auditor: Farm Equipment Industry,* followed by a one- or two-paragraph summary of why you're qualified. Think of a summary as a salesperson's hook. It describes some of your special skills, how you stand out from the competition for your target, your familiarity with the target industry, and your top accomplishments (see Chapter 8).

>> **Not supplementing a high school education:** If your highest education attainment is high school, don't forget to mention any continuing education, including seminars and workshops related to your work, if those studies apply to what you want to do next. Never list high school on your resume unless you're currently a young cub attending.

Moving from Military Work to Civilian Employment

Transitioning from the military into a civilian role can be an extremely daunting experience. You suddenly find yourself going from a very structured world into one of unstructured chaos where it seems "anything goes." But, when it comes to the resume, that's not the case.

TIP

If you're trading military life for your first civilian gig, be sure to sign up for the federal government's invaluable Transition Assistance Program (TAP). TAP offers a three-day class to help active-duty personnel write resumes and prepare for interviews.

Highlighting your military strengths

Having recently transitioned from the military, you have six key selling points:

>> You're highly disciplined and understand the chain of command.

>> You're a hard worker who understands a day's work for a day's pay.

>> You are likely well traveled and have gained cultural experience.

>> You understand teamwork as well as being accountable.

>> You likely held new positions in new geographies on a regular basis, causing you to develop a variety of diverse and transferable skillsets.

>> You're accustomed to changes in responsibility, title, and position.

Identifying potential strikes against you

Your key weaknesses can easily be overcome. They include:

>> You likely speak and write using jargon, titles, and acronyms that may be unfamiliar and intimidating to employers.

>> Your confidence and discipline may come across as arrogance, superiority, or inflexibility.

>> You may lack knowledge of how corporations operate.

>> You may fall into a common misperception held by some employers that you need constant structure and guidance to function.

>> Corporate America believes you operated without concern of budgets.

Tips for transitioners

When transitioning from the military, you are going to want to do four things:

» Gather together all the resources you need to review your career path (see the "Resources to consider" section later in this chapter).

» Get all your responsibilities and accomplishments on paper in a brain dump (see Chapter 8).

» Look at civilian job descriptions to understand target wording when translating your military experience.

» Write your experience to speak to your target audience and positions (see the following section).

Writing for civilian markets

Most civilian employers aren't familiar with military speak and need you to use crossover language that they understand and to which they can relate. This means taking the time to change your word choice from milspeak to civilian language that targets the target job description. If you get stuck using acronyms and military titles they don't know, you may get passed over.

TIP

To determine how to word your resume for civilian speak, do one of the following:

» Access your military branch's transition assistance center for workshops or personal assistance in writing your resume.

» Go over what you did with a friend or family member who has been in the civilian world and can advise you on accurately wording the description.

» Check out military transition websites as suggested by Master Military Resume Writer Billie Parker Jordan of Advantage Resumes and Career Services:

  • Use skill translator websites that show you corresponding civilian and federal employment roles.

  MOS (www.onetonline.org/crosswalk)

  Mil2FedJobs Federal Jobs Crosswalk (www.Mil2FedJobs.com)

  Department of Labor Military to Civilian Occupation Translator (www.careerinfonet.org/moc)

  • Explore transition options for veterans to help determine what you would like to do next and where you fit best.

  My Next Move for Veterans (www.mynextmove.org/vets/)

Resources to consider

These are the military transition documents you will likely need to review:

» Evaluation Reports

- USMC: Fitness Reports (E-5 & above) or Proficiency Conduct Marks (E-4 & Below)
- Navy: Fitness Reports (Officers)/Performance Evaluations (Enlisted)
- Army: Evaluation Reports (Officer, NCO, or Enlisted)
- Air Force: Officer Performance Evaluation Report or Enlisted Performance Appraisal
- Coast Guard: Performance Reviews

» List of medals and certificates describing what you did to receive them

» Military Occupational Specialty (MOS)

» Smart Transcript

» VMet (DD2586): Verification of Military Experience and Training

» Job descriptions for potential job targets

» Training certificates/transcripts (non-military)

» Brief Sheet (originates from MCTFS)

» Education Information Report

TIP

If you don't have your records, go to the National Personnel Records Center (www.archives.gov/personnel-records-center/ompf-access) to learn how to obtain your OMPF (Official Military Personnel File).

Getting the message about milspeak

Bill Gaul, a former military officer and placement specialist, popular media commentator, and acknowledged expert on the military transitioning job market, answers questions about demilitarizing your resume.

Q: Can you give an example of what you call milspeak?

A: An Army officer's resume read: "As commanding officer of a 500-person organization, I was responsible for the health, morale, and welfare of all personnel." Health, morale, and welfare? Just think of the incredible range of skills and experience completely overlooked in that milspeak phrase. Far-reaching accomplishments and important responsibilities are whitewashed into boilerplate terms that mean nothing to a civilian hiring manager.

For example, digging into "health, morale, and welfare," we found "policy development, human resource management, budget planning and administration, process improvement, operations management, and staff development."

Q: What's the deal with job titles?

A: Some military job titles are ambiguous, some misleading. For example, a Navy fire control technician does not put out fires but operates and maintains electronic weapons targeting systems.

Translate your job title without misleading the employer:

>> Mess cook (food service specialist)

>> Fire control technician (electronic weapons systems technician)

>> Motor pool specialist (automotive maintenance technician)

>> Provost marshal (law enforcement officer)

>> Quartermaster (supply clerk)

>> Base commander (mayor of a small city)

When in doubt about the ethics or clarity of "civilianizing" your job title, you can list it like this: Functional Job Title: Mayor of Small City.

TIP

When you need a tool to help you translate military job titles to their civilian counterparts, find the Military Occupational Classification Crosswalk at the O*NET Resource Center (www.onetonline.org/crosswalk/MOC/), a free Department of Labor website.

Q: What can you do in situations where your specific work experience doesn't closely relate to the job you're applying for?

A: You can communicate your organizational position instead of your job title. An E-5 Marine Corps embassy guard applying for a management position in the security industry listed his job title as "facility supervisor." He added the details of his experience within the body of his resume. This drew readers because it represented more of a fit than someone who kept people in proper lines applying for visas.

Q: Aren't most military members in combat-related jobs?

A: Yes, and that can be a problem, trying to relate the job you've had to the job you want, unless you're applying for law enforcement positions. But for the straight combat MOS (military occupational specialty) — infantry, tank gunner, reconnaissance Marine, and the like — there are several options.

List your relative position in an organization — "unit supervisor" instead of "platoon sergeant" as your title. Your work in collateral duties may be the key. A platoon sergeant seeking a position in staff development and training, based on duty as a training NCO (noncommissioned officer), can list "training supervisor" as her title.

The dates listed must accurately reflect the time you spent in the specific collateral duties, of course. As you know, it is often the case that you will have more than one collateral duty while performing a key role for an organization.

Q: How should you list your level of authority?

A: Omit references to rank or grade such as "NCO," "petty officer," and "sergeant." Unless an employer has military experience, these terms won't communicate your relative position within an organization. Instead, list civilianized equivalents appropriate to your level of authority:

>> Safety Warrant Officer OSHA (coordinator)

>> Training NCO (training supervisor)

>> Barracks sergeant (property manager)

Q: What about education and training?

A: Many courses and schools leave recruiters wondering exactly what you trained for because the course titles can be esoteric and arcane. The rule is this: List your training in a way that will provide immediately apparent support for your job objective.

If the name of a school or course doesn't communicate exactly what you were able to do after the course that you couldn't do before, show that value because you are trying to inform, not mystify. You are trying to demilitarize the language to help resume reviewers understand the nature of your military training. Some examples:

- » SNAP II Maintenance School (Honeywell Computer Server Maintenance School)

- » NALCOMIS Training (Automated Maintenance and Material Control System Training)

- » Mess Management School (Food Service Management School)

- » NCO Leadership Training (Leadership and Management Training)

Q: Is that all there is to civilianizing a military background?

A: Not quite. To help resume reviewers understand the depth of your training, list the number of classroom hours you studied. To determine the number of hours, multiply the number of course days by 8, or the number of weeks by 40. If you completed the course within the past 10 years, list the completion date. If the course is older, leave off the date. Here are two examples:

Leadership and Management Training (160 hours)
Organizational Development (120 hours)

IN THIS CHAPTER

» Successfully leaping over gaps to return to your career

» Continuing your career despite other challenges

» Addressing unique life circumstances in your resume

Chapter **14**

Overcoming Career Roadblocks

Chances are that not everything in your career history is a plus. Minuses — either fact or perception — such as a gap in your work history, need to be handled carefully to keep them from setting off alarm bells in prospective employers' minds. It's always better to anticipate and minimize factors in your background that might screen you out of the running.

Nobody's perfect, but rarely are job seekers jammed up against problems so severe that they can't be solved in some way. Careful resume management is a good start.

This chapter gives you ideas on how to turn lemons into lemonade if you have some negatives in your background.

Navigating Job Gaps

Job gaps can happen for any number of reasons, but when it's time to return to work, you can feel like you just stepped over the edge of a cliff. Some of the reasons for job gaps include:

» Unemployment/layoff

» Stay-at-home mom or dad

- » Caring for elderly parents
- » Incarceration
- » Illness/disability
- » Attending school
- » Taking a sabbatical (to write a book or travel)

Regardless of why you have the gap, one thing is for sure: Employers will see recent unaccounted time in your work history as a red flag. So, instead of hoping it will be overlooked, determine how to address it in the most positive light for your situation.

TIP

If the gap was only for a few months or less than a year, list only years in your employment history instead of months and years. This can make a gap disappear on your resume (but not in reality). You still need to be prepared to explain the gap in the interview or in a detailed job application.

Viewing a gap as a good thing

The first step in turning a gap in your work history into a value-added time period is to look for the golden threads that make it valuable. Consider things that may translate into covering the gap:

- » Did you learn anything new from classes, self-study, reading books, earning a certification, or attending professional meetings or conferences?
- » Did you perform unpaid work for a family member or friend?
- » Did you create crafts that you sold online or at local events?
- » Did you volunteer and contribute to projects, leadership, or fundraising?
- » Did you write a book or start and build a blog in your industry?
- » Did you travel extensively and become more culturally aware?
- » Did you stay deeply connected to your industry through professional association and trade memberships, networking, and self-study?
- » Did you help old customers or employers as an unpaid favor?

When you get these details down on paper, you can begin to see how you can cover a gap with true value-added experience.

Minding the gap

How does all this data translate into an appropriate job title, location, and description in your resume? As you likely found when reviewing the questions in the preceding section, many positive elements eclipse the real reason for your employment gap. Put the emphasis on what best positions you for your target.

Covering your gap begins with the job title you use as a placeholder for this time period in your life. Depending on what you were doing this could appear as:

> *Consultant; Fundraiser (Volunteer); Coordinator; Sabbatical; Self-Study, Project Management; or even Bookkeeper.*

Here's how each came to be, with an included explanation of the gap so you can understand the reasoning.

» **Consultant:** *While looking for a new position, I contacted old clients and did some work for them. I also created a blog and advertised myself in my professional association's journal, which led to a few short gigs.*

» **Fundraiser (Volunteer):** *While raising my children, I volunteered for the ULA and was elected to direct their 2017 fundraising initiative, which led to recruitment of team, strategic planning, innovative marketing, and a 300 percent increase in funds over prior years' campaign.*

» **Coordinator:** *As a stay-at-home mom, I maintained time management and organization despite challenging personalities and schedule conflicts. I directed daily activities ranging from study groups to field trips.*

» **Self-Study, Project Management:** *I utilized my employment gap to stay-up-to-date on trends through PMI and continued pursuit of PMP credential. Presented the Project Gap to 30 attendees at local PMI chapter meeting. Contributed extensively to support discussions on PMI web forum.*

» **Bookkeeper:** *I kept the books for my husband's business, ABC Trucking, which included processing accounts payables and accounts receivables, handling all cash receipts, and bank balancing. I set company up on QuickBooks, which reduced processing time by over 40 percent monthly and cut out third-party fees of $500 monthly.*

REMEMBER

The reasons for the gaps I include in the preceding list wouldn't go in your resume. The idea is to cover the gap without exploiting the why. Know that if you are covering a gap, you'll have a chance to discuss it in the interview. That's the appropriate time for discussing the "why" of a job gap. If it gets out in your resume, you likely won't get the interview.

Instead, position yourself, truthfully, as a great candidate with the positive elements of your gap and be prepared to discuss the reason for the gap in your interviews.

Resume antidotes: Describe yourself as "manager," not "CEO" or "president," and if you have time, rename your business something other than your own name: "River's End Associates, Inc.," not "Theresa K. Bronz, Inc."

WARNING

The chief mistake people make is assuming that a positive explanation won't sell. Instead, they fudge dates from legitimate jobs to cover the gaps. You may get away with it in the beginning. But ultimately, you'll be asked to sign a formal application — a legal document. When a company wants to chop staff without paying severance benefits, the first thing that happens is an intense investigation of the company's database of application forms. People who lied on their applications can be sent out into the mean streets with nothing but their current paychecks on their backs. Lying isn't worth the risk.

Work history breaks are less obvious in a functional or hybrid format, which I discuss in Chapter 6.

Returning to the Workforce after Being a Caregiver

Whether you were taking care of your children or your aging parents, if you have taken time off and are now ready to return to work, you need to effectively cover that gap.

After taking a career break to care for your family, trying to reenter the workforce — whether by choice or economic necessity — may make you feel as though you've been living on another planet. A reader writes:

> Employers don't want to hire men or women who've been out of the market for more than a year or two. But for the last ten years, I've worked my tail off! Don't they understand that? Doesn't intelligence, willingness to work hard, creativity, attention to detail, drive, efficiency, grace under pressure, initiative, leadership, persistence, resourcefulness, responsibility, teamwork, and a sense of humor mean anything these days?

Every characteristic that this reader mentions is still a hot ticket in the job market, but the burden is on you to interpret these virtues as marketable skills:

>> Grace under pressure, for example, translates to *crisis manager,* a valuable person when the electricity fails in a computer-driven office.

>> Resourcefulness translates to *office manager,* who is able to ward off crank calls from credit collection agencies.

>> A sense of humor translates to *data communications manager,* who joshes a sleepy technical whiz into reporting for work at 2 a.m. for emergency repair of a busted satellite hovering over Europe.

You can't, of course, claim those job titles on your resume, but you can make equivalency statements:

> Like a crisis manager, I've had front-lines experience handling such problems as electrical failures, including computer crashes.

REMEMBER

Fill the home-management period with crossover (transferable) skills relevant to the targeted position. Examples range from time management (developing the ability to do more with less time) and negotiation skills (creating compromises with difficult people and in challenging situations) to budgeting experience (developing a sophisticated understanding of priority allocation of financial resources). Other examples include using a smartphone in drumming up support for a favorite charity (developing confidence, improving sales skills, and cultivating a businesslike telephone technique) and leadership positions in the PTA (developing a sense of authority, attaining management strengths, and establishing the ability to guide others).

REMEMBER

Omit all information that the employer isn't entitled to, including your age, marital status, physical condition, number and ages of children, and partner's name. Even though the law is on your side, why drag in facts on your resume that can stir up bias? Your resume's job is to open interview doors.

SELECTED HOME-BASED SKILLS

Don't overlook skills that you may have acquired inside the home. Here are a few examples of occupations in which they can be used. This illustration assumes that you lack formal credentials for professional-level work. If you do have the credentials, upgrade the following examples to the appropriate job level:

- **Juggling schedules:** Paraprofessional assistant to business executives or physicians, small service business operator, dispatching staff of technicians

- **Peer counseling:** Human resources department employee benefits assistant, substance abuse program manager

- **Arranging social events:** Party coordinator, nonprofit organization fundraiser, art gallery employee

- **Conflict resolution:** Administrative assistant, customer service representative, school secretary

- **Problem-solving:** Any job

- **Decorating:** Interior decorator, fabric shop salesperson

- **Nursing:** Medical or dental office assistant

- **Solid purchasing judgment:** Purchasing agent, merchandiser, retail sales associate

- **Planning trips, relocations:** Travel agent, corporate employee relocation coordinator

- **Communicating:** Any job

- **Shaping budgets:** Office manager, department head, accounting clerk

- **Maximizing interior spaces:** Commercial-office real estate agent, business furniture store operator

To help in your quest, seek out seminars, workshops, and services offered to on-ramping individuals. Women will want to discover such websites as Fairy God Boss (https://fairygodboss.com) and the forum Dad Stays Home (www.dadstayshome.com), which includes a section on working from home.

Seeking a Job When You Have a Disability

Millions of job seekers are protected by the *Americans with Disabilities Act* (ADA), which makes it illegal for an employer to refuse to hire (or to discriminate against) a person simply because that person has one or more disabilities.

ADA protection covers a wide spectrum of disabilities, including acquired immunodeficiency syndrome (AIDS) and human immunodeficiency virus (HIV), alcoholism, cancer, cerebral palsy, diabetes, emotional illness, epilepsy, hearing and speech disorders, heart disorders, learning disabilities (such as dyslexia), intellectual disabilities, muscular dystrophy, and visual impairments. The act does not cover conditions that impose short-term limitations, such as pregnancy or broken bones.

Generally, the ADA forbids employers that have more than 15 employees from doing the following:

>> Discriminating on the basis of any physical or mental disability

>> Requiring applicants to take pre-employment medical exams

The ADA requires that an employer make reasonable accommodations for qualified individuals who have disabilities, unless doing so would cause the employer undue hardship. The undue hardship provision is still open to interpretation by the courts.

TIP

If you have a disability that you believe is covered by the ADA, familiarize yourself with the law's specifics. The U.S. Department of Justice's ADA home page can be found at www.ada.gov. For even more information, call your member of Congress, visit your library, or obtain free comprehensive ADA guides and supporting materials from the splendid website maintained by the Job Accommodation Network (https://askjan.org).

The following section offers advice on building an effective resume while navigating disability-related issues.

Deciding whether to disclose a disability

Do not disclose your disability on your resume. Remember, your objective is to get an interview. Save disclosure until a better time, if at all. Here are a couple of guidelines for deciding when and whether to disclose a disability:

>> If your disability is visible, the best time to disclose it is after the interview has been set and you telephone to confirm the arrangements. Pass the message in an offhanded manner: "Because I use a wheelchair for mobility, can you suggest which entrance to your building would be the most convenient?" Alternatively, you may want to do a drive-by to determine this for yourself and reserve disclosure for the interview.

>> If your disability is not visible, such as mental illness or epilepsy, you need not disclose it unless you'll need special accommodations. Even then, you can hold the disclosure until the negotiating stage after you've received a potential job offer.

No matter what you decide to do, be confident, unapologetic, unimpaired, and positive.

Explaining gaps in work history

What can you do about gaps in your work history caused by disability? Stay the course I recommend earlier in this chapter. You cannot permanently obscure the issue, but your goal is to get to the interview. If you have nothing to cover the time outside of recovering from your illness, list it as "Sabbatical" in your timeline and then be prepared to discuss it.

While you are prepping for your job search, also spend some time getting up to speed on your industry and area of expertise so you can confidently feel and be prepared to return to work.

If you have too many episodes of gaps your work history will look less shaky in a functional or hybrid format, which I discuss in Chapter 6. Online resume discussion groups, which you can find through the Job Accommodation Network (https://askjan.org), can serve as further sources of guidance on this difficult issue.

When substance abuse is the problem

Substance abuse is a disability under the Americans with Disabilities Act. If you're recovered from the addiction, you're entitled to all the act's protections. If you're still abusing a substance, such as alcohol or illegal narcotics, you're not covered by the act. Don't disclose previous substance abuse on your resume, and cover gaps in your work history as described earlier in this chapter.

REMEMBER

Avoid mentioning alcohol or drugs, be careful about application forms, and be honest at interviews *if* you have recovered or *if* the experience was a brief fling or two. In being honest, also remember that you still need to sell yourself. Write up an addendum that explains your mistake and how you have changed, and have letters of recommendation, proof of employment, and any recognition since that time with you to further prove your character.

However, if you're still held prisoner by a chronic, destructive, or debilitating overuse of a chemical substance that interferes with your life or employment, no resume tweaks can benefit you. Get help for your addiction.

Seeking a Job When You're an Ex-Offender

Each year millions of offenders leave state and local prisons for the free world or circulate in and out of American jails and detention centers at the city and county levels. If you're one of these people, this book can help you — especially when it comes to meeting today's need to customize and send out your digital resume — but you need specialized help of the type that I describe here.

Negative info kills your chances

Never forget that the purpose of your resume is to get a job interview. Period. Your resume is not the place to confess your sins, accentuate your weaknesses, or lie about yourself. Make sure your resume is future-oriented and employer-centered. Use your resume to clearly communicate to employers what you can do for them. Issues concerning your criminal record are best dealt with during the job interview.

Avoid the chronological format

The reverse chronological format (see Chapter 6) is not your friend. This format, with its emphasis on employers and dates, tends to point up the two major weaknesses of ex-offenders — limited work experience and major employment time gaps. Instead, choose a functional or hybrid combination format (also in Chapter 6) that emphasizes your qualifications as they relate to the job you seek — skills, competencies, and personal qualities.

Present prison experience in nonprison terms

If you acquired education, training, and work experience in prison, be careful how you list that experience on your resume. Instead of saying that you worked at "Kentucky State Prison," say you worked for the "State of Kentucky." Both statements are truthful, but the first statement immediately raises a red flag that can prematurely screen you out before you get an interview.

Get help with job search moves

Resources are available to help you. Following are a few:

>> Find the best specialized books at www.exoffenderreentry.com.

>> Discover re-entry resources in all 50 states at the National Hire Network (www.hirenetwork.org).

>> Visit the CareerOneStop's Job Search Help for Ex-Offenders site (www.careeronestop.org/ExOffender).

>> Consider hiring a professional resume writer; see the appendix.

Addressing Experience Dilemmas

Most job listings you look at include a line that details how much experience the employer wants the ideal candidate to have. If you're like most job seekers, you may feel like Goldilocks whenever you read this line. It always seems as though you have too much experience or too little experience — never just the right amount. So what's a job seeker to do? This section has the answers.

Too much experience in one job

A reader writes:

I've stayed in my current and only job too long. When my company cut thousands of workers, we received outplacement classes. I was told that job overstayers are perceived as lacking ambition, uninterested in learning new things, and too narrowly focused. What can I do about this?

Here are several strategies for meeting this issue head-on.

Divide your job into modules

Show that you successfully moved up and up, meeting new challenges and accepting ever more responsibility. Divide your job into realistic segments, which you label as Level 1, Level 2, Level 3, and so on. Describe each level as a separate position, just as you would if the levels had been different positions within the same company or with different employers. If your job titles changed as you moved up, your writing task is a lot easier.

Deal honestly with job titles

If your job title never changed, should you just make up job titles? *No.* The only truthful way to inaugurate fictional job titles is to parenthetically introduce them as "equivalent to . . ." Suppose that you're an accountant and have been in the same job for 25 years. Your segments might be titled like this:

>> Level 3 (equivalent to supervising accountant)

>> Level 2 (equivalent to senior accountant)

>> Level 1 (equivalent to accountant)

To mitigate the lack of being knighted with increasingly senior job titles, fill your resume with references to your contributions and accomplishments.

Tackle deadly perceptions head-on

Diminish a perception that you became fat and lazy while staying in the same job too long by specifically describing challenges faced, actions taken, and results attained (see Chapter 8).

Derail a perception that you don't want to learn new things or that you are too narrowly focused by including learning initiatives in your training and education section and active affiliations in either your summary or affiliations section of your resume.

TIP

You will likely want to highlight the reason why you are now leaving this job and making a change — don't. Your resume is for selling you, not excusing you. The closest you can come is to simply align yourself in the cover letter with a passion for what the prospective employer is doing. For example:

> *I'm excited to apply for the advertised position of Department Manager with your company. As an organization with contemporary viewpoints and green practices, you align exactly with my personal beliefs and professional goals.*

Otherwise, save talk of why you left for the interview.

Too little experience

When a job posting calls for a specific number of years of experience — say, five years' experience and you come up short with only three years' experience — but you know you can do the job, the basic technique is to work with what you've got. Dissect your three years' experience for all you're worth. Use the strategies in Chapter 8 to use all the appropriate bells and whistles to show how you are equivalent to someone with five years based on what you have done and accomplished.

Addressing Situations Not in Your Control

In today's quick-changing day and age, companies often make decisions to improve the bottom line, but in the process, employees take a hit. Usually, you can't do much when you're told you're going to be laid off or that your company has been swallowed up by a larger one. You have to pick yourself up, dust off your resume, and put your best foot forward. In the following sections, I explain how to handle things such as layoffs, mergers, and acquisitions on your resume.

Several layoffs

Hard to believe, but good workers sometimes experience one layoff after another. A reader writes that he'd experienced four no-fault severances within seven years.

When you've been to the chopping block a few too many times, explain the circumstances after each listing of the company name:

> Carol Interiors (company closed doors) . . . Salamander Furnishings (multiple rounds of downsizings) . . . Brandon Fine Furniture (company relocated out of town) . . . Kelly Fixture Co. (plant sold and moved overseas).

Offering brief explanations takes the blame from your shoulders. When you combine this with strong accomplishment stories (see Chapter 8), you can overcome any negative stigma from the layoffs.

Mergers and acquisitions

A reader writes:

> Upon graduating from college, I went to work for Company A. Several years later, Company A was acquired by Company B. More years passed, and Company B was acquired by Company C. Eventually, Company C merged with Company D, and as a result, after ten years with the four companies, I was laid off.

My question is how best to handle this work history on my resume? I worked for four different corporate entities, with four different names, without ever changing jobs. Do I list all four on my resume? Or just the last one?

Always try to show an upward track record — that you acquired new knowledge and skills and just didn't do the same thing over and over each year. And you don't want the reader to assume that you worked for only one company that laid you off after a decade.

Taking these two factors into consideration, can you show correlation between your job titles and responsibilities with the changes in ownership? If yes, identify all four owners:

Job title, Company D (formerly Company C), years Job title, Company C (formerly Company B), years Job title, Company B (formerly Company A), years Job title, Company A, years

If you can't show an upward track record that correlates with changes in ownership, just use the current owner name with a short explanation:

Job title, Company D, years (Through a series of mergers and acquisitions, the entities for which I have worked include Company A, Company B, and Company C.)

The reason for naming every entity is perception. Background and credit checks will turn up those company names, and if your resume doesn't mention them, it sends up a red flag for your potential employer!

Handling Red-Flag Circumstances

Only the luckiest job seekers have a straight-line career path upward. The rest of us have steps back (whether by choice or by force), and some of us change jobs like the British royals change hats.

Employers can detect demotions or backward job steps with just a glance, and they often frown on them — or at the very least, wonder what happened. You know you're going to be asked about it, so there's no better time than when you're putting together your resume to decide how to put a positive face on the situation.

As for job hopping these days, the notion is as far out of a reality circle as the concepts of job security, company loyalty, and a guaranteed company pension.

Adding insult to injury, some employers cling to a double standard — hiring and firing employees like commodities, then looking with disfavor on applicants who have had a glut of jobs by circumstance, not by choice.

In the following sections, I explain how to address job issues that may cause potential employers to raise an eyebrow, if not handled well.

Demotion

You've been demoted. There are myriad reasons that could range from the employer no longer thinks you are a fit and wants you out to the employer wants to keep you but budgets are an issue. But in either case, if you have to show a progression that shows a chronology with the company of a lower-level position, it can raise red flags with the prospective employer.

REMEMBER

The basic way to handle demotions throughout the job-hunting process is akin to how you handle being fired: by accentuating the positive contributions and results for which you are responsible. But being demoted is trickier to handle than being fired. Being let go no longer automatically suggests personal failure — but being demoted does.

Unless you are still with the company or left on bad terms, now is the time to speak with your former employer about your resume and her reference. If the situation wasn't your fault, your employer may work with you to develop what she will say and what title you can put on the resume. Your employer may agree that you can list the higher-level title for the full time frame or agree to let you group your roles under a broader title. You won't know if you don't ask.

But what if you can't do that? Don't worry because you still have options.

Option one: Use the big umbrella

Group all jobs under one big time umbrella and don't include dates on any of them. This approach lets you sell what you've done but takes the emphasis off exactly when you did it. Of course, you still need to be prepared to present it in a positive light when they ask you about it in the interview. Check out Figure 14-1 for how this looks.

Option two: Group like with like

While not all that different from option one, grouping like with like means that you put the two management jobs together with one set of dates to cover the entire time, and then you list the prior positions with that company by their correct dates. It has a similar effect, but now with some dates connecting it, it makes it feel more factual. Figure 14-2 gives you an example of grouping like with like.

FIGURE 14-1:
This snapshot shows the umbrella concept at work.

XYZ Company, City, ST　　　　　　　　　　　　　　　　[Date – Date]

Manager of Operations
Regional Manager
Sales Associate

Spearheaded a variety of challenges during tenure which ranged from turning around 5-facility region to triple productivity and reduce product churn by 47% to guiding departmental operations for one under-performing facility, which was then positioned as a #3 performer out of 27 facilities in just 10 month. Key actions included:

- ………
- ………
- ………

FIGURE 14-2:
This snapshot shows grouping like with like.

XYZ Company, City, ST　　　　　　　　　　　　　　　　[Date – Date]

Manager of Operations / Regional Manager – Date - Date
Spearheaded a variety of challenges during tenure which ranged from turning around 5-facility region to triple productivity and reduce product churn by 47% to guiding departmental operations for one under-performing facility, which was then positioned as a #3 performer out of 27 facilities in just 10 month. Key actions included:

- ………
- ………
- ………

Sales Associate – Date – Date
Recruited to perform outside sales in a recently opened territory. Tasked with identifying prospective clients, opening lines of discussion, and creating excitement and opportunity for high-end corporate data solutions. Rapidly eclipsed competition to capture 30% marketshare representing $1 million in sales in first year.

Option three: Explain it away

Proceed with caution here! Perhaps you have this demotion as a favor to you (yes, it happens) or a major change happened internally in the company that had nothing to do with your performance. You went back to school to get your MBA and needed less responsibility, you had an aging parent in hospice three hours from home, or you landed a book contract and needed breathing room but not so much you would leave your job. On the other end, your company was bought out or taken over, and it didn't need you in that role but saw the value of keeping you.

When the demotion lets you function and perform, go ahead and play it up carefully. This can be as simple as adding the statement, "Assumed role with lesser accountability in order to complete company-required MBA." See Figure 14-3 to get an idea of how you can explain away a demotion.

A – Getting an advanced degree

XYZ Company, City, ST   [Date – Date]

Manager of Operations / Regional Manager – Date - Date
Spearheaded turnaround of 5-facility region to triple productivity and reduce product churn by 47% as Regional Manager. Requested and granted assignment to Manager of Operations role to decrease 50-hour accountability while completing MBA. Successfully guided operational of single under-performing facility from #22 to #3 out of 27 facilities in just 10 months. Key actions included:

B – Writing a book

XYZ Company, City, ST   [Date – Date]

Manager of Operations / Regional Manager – Date - Date
Spearheaded turnaround of 5-facility region to triple productivity and reduce product churn by 47% as Regional Manager. Requested and granted assignment to Manager of Operations role to decrease 50-hour accountability while working to meet publisher deadlines on my first book, *Operational Excellence.* Successfully guided operational of single under-performing facility from #22 to #3 out of 27 facilities in just 10 months. Key actions included:

C – Handling an external personal challenge

XYZ Company, City, ST   [Date – Date]

Manager of Operations / Regional Manager – Date - Date
Spearheaded turnaround of 5-facility region to triple productivity and reduce product churn by 47% as Regional Manager. Requested and granted assignment to Manager of Operations role to decrease 50-hour accountability while traveling to handle a person emergency which has now been addressed and completed. Successfully guided operational of single under-performing facility from #22 to #3 out of 27 facilities in just 10 months. Key actions included:

D – Explaining a company change that wasn't your fault

XYZ Company, City, ST   [Date – Date]

Manager of Operations / Regional Manager – Date - Date
Spearheaded turnaround of 5-facility region to triple productivity and reduce product churn by 47% as Regional Manager. Assigned to Manager of Operations role following company buy-out with established regional management team. Successfully guided operational of single under-performing facility from #22 to #3 out of 27 facilities in just 10 months. Key actions included:

FIGURE 14-3:
These four options show you exactly how to account for different demotion challenges.

TIP

No matter how well you handle your resume entry, the reference of the demoting employer may ultimately end your chances of landing a new job that you want. In trying to mend fences, you may appeal to the demoting employer's fairness or go for guilt. Point out how hard you worked and how loyal you've been. Find reasons why your performance record was flawed. Ask for the commitment of a favorable reference and a downplaying of the demotion. If fairness or guilt appeals are denied, see an employment lawyer about sending the demoting employer, on law–firm letterhead, a warning against libel or slander.

Job-hopping

Even when it wasn't at your initiative, holding five or more jobs in ten years can brand you as a job hopper. The fact that you're out of work now underscores that impression. Even employers who are guilty of round after round of employee dismissals instinctively flinch at candidates they perceive to be hopping around.

TIP

Take pains to reverse that disapproval. When you draft your resume, post a list of negative perceptions on your desk; when you're finished writing, compare your resume with the list. Offer information that changes negative perceptions of you as a job hopper. The following list identifies perceptions employers often have of a job hopper and ways to counter them.

Perception	Counter
Is disloyal and self-focused	Perfect attendance, volunteer office gift collector
Will split in a blink for a better offer and take company secrets along	Competition of projects
Doesn't know what he/she wants and is never satisfied	Diverse background that promoted impressive results

After checking for damage control, go back and review your resume for accomplishments that enhance your image, such as the following:

>> **A fast learner:** Give examples of how your skills aren't company-specific and you rapidly adjust to new environments.

>> **A high achiever:** Show favored skills much courted by headhunters. When true, emphasize, "Recruited for advanced position."

>> **A quick adapter:** Mention examples of agreeable flexibility in adjusting to new ideas, technology, and position requirements.

>> **A relationship builder:** List praise from coworkers or bosses for commitment to team success. Quotes, as shown in Chapter 7, are a great way to do this.

>> **A determined worker:** Use examples of accomplishments and contributions that show your commitment to meeting standards of superior workplace performance despite the tough job market of recent years.

TIP

When your current joblessness comes after a background that a quick-change artist would admire, use your resume to prepare the way to acceptance. Emphasize project completion and career progression, using years not months. If you still have trouble landing interviews, include more positive statements in your cover letter to tackle your history. For ideas, read Joyce Lain Kennedy's book, *Job Search Letters For Dummies* (Wiley).

Concurrent positions

Sometimes you find that you're doing work for a specific company (or companies — such as with temporary work) but are being paid through a staffing firm or other intermediary. Putting this on your resume can feel sticky and overwhelming. Do you list all companies and months you worked for them individually? No! That can make you look like an inconsistent, noncommittal job hopper.

Luckily, reporting this information on your resume is easy. You can group them all together under one date umbrella with the agency and then separate out each company below it with descriptions and accomplishments. For example:

XYZ Agency   [date] to present

Marketing Representative

Stepped into challenging marketing assignments with Company A, Company B, and Company C with the goal of raising consumer awareness and profits.

For **Company A,** Name of Department/Division

As **job title,** performed:

    *accomplishment

    *accomplishment

    *accomplishment

In the same format as I show for Company A, offer the company, department/division, job title, and accomplishment information for Companies B and C.

TIP

If your job assignments were virtually the same, you can just list the bullets about the assignments together. Just be sure to clarify the particular company where any results took place.

Self-employed or family-employed

You likely didn't even realize a potential time bomb in this one, but there is! When your resume shares that you worked for a family business, it can send up red flags to prospective employers that you had it easy. While the reality is that you probably put in long hours, you need to make sure this negative perception doesn't get in the way of your chances at the interview.

Conversely, if you were self-employed, chances are you wore many hats and gave yourself the title of director, president, or even CEO. Unless you have a professional track record in those roles and the responsibilities they encompass, using them to land your next job as technical writer, marketing manager, or production manager won't work. You'll be labeled overqualified and ignored.

Luckily, it only takes little wording tweaks to overcome these challenges.

>> **Worked for the family:** Abolish any mention of family-owned, inherited, next-generation, parents, or siblings. Instead talk about it like any company you joined (or built) and the challenges, action, and results that it took to do so. If you are concerned you are assuming too much about the position, get on the Internet and look at job descriptions for similar jobs (such as chef, operations manager, bookkeeper, general manager, front-of-house manager, and so on).

>> **Had your own business and it was a multi-million dollar success:** Yes, you can call yourself CEO and go on to manage another multi-million dollar operation for another company.

>> **Had your own business and now it's time for a 9-to-5 position:** Whether you were successful or not, you realize you need to go back to your profession. If that isn't as an executive, then don't label yourself as one with your job title. Aim for something as parallel to your target as possible by looking at your areas of accountability. For instance, if you are trying to go back to Marketing Manager, your title may be Marketing Manager, and those skills are what you play up first and foremost in having run your own business.

TIP

Check out Chapter 9 for ideas on how to target your resume for career changes and Part 4 of this book for effective resume samples.

4

Bringing It All Together with Sample Resumes

Chapter **15**

OnTarget Resumes by Industry and Career Field

The sample resumes in this chapter are set up to highlight a variety of positions and professions, from restaurant service and office manager to IT tech and logistics manager. You'll find examples for individuals of all levels with straight-forward careers as well as curveballs.

A text box atop each sample resume in this chapter tells you the job being targeted, shares any key details, and provides the author of the resume sample. Each author is a professional resume writer, and you can find their contact information in the appendix.

REMEMBER

These examples represent individual people and their unique experiences; they are provided only as an example of what is possible in a resume. Please consider them as roadmaps — not rules — in creating your next resume.

TIP

As you review these resumes, note that I have made it possible for you to see yourself in them while also protecting the identity of the original job seekers who agreed to have their resumes fictionalized. To do this, I have made certain stylistic choices for all the resumes:

» The job seeker's name appears as *Your Name* at the top of the resume and as *NAME* when mentioned in a testimonial quote. These indicate where you should refer to yourself.

» Contact information is shown with the words *City, State, Zip Code, Phone,* and *Email.* This is where you would place your contact information.

» Employment dates (and education dates, when included) use the word *Date.* This is where you would list your years of employment or the year you earned a credential.

» Job descriptions do not list actual company names. Instead, you'll see *Company Name, Hospital Name,* and the like. This is where you would list your employer's company name.

» If a year is stipulated, such as *Won this award in 2015,* the word *Year* has been substituted for the actual date.

YOUR NAME

City, State, Zip Code | Email |Phone | LinkedIn URL

MEDICAL OFFICE MANAGER

Conscientious professional with experience delivering quality office management and administration in the healthcare industry. Emphasis on streamlining and process improvement. Inspire confidentiality, teamwork and excellence in patient care.

Office Administration | Conflict Management
Customer Service | Regulatory Compliance
Problem Solving | Discretion and Ethics
Recruitment, Retention, and Training
Employee Relations | Policies and Procedures
EEO, ADA, HIPAA, DOL, OSHA
Multi-Project Management | MS Office Suite
Medical Billing and Scheduling software

PROFESSIONAL EXPERIENCE

OFFICE MANAGEMENT (ADMINISTRATOR), Company Name, City, ST   Date–Date

Recruited to provide quality administrative support to four management and 10 agency staff. Challenged to increase records accuracy and efficiency while also managing and reducing employee conflicts.

- **Manage Daily Office Operations** – Handled scheduling, records management, equipment and stock, client appointment scheduling, marketing projects and corporate events within deadlines. Reported to COO and CFO.
- **Accuracy and Attention to Detail** - Performed quality assurance audits and assessments to ensure compliance of personnel files and client medical records. Developed audit tools to ensure complete chart information.
- **Discretion, Confidentiality and Ethics** - Inspired and maintained an ethical and confidential work environment where employees used discretion while discussing business / client information.
- **Monitoring & Controls** - Conceived and initiated monitoring system to track employee use of medical records. Restricted record access to designated areas. Required security measures for records moving between locations.
- **Employee Conflict Management** - Resolved grievances by meditating between staff and management.
- **Problem Solving** - Facilitated correction of pay discrepancy with an unhappy employee and negotiated with disgruntled employee to elicit her help to resolve deficiencies discovered during client chart auditing.

OFFICE ADMINISTRATION and HUMAN RESOURCES, Company Name, City, ST   Date–Date

Promoted through increasingly responsible positions based on team leadership, office process improvement, and HR administration. *Company transitioned through contracts provided initially by Company Name and then Company Name.*

- **Recruitment and Retention** - Directed full life cycle recruiting process, assessed staff needs, made hiring recommendations, and ensured regulatory compliance of EEO, AA, ADA, DOL, and state and local regulations.
  - Executed recruitment and head hunting, managed job announcement postings, and tracked expiration dates.
  - Reviewed candidate resumes and applications. Performed employment screenings (background check, drug testing and reference checks) and scheduled and conducted job interviews.
- **Orientation, Training, and Development** - Processed new hires and presented orientation training. Facilitated routine employee training sessions for company procedures, electronic medical records systems, and recurring regulatory trainings: HIPAA, BBP, CPR, First Aid, State Intervention. Administered safety inspections and drills.
- **HR Administration** - Administered bi-annual performance reviews and identified improvements. Coordinated staff meetings, addressed facility issues, approved weekly payroll, monitored daily functioning of facility and maintained appropriate staff to client ratios. Key contributor to facility quality improvement plan.

IMAGING SCHEDULING, Company Name, City, ST   Date–Date

Coordinated schedules for all RAD, CT, and NMRI technicians. Scheduled appointments made by doctors' offices and individual patients for a broad range of medical imaging tests. Made appointment reminder calls and greeted patients.

CAREER CHRONOLOGY

Employer	Job Title	Employment Dates
Company Name, City, ST	Office Administrator	Date–Present
Company Name, City, ST	Medical Records Coordinator	Date–Date
Company Name, City, ST	HR Associate / Quality Assurance	Date–Date
Company Name, City, ST	Office Assistant	Date–Date
Company Name, City, ST	Imaging Scheduler	Date–Date

EDUCATION

Master of Business Administration in Healthcare Administration (M.B.A.), ABC University, City, ST, Date
Bachelor of Science in Healthcare Management (B.S.), XYV University, City, ST, Date

YOUR NAME • SALES & MARKETING DIRECTOR

CITY, COUNTRY | PHONE NUMBER | EMAIL ADDRESS | LINKED IN ADDRESS

Multi-channel Revenue Growth Specialist for World-Leading Sports Brands

Award-winning sales and marketing strategist, recognized by Company Name CEO for encyclopedic knowledge of the sports sector throughout the MENA region and the ability to turn around loss-making business units to full strength.

Career Showcase:

⇨ **Catapulted revenue by over $30M per annum;** directed $MM operational performance U-turn.

⇨ **Motivated Sales and Marketing teams to exceed divisional KPIs by 25%;** drove change initiatives and communicated powerful strategic vision to gain 100% staff buy-in.

⇨ **Engineered exponential rise in profits over five years;** capitalized on unchartered markets and products.

⇨ **Offloaded insolvent business lines to raise $25M in new capital;** balanced risk through exhaustive research to avoid unnecessary losses.

Expertise:

Strategic Leadership	Multi-media Advertising	New Product Development
Process Improvement	Brand Strategy	Digital Marketing
International Business	Above-the-line Marketing	Brand Repositioning
Client Turnaround	Market Growth	Channel Strategies

COMPANY NAME, COUNTRY, DATE - DATE
SALES & MARKETING DIRECTOR, CLOTHING & FOOTWEAR

International sports and leisure retailer | >250 stores | Eight countries | $6B turnover | 18,000 employees

Professional Experience:

Orchestrated revival of declining $200M business. Generated significant and sustainable net revenue growth of 15% ($30M) in first full year, exceeding ambitious targets. Owned P&L across five categories, mobilizing Sales and Marketing team of 75 to implement expansion plan throughout the MENA region.

Transformed Operations in to Market-Leading Center of Excellence

⇨ **Realized sales growth of 26% in all categories.** Masterminded critical culture change program; restructured workforce, and identified and nurtured future stars with accelerated promotion for talented individuals. Inspired team to achieve stretch goals and smash KPIs.

⇨ **Optimized efficiency by 15%.** Streamlined "above and below the line" marketing processes across Footwear and remodeled HQ infrastructure.

⇨ **Doubled sports fashion business profit in one year from $22M to $44M.** Terminated loss-making product lines and sold off distressed segments.

Achieved $MM Profit through Astute Marketing Insights

⇨ **Effected 22% surge in turnover and $33M profit.** Created new profit stream in previously under-marketed kids' apparel. Embedded products in 38 retailers across the region and acquired seven major key accounts.

⇨ **Yielded triple profit** of every other XYZ children's line. Spearheaded launch of "Speedys" to youth footwear market in Saudi Arabia from zero base. Placed product in high profile department stores.

> *"NAME transformed five failing departments to profit centers in record time... an exceptional ability to make effective, critical decisions that positively impact the bottom line."*
>
> CEO, Company Name

COMPANY NAME, COUNTRY, DATE - DATE
SENIOR ACCOUNT MANAGER
German multinational | Sports shoes, clothing and accessories| $10B turnover | 50,000 employees

Parachuted in to revitalize failing account. Promoted twice in three years for performance excellence, maximized wallet share with major buyers and nurtured lucrative relationships with Company A and Company B. Headed team of 15 to achieve 2008 divisional revenue highs of $16.8M from a $1.3M starting point.

Leveraged Growth of Key Accounts with Tactical Customer Approach

⇨ **Delivered revenues of +11%** with E-Sports in 2004, rising to +46% in 2008. Revitalized historic negative relations to renegotiate and renew annual contract.

⇨ **Averted potential loss of 15% of divisional income.** Secured and expanded key accounts and rejuvenated relationship with VIP client.

Captured Extra Sales through Emerging Technologies

Combined YOY Sales Increase

⇨ **Generated online sales with year-on-year growth of 20-37%** as an early e-commerce adopter. Initiated build of transactional website, developed channel-specific digital marketing strategies and led key category management projects.

⇨ **Pioneered explosive growth of 8% in new business acquisition** in just six weeks; designed and executed sales campaign using cutting-edge cloud technology to target specific sectors. Company 123 went on to win prestigious CIO award for high-impact use of technology.

COMPANY NAME, COUNTRY, DATE - DATE
BRAND MANAGER, SUPER SNEAKERS
American multinational | Sports shoes, clothing, equipment and accessories |$20B turnover | 44,000 employees

Captured 28% of the $36M Kuwaiti 'sneakers' market from a static 8% legacy start, during a period of falling sales industry-wide. Created opening for entry of new brand and devised successful imaginative marketing plan, including multichannel brand storytelling.

Won Territorial Gains in Stagnant Market and Globally Recognized Marketing Honors

⇨ **Optimized competitive advantage** through in-depth SWOT analysis; identified opportunity to expand into the Qatar and Saudi geographies; destabilized four major rivals. Recommendations formed future brand strategy for the MENA region that saw threefold upsurge in revenues.

⇨ **Originated award-winning brand marketing strategy**, including TV, print and poster campaigns. Won Adwin's "Best New Ad Campaign, 2002" and "Best ATL Strategy, 2003."

Education:
✔ **University of State, City**
⇨ **Master of Business Administration (MBA)**
⇨ **Bachelor of Arts (BA), Marketing with honors**
⇨ **Dean's list for three successive years**

Global Reach:
✔ **UAE national, US green card, EU resident**
⇨ **Fluency in English, Arabic, French**
⇨ **Cross-cultural – lived in UK, US, Middle East**
⇨ **Globally relocatable**

R.T. (R)

YOUR NAME
Phone Number | Email Address | City, State

RADIOLOGIC TECHNOLOGIST

☑ Patient Advocate
☑ Inpatient/Outpatient
☑ Home Health Care
☑ Rehabilitation
☑ Occupational Health
☑ Urgent Care
☑ Specialty Clinics
☑ Portable
☑ Stationary

Specialize in providing compassionate, quality health care support and imaging services; perform all aspects of inpatient and outpatient radiologic diagnostic imaging, emergency room, post-operative, mobile, and portable radiography.

Flexible, punctual and dedicated – awarded for attendance. Recognized for ability to build productive relationships with patients, multidisciplinary physicians, diverse healthcare practitioners, and cross-functional medical staff. Strong early career technology grounding with positions in information management, network administration and security.

Relevant Education / Certifications

Certified Registered Technologist – Radiography - *American Registry of Radiologic Technologists*
Certified in Cardio Pulmonary Resuscitation, Basic Life Support, Advanced Life Support - *American Heart Association*
Certificate of Training - Blood Borne Pathogens
AA, Major in Radiologic Sciences – *University Name, City, State*
BS, Major in Computer Science, Minor in Health Care Administration – *College Name, City, State*

Employment History

RADIOLOGIC TECHNICIAN
Company Name, City, State (Date-Date)

Provided radiology services for this healthcare organization consisting of seven nationally accredited hospitals, the only children's hospital within a tri state area, a network of more than 265 primary care and specialty physician practices.

- X-rayed <25 patients daily and perform inpatient and outpatient radiologic diagnostic imaging, emergency room, post-operative, mobile, or portable radiography.

- Performed radiographic exams including bone densitometry/bone density scanning, fluoroscopy procedures; comfortable with C-Arm procedures and protocols.

- Facilitated quality management and workflow within radiology department through efficient communication and information management with radiology information systems (RIS), hospital information systems (HIS), picture archiving and communication systems (PACS) and electronic health records (EHR).

- Leveraged knowledge of medical terminology, diagnoses, physiology, and general anatomy on a daily basis.

- Collaborated with radiologists, subject matter experts, and radiological specialties, which included medical sonographers, nuclear medicine, and cardiovascular technologists on aspects of diagnostic imaging.

- Performed routine maintenance on radiology equipment; identified and reported a serious malfunction, prevented significant exposure to radiation for critical radiological staff.

- Ensured compliance with internal / external regulations; maintained operational processes put forth by established policies, standard operating procedures (SOP) and regulatory agencies such as the Joint Commission on Accreditation of Healthcare Organizations (JACHO) and the Occupational Safety and Health Association (OSHA).

☑ Radiologic Diagnostic Imaging
☑ Emergency Room
☑ Post-Operative
☑ Portable Radiography
☑ Bone Densitometry
☑ Fluoroscopy
☑ Radiographic Equipment
☑ Computed Radiography (CR)
☑ Imaging Plates (IP)
☑ Computed Tomography (CT)
☑ Magnetic Resonance Imaging (MRI)
☑ Medical Terminology

NETWORK AND SYSTEMS ADMINISTRATOR - *Company Name, City, State (Date-Date)*

LEAD NETWORK AND SYSTEMS TECHNICIAN - *Company Name, City, State (Date-Date)*

Your Name

▶▶◀◀

City, State   Email: Cell:

SENIOR ACCOUNTING & FINANCE MANAGER
Charting New Waters....Championing Multi-Million Dollar Growth

Entrepreneurial and results-focused professional with a reputation for driving multimillion dollar revenue growth through strategic management of premier merger and acquisition opportunities, skillful negotiation of lucrative international service contracts, and development of commonsense cost control initiatives.

Proven ability to guide the formulation of realistic corporate growth targets in collaboration with the senior executive team by leveraging an innate business acumen and encyclopedic knowledge of national and international taxation structures. Inspirational leader, communicator, negotiator, and facilitator.

Key Areas of Expertise

- Mergers & Acquisitions
- Strategic & Tactical Planning
- National/International Taxation
- Stakeholder Engagement

- Management & Financial Reporting
- Risk Management / Internal Controls
- Corporate Growth & Development
- Productivity/Efficiency Improvements

- Employee Leadership
- Debt/Equity Financing
- Regulatory Compliance
- System Implementation

PROFESSIONAL EXPERIENCE

NEWCO SHIPPING COMPANY, Vancouver, BC   Date to Date

Corporate Controller

Handpicked by the executive team to pioneer growth and expansion of the business by leading an ambitious program of M&A activity to crystallize strategic vision of the CEO.

Key results: Facilitated acquisition of three core competitors which **increased revenues by 100%** over a 5-year period, and thrust company onto the global stage as a **major international industry player.**

- **Corporate Growth & Development:** Instructed to engineer the design, development, and implementation of internal controls and structures capable of handling rapid growth. **Revamped accounting structure to ensure ongoing compliance with changing industry standards, reduced departmental attrition rate by 100%, and capitalized on new software technology to increase operational efficiencies.**

- **Accounting & Finance:** Played instrumental role in managing all accounting and finance functions for multiple international locations. **Recommended benchmarks for measuring financial and operating performance of all domestic international divisions.**

- **Taxation:** Commended by senior executive team for successful development and execution of multiple audit defense strategies against tax authorities of all levels in a number of jurisdictions. **Saved company upwards of $25M in potential tax liabilities stretching back 10 years.**

- **Internal Controls:** Chaired a multidisciplinary committee convened to analyze and document existing and potential risks to business. Instituted a comprehensive risk management framework with accompanying learning resources. **Reduced external auditor consulting fees by 25% as a direct result of this initiative.**

▶▶◀◀
Your Name – Page 1/2

Corporate Controller, *continued*

- **System Implementation:** Developed a sound business case for replacement of an archaic accounting system incapable of delivering the functionality or value essential to the needs of a growing enterprise. **Led the entire program to successful completion and launch to rapturous approval from executive team.**

- **Leadership & Mentoring:** Commended by the senior executive team for reducing departmental attrition by 100% (2010 to present). **Cultivated an environment based on mutual trust and respect, and implemented skills development program to realize employee professional growth ambitions.**

NEW TECHNOLOGY COMPANY, Vancouver, BC   Date to Date

Financial Controller

Recruited by CEO of this entrepreneurial technology company with revenues in excess of $80M to exercise control over corporate growth by raising debt and equity capital, structuring strategic M&A deals, and monitoring financial KPIs to achieve long-term growth objectives. **Achieved double digit growth and developed cost-efficient international taxation structure.**

- **Process Development:** Provided catalyst for driving the development of new strategic key performance indicators to provide high-level visibility into national and international operations for executive team, and set clear employee performance expectations.

- **Internal Processes:** Strengthened internal controls and restructured all financial reporting processes to mitigate risk and ensure company was positioned for explosive growth from a financial perspective.

ERNST & YOUNG, Vancouver, BC   Date to Date

Manager, Audit & Assurance (Date to Date)
Articling Student / Audit Senior (Date to Date)

- **Delivered strong operational leadership** to a team of developing professionals in the timely & effective management of audit & review engagements for a diverse selection of public/private company clients.

EDUCATION & TRAINING

Chartered Accountant (CA) - Chartered Accountants Association
Bachelor of Commerce in Accounting – University Name

PROFESSIONAL AFFFILIATIONS & COMMUNITY INVOLVEMENT

Member (Since Date) - Chartered Accountants Association
Member Since Date / Treasurer (Current) / Past Chair, Development (Date to Date) - Board of Trade
Chair, Competition & Assessment (Date to Present) - Young Entrepreneurs Association

Your Name – Page 2/2

Your Name

Address, City, State | Email Address
h: Number | m: Number

Customer Service Supervisor

Telecommunications | Call Center Specialist

Accomplished leader, with more than ten years of high-volume call center expertise and a reputation for "making things happen." A genuine diplomat and communicator, passionate about exceeding expectations and achieving winning outcomes for everyone.

↗ Acknowledged for providing first-class call service to deliver total customer satisfaction and win ongoing loyalty.

↗ Reputation for empowering support teams and driving call center strategies to surpass targets and maximize profits.

"Every customer service department needs a NAME. She has an insatiable desire to solve problems and reach targets, while at the same time, she maintains calm to create a truly harmonious environment - a rarity in high pressure environments." - *Customer Service Manager*

Expertise

☐ **Service Team Management**
☐ **Cross Selling Strategies**
☐ **Telemonitoring Feedback**
☐ **Conflict Resolution**
☐ **Inbound/Outbound Calls**
☐ **Uncompromised Customer Service**
☐ **Training and Development**
☐ **Employee Recognition Initiatives**
☐ **Above Average Record Keeping**
☐ **Procedural Improvements**
☐ **Sales and Target Focused**
☐ **Key Account Management**
☐ **Phone and Data Plan Solutions**

Career Highlights

Company Name, City, ST   Date - Date
TEAM LEADER | CUSTOMER SERVICE
Leading telecommunications company, providing communications and technology solutions.

Recruited during an unprecedented period of poor performance, absenteeism and low staff morale which directly impacted on customer satisfaction and relations. Charged with energizing productivity across 14 staff, to deliver high-level smartphone, telephone and data plan support to 4,500 customers.

Key Contributions:

↗ **Boosted call center productivity by 30%, within six months** through reallocating staff to overhaul inaccurate customer account information and outdated database system.

↗ **Steered turnaround of customer satisfaction levels from an all-time low of 35% to 89%,** initiating improvements across call procedures and customer response times, to exceed set targets.

↗ **Transformed employee morale to significantly reduce staff absenteeism by 90%,** implementing optimistic employee engagement processes and reward / recognition incentive programs.

Company Name, City, ST   Date - Date
CUSTOMER SERVICE REPRESENTATIVE
Fortune 500 company operating in 150 countries and delivering the fastest, most reliable 4G network in America.

Recognized for exceptional ability to handle high-volume service inquiries across 5,000 business customers within local area, as part of a team of 90 representatives. Constantly exceeded weekly call targets by 25%, providing service options, changes and cross-selling of additional plans and packages.

Your Name

Career Highlights | cont...

Company Name, City, ST
Key Contributions:

↗ **Overachieved performance benchmarks** across call monitoring, sales, document control and reporting records to average 250 calls per week and achieve 40% more additional service sales.

↗ **Promptly and reassuringly resolved customer issues** including service errors to retain $1 million in business and receive customer letter of appreciation, acknowledged by company president.

↗ **Awarded Employee of the Month** in [Year] for exceeding call targets by 25% and increasing productivity by 50%, over a one-month understaffing period, servicing in excess of 60 clients.

↗ **Convincingly resolved 90% of inquiries on a first-call basis,** through prompt service identification and resolution, to rapidly reduce average handling times by 16%.

Company Name, City, ST   Date - Date
CUSTOMER SERVICE REPRESENTATIVE
Women's bathing suits and sportswear wholesale and manufacturer.

Promoted to Acting Supervisor for a three-month period; involved telemonitoring of five customer service representatives and providing detailed feedback. Selected to train more than 15 employees over a four-year span and utilize proven performance results to conduct ongoing training for new employees.

↗ **Constantly exceeded sales and call targets by 15%,** to be recognized as top seller in 2002, utilizing strong product knowledge, cross-selling strategies and proposing alternative options.

↗ **Reduced average call length by 45 seconds per call** through development of an intranet site and transferring of all catalog product information from hard to soft copy.

↗ **Developed and piloted employee recognition program,** successfully adopted as standard practice company-wide, rewarding top salespeople with cash incentives and lunch with company president.

Professional Development

Internal Training: Supervising Teams | Advanced Communication and Interpersonal Skills | Cross-Selling Strategies | Verizon Product Suite | Closing the Sale | Telemonitoring Procedures

Computer Skills: Microsoft Office 2010/XP: Excel, Word, Outlook - Advanced | Typing speed: 64wpm

YOUR Name, RN, BSN, CMSN

CITY, STATE ZIP CODE • PHONE NUMBER • EMAIL ADDRESS

PROFESSIONAL PROFILE

➲ Pro-active and collaborative **REGISTERED NURSE** with 15+ years' experience in acute care settings. Recognized as a diplomatic bed-side nurse and high-impact clinical leader.

➲ Member in good standing with the **College of Registered Nurses of South City State** and the **State United Nurses Union.** Successful track record managing complex patient challenges in a specialized interdisciplinary environment.

➲ Go-to resource for nurses and physicians for issues relating to wound care and discharge planning. Demonstrated leadership skills rewarded by repeated invited assignments as clinical leader in a dynamic medical/surgical setting.

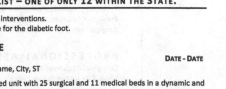

➲ Solid and effective communication skills advising patients and families in preparation for discharge into the community, ensuring safe continuity of care while consistently, and expertly applying hospital policies and procedures.

CRITICAL SKILL SET

- Acute Care Clinical Expertise
- Basic Life Support / Health Care
- Comprehensive Discharge Planning
- Win-Win Negotiation Style
- Quality Management and Auditing
- Social Needs Awareness / Assessment
- Patient and Family Education
- Strong Coordination / Facilitation Skills
- Leadership and Communication Skills
- Decision Making and Problem Solving
- High-Risk Medication Advising
- Cognitive Screening/Patient Risks

NOTABLE ACHIEVEMENTS

- Complex Discharge Coordinator, General Support, and Auditor for Bed Utilization Management Program – BUMP | first RN to formally audit UMS/BUMP.
- Preceptor for new staff and nursing students with 6+ years in clinical leader role.
- Medical/Surgical Nursing Specialty – American Association of Medical Surgical Nurses.

CERTIFIED WOUND CARE SPECIALIST – ONE OF ONLY 12 WITHIN THE STATE.

- Nurse adviser to physicians for wound-care interventions.
- Advanced Foot Care Course – including care for the diabetic foot.

PROFESSIONAL EXPERIENCE

STAFF NURSE AND CLINICAL LEADER | ROTATIONAL   DATE - DATE
South State District Health Authority – Hospital Name, City, ST

Reporting to Director of Nursing, managed a 36-bed unit with 25 surgical and 11 medical beds in a dynamic and challenging unit. Processed 12+ new admissions in a 12-hour shift and led 10 staff per shift. Supervised 12-hour shift, facilitated patient flow, organized team assignments, and led team for daily multi-disciplinary rounds. Assumed accountability for efficient discharge of resources including a keen understanding unit operations at all times evaluating patients' stability and responding accordingly.

- Invited by **Chief of Staff** to assume the role of **Complex Discharge Planning Nurse** which resulted in improved patient flow, reduced operating costs, discharge planning, and robust care plans for patients. Scope of position included patient teaching and organizing required community supports and resources while managing length-of-stay expectations with patients and caregivers.

LEADERSHIP • ACCOUNTABILITY • SUCCESSFUL OUTCOMES

YOUR NAME, RN, BSN, CMSN

ABC General Hospital | Staff Nurse and Clinical Leader continued

- Carefully managed the human and financial resources on the unit, including unit patient attendants subsequently reducing operating costs exponentially year over year for 4 years.

25% REDUCTION IN OPERATING EXPENSES AND 20% IMPROVEMENT IN BED FLOW IN 4 YEARS

- Developed innovative approach to team assignment in collaboration with nurse manager, nurse educator, and professional practice leaders which ensured appropriate nursing staff are assigned to appropriate patient and resulted in safer and more cost-effective care.
- Identified as "super user" of several critical resources and subsequently invited to participate in upgrade projects, which included PYXIS machine (medication delivery system) as well as Emerald software program (workload measurement) and BUMP (Bed Utilization Management Program).
- Recognized as go-to resource for all aspects of shift, which included collaborating with physicians, physiotherapist, nurse practitioner, pharmacy, dietician, occupational therapist, therapeutic assistants, social worker, and continuing care coordinators in support of safe and effective patient outcomes.

PREVIOUS PROFESSIONAL EXPERIENCE

NURSING SUPERVISOR   DATE - DATE
Nursing Home Name, City, ST

STAFF NURSE   DATE - DATE
Hospital Name, City, ST

STAFF NURSE   DATE - DATE
Center Name, City, ST

FORMAL EDUCATION AND PROFESSIONAL DEVELOPMENT

Wound Care Management Seminar – State Public Health Board | Date
Advanced Foot Care Course—including care for the diabetic foot—American Diabetic Association | Date
Wound Care Management – American Association of Wound Care (AAWC) | Date
Perioperative Nursing Seminar – District Health Association | Date
Bachelor of Science in Nursing (BSN) – University Name | Date

COMMITTEES, CONFERENCES AND WORKING GROUPS

Better Outcomes for Older Adults Through Safe Transition (BOOST) | Date
Family Practice Quality Committee | Date
Presenter, "Classification of Stones" | American Urology Nurses Association Conference | Date
Presenter, "Radiation in Muscle-Invasive Bladder Cancer" | Urology Nurses of America Conference | Date
Surgical Care Committee | Date - Present

PROFESSIONAL ASSOCIATIONS

College of Registered Nurses of State – Member # 08000   DATE – Present
South City United Nurses Union   DATE – Present

"NAME is a great team player who respects others. Competent and efficient at her work, she strives to do a good job and is interested in improving and making things better in the work environment and for patient care."
W.R.W., Chief of Staff

LEADERSHIP • ACCOUNTABILITY • SUCCESSFUL PATIENT OUTCOMES

YOUR NAME

City, ST   Email Address   Phone Number

IT SUPPORT SENIOR MANAGER

Advanced Global Service Delivery and Cross-Functional Team Support

Forging a Link between Business and IT to Advance the Company Name Corporate Mission to Provide Clients with Long-Term Financial Success

Accomplished **Senior Global Technology Support Manager** with solid progressive experience managing and delivering multiple large-scale projects on time and budget. Build, train, lead, and coordinate with multilevel technology teams and business units to support company objectives. Proven success at reducing costs, improving operations, and enhancing bottom-line growth. **Currently leading Windows 10 / Office 365 Migration.** Areas of expertise include:

- Team Building and Leadership
- Resource Planning / Management
- IS Strategic Planning
- Consensus Building
- Change Management
- Policy & Procedural Design

- Global Operations Management
- System Design Life Cycle (SDLC)
- Global Project Management
- Cross-Functional Team Coordination
- Cost Reductions & Avoidance
- Systems Installation & Integration

- Service Delivery Control
- End User Support
- Budgeting & Finance
- Strategic Sourcing
- Communications
- Conversions & Migrations

* Promoted Based on Strong Leadership and Service Delivery Management *
* Coordinate with Business Units, Multilevel Staff, and Vendors to Align Deliverables with Company Goals *

Professional Experience

COMPANY NAME, City, ST   Date–Date

Senior Manager, Global Technology Support *(Date-Date)*

Progressed through a series of increasingly responsible positions on the basis of strong leadership and technology performance. Directed 4 managers, support teams, and internal business units across 3 locations (X, Y, Z) to develop, implement, and align global business and ITG support strategies. Managed resource and project planning, and adhered to global strategy and budget constraints.

Global Projects and Achievements:

- **MS Windows 10 Office 365 Migration:** Facilitated resource planning, team training, and vendor sourcing functions.
  - Replaced outdated systems and tools with state-of-the-art technologies which improved productivity, facilitated systems integration, increased efficiencies, and generated substantial cost savings.

- **IP Telephony Phone Rollout and Voice Mail Update:** Tasked with resource planning and vendor management, as well as team training, scheduling, and oversight.
  - Replaced company voice analog systems with leading edge VoIP technology, which improved corporate-wide communications and operational efficiency.

- **Service Desk Support Conversion for Company Name Offices:** Led business needs, requirements, and case analysis development and presentation to align project with company goals. Also developed communication plans and handled budgeting, scope, and scheduling needs.
  - Held follow-up meetings with business units to assess model effectiveness and potential modifications.
  - Boosted support team morale by communicating need for conversion and continuing value of their efforts.

...continued...

Professional Experience

Senior Manager, Global Technology Support *continued*

- **Global Data Destruction:** Managed global process development and vendor sourcing project to certify destruction of laptop, desktop, and server hard drives.
  - Increased data security, lowered risk exposure, and enhanced revenue-producing life cycle.
- **MS XP Migration Lead:** Managed resource planning, team training, and vendor sourcing.
  - Upgraded systems and tools which improved productivity, enabled systems integration, enhanced efficiencies, and generated significant cost savings.
- **Support Team Consolidation:** Assessed capabilities and benefits of merging Financial and Nonfinancial support teams to replace independent help desk support structure with one business-aligned team. Collaborated with senior associates on both teams to develop consolidation plan and explained new job responsibilities to all support associates.
  - Participated in meetings to assess business needs and to ensure effectiveness of new support model.
  - Consolidation increased support efficiencies and allowed for workforce reduction in the coming years.

Manager, Global Service Delivery Technology Support *(Date-Date)*

Managed a 10-12 member associate support team for financial operations and trading rooms.

Global Projects and Achievements:

- **Global Investment Sales Office Y2K Desktop Hardware Remediation Efforts (1999):** Led critical operation to check, fix, and upgrade Desktop Hardware components to ward off potential problems related to the millennium rollover.
- **Global Investment Office Token Ring to Ethernet Conversion (2000-2001):** Coordinated resources for replacement and testing of new Ethernet hardware.
  - Reduced hardware costs by synchronizing technologies and paved the way for broadband use.
- Promoted to Senior Manager of End User Support, with oversight of 4 Managers and their Support Teams.

Technology Support Associate *(Date-Date)*

Provided support to associates with focus on Fixed Income Associates and Fixed Income Trading.

* * *

Served in prior role as Director of Research for Company Name of City, ST

Education and Credentials

Bachelor of Science in Economics
University Name – City, ST

Computer Communications Certification　　　　**Teaching Certification**
College Name – City, ST　　　　　　　　　　　　　University Name – City, ST

Your Name

City, ST Zip • Phone Number • Email Address

"...Whether it's increasing revenues, attracting sponsors, retaining members, or building raving fans, NAME always gets it done while exceeding our expectations and helping build unheard of profits." — Reference Name, Company Name

Seasoned Director of Development & Outreach

Bottom-line focused Director with a knack for driving profitability through knack for building relationships with clients and users by homing in on organizational needs and building bridges. Leverages complex data set analysis to create directives, optimize services, and exceed bottom line goals.

Display phenomenal business and cross-cultural etiquette to cultivate positive relationships among stakeholders, along with a positive, upbeat nature to attract diverse clients.

Highly versatile and adaptable main point of contact, representative, and team lead: Collaborate with staff to meet and exceed eclectic corporate goals within allotted times. Actively involved at all levels of the company to navigate trends and change. Known department-wide for generating a "6X" increase in corporate efficiency.

KEY SKILLS MATCH

- ✓ Strong comprehension of talent acquisition, communications, outreach, and content strategy
- ✓ Leader in project management
- ✓ Highly adaptable / flexible, with capacity to work under pressure
- ✓ Skilled in tracking trends and fulfilling high-priority projects
- ✓ Expert in landing lucrative deals via negotiation and team building
- ✓ Adept at applying qualitative and quantitative research analysis

Professional Experience

COMPANY NAME, CITY, ST   *Date - Date*
Director of Development and Outreach *(Date - Date)*
Challenged to drive turnaround while overseeing strategic operations at a company with 30+ staff and $7M in revenue. Monitored company's strengths, weaknesses, opportunities, and threats, and liaised with team members and administrators at meetings to devise action plans that brought the business up to par. Quickly turned the organization around via multi-level communication and marketing strategies, which attracted corporate sponsorship and sealed lucrative partnerships.

Key Achievements:
- Spearheaded developments to launch sponsorship and membership development (+$1.2M), **retention** (from 28% to 78%), membership services, and outreach for 160 academic and cultural institutions across the United States, Canada, and Europe.
- Implemented multi-level communication and marketing strategy which attracted corporate sponsorships and **increased corporate giving by 400%** within less than five years. (Repeatedly lauded for role in designing this profitable initiative.)
- Streamlined services through centralizing outreach to measure individual, administrative, and departmental performance.
- **Quadrupled memberships** since YEAR as result of extensive target marketing strategies, which led to acquiring lucrative markets in international cultural heritage organizations, liberal arts colleges, banks, libraries, and museums.

Senior Program Associate (Previously Program Assistant) *(Date - Date)*
Collaborated with cross-functional team members to drive research, social justice, and the public good through creative design and best application of digital library technologies. Quickly built rapport for strong attention to detail while collecting market intelligence, inputting information into charts and graphs, addressing concerns, and assessing accounts. Attained significant improvement in retention rates, company revenue, and returns on investment within less than a year.

Key Achievements:
- Implemented cost reduction solution while conducting risk / impact assessments and determining weaknesses / threats.
- Spearheaded developments to launch new and improve programming and generate new lucrative target markets.
- Streamlined services through identifying areas in need of improvement and taking corrective action: Restructured outdated user groups and technologies and expanded social media and communications outreach, which **generated $5M in profit.**
- Acted as primary point of contact on **memberships growth (+$800K)** and development and target marketing goals.
- **Grew annual meetings by more than 50%** due to strategic, targeted outreach to speakers, sponsors, and attendees.
- Earned recognition from upper management due to strong capacity to see the bigger picture and bring about change: Advanced from Program Associate to Senior Program Associate to Director of Development & Outreach in three years.

COMPANY NAME, CITY, ST
Director of Marketing & Business Development (*Date - Date*)
Oversaw operations and logistics across locations to streamline services, avoid lag time, and maintain consistency and efficiency. Met with staff to discuss and evaluate best practices for implementation in B2B direct marketing campaigns. Assessed process reports, integrated data to master files, and documented data analyses and/or specs for system processing; reported key process improvements or escalated extenuating circumstances to appropriate departments.

Key Achievements:
- Designed a strategic marketing proposal strategy and sales pitch, which secured a multi-million-dollar contract.
- Exceeded target revenue by at least 110% by producing well-researched proposals and expanding client base.
- Headed national and international initiatives, which included social media presence and outreach, potential client meetings, and growth factors assessments. Achieved 5 million new memberships in less than two years.
- Devised an annual Giving Plan, which met its goal of $10K in its first-year launch.
- Partnered with teams to generate a ten-year capital plan, which is anticipated to generate record breaking growth.

Business Development Manager (*Date - Date*)
Held a strategic role developing, implementing, and leading public awareness campaigns. Cultivated strategic relationships among alliances to further corporate awareness and develop and engage unique tools, programs, and resources. Headed communications and marketing teams' initiatives, which included preparing new financial opportunities and contracts. Based on research, devised strategic plans and facilitated collaboration among marketing teams to launch new potential outlets.

Key Achievement:
- Advocated for additional resources and funding from international clients, traveling as required to meet industry heads.

COMPANY NAME, CITY, ST
Recruitment Specialist & Internet Researcher
Merged five locations under one umbrella due to efficient process management while working under pressure to meet deadlines. Acquired repeat praise from senior heads, along with additional tasks, including training direct reports. Instrumentally reviewed incoming resumes and job search letters to source talent for exempt and non-exempt positions. Made extensive use of Boolean searches and Applicant Tracking Systems (ATS) while working to generate key words.

Key Achievement:
- Streamlined operations across five locations due to collaborative, analytical, and organizational competency.

Education

Master of Science in Library and Information Science • University Name, City, ST
Bachelor of Science in Business Administration • University Name, City, ST

YOUR NAME
Senior Sales Management • Chemical Industry

City, ST Zip • Telephone Number • Email Address

The Chemical Industry's Charismatic Sales Phenomenon
"If We Could Figure Out Her Secret, We'd Bottle It for the Worldwide Sales Force"

Chemical industry veteran who defies the conventional wisdom about selling commodities. Lead teams that consistently out-perform competitors – at higher profit margins – in hotly contested markets. Instantly connect, build trust, and deliver 100% on commitments.

- **Sales Performance:** Ranked #1 salesperson-of-the year for 18 straight years for 4 employers.

- **Dual Expertise:** Chemical engineer and financial ace – BS Ch.E & MBA – with encyclopedic knowledge of the chemical industry: R&D, markets, financing, manufacturing, and sales.

- **Turnaround:** Within 10 years of graduation, took charge as Acting President for Company Name – a distributor in danger of collapse – and negotiated with banks, suppliers, and sales force. Rescued the company (still in business today).

- **Team Leader:** Natural talent for inspiring a team to see untapped opportunities and accomplish "impossible" goals.

Chemical Industry Cumulative Career Sales Nearly $700 Million

---

AREAS OF EXPERTISE

Sales Team Leadership	Chemical Industry	General Management (P&L)
Top Sales Producer	P&L and Cost Cutting	Acting President and CEO
Motivation Public Speaker	Financial Modeling	Product Development

SALES AND SALES MANAGEMENT EXPERIENCE

COMPANY NAME, City, ST   **Date–Present**
Global chemical distributor for pharma, oil-and-gas, food processing, and environment • $11 billion total sales & 7,700 emp.
Vice President of Sales for Central US & Canada
Leading an 860-Person Sales Org | $120M Direct and Distributor Sales | Member of Executive Leadership Team

Transitioned from distributor management within former employer to senior sales role for this leading chemical distributor and #1 customer. Reversed 4-year trend of declining sales and profits.

- **Challenge:** Over 4-year period, prior sales management had attempted to implement a sales reorg that was not appropriate for chemical industry. Sales and market share had been declining for four years.

- **Actions:** Implemented a 3-part turnaround: "Bend-over-backwards" service, a "war game" mindset, aggressive commercial strategy to grow market share, and a new sales ethos called "freedom to sell."

  ✓ **Margins & Pricing:** Introduced Lean Six Sigma and hired a 6-person strategic pricing team that developed analytics and real-time pricing tools similar to Amazon.com.

  ✓ **Sales:** Cut sales admin-overhead by 30%, which doubled individual sales calls – on average – from 10 to 20. Restored geographical territories and key accounts.

  ✓ **Reporting:** Enforced disciplined sales tracking via Salesforce.com. Directed creation of a proprietary executive dashboard to personally engage each sales manager each week.

- **Results:** Year-over-year, increased sales by 5% and margins by multiple points. Improved delivery reliability, cut operating costs, and improved employee morale (increased Net Promoter Score 10 points).

SALES AND SALES MANAGEMENT EXPERIENCE

COMPANY NAME, City, ST   **Date-Date**
One of the world's largest chemical companies • $30B revenue and 60,500 employees.
Business Development Director for Oxygenated Solvents (Date-Date)
450-person organization | $80M budget | Global manufacturing & sales | Member of Elite Corp Leadership Team

Continually improved sales, profit, strategic positioning, financial forecasting & investor relations.

- **Challenges and Opportunities**: Oxygenated Solvents BU was a profitable "cash cow" that was not performing at its peak earnings potential. Exploited profitable niches ("talent pools") that were ignored.
  - ✓ Analyzed "value chains" – identified how company creates value in each industry served by BU.
  - ✓ Increased earnings by 20%, met all P&L and KPI targets, and improved worldwide morale of BU.
- **Actions**: Shifted sales focus to the most profitable niches, for example, increased sales of proprionic acid to food-preservative makers instead of agricultural companies.
- **Results**: Achieved a turnaround for Monsanto and met the key target (grew earnings over 20%).

Director of Sales / Director of Distribution, Oxygenated Solvents (Date–Date)
Based on success with the Oil & Gas project, promoted to Director and contributed a leading role during the turnaround of an underperforming sales force (roughly 450 people in NA, 2,000 people worldwide).

- **Challenges**: Over a 10-year period, sales had degenerated into a dead-end career path at Company D – top talent avoided sales, so Company D lost market share and opportunities. After acquisition of new company, Company D integrated 2 disparate sales forces, which posed a major retention problem: top talent was leaving, and remaining 2,000 salespeople were isolated in "silos" with little interaction.
- **Actions & Results**: Achieved a second turnaround #1 for Company D: Transformed sales culture from mediocrity to excellence. Promoted 3X and shifted new team from "commodity" sales to "solution" sales.
  - ✓ Scaled up size and quality of sales force, which increased sales from $14B to $20B during 2008–2010.
  - ✓ Relocated to City, ST to manage Midwest, which drove regional sales from $50M to $200M.

Strategic Sales Team Leader (Date)
Sales Manager, Specialty Chemicals (Date)

ADDITIONAL EXPERIENCE

COMPANY Name, City, ST (Date–Date): Vice President for a privately held, full-line chemical distributor focused on MI, OH, and IN. Orchestrated complete turnaround of company: Joined PVS while struggling.

- Promoted three times, from Sales Manager to VP: Drove all aspects of the business: acquisitions, capital investment, customer service, price negotiations & P&L. Took charge as Acting President for one year.

COMPANY Name, City, ST (Date–Date), Distribution Sales Manager: Led a 7-person sales team ($40M goal) for 3 plants (made pulp, paper, and coatings). Achieved #1 regional ranking for profit.

COMPANY Name, City, ST (Date–Date), Technical Sales Rep: Promoted twice. Created a "Blanket Hazardous Waste Treatment Permit" that cut permitting time from 90 days to less than 30.

EDUCATION

MBA, UNIVERSITY NAME, City, ST

MS, Chemistry, UNIVERSITY NAME, City, ST

BS, Chemistry, UNIVERSITY NAME, City, ST

Administrative Assistant authored by Posey Salem. This resume homes right in on the job target by using it as an objective header. The summary draws attention to her unique value. The work history draws the eye with bold entries. Note that the two jobs on page one have *Volunteer* after the title, which allowed a stay-at-home mom to cover an employment gap.

Phone ▪ Email ▪ City ▪ ST ▪ Zip Code
LinkedIn URL

Your Name

Ethics Committee Administrative Assistant

Top-notch bilingual administrative assistant with excellent ethics, service, and office skills accustomed to working in fast-paced environments. Known for discretion when handling confidential information, processes, and procedures. Recognized for providing superior support and service to all levels of management, staff and outside clients. Excel at identifying opportunities to streamline processes. *Key competencies include:*

✓ Office Administration	✓ Bilingual: English-Spanish	✓ Cross-functional Collaboration
✓ Discretion and Confidentiality	✓ Multi-cultural Experience	✓ Prioritization and Multi-tasking
✓ Integrity Dependability	✓ Fast-paced Environments	✓ Organization and Coordination
✓ Detailed and Accurate	✓ Customer and Information Services	✓ Microsoft Office: Word, Excel,
✓ Problem Solver	✓ Client Interviewing and Screening	PowerPoint, Outlook

Professional History

Client Intake Interviewer / Administrative Assistant (Volunteer), Company, City, ST   Date–Date
Company is a non-profit agency serving low-income individuals by providing food, shelter, and financial assistance for individuals and families in crisis. Hired to assist senior staff by interviewing and screening applicants from various cultural backgrounds who request food and assistance — especially Spanish-speaking individuals. Obtain required documentation regarding family composition, financial, medical, and employment.

- **Reviewed and processed applicant's documentation to determine compliance** with agency rules and policies and advised them of their eligibility status.
- **Explained agency procedures and policies to applicants.** Responded to inquiries; provided resource information and referred applicant to agencies providing additional assistance.
- **Increased efficiency and decreased application processing time** by translating and reformatting intake forms for Spanish-speaking applicants.
- **Selected to be a contributing member** of the Advisory Committee that analyzes, interprets, and implements policy and procedural guidelines for operations, fraud reduction, staff, and client eligibility.
- **Entered and updated client data into computer system.** Filed paper applications for qualified clients and followed-up on applications. Tracked, completed, and entered demographic data into computer database.
- **Researched, compiled, and updated** resource listings for governmental, community, and private agencies that provide additional assistance to County residents in financial crisis.
- **Trained new volunteers** as client intake interviewers. Participated in community events which included setup and tear down of agency booth, information distribution, and answering of general public inquiries.

Administrative Assistant / Spanish Interpreter (Volunteer), Company, City, ST   Date–Date
Hired to assist medical professionals and office staff by providing Spanish-English interpreting services to non-English speaking patients. Integrated education, preventive services, and medical care for County citizens.

- **Scheduled appointments** and handled phone calls from Spanish speaking patients.
- **Interviewed patients**, gathered critical and confidential medical data, explained information, and aided patients who required help to complete agency forms. Reviewed and processed forms.
- **Assisted doctors, nurses, and staff**, when working with Spanish speaking patients, for the following departments: Maternity, Pediatrics, Family Planning and Nutrition.

Continued on Page 2

Professional History
Continued

Office Manager, Company, City, ST   Date–Date
Family owned company that is an authorized independent representative for a major equipment company, servicing customers in nine southeastern states. Provided clients with genuine Company Name equipment, customer service, and expert product support.

- **Saved $100 per month** by researching and analyzing telephone provider options. Determined best phone service solution and implemented changes.

- **Averted a 40% insurance premium increase** by negotiating with a different provider resulting in a lower annual premium with additional benefits.

- **Supported the president and company operations** by managing office systems, operations, and equipment. Maintained office efficiency by prioritizing tasks, organizing workflow, coordinating daily activities, and collaboratively developed and implemented policy and procedure guidelines.

- **Responded to customer inquiries and orders** via telephone, email, and facsimile. Entered and retrieved critical customer sales data, placed orders with XYZ Company and provided customer service.

- **Recorded, analyzed, and summarized data** to prepare monthly and special reports that informed management of sales statistics, customer purchase history, financial information, budgeting, and new product offerings from suppliers. Reviewed, processed and filed correspondence and vendor information.

- **Created and typed letters and memos,** opened and distributed mail, answered and responded to phone calls, scheduled appointments, and maintained databases. Booked travel arrangements and provided administrative support for out-of-town sales promotions.

Human Resources Staff, Company, City, ST   Date–Date
Administered biannual performance reviews and determined improvement recommendations. Coordinated staff meetings, addressed facility issues, approved weekly payroll, monitored daily functioning of facility and maintained appropriate staff ratios. Key contributor to facility quality improvement plan.

- **Recruitment and Retention** - Directed full life cycle recruitment process (assessed staffing needs in collaboration with hiring managers, made hiring recommendations) and ensured regulatory compliance of EEO, AA, ADA, DOL, and state and local employment regulations.

- **Orientation, Training and Development** - Created training modules, visuals, and participant materials. Supervised the processing of new hires and presented orientation training. Facilitated routine employee and recurring regulatory training sessions for company procedures, electronic medical records systems.

Education & Professional Development

Bachelor of Arts in Psychology (B.A.), University Name, City, ST   Date
- **Minor in Communications**

Professional Development Seminars
- Human Resources Systems
- Supervisory Skills
- Public Speaking
- Violence in the Workplace
- Sexual Harassment
- Zero Tolerance
- Diversity
- Conflict Management
- Computer Skills

Your Name

City, State Zip | Phone Number | Email Address

Retail Sales & Marketing Professional

Award-winning Marketing and Sales professional with proven ability to exceed year over year (YoY) sales goals.

- ☑ Excel at leveraging broad expertise in leading merchandising and branding campaigns for large retail outlets.
- ☑ Media savvy, seamlessly integrating technical expertise with innovative and imaginative promotional strategies to transform customer experience and service while consistently exceeding key company sales metrics.
- ☑ Keen business acumen, planning skills, and relationship management aptitude combine to drive adaptable business plans that are profitable and sustainable.
- ☑ Customer-focused and company-centric, leading by example to inspire team to succeed.

KEY AREAS OF EXPERTISE

⚲ Relationship Management	⚲ Sales Presentations	⚲ Marketing Strategies
⚲ Sales and Business Analysis	⚲ Merchandising/Business Plans	⚲ Account Management
⚲ New Product Launches	⚲ Staff Training and Development	⚲ Customer Service

EDUCATION / MEMBERSHIP

Bachelor of Arts in Marketing, University Name, City, ST
Member - American Marketing Association

PROFESSIONAL EXPERIENCE

COMPANY NAME   Date to Date
Solutions Consultant (In-Store Sales & Marketing)

Challenge: To set up and direct sales, merchandising, and operations of a branded "store-in-a-store" concept in a single unit reseller (Retail Store Name). Tasked with increasing revenue by achieving quarterly sales quotas and by meeting additional financial metrics.

Actions: Established successful merchandising plans and analyzed business results in order to create and modify business plans to achieve goals. Trained resellers and other store associates. Introduced customers to the newest company technology, delivering a transformational customer experience through sales contact and merchandising.

Selected Results:

- ☑ Partnered with reseller store management to create a 'win-win' relationship through in-store initiatives and merchandising strategies that significantly contributed to significant sales growth.
- ☑ Increased Year YoY revenue by 27% and unit sales by 26% in a declining economic market.
- ☑ Achieved 115% of target revenue for Year, and 108% for Year.
- ☑ Awarded Company Sales Professional recognition from Year-Year.
- ☑ Successfully launched major new product initiatives, including Galaxy S9+ Phone and Galaxy Tab S4 Android Tablet.
- ☑ Oversaw additional reseller location for limited support role, achieving 103% of target revenue for Year.

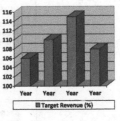

COMPANY NAME   Date to Date
Senior Product Specialist
Supervised day-to-day operations of computer and digital camera department. Resolved escalated customer service issues. Scheduled labor and trained and developed associates. Cross-trained to work in all departments of the store. Promoted twice within 13 months of service.

Your Name

Phone Number · Email · City, State · LinkedIn

HR GENERALIST
· Committed to improving processes in human resources ·

Award- Winning, Lean 5S certified HR professional with 10+ years of payroll experience known for remedying inefficiencies. Seasoned in HR transactions and proficient in Microsoft Office Suite & Human Resource Information Systems: Hours Balanced & Socrates.

Human Resources Core Competencies

Payroll	FMLA	Tuition Assistance Program
Employee Relations	Time/Attendance	Onboarding
Reporting/Tracking	Benefits Administration	Hire/Termination
Social Media Recruiting	AAP/EEO	Workers' Compensation

Professional Experience

Company Name, City, State   [Date – Date]

OFFICE & HUMAN RESOURCES MANAGER - [Date – Date]

Spearheaded administrative and human resource functions for a 600+ employee department. Supervisor noted knack for "managing all people movement" within facility. *Promoted to position from Production Worker role [Date-Date].*

- Created 330 new employee files eliminating HR process inefficiencies for tracking attendance, vacation, training, FMLA, tuition assistance (TAP), benefits and transfers.
- Won 5S Outstanding Award for $200,000 savings for implementing new, all-factory lean system reducing office and production floor footprint.
- Supported 15+ managers in HR transactions via accurate employee documentation / reporting ensuring federal, state and local employment law compliance.
- Monitored weekly payroll, benefits and multiple shift schedules for 630 employees.
- Onboarded new employees through facility tours, new- hire paperwork/processes and setup.

Company Name, City, State   [Date – Date]

HUMAN RESOURCES MANAGER · PROJECT COORDINATOR

Directed and performed administrative tasks for this family- owned business in areas of human resources, financial/ budgetary activities and project coordination. Handled tax preparation, project pricing, budgeting, compensation, hire/termination & employment law compliance.

- Orchestrated employee hiring process from recruiting, interviewing to hire.
- Managed payroll, employee bonus/recognition, time and HR paperwork for six employees.
- Prepared project quotes/proposals in collaboration with contractors for 400+ jobs annually.

Education and Certification

Bachelor of Science, Human Resources · XYZ University	[Date]
Associate of Science, Business Management · State University	[Date]
Lean 5S Manufacturing Certification · ABC Company	[Date]
Category: Late-career - Career change	

YOUR NAME

City, State Zip   Telephone Number   Email Address

INVESTMENT BANKING ASSOCIATE

Investment Banking ♦ Financial Associate ♦ Proprietary Trading

➤ Top performer with a proven track record of successive advancement through proactive leadership and development of multi-million dollar positive revenue growth and bottom-line results for global leaders in the financial services / banking industry.

➤ Expertise in origination, investment and sales of emerging markets fixed income securities for U.S. and European institutional investors with highly profitable results that outperform emerging market equity indices. Proficient in electronic trading.

➤ Solid network of senior-level contacts in banks, corporations and government, and originated debt capital markets transactions.

PROFESSIONAL EXPERIENCE

COMPANY NAME – CITY, ST   Date - Date
Investment Banking Associate & Proprietary Trader

Selected to join senior executive team in emerging markets Proprietary Trading Division that managed U.S. $3+ billion in Bank capital. Originated and managed investments for several books: debt, equity, local currency and structured financing with a primary focus on equity investments and structured financing. Comanaged U.S. $1 billion financing book of emerging markets fixed income securities as well as U.S. $100 million equity special situation book. *Results included:*

♦ Delivered **$30 million in net profits** for the Proprietary Trading Division of ABC Company in YEAR and YEAR as the top contributor to the special situation equity and financing books. **Instrumental in division's ranking #1 in profitability** during YEAR.

♦ **Originated and managed several debt Private Placements** for ABC Company and for clients of the financing book.

♦ Achieved **top ranking in division** at ABC Co for 3 consecutive years: **#1 producer in emerging markets** institutional fixed income sales, **#1 producer of derivatives sales, #1 producer in Eurobond sales and #1 in structured financing.** Generated **$15 million in annual profits.**

♦ Produced **$45 million in profits** over 3-year period for most profitable division at ABC Co.

♦ Spearheaded Eurobond syndication activity, which became **#1 European bank involved in Eurobond underwriting** over 2-year period. Participated in the **syndication of 30% of all new issues** – the Bank's first participation in international new issues.

♦ **Initiated entire distribution of Eurobonds,** successfully cultivating relationships with over 40 institutional investors in Eurobonds and emerging markets fixed income securities.

EDUCATION & LICENSES

B.S. in Financial Management - University Name
NASD licenses: Series 7 and 63

YOUR NAME

City, State
Phone: ● Email:

INFORMATION TECHNOLOGY SECURITY GURU

● Ranked #1 Information Security Consultant ● Trusted Advisor to Banking Powerhouse ●

Visionary technology executive with a strong track record of success in leading national, regional, and global teams in establishment and maintenance of robust information security management programs for a global banking powerhouse.

Inspirational and influential leader and team builder with a proven ability to secure executive-level buy-in for major information security programs.

Ranked #1 Information Security Consultant by Intell IT Security Magazine as voted by a panel of peers.

Hand-picked by members of executive team to set up information security function at global HQ in Geneva.
Drove threat risk down 65% by deploying cutting edge technologies.
Catalyst for significantly improving information security at world's second largest bank.

Key Areas of Expertise

▪ Strategic & Tactical Planning	▪ IT Security Management Framework Usage	▪ Employee Leadership
▪ Risk Assessment & Mitigation	▪ Internal Control Standards Development	▪ Project Management
▪ Stakeholder Engagement	▪ Departmental Start-Up & Development	▪ Regulatory Affairs
▪ International Compliance	▪ Policy & Procedure Development	▪ KPI Development
▪ Performance Management	▪ Budgeting & Resource Management	▪ Change Management

PROFESSIONAL EXPERIENCE

BANKING CONGLOMERATE NAME   Date to Date

Director, Information Security (Date to Date)

Handpicked by senior executive team to establish Worldwide Information Security function with a mandate to manage all aspects of information security for three major Internet points of presence, to include: e-commerce infrastructure, 12,000+ desktops, 400+ Windows Servers, and 30 iSeries LPARs. **Reduced documented security threats by 65%, and instituted world-class proactive threat detection mechanisms.**

- **Project Management:** Significantly improved IT security and minimized system vulnerability by implementing major projects spanning security event management, database vulnerability scanning, risk based application security methodology, access management workflow, and InTrust for Active Directory.

- **Corporate Leadership:** Initiated country involvement in Global IT Architecture team responsible for defining global business standards. **Played a key role in defining international information security standards for entire group which were heralded by executive team as a significant achievement.**

- **Compliance:** Developed PCI compliance strategy focusing on integrating security controls within standard operational models. **Achieved and maintained merchant 1 compliance status since 2009.**

- **Mentorship & Training:** Deliver inspirational leadership & training to a staff complement of 55 cross-functional professionals based in 6 countries. **Improved key staff retention rate by 35% (2007-Present).**

▪ ▪ ▪ ▪

Global Head of IT Security, Risk & Control (Date to Date)

Selected by international executive committee to undertake a secondment to Geneva, Switzerland to provide executive management, leadership, and strategic direction to local Information Security and IT Risk and Control professionals in development and operation of a proactive internal IT security practice.

- **Strategy Development:** Developed and executed strategy for managing IT Security within Group Private Banking and across all business lines, which included: IT infrastructure, access management, incident management, and application security management. **Rendered practice operational within three months.**

- **Operational Leadership:** Ensured IT initiatives aligned to business priorities while balancing resource constraints to optimize investment. **Commended by president, Private Banking for totality of service provided and immediate impact made by security practice.**

- **Regulatory Compliance:** Acted as regulatory representative for matters related to information security, Swiss banking regulation, and other global banking regulators. **Invited to sit as executive member of Group Private Bank Fraud Steering Committee, IT SOX Steering & Operational Risk Committees.**

Manager, IT Security & Compliance (Date to Date)

Recruited by VP, Technology to lead a team of IT professionals in redevelopment of a mission critical IT security function failing to stem tsunami of web-based attacks on bank. **Transformed security practice from legacy control model to a pragmatic, risk-based consultative service, implemented improved perimeter protection and detection services, and reduced security breaches by 95%.**

- **Value-Add:** Initiated Canadian involvement in Global IT Architecture team responsible for defining global business standards. Played a key role in defining international information security standards for entire group.

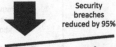
Security breaches reduced by 95%

- **Process Improvement:** Consolidated and/or restructured 50+ individual security policies into five logical security domains providing context to specific audiences, and established infrastructure hardening and assurance program.

Productivity increased by 45%

- **Regulatory Compliance:** Delivered a strategic Active Directory solution that aligned and achieved consistency in security technology, process and practice, and addressed both tactical and regulatory requirements for authentication.

- **Team Lead, IT Security & Compliance (Date to Date)**

EDUCATION

Project Management Professional – Project Management Association
Bachelor of Computer Science – University Name

MEMBERSHIPS & AFFILIATIONS

Founder – Allied IT Professionals, Western Chapter
Board Member – Project Management Association, Western Region

■■■■

Your Name

City, State ❑ Cell Phone ❑ Email Address

PROGRAM MANAGER ~ NONPROFIT
THOUGHTFUL COMMUNICATOR ~ RESOURCEFUL PLANNER ~ CREATIVE LEADER

"When you think you have exhausted all possibilities, remember this: You haven't."
~ Thomas Edison

Track Record of Creative Leadership:

❑ **Innovative & Start-Up Focused:** Created first internship program for students with City Hospital by initiating and cultivating relationships with nursing program management. Program offered students the opportunity to use classroom knowledge in practical situations.

❑ **Focused on Profits & Cost Controls:** Dramatically cut newsletter expenses and venue costs, and increased monthly event fees to move organization from running at a deficit to being self-sustainable.

❑ **Committed to Process Improvement:** Revitalized vocational program by researching additional assessment tools and developing new curriculum for training in basic office skills. Produced original workbooks, worksheets, and tests.

VALUE OFFERED

❑ Strategic Thinker	❑ Creative Leadership	❑ Client Assessment
❑ Curriculum Development	❑ Relationship Building	❑ Program Research
❑ Maintain Confidentiality	❑ Group Facilitation	❑ Program Development
❑ Verbal & Written Communication	❑ Progress Assessment	❑ Deliver Presentations
❑ Recruit & Motivate Volunteers	❑ Manage Volunteer Board	❑ Assessment Processing

PROFESSIONAL EXPERIENCE

Company Name, City, ST   Date—Date
Government Admissions Counselor
Recruited to develop affiliations with government agencies and research additional funding sources. Presented information on Learning Center programs, facilitated group discussions on career options, evaluated students' goals, and recommended appropriate curriculum. Researched, contacted, and built relationships with area businesses to arrange internships for students.

Key Contributions:
❑ Created first internship program for Learning Center students with City Hospital through initiating contact and cultivating relationships with nursing program management. Program designed to give students the opportunity to use their classroom knowledge in practical situations.
❑ Developed newsletter to share Learning Center news and student achievements. Wrote all content, provide input on design and layout. Prepared new program marketing materials.

Company Name, City, ST   Date—Date
Vocational Counselor
Revitalized stagnant vocational program for chronically mentally ill clients by developing new curriculum for office skills classes. Worked closely with program manager on assessing client progress and work readiness. Facilitated career-development workshops, administered and processed assessments and interest inventories; analyzed results and shared with clients. Updated clients' therapists on their progress.

Vocational Counselor *continued*

Contributions:
- ❑ Constructed original workbooks, worksheets, and tests for students to use in basic office skills program. Initiated testing procedures in typing, letter writing, and other office practices. Consulted with program manager to determine additional training needs.
- ❑ Counselled mentally challenged students to help them develop realistic career goals and prepare to secure mainstream positions. Continued to work with students until program completion.

Executive Women's Business Organization, City, ST   Date—Date
Director/Program Chair (Volunteer)
Created much-needed structure to a long-standing organization. Recruited and motivated volunteer Board of Directors, selected a more cost-saving venue for monthly events, transitioned printed newsletter to monthly email announcement, and grew membership by launching first membership drive. Sourced and secured compelling speakers on a variety of topics to spark member interest and participation.

Contributions:
- ❑ Revived languishing Board by recruiting volunteers. Built Board of Directors from two to ten members during first six months as director. Maintained engaged board for duration of term.
- ❑ Dramatically cut newsletter expenses and venue costs, and increased monthly event fees to help organization move from running at deficit to being self-sustainable.
- ❑ Arranged and implemented first-ever Holiday Giving program in conjunction with select local nonprofit where members purchased winter coats for children in-need. Program continued for 5+ years and provided coats to hundreds of children.

Company Name, City, ST   Date—Date
Administrative Support (Temporary)
Worked with a number of agency's key clients serving as administrative assistant, receptionist, and customer service representative. Requested to assist in Chairman's office of financial services firm.

AFFILIATIONS/CREDENTIALS

American Psychological Association ~ American Counseling Association ~
Executive Women's Business Association ~ Domestic Violence Crisis Center ~
National Career Development Association

EDUCATION/CREDENTIALS

Master of Arts: Applied Psychology, University Name, City, ST
Bachelor of Arts: English, University Name, City, ST

Myers-Briggs Type Indicator Professional Qualifying Program

YOUR NAME

City, ST   Phone Number   Email Address

SALES & BUSINESS DEVELOPMENT MANAGER
BUILDING PROFITABLE CUSTOMER RELATIONSHIPS

"If you need a salesman who doesn't just 'talk the talk' but 'walks the walk,' look no further than NAME."

John Smith, CEO, Company Name

Accomplished brand champion and product sales manager who excels at positioning products, companies, and packaged solutions for dramatic triple-digit revenue growth in competitive commercial and retail environments. Performance is underpinned by an energetic, personal passion for surpassing expectations.

▶ Reputation for being able to infiltrate untapped markets and exploit existing relationships to drive sales.

▶ Big picture laser-focus on the details, people, and processes that equal customer, supply, and team loyalty.

▶ Respected by clients, management, and peers for personal ethics and integrity.

AREAS OF EXPERTISE

- Sales Management
- Budgeting & Sales Forecasting
- National Account Management
- Supplier & Retail Relations
- Sales Force Training & Leadership
- New Business Development
- Client Retention Strategies
- Brand Awareness & Development

- Product Development & Launches
- Needs Assessment
- Solution Selling
- Point of Sale Promotions
- Catalogue Sales
- Direct Marketing & Advertising
- Inventory & Stock Control
- Electronic Transfer Delivery (EDI)

CAREER HISTORY

COMPANY NAME   [DATE – DATE]

SALES MANAGER

Manufacture ladies' and children's wear for sale through national department stores and boutiques.

Report to: Chief Executive Officer; Supervise: 4 Sales Agents

Against a backdrop of low morale, high turnover of staff, limited product range, and falling sales, recruited for talents in rapidly solidifying client relationships to increase revenue in retail environments.

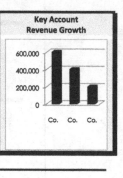

Key Account Management: Developed and grew lucrative accounts including David Jones, Target, and Myer as well as retail accounts in three major regions throughout the country.

Sales Performance: Acquired 40 new accounts and increased personal annual sales budget from $300K to $3M. Drove interstate sales increasing one region's account by 75% and another's by 50%.

Leadership: Managed State Sales Agents; set targets, seasonal / annual budgets, and conducted monthly sales meetings to monitor performance, improve sales techniques, provide guidance and increase market penetration.

Innovation: Developed an exclusive baby gift pack to fill a gap in the retail market, which achieved sales in excess of $220K.

SALES MANAGER, CONTINUED...

Client Retention & Growth: Implemented and coordinated exclusive programs for catalog sales with David Jones, Myer, and Target. Developed distinctive children's ranges for major accounts. Improved existing customer relationships, changed perception of brand and increased sales.

Marketing & Brand Awareness: Designed new company branding and coordinated the launch of contemporary packaging and promotional point of sale items.

Production & Product Development: Developed and implemented new clothing lines, which became best-selling items. Interfaced between design and production teams, and oversaw the development of new ranges including sourcing samples and selecting fabrics, through to production.

Technology: Played an integral role in the development and implementation of the company website and provided ongoing management of Content Management System (CMS).

Stock Control: Entrusted with monthly stock ordering for 38% of clients based on quality relationships.

Warehouse Operations: Assisted with picking, packing and dispatching of stock including electronic transfers (the Target, Myer and David Jones delivery system).

COMPANY NAME   **[DATE – DATE]**
SALES EXECUTIVE

Leading manufacturer of clubwear (school and sports uniforms) with supplementary branding embroidery services.

Report to: Directors (4)

Hand-selected to use existing networks within sporting sector to promote company's wares and secure a foothold in a highly competitive industry. With no customer base, systems or procedures, developed prospect lists and started cold calling to identify needs and present competitive solutions.

New Business Generation: Developed target lists and used direct mailing and cold call techniques to secure appointments. Averaged 8 client visits per day, 75% of which ordered on the spot.

Sales Performance: Consistently met weekly sales budget of $30-$35K. Achieved 200% of budget in second month of employment.

Innovation: Identified need for a customized basketball range for clubs and retail outlets. Worked closely with designers to develop and implement range, which was well received and generated significant revenue, covering development costs in the first month.

Workflow Management: Refined sales strategies as business grew to meet demands of a rapidly increasing customer base including implementation of call cycles and direct marketing campaigns.

Order Processing: Applied a 'hands-on' approach, tracking all orders from input to production and dispatch, with an emphasis on providing quality products with superior levels of customer service.

> " ... a rare find these days; NAME treated this business as if it were his own ... single-handedly opened new markets ... saw a gap in the product range and filled it, adding significant revenue in the process ... we would not be in such a strong financial position if it weren't for NAME ..."
>
> *Excerpt from written reference: Bob Jones, CEO, Company Name*

CERTIFICATES & TRAINING

Sales Strategies Success (Date); **Advanced Sales Training** (Date); **Certificate IV in Business Marketing** (Date)

YOUR NAME

Email Address • Phone Number • City, State Zip

SALES DIRECTOR

Award-winning, magnetic, and solutions-driven sales professional with extensive leadership experience in the automotive industry. Proven strengths in controlling multimillion-dollar inventories, administering budgets / resources, and achieving exceptional levels of growth and profitability. Effective manager with talents in staff hiring, training, and motivation with comprehensive knowledge in both front-of-house and back-of-house operations. Demonstrated integrity, commitment to client satisfaction, and drive for exceeding performance expectations.

AREAS OF EXPERTISE

Customer Relationship Management (CRM) • Program Development • Leadership & Team Building
Multichannel Marketing • Scheduling • Policy & Procedure Design • Lead Generation
Market Analysis • Cost Control • Contract Negotiation • Problem Resolution • Documentation

PROFESSIONAL EXPERIENCE & ACHIEVEMENTS

Company Name, City, State   Date to Date

Director of New Car Sales

Recruited to preside over day-to-day retail and fleet sales operations within leading area dealer. Challenged to improve inventory controls.

Hired, trained, and supervised team of 30. Managed inventory of 400 new cars in cooperation with GM based on sales / market analyses. Held daily and weekly sales meetings. Controlled expenses and assisted with F&I.

> ❖ **Key contributor to company recording highest profit and sales since Date and upholding YOY sales growth of 50%.**
> ❖ **Captured and continue to hold 100% targeted market share.**

- **Streamlined inventory to achieve best levels in company history.**
- Oversaw training for sales employees, ensuring all obtained ABCD certification.

Company Name, City, State   Date to Date

Lead Sales Manager (Date to Date)
Finance Manager (Date to Date)

Promoted based on outstanding contributions as Finance manager to fill newly-created position. Directed sales for new and used Volvo, Scion, Nissan, Lexus, and Jeep dealer ranked 2nd in district.

Led 25+ staff encompassing Sales / Sales Manager, Finance Managers, Service Advisors, Internet Manager, Lot Attendants, and Aftermarket and Accessories Manager. Prepared monthly commission reports for 10+ Sales Reps. Devised/executed integrated multimedia ad campaigns.

> ❖ **Outperformed sales quotas by 25% for XYZ region and increased sales 35% within 2 years.**
> ❖ **Founded successful Volvo Club and achieved ranking as #1 Volvo retailer in State (Date to Date).**

- **Propelled client base 60% through strategic CRM.**
- **Earned Dealer of the Year Award in Date.**
- **Enhanced customer satisfaction 50%** by developing and implementing standardized employee training.
- **Improved employee productivity** by designing / teaching training program on sales processes and procedures.
- Received ABC Motors' **Sales Person of the Year Award in Date** (dealership's top award).

EDUCATION & COMPUTER SKILLS

International Business & Finance Coursework – ABC University
MS Office Suite (Word, Excel, PowerPoint) • Auto Exchange • vAuto • GM Global • DealerTrack • DealerCONNECT

Senior Commercial Banker authored by Kara Varner. You can see in this resume how key accomplishments in each position can be made to stand out with the right-hand column of specific metric-based accomplishments.

YOUR NAME
Focus - Accuracy - Accountability

City, ST ▪ Phone ▪ Email ▪ LinkedIn Profile

SENIOR COMMERCIAL LENDING & BANKING PROFESSIONAL
CORPORATE ACCOUNT MANAGER

Intellectual and progressive Commercial Banking Executive leveraging 20+ year career driving sales and propelling account growth. Capture service dominance in highly competitive markets.

Top-performer ➤ Harness the power of relationships for business success by acquiring new business, dissolving sales barriers, and delivering client solutions that attract and retain profitable clients. Achieve 'win-win' outcomes.

Change catalyst ➤ Optimize market potential and consistently yield high revenue growth.

Progressive career ➤ Account Executive to VP-Relationship Management to VP / Sr. Commercial Banker

> ➤ Consistently in Top 5 of Producers across profitability and Small Business Administration Lending
> ➤ Director's Club / Emerald Award Winner: Record setting commercial and credit transaction closings
> ➤ **BA Degree in Finance**

STRENGTHS & SKILLS

Business Development	Client Relationship Management	Increase Revenue Streams
Portfolio & Cash Management	New Customer Acquisition/Retention	Financial Products & Services
Sales Strategy & Planning	Analysis & Reporting	Implement Best Practices
Leadership & Management	Regulatory Compliance	Risk Management and Control
Forecasting/ Project Budgets / P&L	Technology Integration	Sales Support and Partnership
Accounting Controls / A/P & A/R	High-value Account Management	Prospecting/Influential Selling

CAREER NARRATIVE
Top Performer - Revenue Generator - Service Excellence - Market Expansion & Growth

VP, SENIOR COMMERCIAL BANKER   Date to Present
COMPANY - City, ST
Promoted to Senior Commercial Banker 10 months into tenure

Tasked as key collaborator, relationship partner, and solution generator for family owned, community bank. Actively managed business development opportunities; oversaw ongoing monitoring of client portfolio performance to maximize ROI. Small Business Administration (SBA) lending expert.

- Drove marketing initiatives; developed strategic client solution opportunities within sector and SBA portfolios.
- Directed preparation of lending proposals to prospective clients. Instituted cross-selling initiatives to increase ranking with clients.
- Steered efforts that defined and executed process for the bank to become a SBA Express designated lender.

Notable Impact
➤ Produced $54M in loan volume; $1.8M interest income 1st year of tenure
➤ Newcomer of the Year Award
➤ Director's Club
➤ Top commercial lender for loan volume deposits/fee & interest income
➤ Top SBA lender; resulted in XYZ Bank becoming Top 5 SBA Producer

VP, COMMERICAL BANKER   Date to Date
COMPANY - City, ST

Achieved top Commercial Lender in Southern Market for fast-growing, full-service bank with $19B in assets operating across 10 states. Managed banking portfolio: 380 clients, 98 credit facilities, $102 in deposits.

- Built new business lending relationships with focus on $700K+.
- Spearheaded presentation to high value contacts which significantly boosted referrals.
- Guided efficient work-through process for monitoring bank's loan portfolio which improved regulatory compliance for portfolio management by 40%.

Notable Impact
➤ Produced 15M+ in commercial lending
➤ Achieved Top 3 ranking company-wide for credit production
➤ Achieved Top 3 ranking company-wide for portfolio profitability growth
➤ Acquired multiple new clients: $32M in new lending/$44K in cash management

VP, RELATIONSHIP MANAGEMENT   Date to Date
ZYX Bank - City, ST

**Recognized as Top Performer -
promoted to VP, Relationship Manager**

Architected revenue-generating, strategic relationships for a leading global
financial services firm with $47B in assets spanning 62 countries.

- Managed client portfolio accounting for $39M in balances and $1.8M in
  revenue within the business banking division.
- Drove service and growth within existing book by acquiring new
  business clients with $3-$19M in annual revenue.
- Recognized as: Top Loan Producer on team for Q1 & Q2.

Notable Impact

➤ Produced $8M+ in commercial
  lending facilities in 1st year of tenure
➤ Increased cash management
  revenue by $50K by conducting
  client portfolio needs analysis
➤ Acquired multiple new clients: $3M
  in new deposits/ $8M in new lending

ACCOUNT EXECUTIVE   Date to Date
Company Name - City, ST

Managed $2.3M sales territory with 18 'high touch' accounts for a regional
manufacturer / distributor of food/food-related products - $1.4B in revenue.

- Opened 50 new accounts through cold calling and referrals.
- Dynamic presenter: Tapped as Keynote speaker for 15 District
  Trainings on best practices / time management. Selected as Corporate
  Trainer for account executives at new company branch.
- Appointed Regional / District Trainer for 2 new software rollouts.

Notable Impact

➤ Prestigious Emerald Award Winner
➤ Top performer: In top 10% of 110
  person sales force
➤ Recognized as Top 5% of sales
  force for 6 consecutive years
➤ Upped purchasing loyalty from 25%
  account volume to 100% w/
  inclusion of high-profile accounts.

EDUCATION

Bachelor of Arts Degree in Finance
University - City, ST

License: #5555000

PROFESSIONAL AFFILIATIONS

Small Business Network

Southern Banker's Association

YOUR NAME

City, State, Zip
Phone Number • Email

SENIOR EXECUTIVE • FINANCIAL SERVICES EXPERT • BANKING OPERATIONS MANAGER

"Good management is the art of making problems so interesting and their solutions so constructive that everyone wants to get to work and deal with them." – Peter Hawkins

Dynamic senior executive with 20+ years' experience leading domestic and global financial services operations with small and large-scale banking institutions. Comfortable navigating ambiguous situations to provide strategic direction and change management throughout multifaceted projects and transitions. Iron out deficiencies and extracts the most productive processes to enhance internal structures, improve client satisfaction, and drive revenue.

Secured Asian markets which brought $22B in new business.	Restructured staff operations which saved $1.4M per annum.	Launched new lending product which attained $20B in 2 years.
BUSINESS DEVELOPMENT	CHANGE MANAGEMENT	REVENUE GROWTH

NOTED AUTHORITY IN THE AREAS OF:

- Global & Domestic Custody Banking
- Mortgage Backed Securities & Securities Lending
- Clearance, Letters of Credit & Loans
- Offshore Fund Administration
- Corporate Trust & Transaction Solutions

- Budget Management & Forecasting
- Money Markets & Asset Management
- Recruitment, Mentorship & Team Motivation
- System Upgrades & Technology Integration
- AML/BSA/OFAC Compliance & Reporting

CAREER NARRATIVE

Vice President & Manager, Trust Operations   Date - Date
Company Name, City, State

Relied upon by teams of administrators to provide sound advice and tactical plans for bank's domestic custody business. Oversaw transactions for 400+ accounts. Continuously monitored operations to identify deficiencies in product offerings and service processes and then created improvements that unlocked business potential. Generated a brainstorming powerhouse via team collaboration and open dialogue.

→ **Gained new competitive edge and earned $22B-worth of business for all other Asian markets.** Devised value-added services to transform lackluster offerings into attractive service packages. Retained supranational firm's business for Japanese securities by negotiating ground-breaking 2-year locked contract in exchange for reduced interest rates and 24/7 access to exclusive account manager.

→ **Employed a "show me" management style which saved $1.4M per annum.** Groomed 3 staff for promotions as well as worked with HR to prepare severance packages for 27 staff terminations. Change management sustained a high level of productivity despite halving the headcount.

→ **Spearheaded project to reconcile a 10-year backlog of over 3 million bonds to underlying cash accounts.** Hand-picked team of most dedicated and results-driven staff members and devised a new reporting procedure to track progress. Reduced vault contents to 30,000 with no improprieties.

> "Michael is one of the best managers I have ever worked with and for. He can create a positive culture where people thrive, and he is confident and strong enough to make tough decisions. Michael is a true role model of a contemporary senior executive."
>
> – Chief Operating Officer of ABC Bank

→ **Directed $2M bank system conversion project.** Selected vendor and co-developed a cutting-edge browser-based module which enhanced efficiency of issuing and paying clients' commercial paper and medium-term notes. New system retained business with previously disgruntled clients and is now hailed as the benchmark for other financial institutions.

Page 1 of 2

Career Narrative Continued...

Vice President, Global Investor Services, State Branch   Date - Date
Company Name, City, State
Oversaw 2 large-scale and high-stakes initiatives; launched a global securities lending business to drive revenue and merged 2 corporate trust operations to reduce costs.

➔   Invited by general manager of bank's London branch to launch a global securities lending product. Created comprehensive step-by-step plan to **maximize profitable opportunities** on supply side. **Designed a product profile that enticed buyers** through vigorous reach and establishment of industry contacts.

➔   Handled regulatory approvals, legal agreements, and tax assessments. Obtained credit lines for borrowers and **evaluated market and operational risks for 30 countries**. Assembled team of 5, selected system vendor, directed system installation, and wrote procedures.

➔   **Exceeded $4M per annum** in product revenue, which grew loans from below $1B to $20B in less than 2 years.

➔   Appointed by senior management to **consolidate 2 corporate trust groups**. Developed project roadmap to amalgamate branch and merchant banking subsidiary operations **without compromising service** to corporate issuers of Eurobonds.

➔   Spearheaded system changes, staff re-selection, and client document reviews and revisions. Notified issuers, investors, paying agents, and depositories of revamped procedures. Merged operations which **reduced expenses by 20%**.

> "Michael is a visionary yet is pragmatic. He is a clear, decisive communicator and is highly skilled at building and nurturing relationships with key stakeholders—whether that person is an influential board member, a supplier, a client or a call center operator. From those relationships, he builds trust and loyalty like no other senior executive I have ever seen."
>
> – President at XYZ Bank

Group Manager, State Operations   Date - Date
Company Name, City, State
Rebuilt internal operations from ground up after taking over an unsuccessful merger. Applied balanced scorecard techniques to overhaul internal processes, business position, and product offerings while carefully monitoring effects of changes. Recruited and managed a 12-member team to promote reinvented services and generated positive brand awareness.

➔   Enhanced company functionality while reducing costs, making huge gains in efficiency and performance.

➔   Surpassed the budgeted net profit figure by $300K on a $150.1M revenue base for the fiscal year 01/02.

EDUCATION, TRAINING & TECHNOLOGY

Bachelor of Arts, Economics, College, City, State

Mini MBA – 6-week intensive course in France

Conflict Resolution • Consortium Executive Program • Train the Trainer • Targeted Selection
Interaction Management • Leading Organizational Change • Kepnor-Tregoe Problem Solving/Decision Making

Microsoft Excel & Word • SWIFT • DTC

SPEAKING ENGAGEMENTS & PROFESSIONAL AFFILIATIONS

Guest speaker, Presidents Business Circle Luncheon: *"How the Financial Sector is Fighting the War for Talent"*
Guest speaker, Bankers' Business Annual Conference, President's Luncheon: *"Driving Value in Recession"*
Member, Vice Presidents' Advisory Council
US Representative, Group Executive Panel, ABC Bank

YOUR NAME

City, State | Phone Number | Email Address

SUPPLY CHAIN DIRECTOR

Lean Manufacturing | Internal & External Logistics | Distribution | Scheduling | Process Optimization
KPI Definition | Procurement | Inventory Management | Warehousing | Project Management

Seven-year track record of pioneering solutions and optimizing industrial performance across international markets, spanning numerous industry sectors. History of generating exceptional improvements in costs, quality, lead time and delivery in fast-paced environments. Talent for inspiring teams to deliver on goals.

Speak Native French, Fluent English & Creole, Proficient German.

PROFESSIONAL EXPERIENCE

COMPANY NAME, CITY, STATE   Date–Date

Senior Consultant / Project Manager for premier global consulting company specializing in lean manufacturing and known for expertise in supply chain management. Signature consulting projects:

ABC Company, City, State, Country

Challenge: Spearhead external logistics and scheduling for client's urgent transition to new supplier at a start-up plant and root cause analysis on production side; provide expertise on internal logistics processes.

Actions:
➢ Designed and launched External Logistics System and scheduling processes during supplier transfer.
➢ Directed team to execute Downtime Measuring System for 3 production lines and root cause analysis.

Results:
➢ Ramped-up from 0 to 110 chassis per day within 8 months.
➢ Enhanced internal logistics processes (e.g., supermarket and kitting).
➢ Attained deadline for executing processes and training; seamlessly transitioned with no service disruption.

DEF Company, City, State, Country

Challenge: Define and introduce solutions to improve overall supply chain, including production scheduling process; external / internal logistics; disruption and inventory levels; service quality; and client satisfaction.

Action:
➢ Replaced push system with pull-system on a cab production line.

Results:
➢ Reduced layout surfaces used by 60%. Decreased parts diversity at point of use by 75%. Achieved record of 0 parts disruption since the implementation.

Actions:
➢ Implemented external material controlling process and automated the expediting process; trained 10 expediters and coached their manager.
➢ Initiated system to track and measure supplier performance.
➢ Created and formalized Lean Manufacturing training game used to train management team.
➢ Optimized paint department production booth scheduling process, which included tool and user training.

Results:
➢ Slashed supplier performance analysis processing time from 4 hours to 15 minutes.
➢ Decreased number of suppliers having a delivery precision of less than 80% from 59 to 32 in 34 weeks.
➢ Cut in half number of suppliers disrupting the plant in 34 weeks.
➢ Reduced paint scheduling disturbances from 14 to less than 1.5 per week within 8 weeks.

continued

GHI Company, City, State, Country

Challenge: Provide vision and targets for ramp-up of a new production line with new product. Lead 2 sub-projects: workforce and workflow organization; and total productive maintenance system definition.

Actions:

➤ Designed ramp-up vision and target, which included phases, milestones, volume and product mix.
➤ Created various scenarios for manufacturing workforce which enabled client to choose ideal scheme.
➤ Established physical and information flows for the new production line.
➤ Defined total productive maintenance system; trained TPM leader on deployment / piloting of system.

Results:

➤ Maximized overall equipment efficiency and achieved built in performance.
➤ Enabled successful client deployment by designing appropriate roadmaps.

Challenge: Assess risks / opportunities related to SAP deployment and implement risk mitigation strategies.

Actions:

➤ Coached supply chain manager and provided multi-lingual training to team (German and English) to ensure full autonomy using SAP for distribution activities. Assessed risk and built contingency plan.

Results:

➤ Achieved 95%+ supply chain quality of service during the SAP go-live.

JKL Company, City, State, Country

Challenge: Accept appointment as Chief Quality Project Manager for an entire brand. Implement Quality Journal ("QJ") process (8D process equivalent) to resolve market quality problems. Chair QJ decision body to determine whether to open quality actions.

Actions:

➤ Installed monitoring tools and KPIs to track QJ budget and measure lead time and efficiency.
➤ Implemented change management strategies to transition 2 organizations to new processes.

Results:

➤ Launched the QJ process on target and gained full acceptance for process change in both organizations.
➤ Transitioned process to the internal Quality Chief Project Manager.

MNO Company, City, State, Country

Challenge: As Supply Chain Director, resolve delivery precision and supply chain performance shortcomings having negative effect on relations with a major customer.

Actions:

➤ Designed, implemented and automated procurement management system. Defined KPIs.
➤ Trained and defined roles and responsibilities for procurement team of 10 in German.
➤ Implemented production alerts and supplier backlog management.

Results:

➤ Expedited parts supply; reduced shortages and backlogs; boosted/turned around customer satisfaction.

EDUCATION

Master of Science, (Supply chain management), School, City, State (Date)
Bachelor of Science, (Industrial engineering), School, City, State (Date)

YOUR NAME

Phone Number | Email Address
LinkedIn Profile | City, ST, Zip Code

Targeted Role: **Property Manager**

Leverage Property Management experience along with expertise in learning and implementing new software. Excel at growing revenues, increasing occupancy rates, and employing cost-saving initiatives.

LEASING ♦ PROJECT MANAGEMENT ♦ NEGOTIATION ♦ BUDGETING ♦ VENDOR RELATIONS
ASSET MANAGEMENT ♦ PROBLEM SOLVING ♦ LANDLORD/TENANT LAWS ♦ MARKETING

Process Improvement: Boosted productivity at XYZ AND ZYX companies by optimizing software to systemize lease renewals, vacancy reports, and legal letters.

Project Management: Completed 50+ renovation projects across 15 locations at ZYX company— coming in $45K under projected budget.

Relationship Management: Worked closely with tenants, asset managers, construction teams and vendors, improving tenant satisfaction, upgrading buildings, and surpassing profit goals.

PROFESSIONAL EXPERIENCE

COMPANY NAME, City, ST .... Year-Present
Property Manager
Directed team of 15-20 maintenance, housekeeping, leasing, grounds crew, and contract employees, which included hiring, training, and managing daily work expectations. Managed 900 units at five sites. Monitored quality control through regular inspection of units, grounds, amenities, and common areas.

Streamlined processes through implementation of rent manager software. Created forms for entire office to use that standardized procedures and provided important legal documentation.

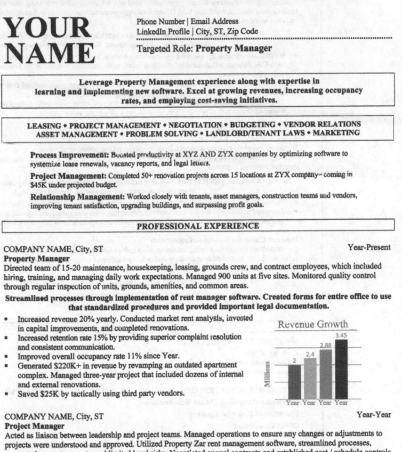

Revenue Growth

- Increased revenue 20% yearly. Conducted market rent analysis, invested in capital improvements, and completed renovations.
- Increased retention rate 15% by providing superior complaint resolution and consistent communication.
- Improved overall occupancy rate 11% since Year.
- Generated $220K+ in revenue by revamping an outdated apartment complex. Managed three-year project that included dozens of internal and external renovations.
- Saved $25K by tactically using third party vendors.

COMPANY NAME, City, ST .... Year-Year
Project Manager
Acted as liaison between leadership and project teams. Managed operations to ensure any changes or adjustments to projects were understood and approved. Utilized Property Zar rent management software, streamlined processes, generated accurate reports, and limited legal risks. Negotiated annual contracts and established cost / schedule controls.

Exceeded goal of 50+ projects (Year). Researched, implemented, and maintained project management tool to organize and track progress for start-ups, inspections, quality monitoring, and invoicing.

- Produced $40K in cost savings on $7M project encompassing 55 locations. Diversified vendors, lowering costs, and trimming completion date by two weeks.
- Saved $4,000/year in labor and part costs by updating antiquated laundry lock cylinders.
- Enhanced functionality and lowered maintenance costs by replacing aging intercom system.

continued

YOUR NAME
Phone Number | Email Address

COMPANY NAME, City, ST   Year-Year
Residential Portfolio Manager
Coordinated operations of 40-unit multi-family property, which included providing customer service, supervising maintenance team, and utilizing YARDI and Realpages property management software. Managed responses to rental inquiries and conducted tours.

**Covered for coworker during six-month leave. Managed both jobs eliminating
the need to hire a replacement. Worked 60-70 hours per week.**

- Revitalized community – serving on University Avenue Redevelopment Committee (Year). Committee partnered with City Planner, which included obtaining public input, deciding best use of the land, and implementing redevelopment plan.
- Oversaw onboarding/offboarding of 80+ properties; fulfilled paperwork, entered data in YARDI software, transferred utilities, and communicated with tenants.
- Decreased work order time-to-fill by 4 days. Instituted new order processing system that prioritized orders by tenant need and risk of problem escalation to more efficiently serve tenants.

COMPANY NAME, City, ST   Year-Year
Account Manager / Logistics Sales   Year-Year
Managed and grew existing accounts. Built long-term relationships, established new services, and expanded service offerings. Used internal tools to develop pricing strategies. Collaborated with leadership, created business reviews, and directed customer meetings.

**Increased revenue $300K (Year) – tripling expectations. Expanded business by cold-calling clients, targeting
start-up customers, and expanding flatbed offerings.**

- Earned **New Employee Spotlight Award** for exceeding performance standards (Year) and contributing to team.
- Recruited to train 35+ team members on implementing sales processes, pricing, and generating leads.
- Studied to understand market / service patterns to better negotiate rates between carriers and customers.

Inbound Customer Service Representative   Year -Year
Developed and maintained strong customer relationships by anticipating problems and working proactively to find solutions. Multi-tasked daily operations and ran 3 to 4 different programs simultaneously while answering customer calls and promoting services.

Selected for high-stress / high-accountability Fortune 500 account.

- Saved $50K annually by devising a creative backhaul utilization plan.
- Answered 40+ inbound calls per day in fast-paced, dynamic environment.

EDUCATION & TRAINING

UNIVERSITY OF NAME | CITY, ST

Bachelor of Arts
Major – Business Administration
Minor – Real Estate

NATIONAL ASSOCIATION OF RESIDENTIAL PROPERTY MANAGERS (NARPM)
Developing Rewarding Owner Relationships   Year
Essentials of Risk Management   Year
OSHA Compliance   Year

YOUR NAME

City, State • Phone Number • Email Address

SENIOR SALES REPRESENTATIVE

Sales authority driving brand awareness, redefining new product possibilities, and nurturing relationships that ensure rapid territory growth and a boost in competitive edge.

Business Development | Sales Territory Expansion | Profit & Revenue Amplification

Award-winning, high-impact business leader and sales expert instrumental in igniting market share, driving industry expansion, outperforming financial guidelines, and surpassing shareholder expectations. Unstoppable world-class negotiator who delivers record wins with exceptional finesse and seals the deal in record time. Recognized for setting strategic direction and employing game-changing sales methodology to guarantee record-pacing market growth.

Core Strengths

Business Transformations | Solution-Based Selling | Contract Negotiations | Strategic Partnership Building
New Product Launches | Lead Generation | Marketing Campaign Management | Global Market Research & Analysis

Accolades

Multiple award recipient throughout stellar sales career:

- → **$300K Commission Club Award (YEAR)**
- → **$200K Commission Club Award (YEAR)**
- → **$100K Commission Club Award (YEAR)**

- → **National Sales Glamour Award (YEAR)**
- → **$150K Commission Club Award (YEAR)**
- → **Breakthrough Sales Rep of the Year Award (YEAR)**

Career & Sales Narrative

COMPANY NAME – City, ST

Membership Manager | Date–Date

Scope & Challenge: Brought on board to accelerate and facilitate growth surge of ~150-member portfolio by utilizing consultative selling approach and offering superb member services. Furnished hands-on leadership and direction in key role affecting retention analysis and corrective action planning. Broke through customer dissatisfaction and inadequate resources to transcend customer retention standards.

- → **Topped member retention benchmarks 95%** by partnering with program directors to create annual strategic retention plan which eradicated member complaints and dissatisfaction.

- → **Launched 5-member committee which developed and engineered marketing strategies,** orchestrated and analyzed member survey results, and safeguarded against program compliance violations.

- → **Yielded revenue boost 12%** which were attained by exceeding member expectations, boosting membership value, increasing workshop sales promotions, and executing foolproof marketing strategies.

Boosted revenue
12%

continued

COMPANY NAME – City, ST

Medical Device Sales Consultant | Date–Date

Scope & Challenge: Handpicked to manage multimillion-dollar pharmaceutical sales territory and execute cutting-edge business methodology that increased profit potential, reduced operational inefficiencies, and propelled client demand. Built and nurtured relationships with medical leaders in orthopedic, pain management, and rheumatology specialties, throughout sales life cycle. Concluded tenure with 20% market share boost.

→ **Sustained 94% close rate** while expanding business territory and securing several high-profile clients in first year, with multiyear renewal commitments.

→ **Expanded value of pharmaceutical accounts $25M** by leading 20-member sales team in performing aggressive and simultaneous promotions during company-sponsored events.

→ **Solidified trust and sales mastery,** penetrated foreign markets and promoted trailblazing, first-to-market products.

→ **Converted multimillion-dollar client** from less expensive and unsanctioned Canadian supplier.

→ **Re-engaged largest US military account as orthopedic drug client** by working one-on-one with physicians and creating value and demand throughout 10-month sales cycle.

Additional Sales Excellence (Date–Date)

COMPANY NAME – City, ST

Served as **Pharmaceutical Sales Representative,** becoming **#1-ranked sales representative** in district for 4 years straight.

→ **Ranked #1 in district** for market share change *(2004, 2003).*

→ **Ranked #1 in district** for national teleconference and e-Detail recruitments *(2002).*

→ **Ranked #1 in district** in national sales contest for market share change *(2001).*

Education

Bachelor of Science in Business Management
School, City, State

Chapter **16**

OnTarget Resumes by Experience and Age

Have reason to think that you have too much experience — or not enough — for the job you want? Or that you're too young — or too old? The sample resumes in this chapter show techniques aimed at making your resume just right for your age and experience level.

REMEMBER

These examples represent individual people and their unique experiences; they are provided only as an example of what is possible in a resume. Please consider them as roadmaps — not rules — in creating your next resume.

TIP

As you review these resumes, note that I have made it possible for you to see yourself in them while also protecting the identity of the original job seekers who agreed to have their resumes fictionalized. To do this, I have made certain stylistic choices for all the resumes:

>> The job seeker's name appears as *Your Name* at the top of the resume and as *NAME* when mentioned in a testimonial quote. These indicate where you should refer to yourself.

>> Contact information is shown with the words *City, State, Zip Code, Phone,* and *Email.* This is where you would place your contact information.

>> Employment dates (and education dates, when included) use the word *Date*. This is where you would list your years of employment or the year you earned a credential.

>> Job descriptions do not list actual company names. Instead, you'll see *Company Name, Hospital Name,* and the like. This is where you would list your employer's company name.

>> If a year is stipulated, such as *Won this award in 2015,* the word *Year* has been substituted for the actual date.

YOUR NAME

Street Address, City, State, Zip
☎ Phone Number | ✉ Email Address

"NAME is truly dedicated to public service and consistently goes above and beyond to assist our constituents and his colleagues...a real asset to our team."
– The Hon. Any Congressman, XYZ District

LEGISLATIVE STAFF ASSISTANT CANDIDATE

Self-motivated political science graduate with experience in demanding, fast-paced legislative environment and knowledge of current policy issues. Proven ability to interface effectively with diverse constituents, handle high volume of correspondence for Congressional District Office, and assist with diverse casework. Known for calm under pressure and strong work ethic; excelled in degree studies and internship while working full-time and earning promotion.

Constituent Communications & Casework ▪ Outreach Campaigns ▪ Research & Statistical Analysis

Event Planning & Organization ▪ Administrative Support ▪ Intranet Quorum / MS Office

Additional Knowledge, Skills, and Training: International Affairs ▪ Labor & American Politics ▪ Urban American Politics ▪ Race, Gender & American Politics ▪ American Foreign Policy ▪ Advanced Topics in Quantitative Research ▪ Design & Analysis of Public Opinion Polls ▪ Independent Research Project on XYZ (presented and debated)

EDUCATION

Bachelor of Science in Political Science, XYZ University, City, State

RELATED EXPERIENCE

OFFICE OF ANY CONGRESSMAN, City, State   Date–Date
Congressional Intern

Office of the U.S. Representative serving five counties of State's ABC Congressional District with diverse population of 200,000.

Key Contributions:

▶ Monitored, accurately summarized, and prioritized constituent phone calls, mail, and faxes, and drafted correspondence utilizing Intranet Quorum; reported opinion trends to Congressman and Press Secretary during weekly meetings.

▶ Entrusted with tasks outside the scope of intern duties based on proven professionalism and knowledge of legislative issues; assisted constituents by responding to questions and concerns relating to ABC Act and XYZ Act.

▶ Selected by supervisor to lead team of four interns on 6-week research project to update outdated contact list, establishing foundation for increased community outreach and engagement.

▶ Instructed constituents on administrative processes to expedite issue resolution with federal agencies including Social Security Administration, Health & Human Services, Veterans Affairs, and Citizenship & Immigration Services.

▶ Praised by Congressman for serving as his representative at community events to raise visibility and generate goodwill.

ADDITIONAL WORK EXPERIENCE (TO SUPPORT STUDY)

COMPANY NAME, City, State   Date–Date
Manager (Date–Date)
Customer Service Associate (Date–Date)

Specialty retailer with 250+ locations across 15 states. Promoted to Manager after only eight months of hire based on demonstrated initiative, reliability, and skill in motivating staff.

Key Contributions:

▶ Ranked among top 10% of employees nationwide in sales.

▶ Earned distinction among peers and improved service quality by volunteering to complete highest level of product training on personal time and proactively researching and analyzing product data to better educate customers.

▶ Sparked 15% increase in targeted brand sales in first year on the job by actively promoting preferred suppliers' products.

▶ Coordinated and disseminated schedules for 10 staff members to ensure adequate coverage, tracked budget, trained all new hires on opening and closing procedures, and managed day-to-day logistics.

Your Name
City, State Zip
Phone Number
Email Address

TARGET ROLE: DOMESTIC BUILDING APPRENTICE – CARPENTRY

Hard-working and extremely motivated domestic building and construction graduate now seeking a carpentry apprenticeship where two years work experience will be an asset to expand on. Easy-going but unafraid to ask questions, with a self-determination to ensure each task is fully understood before commencing.

Experienced and confident in safe use of a variety of building implements (including power tools) across various domestic building duties, as accredited by White Card. Keen to be challenged in an apprenticeship role that enables continual learning about carpentry trade.

KEY SKILLS

- Construction of internal and external carpentry structures
- Qualified in the skills and knowledge to implement healthy and safety in the workplace
- Self-assured power tool usage
- Ability to resolve issues via stakeholder communications
- Proven ability to balance competing work and study commitments
- Capability to self-commute to various locations with ownership of a driver's licence

EDUCATION & TRADE QUALIFICATIONS

- **Construction Industry White Card** to meet the implementation regulations of the National Code of Practice for Induction for Construction Work
- **Certificate I Carpentry Pre-apprenticeship** – College Name, City, ST
- **Certificate II Carpentry Pre-apprenticeship** – College Name, City ST

BUILDING TOOLS EXPERIENCE

Nail gun	Fixer gun	Drill press
Coil gun	Electric drill	Ramset gun
Drill drop saw	Circular saw	Reciprocating saw

EMPLOYMENT HISTORY

COMPANY NAME   Date – Date
Domestic Building Apprentice/Laborer

Working on a part-time basis while completing [Course Name], role involved various labor duties associated with a first-year carpentry apprentice.

- Demolished and cleared former structures.
- Constructed external framing structures, including new homes, extensions, renovations, decks/pergolas and carports.
- Constructed and renovated internal framing structures, including bathrooms and kitchens.
- Assisted in planning stage of projects.

COMPANY NAME   Date – Date
Assistant (part-time)

Worked at [Company Name] while completing studies and gaining experience in the domestic building industry. Various duties included cleaning the store's interior and equipment, including handling and washing of meat trays. Also referred customers to relevant sales staff for product and pricing queries.

COMPANY NAME   Date – Date
Food Preparer/Waiter (part-time)

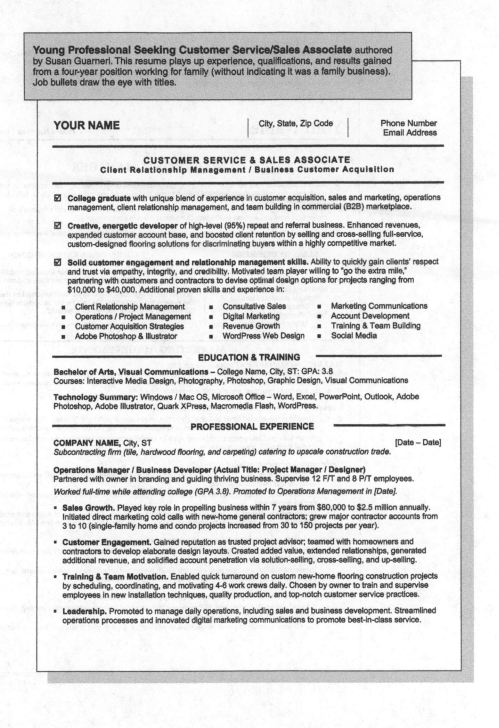

Young Professional Seeking Customer Service/Sales Associate authored by Susan Guarneri. This resume plays up experience, qualifications, and results gained from a four-year position working for family (without indicating it was a family business). Job bullets draw the eye with titles.

YOUR NAME

City, State, Zip Code | Phone Number
Email Address

CUSTOMER SERVICE & SALES ASSOCIATE
Client Relationship Management / Business Customer Acquisition

☑ **College graduate** with unique blend of experience in customer acquisition, sales and marketing, operations management, client relationship management, and team building in commercial (B2B) marketplace.

☑ **Creative, energetic developer** of high-level (95%) repeat and referral business. Enhanced revenues, expanded customer account base, and boosted client retention by selling and cross-selling full-service, custom-designed flooring solutions for discriminating buyers within a highly competitive market.

☑ **Solid customer engagement and relationship management skills.** Ability to quickly gain clients' respect and trust via empathy, integrity, and credibility. Motivated team player willing to "go the extra mile," partnering with customers and contractors to devise optimal design options for projects ranging from $10,000 to $40,000. Additional proven skills and experience in:

- Client Relationship Management
- Operations / Project Management
- Customer Acquisition Strategies
- Adobe Photoshop & Illustrator
- Consultative Sales
- Digital Marketing
- Revenue Growth
- WordPress Web Design
- Marketing Communications
- Account Development
- Training & Team Building
- Social Media

EDUCATION & TRAINING

Bachelor of Arts, Visual Communications – College Name, City, ST: GPA: 3.8
Courses: Interactive Media Design, Photography, Photoshop, Graphic Design, Visual Communications

Technology Summary: Windows / Mac OS, Microsoft Office – Word, Excel, PowerPoint, Outlook, Adobe Photoshop, Adobe Illustrator, Quark XPress, Macromedia Flash, WordPress.

PROFESSIONAL EXPERIENCE

COMPANY NAME, City, ST   [Date – Date]
Subcontracting firm (tile, hardwood flooring, and carpeting) catering to upscale construction trade.

Operations Manager / Business Developer (Actual Title: Project Manager / Designer)
Partnered with owner in branding and guiding thriving business. Supervise 12 F/T and 8 P/T employees.
Worked full-time while attending college (GPA 3.8). Promoted to Operations Management in [Date].

- **Sales Growth.** Played key role in propelling business within 7 years from $80,000 to $2.5 million annually. Initiated direct marketing cold calls with new-home general contractors; grew major contractor accounts from 3 to 10 (single-family home and condo projects increased from 30 to 150 projects per year).

- **Customer Engagement.** Gained reputation as trusted project advisor; teamed with homeowners and contractors to develop elaborate design layouts. Created added value, extended relationships, generated additional revenue, and solidified account penetration via solution-selling, cross-selling, and up-selling.

- **Training & Team Motivation.** Enabled quick turnaround on custom new-home flooring construction projects by scheduling, coordinating, and motivating 4-6 work crews daily. Chosen by owner to train and supervise employees in new installation techniques, quality production, and top-notch customer service practices.

- **Leadership.** Promoted to manage daily operations, including sales and business development. Streamlined operations processes and innovated digital marketing communications to promote best-in-class service.

Your Name

Phone Number | Email Address

MARKETING MANAGER

➢ Savvy professional offering eight years of top marketing leadership experience and repeated success aligning marketing efforts to strategic business goals to grow revenue and company market share. MBA in Marketing.

➢ Excel at bringing structure, standards, and processes to optimize productivity and take marketing organizations to the next level and support businesses in unstable market environments.

➢ Expertise in pushing strategies through the organization and rallying teams around a common goal.

AREAS OF EXPERTISE	PROFESSIONAL ENDORSEMENTS
Corporate Marketing Leadership Brand Management & Communications Marketing Project Management Strategic Business Planning Ecommerce Strategy Email/Promotional Campaigns Content Generation	"She has the **vision, the technical understanding and the management skills** to lead our projects to a successful conclusion." "**I find her marketing mind to be instrumental in the success of the programs I manage.** She sees the big picture quickly and provides the strategic plan, tools and presence needed." ***Read more endorsements on LinkedIn.***

MARKETING ACHIEVEMENTS

MARKETING MANAGER ● Company Name, City, ST   Date–Present

Recruited to improve marketing department through process and positioning for company sales growth. Supervised marketing and ecommerce team of four employees and managed corporate ecommerce strategy, email campaigns, branding, corporate planning, and content generation.

Introduced marketing strategy and structure

- Brought much-needed focus and strategy to the marketing department. Worked with company owner to define expectations, prioritize initiatives, and ensure marketing efforts aligned with corporate goals.
- Expanded email and promotional campaigns by establishing company's first sustained editorial calendar and formal promotion planning process.

Grew annual ecommerce sales 10%–15%

- Enhanced website usability / functionality and customer experience; collaborated with ecommerce manager to define and implement strategy.
- Participated in launch of paid online marketing strategy, which has positively impacted sales and spurred further investment.
- Minimized abandoned shopping carts by initiating and leading development of automated email campaign. Utilized targeted campaign to reminder shoppers of abandoned carts and auto-send discount offer.

Enhanced sales materials to drive market penetration

- Created and planned distribution of integrated card binder that captured 200% first-year revenue growth in the product line.
- Improved quality of sample pack program which supported brand image, reused content, reduced collateral expenses, and represented features of more than 24,000 products.

Championed cross-functional initiatives to support the business

- Selected and implemented new ERP system, which involved cross-departmental planning, discovery, and sourcing during 6-month selection process.
- Coordinated transfer of pre-press position to production department to sharpen focus of marketing group.

Your Name

Marketing Achievements, Continued

MARKETING MANAGER • Company Name, City, ST .... Date–Date
Brought on board to provide strategic marketing and business leadership in a mature industry. Aligned marketing strategy and tactics to meet corporate objectives.

Guided department through a shrinking market
- Maintained marketing functions as budget decreased and department was downsized from 4 to 1 employee.
- Developed company's first-ever new product development process, which enable staged development with limited resources and minimal risk, and helped company better compete in a changing market.
- Enabled 80% annual client retention by creating and distributing packaged collateral and original content, which included data-rich articles, success stories, and tips for maximizing research investment.
- Maximized existing resources by seeking out cost-reduction opportunities:
  o Reduced postage costs by nearly 40% by incorporating postal discounts.
  o Slashed printing costs 50% by integrating more efficient production procedures.

Gained competitive advantages through new product development
- Drove development of an industry-first product that addressed unmet customer needs.
- Played key role in major initiative to develop online gift giving service with automated fulfillment of hundreds of incentives annually.

MARKETING SPECIALIST / MANAGER • Company Name, City, ST .... Date–Date
Promoted from Marketing Assistant to Marketing Specialist/Manager to lead the corporate marketing department of three employees.

Strengthened company-wide marketing efforts
- Coordinated marketing activities for 9 offices throughout the Midwest, including seminar events, trade show/conference exhibits, sales collateral, newsletter generation, direct mailings, and advertising plans.
- Maximized resources at trade shows by auditing participation.

■ ■ ■ ADDITIONAL EXPERIENCE ■ ■ ■

PUBLIC RELATIONS DIRECTOR & PROMOTIONS STAFF • Company Name, City, ST
- Produced and edited monthly newsletter, and coordinated promotional events.

MARKETING ASSISTANT • Company Name, City, ST
- Managed publication of proposals/reports and drafted advertisements for trade publications.

EDUCATION

Master of Business Administration (MBA)
Emphasis in Marketing
University, City, ST

Bachelor of Science in Speech Communication, *cum laude*
Emphasis in Public Relations
University, City, ST

YOUR NAME

Phone Number | Email address

INTERNATIONAL MARKETING & STRATEGY EXECUTIVE

"James is an inspirational powerhouse... his entrepreneurship, initiative and drive to be successful is something to be admired and aspire to..." – Co-Founder, Company Name

Digital Marketing ▪ Global Market Expansion ▪ Business Development ▪ Promotional Campaigns Product Development & Launch ▪ Relationship Management

Commercially focused "intrapreneur" with 14+ years of experience in business start-ups, corporate and agency environments, with a focus on digital marketing arena. Unique combination of business realism and creativity drives marketing and business development projects throughout a multifaceted career spanning product and brand development in the digital marketing space, strategic and tactical B2B sales planning, client and agency relationship development, cross-functional leadership and training.

A strong revenue generator with successes in multinational client development, management, and competitive retention; acknowledged for building and leading powerful marketing, product and business development initiatives globally.

VALUE OFFERED

- Digital Marketing Strategies
- Key Account Management
- Product Marketing & Development
- Project Management
- Business-to-Business Sales
- Human Resources & Talent Management
- Cross-Functional Team Leadership
- Global Market Expansion
- Strategic Planning & Change Management

- Client & Partner Relationship Management
- Business Process Re-engineering
- Campaign & Integrated Marketing Development
- Revenue Generation & Cost Containment
- Brand Marketing & Development
- Public Relations & Stakeholder Engagement
- Business Development & Start-ups
- Networking & Influential Negotiations
- Staff Training & Development

CAREER SNAPSHOT

COMPANY NAME, City, State Country, **Marketing Director / Managing Director,** *Founder*	Date–Present
COMPANY NAME, City, State Country, **Operations Director,** *Founder*	Date–Date
COMPANY NAME, City, State Country, **Head of Digital Marketing**	Date–Date
COMPANY NAME, City, State Country, **Senior Marketing Manager**	Date–Date

EDUCATION

Master of Entrepreneurship and Innovation
University Name

Bachelor of Business, eCommerce
University Name

Diploma of Business, Marketing
College Name

Project Success Story:

Infiltrated the Singapore market to increase **Facebook Likes from zero to 12,500+ in 3 weeks, with 9+ minutes of average engagement**, on the Company "Story Friend" project. Designed a viral story writing competition whereby bookworms could join together to create their own team image, mascot, and story.

YOUR NAME

ACHIEVEMENTS IN-FOCUS

COMPANY NAME   Date–Present

Global leader in app strategy, design and development for mobile, smartphones, tablets, and Facebook application development, operating across Asia, Australia and the UK with apps being launched worldwide.

Marketing Director / Managing Director

Established Effectivity in Year and successfully built social and mobile business into a high margin, lucrative enterprise while travelling extensively worldwide. Designed, developed, and launched custom social media and mobile applications for UK, Asia, and Australian markets for some of the regions' most esteemed corporate brands.

Key Clients:

345 Company |
Your Company |
The Company |
Best Company |

Selected Highlights:

- **Designed a total of 43 sophisticated social and mobile apps** within extremely tight deadlines, all while traveling globally, including concept, architecture, design, development, social integration, testing, and launch. **Achieved product margins in excess of 65% and YOY business growth for every project.**

- **Triumphed over traditional well-established agencies to win business of many high profile, multinational, billion dollar clients** due to outstanding industry reputation and strategic sales / marketing campaigns.

- **Sourced, recruited and developed high quality cross-functional teams** globally and leveraged / developed talent remotely to deliver best of breed solutions.

- **Tracked down and partnered with industry experts** dotted around globe in order to obtain best possible outcomes in app design and development.

- **Achieved Google top 3 position for all high intention keywords** across UK, Singapore, and Australia through developing and executing winning SEO strategies.

Video Company |
Title Company |
Pet Food
Company | Radio
Company | Hotel
& Leisure
Company | Travel
Company |
Finance Company

> **Project Success Story:**
>
> Created Client Name's "Mark My Ride" app, for lovers of modified cars. Due to overwhelming success of app, was engaged to design 2 further versions, resulting in **95,000+ Facebook Likes and 3,500+ insurance leads**.

COMPANY NAME   Date–Date

Full service, multidisciplinary digital agency specializing in all features of digital marketing services including websites, mini-sites, UX web designs, and app development.

Operations Director (Co-Founder)

Partnered with high profile clients to develop strategic multi-channel marketing programs that paved way for rapid business and revenue growth.

Key Clients:

ABC Company |
123 Company |
XYZ Company |
Flowers Company
| Jet Company |
Juice Company |
Temp Agency |
Design Company |
Wine Company

Selected Highlights:

- **Boosted search related sales by 134%** for Client Name through re-establishing powerful PPC campaigns.

- **Increased organic traffic by 51% YOY, and online sales by 42% in 6 months ($2.8 million in attributable PPC sales)** for Client Name.

- Created the Beetroot and Apple campaign for Client Name; the company **won Woman's Weekly magazine's Product of the Year Award** as a direct result.

YOUR NAME, MBA

VP/Director of Contracts

Phone Number ▪ Email Address ▪ City, ST Zip

CORPORATE RISK MITIGATION ▪ GLOBAL OPPORTUNITY BUILDING ▪ INTERCULTURAL RELATIONS

Linchpin negotiator who <u>secured career high $220M international contract</u> and preserved critical year-end fiscal targets
20 Years' Defense Industry Background ▪▪▪ Active Security Clearance

Recognized authority on government, commercial, and international contracts as multidisciplinary business strategist and high-profile tactical leader for Global 500 defense contractors. Advise board and C-level decision makers on the realities and practicalities of diverse business operations affecting enterprise risk management and P&L, embedding policies and procedures to avert legal, financial, reputational, and geopolitical risk. Situational leader, skilled in overcoming performance inertia and project crisis by building solidarity between disparate groups with conflicting agendas.

LEADERSHIP SUCCESS HIGHLIGHTS

- **Won $100M pivotal overseas defense contract** and yielded gross margin of 32% to initial 16% projections as In-Country Program Manager.

- **Prevented termination of 6-year, $300M contract** by traveling to Middle East 9 days after 9/11 to solve technical issues and reclaim client confidence.

- Revived derailed program under threat of shutdown to claim **Most Valued Supplier award** after spearheading rigorous 3–year turnaround.

- **Unlocked gateway for $10s of millions in new defense contract awards** by guiding 5 marginal business units to receive "Superior" defense security ratings—feat achieved by only 6% of all security-cleared companies.

GEOGRAPHIC BUSINESS INSIGHT: Lived and worked in U.S., Germany, Egypt, and UAE with executive business dealings with foreign governments and subcontractors in 24 countries across the Americas, Europe, Africa, the Middle East, and Asia Pacific.

LEADERSHIP STRENGTHS

Strategic Planning / Execution

High-Stakes Negotiations

Risk Analysis / Mitigation

Executive Program Oversight

Business Transformation

9-Figure Budget Administration

Succession Planning

JVs / Strategic Alliances

M&A / Startup Operations

International Business & Diplomatic Protocol

CAREER SUMMARY & SUCCESSES

Corporate Director of Contracts ▪ [Date – Date]
COMPANY NAME ▪ City, ST
$600M U.S. division of U.K.-based, $1.2B world leader in high-tech security solutions; 8 U.S. business units (BUs), 12 sites, and 2,100 staff.

— Negotiated revenue-propelling contracts with **Defense Company, Aeronautical Agency, NATO members, prime defense contractors (Company Name, Company Name),** and various Middle Eastern & Asian governments. —

— Scope of executive authority included: domestic and international contracts/project manager; corporate information security / facility security officer (FSO); corporate export compliance officer (ECO); foreign sales support director. —

Enduring Successes

→ Aligned 8 BUs to system-level compliance, security, and contract standards in record time.

→ Fast-tracked $24M year-end payments; saved $4M contract and company rep.

Capitalized on international contracting and export experience to assist U.S. startup division venture into foreign markets while protecting its contractual position on $600M contracts and briefing BoD, C-suite leadership, and corporate GC on how to avoid various levels of high risk. **Launched corporate-wide export, contracts, and security compliance programs** with security processes and SOPs, and training program for 52-member team to strengthen business processes and realize favorable yearly U.S. government (USG) audits.

- Introduced aggressive Special Security Agreement that aligned entire division under single policy and raised compliance standards in 2 years to **achieve top defense security rating for 5 BUs in the same year**, rare 6% industry accomplishment.

- **Claimed critical $16M year-end invoice from USG**, bypassing normal channels to reverse initial management rejections and realign payment cycle.

continued

YOUR NAME | Page 1 of 2

Enduring Successes

→ Expanded global footprint in Middle Eastern market, securing $60M in contracts to yield 28%+ gross profit.

Corporate Director of Contracts, COMPANY NAME (continued)

- **Rushed $8M in errant invoices 12 hours before fiscal year end to hit profit and sales targets** via face-to-face negotiations with Saudi government and bank; rescued $4M German contract and calmed client via quick resolution of product issues.

- **Mitigated risk during 5 pre-acquisition reviews** as key advisor on merger and integration process; green-lighted $80M Saudi JV project after enforcing U.S. priorities of proposal, negotiations, signing, and management of contract.

Manager of Contracts ▪ [Date – Date]
COMPANY NAME ▪ City, ST
$33.9B Fortune Global 500 security giant providing solutions in unmanned systems, cybersecurity, C4ISR, and logistics.

Enduring Successes

→ Merged & stabilized $500M division, building and retaining high-caliber team.

→ Salvaged $300M at-risk contract to claim Most Valuable Supplier award at contract end and ignited $60M in added program sales.

Sought out to manage high-value commercial and government contracts in Latin America, Eastern Europe, and Middle East. Upon M&A activity, promoted after 1 year to transition and lead newly acquired, 12-person contract administration team from New York to processes and culture of metropolitan-based HQ. Given charge by SVP for 3-year special assignment to protect major international program that posed considerable risk, simultaneously **forecasting and managing budgets for $500M in corporate contracts.**

- **Thwarted cancellation of $300M contract with potential $1.6B in future losses:**
  - Assembled 20-member team for rapid-response technical troubleshooting to rescue tenuous client relationship and company's industry status.
  - **Avoided $35M in overrun penalties and $16M in profit losses** by re-negotiating terms.
  - **Landed and administered $60M in additional contracts,** plus defense offset agreements, after delivering overwhelming program success.

- **Persuaded USG to redact lowering of performance rating for key MG business unit** by bridging divide in communications and instituting weekly status reports between contract administrator and defense client's procurement representative.

- **Built and groomed top-flight group of emerging leaders** in newly merged department—66% of new hires into MG management positions—with culture-shift planning, training, merit programs, and metrics-driven performance management.

▪▪▪

— EARLIER EXPERIENCE —

Senior International Contract Administrator ▪ In-Country Program Manager
COMPANY NAME ▪ City, ST

Recruited by $400M multinational defense vehicle manufacturer based on domain expertise and high-impact sales history. **Structured language to win $100M commercial sale** in Egypt and subsequently selected to assume reins as in-country project manager on 36-month co-production contract. **Saved $3M via contract re-negotiations,** optimized throughput of 3 Egyptian factories, created strong client bonds, and gained deep perspective on international business etiquette and cross-cultural communications while managing contracts in Egypt, Saudi Arabia, Thailand, Kuwait, Greece, Italy, and Morocco; notable highlight includes **negotiating $220M commercial contract and offset program in Thailand.**

Marketing/Sales/Business Development Manager, COMPANY NAME ▪ City, Country

Secured several $10M single contracts, consistently **delivering $15M-20M of total annual revenue** for $65M manufacturer while **raising margins to 25%+** with new pricing strategies. Perfected skills in high-profit contract negotiations with prime contractors, several branches of U.S. armed forces, and foreign governments.

▪▪▪

CREDENTIALS

M.B.A., University Name ▪ **B.S. in Business Management,** University Name

Affiliations: National Contracts Management Association | International Association for Contract & Commercial Management (IACCM) | Society for International Affairs (SIA) | The Society of Industrial Security Professionals

Speaking Engagements: Invited to Year Contract Management in Aerospace & Defense Conference in Washington D.C., presenting on "International Commercial Contracting – Risk Mitigation" and understanding foreign cultures.

YOUR NAME

City, State	Phone Number	Email Address

MASTER OF ENVIRONMENTAL MANAGEMENT | BACHELOR OF SOCIAL SCIENCE & EDUCATION
TARGET: ENVIRONMENTAL SUSTAINABILITY & COMMUNITY ENGAGEMENT

"We are the environment" Quote: Charles Panati

Proactive Graduate offering practical experience in community engagement and education, which is underpinned with a passion for environmental sustainability. Leverages superior communication skills to develop, implement, and manage community presentations, including the creation of materials and resources that resonate with diverse audiences. Acknowledged for strengths disseminating complex information in an engaging manner, and through education, challenge students, and community groups to think about environmental management, raising awareness of critical issues.

- Environmental Sustainability
- Climate Change
- Environmental Impact

- Community Education
- Sustainable Development
- Natural & Water Resources

- Urban Ecology
- Conservation
- Ecosystems

"Name is one of the finest students I've had the pleasure to teach ... superior academic results ... resourceful and tenacious approach to finding opportunities to apply skills and gain experience ... " Dr. Name, University Name

QUALIFICATIONS

Master of Environmental Management | University Name, City ST

Bachelor of Social Science/Education | University Name, City ST
*Commendation for High Academic Achievement: Semesters 1&2 – Year, Year, and Year

RELEVANT EXPERIENCE

National Science Month Presenter | University Name, City ST [Date - Date]
Planned, prepared, and coordinated activities across three campuses to promote National Science Month, a program designed to showcase science. Confidently engaged students, teachers, parents, and community groups; educated, informed and shared knowledge to increase environmental awareness and generate interest in science with 'hands-on' experiments.

▶ Attracted large volumes of students throughout month-long program, exceeding previous year's attendance rate by 71%.

▶ Spearheaded development of innovative social media marketing strategies which increased reach, generated hype, and maximized exposure, resulting in 2,600+ new Facebook followers.

World Environment Day Coordinator | University Name, City ST [Date - Date]
Led a team of eight students to develop campus activities to promote awareness of World Environment Day (WED), with an emphasis on simple actions that make a difference in caring for the planet. Created and implemented an A-B-C campaign with three simple steps to promote environmental protection: **Ask** to carpool, **Bring** your own bags, and **Consume** smartly. Utilized a series of five strategy meetings to develop a plan, assign tasks, and monitor progress.

▶ Coordinated inaugural WED Car park Event; used space made available from carpooling to set up a mini exhibition complete with catering trucks, entertainment, and informative environmental stalls.

▶ Harnessed social media to create event advertisements, which increased awareness and interest in WED activities.

VOLUNTEER ACTIVITIES & COMMUNITY INVOLVEMENT

Youth Climate Change Council: Selected out of 50 applicants to present three-hour lectures to senior students in high schools across metropolitan area, promoting council's activities and initiatives, as well as membership.

*Commended for first-class presentation skills, engaging manner and ability to instill environmental awareness in youth.

YOUR NAME, MBA, CA

City, State | Phone | Email | LinkedIn Profile

SENIOR EXECUTIVE
CFO | President | CEO

Driving Organizational Change, Success, and Rapid Growth

VALUE CREATOR ~ BUSINESS ENABLER

Business Turnaround | Board Influence & Decision | Revenue & Profit Growth | Strategic Direction

Dedicated leader with a record of mastering tremendous growth and crisis challenges, leveraging a rich mix of operational and financial expertise in both publicly-traded and private equity-owned organizations. Recognized for driving improvements, advancements, and best practices to reach aggressive goals. Excel at building business models and teams based on sound strategy and vision, and boosting motivation and customer satisfaction. Highly ethical and articulate communicator; trusted advisor to a network of stakeholders.

Leadership & Financial Highlights from Company Name	Valued Expert in:
☑ Grew sales by $210M in six years.	Organizational Leadership
☑ Increased enterprise value by 102% in eight months.	Performance Management
☑ Captured 76% market share in six months.	Business & Market Development
☑ Championed 16 acquisitions to add $155M in sales.	Financial Planning & Analysis
☑ Spearheaded $95M initial public offering.	Productivity Initiatives
☑ Slashed $8.6M in costs with financial and operational improvements.	Mergers, Acquisitions & Integrations
☑ Refinanced $585M in syndicated debt facilities with U.S. and Canadian lenders.	Investor Relations
	Crisis Management

LEADERSHIP EVOLUTION

COMPANY NAME, City, State | Date – Date
North America's second largest manufacturer, marketer, and distributor of packaged salt.

Recruited to take financial reigns and lead recapitalization and restructuring; turned around underperforming financials and struggling lender relations, which rapidly expanded revenues and created strategic and tactical blueprints for continued growth. Promoted to CEO; helmed organization during period of financial crisis and eventual company sale in Year.

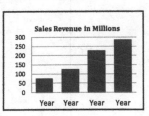

Sales Revenue in Millions

PRESIDENT & CHIEF EXECUTIVE OFFCER (CEO), Date – Date
EXECUTIVE VP & CHIEF FINANCIAL OFFICER (CFO), Date – Date
CHIEF FINANCIAL OFFICER (CFO), Date – Date

8 Direct Reports | 2,500 Employees | $285M Peak Sales | 75 Manufacturing Plants in North America

COMPANY NAME continued...

Financial Savvy:

- Painstakingly re-built lender relationships within first eight months and coordinated three-prong recapitalization; completed successful $95M IPO and magnified enterprise value by 102%.
- Raised profitability and reduced capital invested by $5M; led divestitures of four non-strategic business operations in Canada and U.S.

Strategic Leadership and Improvement:

- Delivered $8.6M in annual savings from operational efficiencies, productivity improvements, lower input costs, and 6% headcount reduction; implemented company-wide restructuring plan after sale.
- Updated and streamlined outdated accounting and reporting systems and processes; centralized 12 systems, which reduced month end closing from 60+ days to 8 days.

Business Expansion and Development:

- Acquired 16 companies, adding $155M in sales; coordinated $185M investment and corporate growth strategy, including valuating, due diligence, implementation, and integration.
- Captured $5.5M in revenue and 76% market share from competitors within six months; facilitated rapid and aggressive launch into new geographic market.

COMPANY NAME, City, State | **Date – Date**
Global business marketing meat products to over 70 countries around the world.

Promoted to direct all financial administration and reporting; managed financial controls, reporting, planning and budgeting. Reported to executive staff and Board and communicated with a variety of external stakeholders.

VP, ACCOUNTING & CORPORATE CONTROLLER, Date – Date
CORPORATE CONTROLLER, Date – Date

15 Direct Reports | 1,200 Employees | $3B Annual Sales | $6B in Assets and Investments

- Improved clarity and compliance of public company reporting; revised financial disclosure and introduced Management Discussion and Analysis of Operating Results (MD&A) reporting.
- Spearheaded introduction of first integrated accounting system; finalized multi-million dollar, multi-year ERP implementation ahead of schedule and 15% under budget.
- Re-engineered numerous financial and business processes; secured annual interest savings of $850K, increased working capital by $8M, and reduced staffing by 18%.

EDUCATION

Master of Business Administration; Finance – University Name
Bachelor of Commerce; Accounting (Honors) – University Name
Chartered Accountant – Association Name

YOUR NAME

Phone Number | Email Address
City, State Zip

SENIOR SALES & MERCHANDISING LEADER

Driving sales growth and brand awareness in highly competitive markets

Sales & Profit Growth
New Business Development
Marketing Campaigns
New Product Launch
People Development
Promotional Consumer Events
Industry Relationships

Industries: Beverage, Clothing, Beauty

Top-performing manager with repeated success driving double-digit sales growth by planning and implementing sales, marketing, merchandising, and buying programs.

History of penetrating new markets, launching new products, and collaborating with internal and external partners to consistently meet and/or exceed revenue and profitability goals.

CAREER HISTORY & ACHIEVEMENTS

COMPANY NAME   City, ST | Date–Present

Drive double-digit sales growth in $240M division with 1,450 brands sold in 40 markets nationwide

SENIOR MERCHANDISE MANAGER, BEER DIVISION (Date–Date)

Developed merchandising and product assortment strategies for division with $200 million annual revenue across three categories. Managed 1,450 brands from 500+ suppliers distributed to stores in 16 states.

- **Outperformed strong company growth**, beating sales and margin numbers for year to date:

Year to Date Performance	Sales Growth	Margin Growth
Beer Division	+20.9%	+34.5%
Company	+18.5%	+26.6%

- **Grew sales of seasonal beers 25% with 56% margin improvement** by streamlining store operations, launching new ordering system, and reducing markdowns by 43%.

- **Penetrated microbrew beer market to add $24 million in new sales.** Researched new breweries in 32 markets and adopted products from 300+ new suppliers.

- **Organized statewide event of unprecedented scale** which increased store traffic and sale, built awareness among customers, and created experiential events as a niche differentiator.
  - Worked with local and national breweries to offer limited-release products, consumer classes, and other events.
  - Achieved 23 publicity stories from 44 classroom events and 220+ in-store tastings with 30+ breweries in 5 stores.

SENIOR MERCHANDISE MANAGER, IMPORT DIVISION (Date–Date)
CATEGORY MANAGER, ASIA PACIFIC (Date–Date)

Developed and led team of nine import buyers to drive $350 million in annual revenue through an assortment of 8,000 wines from 500+ suppliers. Drove sales and margin improvements by establishing category review programs, championing cross-functional process improvements, and negotiating with producers, vendors, and distributors.

- **Launched new brand to U.S. market to generate $450,000 in first-year sales.** Created platform that was immediately adopted as a best practice and was used as a model for other major product launches in the company.

- **Grew gross margin opportunities for "white label" products from 0%-25% to 45%-70%** with some programs reaching as much as 90% penetration in selected categories.

- **Slashed $500K in costs** by revising ordering parameters and negotiating better payment dates with key vendor.

- **Developed strategic sales and marketing opportunities across multiple countries in the Asia Pacific region** and negotiated discounts to promote products without margin loss.

- **Negotiated $100,000 increase in annual government funding** to bolster advertising efforts in key/niche regions.

COMPANY NAME   City, ST | Date–Date

Transformed retail sales from a downward trend to represent 10% of total company sales

BRAND MANAGER

Challenged to grow retail sales for the nation's largest family-owned and operated chain of tanning salons with 800 locations in 16 states. Integrated merchandising and retail teams into this service-oriented business by introducing cross-team meetings, monthly field communications, and product training.

- **Grew retail sales to 10% of total company sales,** which halted a negative trend (-2.2% in 2006) to capture 4% growth in 2007 while simultaneously increasing margins by 2.1%.
- **Reduced overall inventory by 8% without impacting sales** by focusing on SKUs, representing top 50% of retail business and eliminating products at the bottom 20%.
- **Increased mark-up by 3.1% and gained vendor allowance of $165,000 over plan** by negotiating additional vendor support to fuel retail and service promotions.
- **Won Salesperson of the Year Award** in Year.

COMPANY NAME   City, ST | Date–Date

Ranked in top 10% in performance of all buyers companywide for 13 consecutive years

BUYER, PLANNER & ANALYST, HAIR CARE (Date–Date)

Promoted to manager of purchasing for a $61 million division, the company's largest office by volume. Managed and negotiated with eight vendors, each with distinct strategies and branding, in 81 stores and 19 markets.

- **Increased profitability by $800,000 in the first year** by streamlining processes and gaining promotional efficiencies.
- **Grew sales within the category's #3 vendor to $1.7 million (a 6.6% increase),** driving growth through promotions, education, and replenishment synergies.
- **Pushed revenue of ABC products to $8.6 million (a 179% increase)** by negotiating placement in 5 new locations.

BUYER, PLANNER & ANALYST, MEN'S SHOES (Date–Date)

Managed purchasing for the fastest-growing category across all ABC Company divisions with $7.6 million profit growth and 115% volume growth over 6 years. Managed relationships with 10 suppliers.

- **Assumed responsibility for Men's Shoes office that grew to $40 million,** largest shoes division in Company Name, which included 10 suppliers and a private label program.
- **Earned Buyer of the Year Award** for two consecutive years.

Early Career with Company Name includes roles as Buyer in the Shoes Category and Associate Business Manager in Hair Care Category. Additional experience included serving as Buyer and Area Sales Manager with Company Name.

EDUCATION & TRAINING

UNIVERSITY NAME, City, ST
BACHELOR OF SCIENCE IN MERCHANDISING

Completed management training courses/seminars, which included Divisional Management, Category Management, People Development, and Leadership Essentials

YOUR NAME

City, State | Phone Number | Email Address

QUALIFIED FOR CAPITAL MARKETS INTERNSHIP

IVY LEAGUE SCHOLARSHIP STUDENT
A-grade, trilingual student currently pursuing Master of Banking and Finance.

OUTSTANDING INTELLECT
Mensa member. Well-balanced qualitative and quantitative skills with exceptional research capabilities.

PRODUCT EXPERTISE
Cosmopolitan awareness of commodities markets, gained through specialist dissertation on commodity futures' prices combined with three internships in global investment banks.

FINANCIAL ACUMEN
Manage own lucrative equity portfolio with focus on banking and commodity sectors, generated 67% ROI in four years.

> "Name quickly became known as the intern to have on your team... sharp and commercially astute... with a natural aptitude for financial modeling and an advanced understanding of market forces on commodities pricing."
> Vice President,
> Company 123, NYC

PORTFOLIO OF KNOWLEDGE, EXPERIENCE & SKILLS

INTERNED AT:
COMPANY NAME,
COMPANY NAME,
COMPANY NAME

✓ FINANCIAL MODELING AND VALUATIONS ✓ EXCEL GURU

✓ COMMODITIES FUTURES ✓ MONTE CARLO SIMULATION

✓ FINANCIAL REGULATION ✓ GLOBAL CAPITAL MARKETS

ACADEMIC QUALIFICATIONS

DEAN'S LIST

WINNER, CITI
TRADING GAME

AWARDED KENNEDY
SCHOLARSHIP

CHARTERED FINANCIAL ANALYST PROGRAM
CFA Level III - Candidate Date
STATE UNIVERSITY - Date to Date
Master of Banking and Finance - GPA 3.89
- Specialization in Pricing Financial Instruments, Corporate Finance, Investment Management and Fixed Income
- Dissertation: "The Impact of Natural Disasters on Commodities Pricing."
Bachelor of Science, Economics and Banking, Joint Honors - *Summa Cum Laude*

KEY EXPERIENCE HIGHLIGHTS

COMPANY NAME, City, ST, Date to Date
SUMMER INTERN / TRADE SUPPORT, OIL FUTURES, COMMODITIES
Quickly positioned as "Lead Intern" to oversee all deal allocation for Oil Futures team in pressurized trading environment.
Analyzed large volumes of data and reported on divisional results to desk head.
Commercial Focus: Enabled sales teams to manage performance, enhance efficiency, and grow revenue by providing insightful risk and pricing analysis.
Error Minimization: Attained 100% accuracy of time critical, transaction data.
Innovation: Enhanced key investment decisions; generated clear advice to traders on the daily flows of their individual P&Ls; originated distribution of weekly MI report across team.

> Project managed and meticulously reconciled migration of all team transactions into new system.

continued

KEY EXPERIENCE HIGHLIGHTS (CONTINUED)

COMPANY NAME, CITY, ST, Date to Date

SUMMER INTERN, INVESTMENT BANKING DIVISION, OIL AND GAS

Specially selected to assist on high profile transaction. Exploited DCF methodology to model potential gas acquisition. Data produced was integral to subsequent deal execution of >$100M.

Financial Analysis: Performed P&L analysis of existing clients to ensure revenue projections on target. Included financial statement breakdown of one of Texas's most prominent oil companies.

Research and Reporting: Investigated the implications of Global Financial Crisis on the US oil markets. Delivered presentation of findings to management.

> Fast-tracked to deliver transaction support to senior bankers in all aspects of deal origination and execution following resignation of existing analyst.

COMPANY NAME, CITY, ST, Date to Date

SUMMER INTERN, COMMODITIES SETTLEMENTS

Challenged to respond to high-volume queries on outstanding trades and pricing valuations. Championed as "Top Performer" in the intern cohort and identified as "Rising Star" by management team.

Relationship Management: Closed all enquiries in record time. Encouraged client retention, generating additional revenue as a result.

Reporting Accuracy: Expanded role to include production of management reporting, which included full range of commodity instruments. Enjoyed flawless record with zero errors.

PART TIME EMPLOYMENT (TO SUPPORT STUDY)

COMPANY NAME, CITY, ST, Date to Date

MARKET RESEARCHER / TEAM LEADER

Doubled personal call targets for international market research firm.
Specially commended by MD for accuracy.

Communication Excellence: Smashed KPIs by building instant interview rapport. Ranked in the "Top 5 Departmental Performers."

Commercial Drive: Accomplished 25% year-on-year growth in departmental interview numbers.

Transformed Company Culture: Initiated weekly in-house competition and incentivized personnel to exceed targets.

> Boosted applications for market research roles by 50%.

ADDITIONAL LEADERSHIP EXPERIENCE

UNIVERSITY NAME, CITY, ST, Date to Date

MASTER OF BANKING AND FINANCE STUDENT, FULL TIME

Selected for leadership positions throughout study, including:

Communication: Inspired Princeton Debating Team to win two inter-collegiate awards.
Personally awarded 'Best Speaker of the Day' in heated political debate.

Finance: Elected treasurer of SIMS, State Investment Management Society.
Fantasy investment in the NASDAQ with an initial stake of $100K for 12 months. Achieved 137% ROI.

Responsible Citizenship: Singled out to spend the summer on Red Cross volunteer teacher program in Ethiopia, resulting in highest English language results in five years.

ADDITIONAL SKILLS

IT: ADVANCED MS OFFICE, SPSS, CITYBERG, MS PROJECT, VBA, MACROS
LANGUAGES: TRILINGUAL - ENGLISH, FRENCH, SPANISH

Your Name

City, Sate Zip   Email: Cell:

CHIEF EXECUTIVE OFFICER

Billion Dollar Growth • Market Penetration & Domination • Industry Pioneer

"If there is a glass ceiling, then I'm standing on top of it. There are no limits to where I can take this company." – Excerpt from best-selling book.

Entrepreneurial game changer with a sparkling track record of success in generating revenue, cutting costs, and rescuing ailing monoliths of the corporate world. Widely recognized as a leading light with a Midas touch and raw magnetism needed to inspire confidence in the attainment of operational objectives.

Awards & Adulation

Named on Fortune's list of the 50 Most Powerful Women in Business
Listed as one of Time's 100 Most Influential People in the World
Author of Best Selling Book

Attributes & Abilities

- Mergers & Acquisitions
- Strategic & Tactical Planning
- Cost Control & Consolidation
- New Product Development
- Corporate Turnaround & Expansion
- Organizational Growth & Development
- New Market Penetration & Domination
- Management & Financial Reporting
- Visionary Leadership
- Debt / Equity Financing
- Revenue Generation
- Regulatory Compliance

Achievements

Championed need to diversify Company Name corporate product offering in face of ever-increasing competition and challenging economic conditions. **Pioneered development of two patent-protected products which have both become billion dollar brands in their own right.**

Crystallized a vision for Company Name who was facing extinction due to breathtaking speed of change in technological realm. **Saved life of a grand old brand name by performing triage via immediate divestment of underperforming entities and drastic portfolio diversification.**

EMPLOYMENT NARRATIVE

COMPANY NAME, City, ST   Date to Date
Premier global agricultural processing powerhouse with $55B in revenues and 25,000 employees in 120 countries.

Chief Executive Officer
Handpicked by company president to deliver unbreakable forward momentum and inspirational leadership to a global powerhouse entering a period of stagnation and slow decline. **Melted mental chains inhibiting progressive boardroom visioning, revolutionized corporate structure and product offering, and pioneered development & launch of two patent-protected products boosting sales by billions.**

Actions & Results:
- **Corporate Growth & Development:** Assembled a core team of exceptional talent with verve and voracious appetite needed to revitalize business. Personally brokered multiple strategic M&A deals to secure dominant market position.

continued

Chief Executive Officer continued

- **Research & Development:** Catalyst for development of patented technology used to refine core commodities. Company now enjoys virtual monopoly on activity in region due to complete control over means of production and patented refinement processes.

- **Strategic & Tactical Planning:** Unchained $2 billion in cash by reducing inventory and selling noncore assets which in turn facilitated completion of $4 billion strategic acquisition of main competitor in key market.

COMPANY NAME, City, ST   Date to Date
Global provider of hardware, software and services to consumers with 30,000 employees and $53B in revenue.

Chief Executive Officer
Personally approached by company president to resuscitate ailing fortunes of a major multi-national suffering from bloated expenditures, wafer-thin internal controls, and a disengaged staff complement. **Embarked on a ruthless course of cost cutting characterized by divestment of multiple underperforming entities unfit to be associated with the core brand. Saved $10 billion over 4 years.**

Actions & Results:
- **Revitalization:** Initiated major review of organizational structure in collaboration with other executives. Championed move towards nimble corporate structure in line with existing cost-cutting ethos.

- **Morale:** Remained cognizant of message corporate austerity programs have on staff and instituted innovative employee incentive programs. Halted 'brain drain' of key technical specialists and succeeded in attracting top-tier talent from domestic and international sources.

- **Future Prosperity:** Left the company in a healthy financial position with the core brand positioned for double-digit growth and a talented complement of core personnel.

COMPANY NAME, City, ST   Date to Date
Document management specialist that produces & sells hardware and consulting services with $70B in revenue.

Chief Operations Manager & Chief Executive Officer
Chosen by board of directors to assume control of global operations in a bid to arrest an alarming decline in revenue resulting from use of alternative emerging technologies by core customers. **Immediately devised a plan to diversify product portfolio to include customer care and IT outsourcing services, which generated a staggering $11 billion within a 5-year period. Boosted stock price by 45%.**

Actions & Results:
- **Turnaround:** Revamped internal processes and procedures to accommodate new product lines. Charted revenue growth from a low of $22 billion in 1995 to a staggering $70 billion by 2002.

- **Leadership:** Boldly charted new waters by forging mutually beneficial partnerships with complementary service providers. Added an additional $950 million in revenue.

- **Cost Reduction:** Directed use of international talent for technical support activities which reduced personnel costs by 18% without impacting end-user service quality.

EDUCATION & TRAINING

Master of Business Administration – University Name
Bachelor of Commerce - Accounting – University Name

PROFESSIONAL AFFILIATIONS

President, Local Chapter (Date to Present) – Women in Business

Your Name
2 | Page

Your Name

PHONE • EMAIL • CITY • STATE • ZIP CODE • LINKEDIN URL

AREAS OF EXPERTISE

✓ Performance Management
✓ Strategic Alliances
✓ Client Acquisition & Retention
✓ Negotiation and Consensus
✓ Vendor Management
✓ Cross-functional Leadership
✓ Change Management
✓ Tactical Business Solutions
✓ Business Modeling
✓ Continuous Improvement
✓ Problem Solving
✓ Strategic Planning
✓ Product Development
✓ Implementation & Delivery
✓ Technical Acuity
✓ Operating Budgets & ROI

Ad Ops IT Director | Vice President

Results-oriented organizational and technology industry leader. Known for seamlessly coordinating and collaborating with internal organizations and third-party partners to manage, streamline, problem solve, and implement change. Excel at driving business forward through strategic thinking, decision-making, and development of win-win solutions.

Career Highlights

- Women in Technology Leadership Award Recipient in Year
- Amplified revenue 54%+ in 60 days
- Increased advertising revenue 25%
- Repeatedly maximized revenue and streamlined operations
- Increased job performance and satisfaction by 84%

Achievements & Experience

Vice President, Ad Ops, COMPANY NAME, CITY, ST, DATE–PRESENT
Key member of focused management team tasked to increase revenue in mobile app product adoption and advertising revenue growth. Strategized with VPs of Business Development, Engineering, Support, and CFO/COO to successfully drive revenue.

- **Amplified revenue 54% in 60 days** by optimizing remnant inventory that included 12 remnant partners, three which were programmatic /RTB (real time bidding) in Year.
- **Increased advertising revenue 25%** by generating new income streams and initiating, developing, installing, and launching system that effectively monetized unsold inventory.
- **Improved efficiency and assisted CEO/CFO** by developing clear methods to present revenue and trend reporting to the Board.
- **Filled the gap, increased profits and streamlined processes** by taking on additional responsibilities in two understaffed departments: Business Development and Finance.
- **Received Women in Technology Leadership Award** presented at National Association of Broadcasters convention recognizing significant contributions toward industry technological advancement.

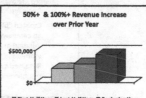

50%+ & 100%+ Revenue Increase over Prior Year

☑ First Half Year ☑ Last Half Year ■ Beginning Year

"Name is a dedicated professional who is one of my most trusted and valuable senior leaders...(she) took a department that was in chaos and turned it into one of the most efficient and productive departments in the company almost single-handedly...name established processes and procedures to streamline workflow and maximized revenue..."
Name, CEO, ABC Company

Senior Director, Ad Ops, COMPANY NAME, CITY, ST, DATE–DATE
Directed largest revenue-generating department supplying broadcast TV-news mobile apps. Successfully administrated local broadcast TV customer ad campaigns and national campaigns across all StepLeader properties.

- **Pioneered use of new cloud-based technology to foster virtual collaboration** and created web-based processes that guide business intelligence and drive business forward.
- **Generated $2.6M in sales** by spearheading team that assisted new national ad sales director to attract new clients and retain existing clients. Enabled team to successfully maintain ad campaigns and boosted revenue.
- **Skyrocketed employee performance and job satisfaction by 85% in only six months** by turning around negative performance, low morale, and high turnover caused by poor prior management.

MORE FOLLOWING PAGE ➞

Manager, Ad Ops, COMPANY, CITY, ST, DATE–DATE
Piloted staff through corporate merger and multiple software platforms and migrations. Maintained multiple workflows alongside migration, mentored team of 12 traffickers, and guided national advertising operational team.

- **Built more cohesive and assimilated workforce** by seamlessly managing merger, migration, and training of two departments and two ad servers post acquisition. Improved customer satisfaction and reduced expenses.
- **Resolved complex workflow process redundancy problem** (post merger) used analysis, critical thinking, and problem solving abilities that removed confusion, established clear responsibilities, eliminated unproductive time, and increased employee satisfaction and retention.
- **Spearheaded collaboration** that produced a robust tagging and taxonomy structure supporting 30 daily newspapers by partnering with internal development, analytics, content management, and support teams.

> *"Name is hardworking, energetic, and methodical. She dealt with daily tasks with ease, and also handled exceptional situations with aplomb...is an influential leader who always moves the needle forward and higher...delivers and expects high-quality results and sets the bar for colleagues and direct/indirect reports.*
> *She is described by many of her reports as 'The best manager I've ever had.'"*
> **Name, Ad Ops Manager, Business Intelligence, XYZ Company**

Ad Ops Specialist, COMPANY, CITY, ST, DATE–DATE
Managed dovetailed migrations of content and ad ops departments. Resolved daily customer emergencies, needs, and questions. Directed trafficking operations for 15 affiliate newspapers and external customers.

- **Increased efficiency and time savings** by orchestrating the centralization of 15 DEF Company affiliate newspaper online ad departments.
- **Salvaged an at-risk client relationship/contract** by consistently providing solutions for their business needs.
- **Tenaciously investigated and resolved key client's allegations and mistrust** due to a technical problem in ad server that caused a counting methodology anomaly, which resulted in increased trust and a happy client.

Web Admin / Ad Traffic Manager, COMPANY, CITY, ST, DATE–DATE
Audited site traffic, scheduled and managed static and rich media ads. Orchestrated conversion of user registration database, email newsletters, SEO/SEM maintenance, classified listings, and worked with emerging behavioral targeting for banner ads.

- Created "bleeding edge" behavioral targeting segments using Tacoda's software that produced first successful ad campaigns of this kind in company history.
- **Pursued and landed new NHL contract** to update advertising options, which included third-party tags with embedded flash, and overcame outdated ad department restrictions.
- **Retained key account and a significant amount of repeat business revenue** by working additional hours to troubleshoot ad tags so that "kid-glove" customer's ads would run properly on their company's website.

➤ Education ◄

Bachelor of Science in Information Architecture (B.S.) XYZ SCHOOL OF COMPUTER DESIGN, CITY, ST, DATE
Continuing Education - Ad Ops Management, Apple Hardware Service, Configuration Management, Electronic Publishing, Font Management, Unix/Sun/Solaris system administration, MCSE coursework, Novell Network administration, Perl scripting, Quality Assurance, QuarkXpress, Technical writing, Unix shell scripting

➤ Technology & Tools ◄

Adinterax, AdMarvel, Classified Ventures, DFA, DFP, DSM, Flash, Google Analytics, Insite, LiveRail, Lyris, MS Office, Mocean Mobile, Multi-Ad Creator, Nexage, Novell, OAS, Omniture, Operative, Parature, Perl, Planet Discover, PubMatic, QuarkXpress, Rubicon, Salesforce, Smaato, Solbright, Tacoda, Unix, VMIX, Yahoo Apt, Yume

YOUR NAME

City, State Zip
Phone ▪ Email

TARGET POSITION: **ASSISTANT MANAGER / EVENT COORDINATOR**

AREAS OF INTEREST: **HOSPITALITY / CORPORATE EVENTS**

Recent graduated who is ready to hit the ground running! Future leader with valuable hands-on experience in hospitality (both front and back of house), event planning, project coordination, customer service, and problem solving. Highly organized with success working within a professional organizing company.

Combine a degree in Hospitality Management with practical internships and positions held within the industry – a true asset to any organization seeking a "go-getter with a position disposition who is ready to contribute and make a difference.

Key Areas of Knowledge Skills, & Training: Operations Management, Hospitality Management, Marketing, Food Service Operations, Event Coordination, Financial Management, Human Resource Management, and Accounting.

EDUCATION

B.S. in Business; Concentration in Hospitality Management
College of Business and Management, University Name, City, ST

VALUE OFFERED

★ **Project Management and Execution**
★ **Self-Directed**
★ **Strong Organizational Skills**
★ **Detail-Oriented**
★ **Problem Solving**
★ **Client Relations**
★ **Event Planning**
★ **Customer Service**
★ **Team Leadership and Motivation**

TECHNICAL SKILLS

Microsoft Excel, Word, PowerPoint;
Auto Clerk; Social Media

PROFESSIONAL EXPERIENCE

Company Name, City, ST   Date to Date
Hotel chain. Location has staff of 20 and 82 rooms.
FRONT DESK AGENT
Served as face and voice for hotel and ensured customers received service excellence from their first touch point with company and on-going.

- Assessed customer needs both in person and by phone.
- Delivered efficient and friendly service to guests during check-in and check-out.
- Problem-solved issues with reservations; utilized reservation system. Booked new reservations; paid close attention to details to meet guest requests.
- Served as concierge.

VALUABLE INTERNSHIPS

Company Name, City, ST   Date to Date
Hospitality support company serving top New York City restaurants and hotels.
PAID INTERN

- Implemented processes that improved productivity within accounts receivable department.
- Managed accounts receivable; developed program to track monthly customer spending trends for reporting and further analysis.

continued

Valuable Internships Continued...

Company Name, City, ST   Date to Date
INTERN
Leading Texas marketing and event management company.
- Provided administrative and project planning support to project managers in event planning, budgeting, and database management.
- Assisted with drafting proposals, applying for grants, and conducting research.

COMPANY NAME, City, ST   Date to Date
INTERN
Los Angeles hotel and event space; recognized as one of the most fashionable in the world.
- Served as Manager's Assistant; helped to oversee housekeeper, hotel upkeep, and maintenance.

OTHER EXPERIENCE

COMPANY NAME, City, ST   Date to Date
PROJECT COORDINATOR
Professional Organizing Company.
- Managed multiple projects (logistics, scheduling, product) for ten separate clients.

COMPANY NAME, City, ST   Date to Date
GREETER
- Managed reservations; ensured all guests received a positive first impression of the establishment and highest standard of service.

COMPANY NAME, City, ST   Date to Date
SHIFT LEADER
- Coordinated staff responsibilities for all shifts; provided staff briefings for monthly promotions.

COMMUNITY SERVICE & LEADERSHIP

Girl Scout Silver and Gold Awards – the highest honor awarded to less than 6% of all scouts, which recognized outstanding leadership and contributions to the community.

Your Name

City, State Zip ◘ Email Address ◘ Phone Number

Customer Service | Waitress | Kitchen Hand

Exceptional Customer Service	Waitressing	Professional Phone Manner
Accurate Order Taking	Fast and Efficient	Security Procedures
Housekeeping	Safe Food Handling	Cash Handling
Friendly	High Presentation Standards	EFTPOS
⌘⌘⌘	⌘⌘⌘	⌘⌘⌘

Strengths & Extra Curricular Activities

Showed natural leadership, sportsmanship, and a mature work ethic across study, teamwork, and part-time employment. Created a respectful culture of empowerment and continuous improvement through sharing of game tactics and maintaining performance expectations.

Captain | School Swimming Team, Date; Captain | School Mixed Netball Team, Date | Grand Final Winners

Work History

Company Name | City, ST | **Date - Date**

CUSTOMER SERVICE | SALES (Actual titles: WAITRESS | KITCHEN HAND)

Date to Date:

Maintained part-time / casual rosters throughout studies on weekends (breakfast, lunch, dinner) and school holidays, always showing flexibility to cover extra shifts at short notice, cooking meals and waitressing.

- ✓ Ensured all dining (inside / outside) and kitchen areas properly set up, cleaned, and presentable while providing attentive and prompt customer service.
- ✓ Supported management and other staff members, to smoothly keep orders moving from kitchen to table, working under pressure, and assisting to resolve issues and/or complaints.
- ✓ Prepared a broad range of drinks, sandwiches and light meals, clearly communicating daily specials as well as encouraging customers to purchase additional items.
- ✓ Accurately processed payments, then followed through on ensuring tables were cleared quickly for next customer, without anyone feeling rushed.

Date to Date:

Built a strong customer base with regulars requesting service across food preparation working as a Junior Kitchen Hand / Waitress on Saturdays (8am-5pm) and one day a week after school (2pm-5:30pm). Always first staff member to be called if someone cancels a shift, helping get food out quickly and clear tables to keep premises in top condition.

- ✓ Prepared cold drinks and cooked big breakfasts (eight elements), omelet, baguette, eggs benedict, sandwiches, and an assortment of light meals menu items, helping out within the barista area.
- ✓ Served customers efficiently, always suggesting additional dishes such as cakes to go with coffee and assisted with chopping of produce, food preparation, and storage within the kitchen.
- ✓ Completed Company Online Training modules within three months, covering all aspects of the business including frontline food safety, meal preparation, and creating a professional atmosphere.

YOUR NAME

City, State Zip | Phone | Email

SENIOR SALES REPRESENTATIVE

Customer-Centric Solution Seller
Driving Rapid Revenue Growth

Secure client loyalty through effective relationship selling and customized sales solution campaigns

Sales leader who excels at driving revenue growth by quickly identifying opportunity and turning untapped potential into lucrative results.

Sales in Millions

→ **Consensus-builder;** transform customer perceptions from something they want into something they need; establish trust to create high ROI relationships.

→ **Solution-generator;** quickly adapt to diverse sales environments to realize revenue growth; instrumental in both start-up development and established business expansion.

→ **Strategic high-achiever;** consistently exceed targets and surpass expectations to secure top sales year after year; develop customized sales approaches to modify operations, proving "the impossible is possible."

PERSONAL SALES METHODOLOGY:

ADAPT TO AUDIENCE → EXPLORE EVERY AVENUE → DEFINE SALES PITCH → PRESENT WITH PERSUASION

SALES RECOGNITIONS AND RESULTS

✓ **Increased sales revenues by 117%** in two years at Company Name.

✓ **Achieved #1 in sales every year** in both profit and gross margin at Company Name.

✓ **Exceeded sales targets, every year, by as much as 190%** at Company Name.

✓ **Expanded tradeshow revenue to $20M** at Company Name.

✓ **Launched company from start-up to $680K** within first 12 months at Company Name.

✓ **Amplified start-up profits by 210%** in two years at Company Name.

> *"Name orchestrated a fundamental change in our sales approach, generating millions of dollars in previously untapped markets."*
>
> - Regional Manager, Company Name

Signature Sales Strengths:

- Business Development
- Customer Needs Analysis
- Strategic Sales & Marketing
- Cold Calling & Prospecting

- Revenue Acceleration
- Relationship Management
- Solution Selling
- Negotiations

- Policy Development
- Sales Force Training
- Market Analysis
- Tradeshow Representation

continued

YOUR NAME

PROFESSIONAL EXPERIENCE

Company Name – City, ST

Sales Representative, Date – Date

As top sales performer, promoted to oversee over $11M worth of business and motivate most profitable region to exceed top sales numbers; *accelerated revenues from $23M to $50M in two years*. Managed policy and procedure development, drove new business pursuit, developed new sales talent, spearheaded tradeshow selling, directed inventory control, and administered staff training, scheduling, and direction.

Overshot sales targets every single year by as much as 190%:

	Year 1	Year 2	Year 3	Year 4	Year 5
% Over Target	153%	188%	190%	189%	185%

- **Redefining Sales:** Increased regional revenues by up to 58% each year; re-architected sales strategy from traditional client model to transformative approach; developed advanced sales training techniques which were adopted company-wide.

- **Team Training and Leadership:** Coached senior sales staff to increase personal revenues by as much as 25% year over year; invigorated sales team by defining new sales vision and introducing innovative business development strategies.

- **Competitive Positioning:** Initiated new sales process to close cold leads at tradeshows; trained top 1% of sales talent to expand tradeshow revenues from almost nothing to $20M and counting.

- **New Business Development:** Captured $17M worth of new market and previously untapped revenue opportunities; established opportunities with hospitals, universities, and nursing homes.

Company Name – City, ST

Operations and Marketing Representative, Date – Date

Recruited to build brand and market campaign for new product launch for local manufacturing and distribution start-up; spearheaded product positioning and platform development. Managed warehouse and production staff; hired and trained sales and manufacturing members.

- **Product Strategies:** Grew revenues by 68%; developed product marketing campaign to promote product through in-store promotions; secured shelf space in over 30 locations in 24 months.

- **Contract Negotiations:** Pursued and acquired all contracts for distribution; signed original strategic partners that launched company from zero to $680K in one year.

- **Cost-Savings Initiatives:** Streamlined manufacturing through automation to increase profits from 10% to 31% in two years; orchestrated equipment purchasing to aid product production without impact to profit.

EDUCATION

Bachelor of Commerce – *University Name, Date*

YOUR NAME

City, State Zip
Email address

SENIOR MARKETING DIRECTOR
TRANSFORMING VISION TO OUTCOMES
EMBEDDING INNOVATION INTO OPERATIONS
SHAPING COMMITMENT TO EVERYDAY EXCELLENCE

"To bring sustained excellence within a business you need more than strategies and training, you have to connect people to the reason 'why' they are doing what they are doing. Once they believe in the 'why,' the 'how' is a natural next step."

Senior Executive with a highly results-driven marketing and general management background for industry-leading technology brands – excels in challenging market conditions. Orchestrator of market strategy that has seen companies post ten-year profit-highs coupled with market domination.

Lifelong technology evangelist with strong instincts for identifying potential products with proven ability to turn 'possibility' to 'profitability.' Repeated successes designing marketing strategies that have improved viability, profits, and prospects for emerging and established technology operations.

EXECUTIVE LEADERSHIP HIGHLIGHTS

As Marketing Director for Company Name, designed business-to-business (B2B) strategy that averted potential risks to its cash cow product, safeguarding a multi-million dollar annual revenue stream.

As Global Brand Manager for Company Name, delivered the company's most successful period for performance in over a decade through new strategic directions aligned to market opportunities.

As Managing Director for Company Name, improved business agility and commercial capability positioning it to be continually poised for innovation and market opportunities.

PROVEN EXPERTISE

Strategic Leadership| P&L Management | Marketing Strategy | Business Turnaround | Change Management |Business Transformation| Cultural Change | Cross-functional Team Building

PROFESSIONAL EXPERIENCE

MARKETING DIRECTOR, COMPANY NAME, COUNTRY, DATES TO DATES
$250 Million sales per annum | $90 Million OPEX per annum | 25 direct reports

Appointed to design commercial strategy for company's entire brand portfolio with a focus on protecting market share and profitability during a period of anticipated market volatility.

Drove a visible transformation in culture, operating practices and marketing strategies delivering business performance that outstripped expectations in a highly price-sensitive market.

> **Strategy:** Introduced a first-of-its-kind strategy aimed at countering a potential market hit to company's biggest brand in lead up to competitor global product launch. **New B2B strategy saw New Zealand as only division globally to maintain market share in face of unprecedented competition levels.**

> **Leadership:** Trained entire marketing team in business planning and resilience, which contributed to sustained team morale and a 100% retention rate despite company facing record levels of sales pressure.

> **Market Evaluation:** Coordinated strategic review of core products, which identified critical market data that reshaped priorities. Revised pricing, which grew profitability in mature lines and divested non-profitable brands.

> **Cost Reduction:** Reduced operational expenditure through restructuring operations to high-value activities and prudent cutting of discretionary expenditure. **Shaved 20% off annual OPEX budget.**

> **Integration:** Halted disconnect between sales and marketing teams, and introduced new planning models and performance measures. **New structures brought better collaboration, brand clarity, and marketing ROI.**

GLOBAL BRAND MANAGER, COMPANY NAME, COUNTRY, DATES TO DATES
$150 Million sales per annum | $70 Million OPEX per annum | |10 direct reports and a total of 20 people within marketing function.

Headhunted to lead marketing function globally for this industrial technology market leader. Managed eight brands and credited with new marketing strategies and models that:

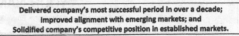

Delivered company's most successful period in over a decade;
Improved alignment with emerging markets; and
Solidified company's competitive position in established markets.

> **Sales:** Managed sales performance of eight brands at different stages of product lifecycle and operating in increasingly crowded markets. **Exceeded country sales plan by a minimum of 10% year-on-year.**
> **Leadership:** Worked with leadership team to develop a 5-year excellence plan with customer-centricity as its underpinning value. **New culture of excellence lifted service ratings 10 points** *above* **global averages.**
> **Turnaround:** Revitalized product line operating at less than 50% to-plan. Implemented branding strategies that set the product on a **growth trajectory and saw it achieve market leader status in its category within six months.**
> **Strategy:** Devised long term marketing plans for the four brands which delivered strong sales performance across key emerging markets and **producing strongest profit performance in over ten years.**
> **Profitability:** Restructured business funding and resourcing model to realign with current market conditions and areas of opportunity. **Accelerated investment in key emerging markets and addressed resourcing deficiencies in key countries / regions halting sales progress.**

MANAGING DIRECTOR, COMPANY NAME, COUNTRY, DATES TO DATES
$280 Million sales per annum. | $80 Million OPEX per annum. |80 staff across 6 offices

Recruited to reinvigorate operations in a stagnant domestic market. Implemented new operational structures, strategic directions and product innovations that activated new market growth and produced year-on-year EBIT increases.

Transformed business into a leaner, more agile operation poised for continual opportunity capitalization.

> **Change:** Led business-wide review pinpointing opportunities for cost control, efficiency enhancement, and revenue growth. **Designed transformation agenda that delivered leaner, more agile operations.**
> **Cost Reduction:** Restructured operations and executed across-the-board review of costs and staffing structures, which resulted in changes that **removed $3M in costs from bottom line without impacts to operations.**
> **Revenue Growth:** Launched new advanced technology research and development hub aligned to emerging market hotspots, which **improved product development pipeline.**

EARLY CAREER HIGHLIGHTS

> As National Sales & Marketing Manager with Company Name (date-date) led New Zealand to be one of only four countries that surpassed revenue targets following the Global Financial Crisis.
> Established and managed successful start-up technology business with recognized product pipeline. Operated as Managing Director until the business was acquired by Company Name (date – date).

EDUCATION

MBA, University Name   **Bachelor of Marketing & Innovation,** University Name

James is a business leader that creates momentum. His track record in marketing is indisputable and in leadership circles he is thoroughly respected for his instincts, intelligence and integrity.
NAME, CEO, Alpha Technology

YOUR NAME

City, State • Phone Number • Email Address • LinkedIn URL

Qualified for Data Analyst Role

Interdisciplinary data-obsessed analyst with unique and refreshing perspective on data science. Excel at bridging gap between techies and fuzzies by utilizing transferable skills gained from journalism to take a deep dive into analytical solutions management and data science across full digital spectrum. Recognized with Women's International Leadership Award. Well positioned to leverage significant academic achievements and success with product mindset to design and deliver transformational solutions.

— Areas of Key Emphasis —

- Data Science
- Digital Analytics
- Research & Analysis
- Data Testing & Integrity

- Data Cleansing
- Tool Prototyping
- Complex Problems
- A/B & Multivariate Testing

- SQL Database
- Program Management
- Matrixed Organizations
- Multi-Lingual Communication

Data Science Project Portfolio

School Name – City, ST

Projects sought to understand and solve existing problems through the transformational power of data & technology.

Declassification Engine Project (History Lab), 1/2017 – 5/2018

Created R package for API client allowing users to explore vast archival collections. Queried 3.2M data in SQL, extracted new field of data from raw body texts, and transformed them into data tables using regular expression in Python with little direction from Professor.

Follow the Money Project, 5/2017 – 7/2017

Designed and built innovative mock-up relational database using SQL and Google Cloud to track influence of money on NY state legislation, connecting silo data sources of campaign contribution, outside income, lobbying, and sponsorship of bills.

Academic Qualifications

Master of Arts, Quantitative Methods in the Social Sciences, Data Science – YEAR
School Name, City, ST
Specialization: Data Structure, Databases, Applied Machine Learning, Data Visualization, Mapping, Social Network Analysis, Time Series
Award: Women's International Leadership, International House (Year)

Master of Science in Journalism, Data Specialization – YEAR
School Name, City, ST ♦ Hearst Scholarship
Award: First Prize - MINDS Innovation Challenge (Year)

Bachelor of Arts in Media Studies, Statistics – YEAR
School Name, City, ST ♦ with Distinction ♦ Phi Kappa Phi ♦ Mu Sigma Rho

Continued

Key Experience Highlights

COMPANY NAME, CITY, ST

Data Science Intern, MO/YEAR – Present

Technologies: SQL Database, Tableau, API call in R

Supported development of analytical products to guide human-led process of monitoring, analyzing, and reporting within Crisis Response Unit. Built new data models and identified inconsistency in past data schemas; configured multiple natural language processing applications using API call in R. Investigated new strategies to improve early warning systems using learning and natural language processing tools.

- Independently designed and delivered innovative crisis risk dashboards using Tableau for UNDP country offices in Cameroon, Sierra Leonne, and Tanzania.
- Worked with little direction and oversight, created detailed reports on Artificial Intelligence for Crisis Risk Dashboard; identified why, what, and how of machine learning implementation and natural language processing to optimize early warning system.
- Recognized for improving team efficiency score by 25% after identifying inefficiencies and building process improvements within cross-functional team dynamic.

COMPANY NAME, CITY, ST

Product Analytics Intern, MO/YEAR – MO/YEAR

Technologies: Google Analytics, Chartbeat, R, Tableau

Analyzed patterns of user behaviors on Company website and mobile applications. Reported on Google Analytics and Chartbeat; delivered actionable insights via Tableau to VP Digital Product and managing editors, and deployed resources to high-performing fields.

- Recognized for creatively identifying key factors driving increased product engagement and traffic across time after constructing and fitting statistical models in R.

COMPANY NAME, CITY, ST

Program Manager, MO/YEAR – MO/YEAR

Planned monthly startup Founder's programs in San Francisco Bay Area; managed budgets and fundraising to grow and expand network of tech entrepreneurs and facilitate exchange of resources and knowledge.

- Directed, organized, and successfully delivered annual Smart City Innovation Summit in Hangzhou, China.

Additional Skills

R, SQL, Python, Tableau, HTML5/CSS, QGIS, Carto, SPSS, JavaScript, Google Cloud, Microsoft Azure, Digital Analytics, Tagging, Social Media, Data Cleansing, ETL

Languages: Fluent – English & Mandarin; Intermediate - Arabic; Basic - French, Spanish

YOUR NAME

Phone | Email | LinkedIn Profile URL | City, ST

EXECUTIVE DIRECTOR
FINANCE AND BANKING INDUSTRY LEADER

Expertise in Corporate Strategy, Complex Analytics, National Sales, Pricing and Staffing Models

- Nationally respected senior executive with unique combination of astute financial prowess, keen economic trend awareness, and disruptive national sales strategy expertise to drive revenue growth, capture new markets, and exceed business book goals.
- Thoughtful and effective leader with reputation for quickly recognizing opportunities for staff and customer behavior changes, aligning services with customer needs, and implementing profitable shifts in status quo.
- Entrepreneurial-minded professional who is highly adept at building innovative models that drive organizational decision making, maximize returns, and driving growth, even during volatile economic times.

Executive Expertise

$MM Revenue Growth	Analytics	Behavior Design
Budgeting / Annual Planning	Business Intelligence	Corporate Strategy
Customer Segmentation	Disruptive Innovation	KPIs
National Sales Strategy	Risk Management	Staffing Models

EXECUTIVE CAREER HIGHLIGHTS

Company Name, City, ST, Date - Date
Leading global financial services firm and one of the largest banking institutions in U.S., with operations worldwide.

Executive Director, Business Banking Finance   Date - Date
Developed annual volume, balance, and revenue plans for Business Banking Loan Book, totaling $22B+ in outstanding balances and $1B in annual revenue. Led 5 direct reports with oversight of 300+ managers and 2,500+ bankers in field.

NATIONAL SALES
- Fueled new loan origination volumes to $7B annually, highest level in company history.
- Disrupted status quo among field bankers and management that initiated positive behavior change through extensive, national mentoring, coaching, and training efforts.

CORPORATE STRATEGY
- Analyzed market behavior and defined packages for $86M revenue stream and personally delivered program and key messages to 300+ managers nationwide annually.
- Crafted communication plan for unavoidable regulatory price increase passed on to customer base, which reversed typical practice of pushing out cost increases without explanation.

COMPLEX ANALYTICS
- Maintained role of corporate point person for evaluating potential effects of adverse economic and financial market conditions, which set strategy and KPIs for all national bank branch managers.
- Revealed untapped, multimillion-dollar revenue potential and unique market offerings after partnering with corporate Finance, Risk, and Macroeconomics teams to develop highly complex measures.
- Architected and achieved federal approval for quantitative models in response to Federal Reserve Bank stress testing requirements for CCAR, ICAAP, and Risk Appetite exercises.

continued

CFO, National Sales, Business Banking   Date - Date

Selected after major business unit merger to provide analytic, strategic, and financial support to Business Banking sales organization, which consisted of 7 regions, 2,700+ bankers and 300+ managers, and served 600k customers with $65B in deposits, $18B in loans and over $2B in annual revenue. Merger combined ~800 bankers in Relationship Managed (RM) channel with ~2,000 bankers in branch channel.

CORPORATE SALES & STAFFING STRATEGY

- Restructured production / sales targets and built annual financial plan, which increased accountability among bankers, improved customer service, and aligned metrics at region, market, and area levels.
- Established monthly analysis, which linked revenue growth to banker production and calling activity, and resulted in 36% increase in new business and 24% desired attrition.
- Implemented analytics, staffing model, and segmentation projects to evaluate portfolio loads, prospect density, and branch coverage. Corrected alignment for tens of 1,000s of customers to appropriate banker expertise.

CFO, Relationship Managed (RM) Channel, Business Banking   Date - Date

Directed strategic and operational financial management for $1B per year business with $30B in deposits, and $12B in credit balances, focused on small- and mid-sized business with $3-$20MM annual sales in highly volatile economy.

CORPORATE SALES & REPORTING STRATEGY

- Initiated and created monthly management reporting process to correct glaring inconsistencies and accountability across 9 sales regions and 94 markets, which combined financial results with branch productivity, calling / prospecting activity, and credit quality metrics.

CORPORATE STRATEGY HIGHLIGHTS

- Built robust RM staffing model to handle not only RM channel requirements, but also acquisition of and unpredictable growth from former Wells Mutual customers. Used average portfolio size, prospect density and branch penetration to determine optimal staffing levels in all markets; grew from 0 to 500 bankers.
- Rectified 100s of millions of dollars of mismatched commercial / retail customers and bankers through collaborative effort with senior banking managers companywide.
- Improved individual productivity per banker and brought banks into corporate alignment by analyzing national, regional, and branch customer base and implementing relevant, market-specific targets for all sales teams. Achieved buy-in to new, more meaningful program through heavy collaboration with bank management.

NATIONAL SALES STRATEGY IMPACT

- Experienced 10% growth year over year (YOY) in existing markets and 30% YOY growth in expansion markets, despite consumer lack of trust in banking industry during volatile time.
- Drove 200+% new customer acquisition growth within first year by changing banker incentive plans to better align with RM Channel strategy.

Vice President – Business Banking Finance   Date - Date

Regional finance manager for Central, Midwest and East region branch-based business sales organizations.

REGIONAL SALES STRATEGY

- Provided insights and analysis from sales production results to the sales force to drive increased acquisition and retention. Sales force focused on customers with < $3M annually in sales.
- Researched and analyzed regional business differences, sales strategies for each, and effectiveness of current KPIs. Defined / refined data, revamped KPIs, and designed meaningful sales reporting scorecards to assist regional managers and sales force to make bigger impact.

EDUCATION

UNIVERSITY NAME

B.S. in Business Accounting ~ Minor: Economics

New Graduate Seeking Sports Broadcaster by Jeri Hird Dutcher. This resume hammers home the qualifications of the new grad by including a recommendation quote and using page one to deeply highlight qualifications and recent accomplishment-laden college-based roles.

Your Name ★ Sports Broadcaster

Phone Number ★ City, State ★ Email Address

Mission: Telling and illustrating exciting, inspiring stories of athletes and games

Student athlete and leader with strong academic record and passion for sports. Eager to learn more of the art of broadcasting toward a career in sports journalism. Available for nationwide work. Meet challenges with enthusiasm, organization, and innovation.

Knowledge and Skills

Newsgathering / Production: Provide coverage of press conferences, fundraisers, and other events ★ Conduct pre/half/post-game interviews ★ Log interviews and game highlights ★ Research, pitch, and tell stories ★ Gather video footage and graphic elements for edit, film on location ★ Script narration to graphic elements ★ Perform final edit and audio mix.

Communication and Interpersonal Skills: Write and speak clearly, concisely, and convincingly ★ Developed strong leadership skills as captain of college basketball team ★ Patient and active listener who helps motivate team toward goals with sincerity, optimism, and positive sense of humor ★ Enjoy meeting, respecting, and working with all personality types ★ Talk with new people easily in small or large groups ★ Often fill teacher role on team. Show high degree of persistence in projects.

Sports Industry Knowledge: Produced, filmed, and provided live radio and TV play-by-play and color for men's and women's soccer, football, basketball, and baseball ★ BA in Communications – Public Relations ★ BA in Broadcast Journalism, minor in Sports Communications anticipated in May.

Administrative and Technical Skills: Mac, PC, and peripherals operation, Sony XD camera operation ★ Avid News Cutter, Final Cut Pro, and Premiere non-linear editing software ★ Social media networks Facebook, Twitter, and Instagram ★ Highly organized and reliable with work ethic for under-promising and over-delivering with "grit" to finish any project.

Recommendation

"Name is a rising star. She communicates well, is highly organized, pays attention to details, is great at building relationships, and understands that the team is bigger than herself. She is passionate about what she does and connects with her peers and colleagues. What continues to impress me most about her are the qualities she possesses of personality, character, integrity, and moral values that I believe distinguish her from many other people."

Name
Women's Basketball Coach
College Name
City, State

Experience

Student News Anchor, State University, City, State　　　　　　　　**[Date] – [Date]**

☆ **News Anchoring:** Won news anchor position over 24 applicants. Completed practice runs in preparation for anchoring half-hour Saturday morning news on local public television station.

☆ **Sports Reporting:** Write stories from sports producer material. Also find and pitch stories to producers.

Play-by-Play Radio Host, Company Name, City, State　　　　　　　　**[Date] – [Date]**

☆ **Announcing:** Hosted live play-by-play and commentary for 16 home games for college men's and women's soccer and 2 basketball games.

☆ **Sports Knowledge:** Prepared for each game by researching other team and statistics, knowing rosters and player histories. Added to lifelong accumulation of information by attending and watching sporting events.

☆ **Soccer Solo:** Provided live play-by-play and color commentary for 6 hours of men's and women's soccer games when partner called in sick immediately before third live experience.

Experience continued

Sports Intern, Company Name, City, State   [Date] – [Date]

☆ **State Tournament Solo Coverage:** Produced footage of all-day state boys baseball tournament airing throughout region under deadline pressure for first solo coverage, by planning and scheduling efficient day of footage and post-game interviews that led 6 pm broadcast. Brought professionalism and enthusiasm to coverage that made fans want to watch show over others. Delivered calmly on deadline despite time crunch produced by game going 12 innings.

☆ **Storytelling:** Attended fundraiser and interviewed teammates of university alumni basketball player diagnosed with brain cancer. Wrote story, selected highlights of interviews that best illustrated history of team and player, raised community awareness of brain cancer, and helped organization receive donations for research and treatment.

☆ **Baseball Package:** Delivered first full package as intern for award-winning television station. Recorded standup on local minor league baseball team used at 6 pm.

☆ **Camera Work:** Shot baseball game highlights solo in second week of internship; footage aired that evening. Later filmed college and high school games, sporting news events, and press conferences.

☆ **Staff Hours Saved:** Saved sports team work by providing highlights used for 6 pm or 10 pm show 4 days per week. Team used all work provided.

☆ **Sports Anchoring Practice:** Rehearsed anchoring and using teleprompter twice weekly. Wrote scripts for highlight clips during reporting and anchoring.

Social Media Intern, Women's Basketball Team, College, City, State   [Date] – [Date]

☆ **Social Media:** Created Women's Basketball Blog with athlete biographies to involve community, families, and younger athletes with team mission and athletic program, telling team stories and experiences. Resulted in uniting basketball community and football community. Elementary schools listened and invited team members to read to them. Blogged weekly in summer and monthly during school year. Invited coach and team members as guest bloggers. Developed surveys and polls and posted / updated on Facebook, Twitter, and Instagram.

☆ **Public Relations:** Maintained community involvement in and support of university sports during games in California by informing parents, professors, and fans back home of daily game results and activities through photos and blog posts.

Sideline Sports Reporter, Company Name, City, State   [Date] – [Date]

☆ **Newsgathering:** Interviewed coaches and players pre/half/post-game. Commentated and updated during home and away games live on field. Logged statistical information on game.

☆ **Hosting:** Commentated for girls AAAA state high school basketball tournament and football games.

Memberships

Association for Women in Sports Media, City, State, [Date] – [Date].

Education

Bachelor of Arts, Broadcast Journalism, Minor in Sports Communications, [Date] – [Date] (Anticipated in May).
    State University, City, State.
Bachelor of Arts, Communications with Emphasis in Public Relations, [Date] – [Date].
    College, City, State.
    ☆ Awarded athletic scholarship for women's basketball program.
    ☆ Captain of women's basketball team.

Chapter 17

OnTarget Resumes for Special Circumstances

J ust because you're changing careers, stepping out of your military uniform, or explaining resume gaps, don't think that you are at a disadvantage. You can create a riveting resume. The samples in this chapter give you some ideas about how to do just that by deftly handling your special circumstances.

REMEMBER

These examples represent individual people and their unique experiences; they are provided only as an example of what is possible in a resume. Please consider them as roadmaps — not rules — in creating your next resume.

TIP

As you review these resumes, note that I have made it possible for you to see yourself in them while also protecting the identity of the original job seekers who agreed to have their resumes fictionalized. To do this, I have made certain stylistic choices for all the resumes:

>> The job seeker's name appears as *Your Name* at the top of the resume and as *NAME* when mentioned in a testimonial quote. These indicate where you should refer to yourself.

>> Contact information is shown with the words *City, State, Zip Code, Phone,* and *Email.* This is where you would place your contact information.

» Employment dates (and education dates, when included) use the word *Date*. This is where you would list your years of employment or the year you earned a credential.

» Job descriptions do not list actual company names. Instead, you'll see *Company Name, Hospital Name,* and the like. This is where you would list your employer's company name.

» If a year is stipulated, such as *Won this award in 2015,* the word *Year* has been substituted for the actual date.

Your Name

City, State Zip Code | Email Address | Phone Number

Sales, Partnerships & Business Development Management

Accomplished and entrepreneurial business champion, motivated by challenge - willing to take fast and calculated action to execute and implement programs, processes, and structure that drive innovation and growth. Passionate with ability to inspire and energize both teams and organizations across global media, marketing, and product launch.

Extensive international experience: traveled, filmed, represented, and competed across Europe (Austria, France, Germany), Japan, Australia, Canada, New Zealand, and United States.

Networking & Referrals	Marketing & Promotions	Sponsorship Growth
Global Sponsorship Market	Project Management	Commercial Retail Sales
Key Alliance & Partnerships	Leadership & Mentoring	Driving Brand Awareness
Contract Negotiations	Stakeholder Relationships	Public Profile & Speaking

Professional Snapshot

Professional Alpine (Downhill) Skier | Date - Date
Short Films Production | Date - Date

Sales & Marketing: Worked closely with major corporations across global sponsorship market, with an ongoing contribution to design, sales, and marketing.

- International Name team member for over nine years, promoting sport as it expanded from an initial 10% participation to grow to 50% nationwide.
  - Provided input into advertising strategies across campaigns and merchandise; liaised with Marketing and Team Managers and various promotional teams.
  - Attended trade shows (Switzerland, Canada, Munich) as company representative; engaged with more than 1,500 attendees over 2 days, and also participated in team photo shoots and endorsement events.
- Collaborated with design and retail teams to design signature range of outer wear; completed both national and international catalogue shoots. Resulted in highest selling range for four years running.
  - Negotiated ongoing contracts with up to six sponsors (Company Name, Company Name, Company Name, etc.) for professional skiing and filming activities.
- Managed distribution and invoicing of professional photos and films to magazines (Europe, Americas, International) and sponsors for more than seven years; maintained accurate accounts.
  - Published articles and interviews in up to 25 issues per year across 23 countries; ensured promotion and participation of sport to inspire newcomers.

Business Development: Proactively maintained key relationships with action sports company CEOs through to sponsorship managers and sports agents; split time between Europe and American bases.

- Pushed boundaries and attempted the impossible; overcame and pushed through injuries and weather conditions to meet sponsorship needs.
  - Noted for excellent communication skills coupled with a strong work ethic and outgoing personality; gained trust and commitment for high-risk projects.

continued

Your Name – Page Two

Professional Snapshot cont...

Elite Action Sports: Began professional career, signed to Company's International Team at 15 years old; rated as one of the best ski competitors in the world and one of Northern Hemisphere's best freestyle riders.

- ☐ Maintained heavy involvement in producing two short films; featured in more than 26. Collaborated with film and photography crew, throughout transport, work schedule, and logistical needs.
    - ☑ Selected and coordinated crew, as part of five athlete team, for *Film Name* - awarded *best documentary* at International Sports Film Festival Year.
- ☐ Invited to co-host *Ski Challenge 2014* (an elite level invitation only heli-accessed free-ride event) in Japan for two TV channels.
    - ☑ Conducted in-depth interviews, introductions, and voiceovers for three-day event; developed and shared a captivating storyline for producers, meeting all deadlines.

Testimonies

"He has a drive to succeed and push himself to reach his full potential. This makes him perfect for any role that includes building strong relationships with clients, sponsors and key stakeholders."

- Sponsorship Manager, Company Name

"His passion for skiing have shaped his life for the good, and the worldwide connections and friends he has made throughout the years, in and out of the industry, are a credit to his likeable demeanor and loyalty."

- Director, Company Name

"Sponsoring many athletes across a diverse amount of action sports, I have never met a person with the same dedication and attitude he has... great enthusiasm and a willingness to learn, super pro-active, not just an athlete but keen to learn on a business angle and approach, to make himself the most rounded of professionals."

- Vice President, Company Name

"I've watched a talented athlete turn into a spokesperson, a leader, and a talent for business. He will continue to go far in whatever he endeavors to pursue. No company can go wrong with his level of drive and dedication to everything he undertakes."

- Marketing Director, Company Name

YOUR NAME

City, State Zip / Phone / Email

OFFICE MANAGEMENT PROFESSIONAL
Office Administration / Sales & Marketing / Coordination & Planning

High energy professional with the strategic vision and tactical implementation skills to:

✓ Increase ROI by negotiation & best practices. ✓ Meet deadlines & budgetary parameters.
✓ Manage concurrent projects efficiently. ✓ Communicate effectively at all levels.
✓ Forecast & plan for proactive management. ✓ Leverage strong economics knowledge.
✓ Ensure world class customer / client service. ✓ Translate ideas into tangible results.

Key areas of experience:

- Contract Development & Negotiation
- Budget Management
- Marketing Collateral
- Profit & Loss (P&L) Management
- Office Management
- Bill & Expense Analysis
- Forecasting, Planning & Analysis
- MS Office Word Processing
- MS Excel Spreadsheets
- Event & Exhibit Management
- Business Writing & Editing
- Direct Mail & Marketing Campaigns
- Program Management
- Logistical Planning
- Records Management
- Report Preparation
- Presentations
- Customer Service

EDUCATION / CERTIFICATION

BS in Economics, Minor in Business Administration – University Name
Currently pursuing Certified Meeting Planner (CMP) credentials

PROFESSIONAL EXPERIENCE

FREELANCE CLERICAL SUPPORT / COMPANY NAME, City, ST   Date to Present

Secretary / Proofreader / VA / Event Manager (Contractor)
Clients / Contracts: Held private clients (Company Name, Company Name, Company Name, and Company Name) and also took on assignments through agencies, which included Company Name, Company Name, and Company Name.

- *Program Management & Contracts:* Consulted with Company Name to manage annual events, which involved extensive contract writing and negotiation; resulted in tens of thousands of dollars in real and potential risk for client. Handled all aspects of events from contracts through scheduling, planning, marketing, and onsite logistics. Renegotiated loan contracts for Company Name and its lenders.

- *Administration:* Performed on-site and virtual administrative support for clients, which included editing, proofreading, customer communications, business correspondence, record keeping, and marketing.

- *Telephone Support & Customer Service:* Furnished telephone customer support and sales to companies such as Company Name and Company Name via contract with Company Name. Attained 90%+ ranking and letters of recognition for service levels and time / goal attainment.

- *Taxes & Finances:* Managed all personal finances for small business which included using tax software and IRS reporting.

- *Management Logistics & Services:* Managed onsite logistics and catering of meetings for 10-2,300 attendees in FL, AL, TX, and NV.

COMPANY NAME, City, ST   Date to Present

Marketing Manager / Sales & Marketing Coordinator
Leveraged extensive administrative, sales, marketing, and business knowledge to participate in driving strategy, design, and implementation for product marketing and positioning with input of co-Marketing Manager and executive direction. Focused on driving company to embrace new strategies in e-marketing including viral strategies, blogging, web video, improved copy, and SEO.

PROFESSIONAL EXPERIENCE

- ***Marketing Collateral & Graphics - Direct Mail & Exhibit:*** Handled creation of specials, promotions, direct mail pieces, brochures, catalogs, comparison charts, literature folders, and spec sheets. Sought to streamline and integrate brand across diverse product lines.

- ***E-Marketing:*** Directed strategy / scheduling of eblasts including creation (from product announcements, technical updates, executive letters) and distribution. Introduced tracking software to track campaigns and make adjustments to improve click-through rates. Researched viral marketing and SEO.

- ***Website Design & Marketing:*** Contributed input, proofreading, sketch designs, and requests around content needed to be posted or created. Spearheaded development of new product site content.

- ***Advertising:*** Oversaw strategy of advertising plan with direction from CEO. Researched free print and Web listings, coordinated publication insertion orders, created ads, and worked with outside agencies.

- ***Public Relations:*** Provided critical media contact as a spokesperson, campaign developer, and creator of press releases. Developed story angles and pitches to capture media interest.

- ***Tradeshow Management:*** Ensured all tradeshow participation was smooth, streamlined, and efficient. Coordinated company participation and exhibition for over 40 region and state tradeshows.

- ***Order System Management:*** Administered company's manufacturing software solution for managing entire order cycle. Set up specials, prices, entered prospect contact information, and tracked marketing campaigns. Provided training in order entry and customer relations management.

- ***Customer Service:*** Interfaced with all customers and end-users (multi-tier corporate, military, gov't). Supported end users who included the US Army, DOT, BLM, and USFS as well as commercial clients.

ADDITIONAL RELEVANT EXPERIENCE

COMPANY NAME, City, ST   Date to Date

Sales Representative
Recruited to spearhead new territory development and aggressive marketing for distributor of a diverse portfolio of domestic and international wines.

COMPANY NAME, City, ST   Date to Date

Corporate Event Planner / Executive Assistant
Office Clerk & Meeting Coordinator – Medicomp (2001)
Handled the planning, budget development and administration, management, and on-site coordination of corporate meetings, conventions, spokesperson tours, tradeshow participation / exhibition, leadership summits, and product launch programs.

Managed website administration (both corporate and convention) and all corporate communications to include daily email newsletters, phone messaging, conference calls, training schedules, weekly meeting updates, distributor event announcement, and US / international promotion logistics.

City, State, Zip
LinkedIn Profile URL

YOUR NAME
Recruiting and HR... without all the drama

Phone Number
Email Address

SUMMARY OF QUALIFICATIONS

Gregarious **Recruiting, Training, and Employee Relations Professional** with a BA in English from Harvard plus 8 years of experience recruiting, hiring, onboarding, and managing employees, stemming from leadership roles as a producer and talent coordinator for 2 beloved Boston performance companies. Previous career in sketch comedy lends well to polished presentation skills and ability to work with strong personalities, not to mention a pretty good sense of humor.

- Recruiting Campaigns
- Phone Screening
- Interview Coordination
- Group Interviews
- Individual Interviews
- Hiring & Onboarding
- Employee Relations
- Employee Engagement
- Training & Development
- Conflict Resolution
- Consensus Building
- Employee Discipline

PROFESSIONAL EXPERIENCE & ACHIEVEMENTS

Company Name — Producer | Director | Trainer   City • Dates-Dates

Became a driving force of recruiting, training, and teambuilding with this renowned Boston sketch comedy company, in addition to writing and acting in several performances. Produced 10 full-length comedy shows, which required top-notch skills in talent acquisition and management, team coordination, mediation, and sales and marketing.

—— RECRUITING, HIRING, AND ONBOARDING ——

- ❖ **Recruiting:** Sourced 500+ actors, crew, and featured artists across 4 years of productions; networked through associations, colleagues, talent databases, job boards, and social media platforms.
- ❖ **Headhunting:** Pitched jobs to top talent, helping candidates see parallels between their work history and open role. Drummed up excitement amongst candidates, despite the low wage offering.
- ❖ **Screening:** Set up and coordinated multi-day initial screenings for 50-75 candidates; selected top 10%-15% of the pool for second-round group auditions to ultimately fill 3-6 spots.
- ❖ **Interviewing:** Conducted formal phone and in-person interviews with potential set design/crew members; developed strong rapport to make inroads for future recruiting opportunities.

—— STAFF RELATIONS AND TEAMBUILDING ——

- ❖ **Conflict Resolution:** Became go-to person for alleviating interpersonal problems amongst some very strong personalities; remained reliably neutral yet empathetic.
- ❖ **Consensus Building:** Called and facilitated town-hall meetings to deliver carefully crafted messaging to all company members in order to reclaim collaboration, creativity, and trust.

—— TRAINING AND TALENT DEVELOPMENT ——

- ❖ **Classroom Training:** Launched new acting workshop, which became a recruiting ground for new members. Designed class strategy and lesson plans to engage groups of 8-12 students.
- ❖ **Individual Coaching:** Developed tailored training programs for high-potential team members.

Company Name — Learning Coordinator | Casting Assistant   City • Dates-Dates

Doubled as a recruiter and training coordinator in the Arts Education division of this well-established theater company. Developed a strong sense of running a non-profit organization from an HR Operations standpoint.

—— RECRUITING, HIRING, AND ONBOARDING ——

- ❖ **Recruiting:** Sourced new talent by attending acting camp job fairs; placed ads, leveraged network, and recruited through existing enrollees. Conducted 100+ interviews every year.
- ❖ **Screening:** Assisted with large-scale rapid-fire general auditions for 300+ professional actors at a time, with more in-depth follow-up sessions for 50 of the most promising candidates.
- ❖ **Onboarding:** Welcomed / processed 30-40 teachers, which included orientation, tours, and paperwork.

—— TRAINING EVENT PRODUCTION ——

- ❖ **Staff Training:** Trained 20 staff, interns, and volunteers in organizing and preparing 550 actors.

EDUCATION & SKILLS

Harvard University: BA English, Certificate in Theater (with honors) – Date
Proficient in MS Office / Fluent Spanish / Basic French

YOUR NAME

City, ST • Phone • Email

SENIOR WELLSITE MANAGER | SUPERVISOR

Systematic Operations → Safety Adherence → Project Execution

- Skilled project leader with progressive hands-on experience in drilling, completions, workovers, and interventions within major oil and gas organizations.
- Experienced in managing daily well site logistics, organizing rig contractor personnel, third-party contractors, and site equipment for multi well pad operations.
- Accomplished in troubleshooting well issues and communicating solutions to clients and multidisciplinary personnel, leveraging a wealth of field expertise to speed diagnosis and recovery.
- Proficient in promoting worksite safety and strictly complying with all safety and environmental regulations, mentoring and training junior staff on performance excellence.

CORE COMPETENCIES

- ✓ Oil and Gas Operations Management
- ✓ Health, Safety, and Environment Compliance
- ✓ Resource Management
- ✓ Scheduling & Logistics
- ✓ Program Development & Implementation
- ✓ Project Management

- ✓ Documentation & Reporting
- ✓ Accident Investigation & Prevention
- ✓ Training & Mentoring
- ✓ Relationship Management & Communications
- ✓ Troubleshooting & Resolution
- ✓ WellView Software

PROFESSIONAL EXPERIENCE

Senior Wellsite Manager   Date – Date
Company A – City, ST

Wellsite Supervisor   Date – Date
Company B – City, ST

Wellsite Manager / Supervisor   Date – Date
Company C – City, ST

Rig Manager   Date – Date
Company D – City, ST

Driller / Rig Manager   Date – Date
Company E – City, ST

Driller   Date – Date
Company F – City, ST

continued

CAREER HIGHLIGHTS & AREAS of EXPERTISE

Operational Management:

- Directed day-to-day operations of drilling, completions, and workovers at Company A, B, and C; organized logistics, personnel, and equipment for simultaneous and multiple well sites throughout State and State.

- Spearheaded work plan implementation for multi-well pad completions valued up to $20M per well at Company A; oversaw cost controls, resource management, and daily workload assignments.

- Performed a wide range of well site activities, including multi-stage fracking, plug and perforate pump downs, and high-pressure high-temperature (HPHT) work at Company A, B, and C; foresaw challenges and adjusted timelines to keep projects on schedule and within budget.

Communications and Logistics:

- Coordinated, monitored, and directed activities of up to 150 site staff, sub-contractors, trades, and suppliers at any one time at Company A; visited sites regularly and encouraged open communications with personnel.

- Acted as a positive company representative towards clients and stakeholders at Company B; developed contingency plans and well site solutions alongside management teams.

Safety Compliance and Technical Expertise:

- Identified and implemented solutions to safety issues, mentoring site staff on proper procedures and safety and environmental regulations at Company D and E; maintained an excellent safety record with no major incidents.

- Leveraged extensive rig expertise at Company E and F to anticipate challenges, identify problems, and streamline procedures that kept projects flowing; technically proficient with a wide range of well site equipment.

EDUCATION & CERTIFICATIONS

Computer Systems, Electronics, Accounting, and Organizational Behavior Courses – Institute Name

Well Workover and Completion Series – University Name

Accident Investigation and Prevention – Organization Name

Oilfield Training and Certificates:

IADC WellCAP Supervisors Level (Completions) • Well Service Blowout Prevention • H2S Alive
Confined Space Entry • Fall Protection • Rig Rescue / High Angle Rescue • Special Oilfield Boiler
Service Rig Assessors • Regulatory Awareness for Well Site Supervisors • Detection of Flammable
Substances • Transportation of Dangerous Goods • Advanced Safety Auditing
WHMIS • Standard First Aid and CPR

YOUR NAME
Cell Phone Number ■ Home Phone Number ■ Email Address

SENIOR AVIONICS TECHNICIAN / TECHNICAL PROGRAM DIRECTOR

Aviation systems technology expert; infuse career-wide experience as an aircraft electrician and avionics specialist to drive operational readiness of diverse aircraft electrical systems and communications platforms. Leverage performance through integration and optimization of aviation maintenance programs, and strategic management of financial capital and resources.

→ **Minimize Downtime**	→ **Cut Costs**	→ **Increase Aircraft Availability**
Quality Systems Management	Developmental Testing	Radar Systems / Navigation
Production Control	Allied Trades	Service Planning Optimization
Supply Chain Management	Aviation Systems Technology	Aviation Systems Sustainment

Professional Experience

Aircraft Maintenance / Avionics Health of Fleet Manager
Branch of Service, Department of Defense [Date-Date]

Program Management – Provided primary liaison between maintenance supervision and electrical engineers; planned, coordinated, and expedited maintenance, overhauls, conversions, and refits on a fleet of F-22 aircraft valued at more than $5.3 billion.

➤ Supplied key leadership and 24-hour management of operations to sustain F22 flying hour program, more than 3K sorties, and 4K in flying hours; increased aircraft reliability by 30%.

➤ Prevented cost expenditures of $158K via system analysis; correction of an electronic warfare defect.

➤ Recognized for averting potential Class A mishap; prevented loss of a $160M jet through eradicating a cabin pressure leak.

➤ Acted as Technical Inspector (TI) for F-22 aircraft; cleared scheduled and unscheduled maintenance procedures (Grounding Red-X and Circled Red-X status) in accordance with technical manuals.

Human Capital Management – Charged with training, discipline, morale, health, and welfare of 90 cross-functional personnel. Increased qualifications by 15% through a robust revamp of department training programs and authored six competitive award packages to expedite promotion of exceptional performers.

Technical Advisor / Avionics System Craftsman
Branch of Service, Department of Defense [Date-Date]

Fleet Relocation - Orchestrated the flawless transfer and transcontinental relocation of fleet aircraft valued in excess of $600M.

Project Development – Stood up new unit of F-22 aircraft; influenced adoption of a new standard for logistics packages to support aircraft specific deployments; authored Installation COMSEC Cryptographic Policies.

Training Program Management – Handpicked to serve as the primary Training Development Instructor for newly assigned aircraft; designed a new aircraft-specific training program from the ground up.

➤ Facilitated training for more than 65 aerospace technicians, journeymen electricians, and electrical apprentices.

➤ Lauded for attaining a 25% increase in production; provided direct oversight, management, and training of 35 new avionics technicians.

continued

Integrated Avionics Journeyman
Branch of Service, Department of Defense [Date-Date]

Operations - Supervised daily operations of six departments and up to 80 occupationally diverse personnel, prioritized scheduled and unscheduled maintenance requirements, communicated scope of work (SOW) as well as mission objectives, and goals. Consistently exceeded operational readiness standards by 8%.

Aircraft Testing – Contributed extensively to developmental testing of newly fielded aircraft, which entailed compiling citation lists, and gathering and documenting the utilization of test data. Successfully improved software suite and attributed to enhanced aircraft war fighting capability by more than 60%.

Cultural Diversity – Completed multiple deployments with tours of duty in five continents; provided critical support to strategically dispersed, global aviation elements.

Career Progression – Held roles with increased responsibility in aspects of aviation maintenance and project management; in-depth knowledge of aviation systems technology, electronics, avionics, radar systems, operational and developmental testing, communications, navigation, flight controls, attack display, utilities, electronic warfare systems, environmental control systems, airworthiness, and quality control inspection protocol. *Key avionics experience:*

➢ Licensed to repair, maintain, or internally adjust ship radar equipment; demonstrated proper installation, servicing, and maintenance of ship radar equipment in general use for maritime navigation.

➢ Qualified to adjust, maintain, or internally repair FCC licensed radiotelephone transmitters in aviation, maritime, and international fixed public radio services (high/low power radio frequency), and operate compulsorily equipped ship radiotelephone stations, voluntarily equipped ship, and aeronautical (including aircraft) stations.

➢ Shared advanced knowledge with colleagues; taught technicians to diagnose, repair, and install electrical, avionic, environmental control, or computer based systems; and troubleshot and conducted functional testing on aircraft systems.

➢ Maintained current certifications; demonstrated working knowledge of risk management processes, hazardous material (HAZMAT) management and handling, occupational safety (OSHA), and the use of personal protection equipment (PPE).

Certifications / Licenses

Licensed General Radiotelegraph Operators (PG), Federal Communications Commission
FCC Ship Radar Endorsement, Federal Communications Commission
Certified in Fiber Optics and Delphi Connection Systems
Aircraft Attach Systems and HTS Systems
Avionics Instruments - Distinguished Graduate
Electronic Principles - Distinguished Graduate
Department of Defense

Education

Bachelor of Science in Avionics Systems Technology
Community College

YOUR NAME

Address ■ City, ST Zip
Phone Number
Email
LinkedIn URL

SALES REPRESENTATIVE

Highly profitable, award-winning sales professional who focuses on strategic solutions that produce annual increases in revenue for employer and consistently amazing results for clients. Valued for securing and maintaining long-term major accounts.

VALUE TO ORGANIZATION

Sales Strategies: Familiar with tried-and-true as well as innovative approaches to client needs.
Relationship Building: Enjoy people and find sales a natural extension of relationships.
Influencing Others: Belief in product / service creates genuine wish to share it with others.
Partnerships: Years of experience collaborating with local and regional companies and industries.

Skills and Expertise

- Product Knowledge
- Customer Information
- Product-Customer Match
- Customer Calls / Service
- Goal Setting / Reaching
- Negotiations

- Computer Skills
- Prioritization
- Post-sales Consultation
- Prospecting
- Funnel Maintenance
- Human Resources

- Market Knowledge
- Sales Closings
- Training
- Follow-through
- Problem Solving
- Organization

PROFESSIONAL EXPERIENCE

COMPANY NAME, CITY, ST   Date to Date
Industry founder and leader providing industry solutions since 1946. District covers northern half of state and northwest third of State, has 3 FTEs and $3 million in Date revenue.

District Manager
Served as primary revenue producer for City District. Assessed needs and created employment solutions for area businesses. Built community awareness through events including job fairs, chamber events, and memberships / offices in other organizations. Developed and implemented diversified and efficient recruiting program and stayed top of mind in community through office relocation, POS, Internet, and proactive customer calls.

Sales Achievements
- Secured three top customers that billed over $2.5 million through consistent contact with employer and employees.
- Improved net sales 25% to $500,000 in fiscal Year.
- Achieved consistent 10% return contribution on sales.

Recognition
- Earned substantial year-end bonus, Division (North and South America) quarterly sales awards, and Q2 Region award, all for 30% YOY increased sales in fiscal Year.
- Won Year Sales Star Division award for strategic teamwork on closing regional account.
- Recognized for sales achievement in three quarters of Year, Q3 in Year, and for consistent growth over three years, an outstanding performance in Division market.
- Singled out for local account growth award, Date.
- Promoted to District Manager for effective sales and management assistance.

continued

Professional Experience (continued)

Resident Branch Manager Date to Date

Sold services to customers and assisted in management of all operations of local branch.

- Increased net sales 200% by closing $1 million sale on No. 1 account to earn Branch Manager position.
- Increased sales, hours, and contributions that resulted in City branch's separating from District for first time since City office opened in 1989.

Company name, City, ST Date to Date

Communication service founded in City, ST in Date, servicing northwestern State.

Territory Manager

Managed all operations and corporate support for sales efforts of direct and indirect representative.

- Secured State athletic sponsorship and communication service of choice.
- Increased indirect sales distribution.

Prior Experience

- **Sales Representative**, Company Name, City, ST
- **Manager**, Company Name, City, ST
- **Sales / Repairs**, Company Name, City, ST

Professional / Community Affiliations

- **State Delegate, Leadership Conference and Member** – Organization Name, City, ST
- **Member** – Organization Name, City, ST
- **Board Member / Member** – Organization Name, City, ST
- **Ambassador / Captain** – Organization Name, City, ST - *"Outstanding Top Hatter" award for event leadership and participation*
- **Ambassador / Captain and Member** – Organization Name, City, ST
- **Member** – Organization Name, City, ST

Education

University name , City, ST
- **Bachelor of Business Management and Marketing,** completed 19 credits

Technical College name, City, ST
- **Associate Degree of Sales and Marketing / Fashion**

Professional Development
- **Franklin Covey Training,** "What Matters Most"
- **Seminars,** Microsoft Office, Date
- **State Human Resources Association,** annual training seminar
- **OSHA** annual training seminar
- **Society for Human Resource Management,** State conference vendor

YOUR NAME

City, State Zip
Phone Number
Email Address

Chief Marketing Officer

Savoring the Sweet Smell of Success: Drove Company A to Worldwide #1 in Luxury Fragrances

Luxury Beauty Products • Haute Couture • Fast Moving Consumer Goods (FMCG)

Negotiated "Media Deal of the Decade" • Legendary Instincts for Fashion's Hottest Trends

Talented Chief Marketing Officer with a solid reputation as a leader in consumer marketing for the worldwide cosmetics and fragrance industry. Stand out among CMO peers in luxury goods by combining three attributes into a single package:

- **Fashion Savvy:** Highly intuitive with a nose for emerging trends and an uncanny ability to exploit opportunities before competitors: In Year, recognized a market change and quickly shifted Company Name's mix from color cosmetics to clear – long before nearest competitors caught on.

- **Entrepreneurial:** Can quickly spot a trend, create business case, rally top management, and implement a winning plan, for example: In Year, Company Name was doing relatively little business in Asia. By Year, Asia was company's #1 growth engine and now does more than $100M annually. Entrepreneurial drive made that happen.

- **Analytical:** MBA trained with keen ability to analyze finances. Excel at conceiving a marketing idea, building an accurate financial model, and ensuring company always makes a profit.

Global Brand Strategist	Fluent in German, French, and English	Product Inventor
Digital Marketer	Team Builder – Retains Top People	Financial Modeler
Supply Chain Optimizer	Master Media Negotiator	Fashion Talent Scout

DISTINGUISHED CAREER IN GLOBAL MARKETING OF LUXURY BEAUTY BRANDS

COMPANY NAME, City, ST · Date-Present

Annual revenue $4B & 1800 employees • ops in 60 countries • fragrances 50%, haute couture 30%, and jewelry 20%

Chief Marketing Officer (Date–Present)

SVP, Worldwide Media and Marketing (Date-Date)

SVP, Asian Markets (Date-Date)

VP, Global Marketing for Cosmetics (Date-Date)

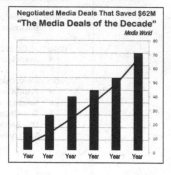

Negotiated Media Deals That Saved $62M
"The Media Deals of the Decade"
Media World

- Advanced through progressively challenging – and overlapping – leadership roles in sales, marketing, and operations.

- Recognized by CEO and Board as company's top sales driver – from $1B to $5B – during ascendance to #1 world ranking in fragrances.

- continued –

HIGHLIGHTS FOR DATE–PRESENT: CHIEF MARKETING OFFICER

Conceived an idea that consolidated company's worldwide media budgets, leveraged big discounts, and will save $62M total during Year-Year (more than any similar program in company's history).

- **"Once-in-a-Decade" Media Deal:** Extended marketing reach despite global financial crisis and shrinking outlays for media spend.
- **Top Results:** Achieved media rates as good or better as top advertisers in key markets.
  - Negotiated across-the-board cuts in US media rates: 31% for TV; 20% for print; and 8% for outdoor. Cut rates in key countries such UK (8%), Germany (13%), and Eastern Europe (20%).
  - Built Global Media Database that provided transparency and insights into key media data and costs for all markets. Secured "best of all" terms despite schedules as short as three months.

HIGHLIGHTS FOR DATE-DATE: SVP WORLDWIDE MEDIA & MARKETING

Handpicked by CEO to create a centralized marketing
organization and accelerate top-line growth throughout the enterprise.

- **Organization:** Set up specialized departments and defined new processes that enabled marketing specialists to focus on competitive business priorities instead of administrative details.
- **Media & Sales:** Turned around low-end image by applying a new PR-and-Event model.
  - Took calculated risks that pushed company's paid celebrities – including some of the highest-profile divas in show business – to work harder for their particular brands.
  - Devised a "PR Model" that generated high-quality publicity at 5% equivalent cost of paid ads. Invented metrics and tracking tools that accurately predict successful fragrances.

HIGHLIGHTS FOR DATE-DATE: SVP ASIAN MARKETS

Promoted to general management, including marketing for all of Asia plus key parts of Asian supply chain. Drove phenomenal growth in Asia that continues into the present.

- **Actions and Results:** Pinpointed opportunities, assessed competitors, and proposed a 5-year plan – including very ambitious $100M Net sales goal – that was approved by CEO and Board.
  - Exceeded all goals – reached $100M sales as forecast – and achieved #1 market position for company across Asia. Achieved 30% CAGR and profitability in first year – Asia became company's #1 growth engine.
  - Turned-around company's low-end image and achieved status as "gold standard" in Asia for marketing mix, speed to market, and distribution.

HIGHLIGHTS FOR DATE-DATE: VP MARKETING FOR COSMETICS

- **Senior Vice President, Global Marketing (Date-Date):** Led 60-person team that reversed declining shares and margins. Achieved #2 ranking for Color in Europe and #1 in UK & Spain (top markets).
- **Vice President, Global Marketing (Date–Date):** Developed a "holistic" marketing idea that was adopted throughout industry. Invited to present campaign World Conference in Le Hague.

EDUCATION

MBA Equivalent, Marketing and Finance, UNIVERSITY Name, City, Country
Licence en Sciences Economiques et Commerciales, UNIVERSITY Name, City, Country

♟ Your Name

CITY | STATE | EMAIL | PHONE | LINKEDIN URL

LUXURY HOSPITALITY INDUSTRY

UPSCALE BARS & NIGHTCLUBS

PROFESSIONAL BAR MANAGER | BAR CHEF

"Focused to achieve business excellence in hospitality/bar industry while passionately exceeding guest expectations every time" Your Name

Professional bartender with positive attitude and high energy known for quickly building rapport with clientele, providing them with premier customer service, and surpassing their expectations. Anticipate, identify, and fulfill food and beverage needs in a guest-centric environment.

"Name's innovative craft cocktail creations, his familiarity of beverages, high-class service, and his ability to maintain a calm and professional demeanor, at all times, were definitely an asset to our enterprise.

I truly feel that Name will propel your organization to new heights."

Name, CEO, Company Name, City, ST

HALLMARKED ACHIEVEMENTS

➢ **Commended by Executive Chef:** Created original handcrafted cocktails containing fresh, original ingredients including:
- Bleu Cheese stuffed olives ▪ Homemade brandied cherries
- Fresh herbs picked daily from the hotel garden
- Handcrafted cocktails at bar, dining room, and by guest request

➢ **Increased Customer Base and Revenue:** Instituted and provided a complimentary premium cigar service at no cost to hotel or guests. **Generated $5,900 on one individual bar tab** and an additional 20 percent in bar revenues/yr.

➢ **100% Top Marks Earned:** Personally received 100/100 by a third-party firm hired to evaluate bar facilities and bartenders against key industry descriptors.

CORE CAREER COMPETENCIES

★ Bar Industry	★ Advancing Business Image & Profits	★ Customer and Team Relations
▪ 5-Star–5-Diamond Experience	▪ Exceed Business Objectives	▪ Food Service Multitasking
▪ State TIPS certified	▪ Innovative Business Building Strategies	▪ High-Volume, Fast-Paced Environment
▪ Original & Recipe Cocktails	▪ Increase Profits and Minimize Losses	▪ Superior Customer Service
▪ Exceptional Memory	▪ Adhere to Company Standards	▪ Go Beyond Call of Duty
▪ Attention to Detail	▪ Solve Problems & Take Corrective Action	▪ Resolve Complaints
▪ Micros POS System	▪ Build Customer Rapport	▪ Foster Team Excellence
▪ Defuse Volatile Situations	▪ Facilitate Cross-Departmental Cooperation	▪ Exceed Guest Expectations

PROFESSIONAL EXPERIENCE

BAR CHEF / BAR MANAGER   Date–Date

Company Name, City, ST

Five-star, five-diamond luxury hotel complex serving high net worth clientele. Bar revenue exceeds $1M/yr. Prepared and presented specialty drinks served at bar and tableside. Monitored guest alcohol consumption, activities and ensured compliance with liquor laws, regulations, and codes. Maintained bar top / back, prep duties, and processed payments.

Increased Revenue

Grew "Double" Volume Drink Revenue 40 Percent within six months by recognizing and correcting pricing inconsistencies between double- and single-volume drinks. Yielded a higher profit margin.

Foresight Results in Good Public Relations and Increased Revenues

➢ Expanded vodka cocktail revenues and satisfied hotel guest professional golf celebrity by stocking and selling top shelf vodka in anticipation of hotel's championship golf tournament. Exceeded weekend bar sales goal by $10,000 during three-day event.

➢➢➢ *MORE ON NEXT PAGE*

PROFESSIONAL EXPERIENCE CONTINUED

BAR CHEF / BARTENDER Continued

Slashed Costs

⇒ **Decreased Liquor Cost by Four Percent/Yr:** While increasing bar profits by initiating measuring and pouring consistency through requisition of new bottle pour spouts.

Expanded and Retained Customer Base and Industry Rating

⇒ **Listen and Respond:** Won over and delighted a challenging, prominent guest by listening and taking immediate action, without his knowledge, when he expressed certain hotel wishes to his companions. This guest continued to frequent hotel and bar with more than 100 enthusiastic visits accumulating over $350,000 in hotel/bar sales over a four-year period.

⇒ **Four-Star to Five-Star Rating:** Advanced hotel complex rating from four to five stars within 24 months of grand opening by working in partnership with key team members.

⇒ **Four-Time Shining Star Award Winner:** Received for outstanding performance, guest service, and interdepartmental collaboration property-wide (one of five out of 350 employees).

> *"Name, thank you for your enthusiasm and participation in the development of the seasonal cocktail (menu)...*
> *I truly appreciate the level of interest and creativity you display—each list sounds fantastic.*
> *Keep up the great work!"*
>
> **Name, Executive Chef, Restaurant, Name (Company Name)**

OWNER, PHOTOGRAPHER, GRAPHIC DESIGNER   Date–Date
Company Name, City, ST
Provided advertising photography, graphic design, and print advertising campaigns

⇒ Planned, designed and executed extensive marketing campaigns for bar and nightclub industry in Metro City Name area.
  - Generated revenues in excess of $70K, for a one-night event at Company Name.
  - Increased customer connection and revenues during a public photo shoot event.
⇒ Provided fashion photography and catalog work for retail stores and a jeans manufacturer.
⇒ Computer proficiencies: Photoshop, Dreamweaver, Flash, CSS, HTML, and PHP using MySQL databases.

BARTENDER   Date–Date
Company Name, City, ST
High-energy, high-volume, fast-paced disco and nightclub. Managed general bar functions: performed prep tasks, prepared and served drinks, and maintained a clean bar top and bar back area to comply with health department standards.

⇒ Limited liability and problems related to guest intoxication by monitoring and controlling customer alcohol consumption and taking appropriate proactive steps.
⇒ Ensured customer satisfaction via exceptional memory of names and drink preferences, which drove nightly production and guest experience quality by increasing customers' perception of personal attention.
⇒ Managed bar tabs, processed customer payments.

EDUCATION AND CERTIFICATIONS

State TIPS Certification   current until / Date
Bachelor of Science Degree in Business Administration (B.S.B.A.), College Name, City, ST   Date

Your Name

City, ST Zip | Phone Number | Email Address

Senior Horticulture & Sales Manager

Master coordinator, manager, and closer of high value field projects across diverse markets.

Sharp analyst, proactive organizer, and savvy definer of specifications, resources, and people that meet project objectives on time and within budget.

Accustomed to roles requiring a high degree of self-motivation, ability to work under pressure, and a firm, yet diplomatic approach to what constitutes "done."

Equally talented cross-functional operations manager who fuels pathways to success using strong account management, sales, budgeting, quality control, and administrative skills.

Patient listener, industrious thought leader, and diligent problem solver who maximizes resources, mitigates risk, and delivers an exponential Return on Investment (ROI).

KEY SUCCESS FACTORS

- ✓ B2B & B2C Sales
- ✓ Project Lifecycle Management
- ✓ Cost Control & Reduction
- ✓ Estimates & Proposals
- ✓ Workforce Planning & Scheduling
- ✓ Performance Metrics & Deliverables
- ✓ Safety & Compliance (OSHA)
- ✓ Vendor Sourcing & Relations
- ✓ Equipment & Materials Management
- ✓ Hiring, Training & Mentorship

Career & Achievements

COMPANY NAME — City, ST   Date to Date

Horticulture Project Manager and Senior Operations Lead

Principal orchestrator of daily operations and field projects for a full service landscaping company for residential and commercial properties. Drove marketing, business development, sales, estimates, proposals, and contract negotiations. Oversaw project lifecycle from conceptual design, workforce planning, and resource management through budgeting, project execution, quality control, and closeout. Managed equipment, vendor relations, inventory, purchasing, and customer retention and upgrades. Hired, trained, and managed performance of 30 staff members.

Select Achievements:

- Grew revenue from zero to more than $220K in three years for a new landscape installation division by solely securing and retaining 30-60 new accounts per year.

- Cut costs 30% and increased quality and efficiency after improving installation methods.

- Eliminated divisional start-up debt in five years after developing and implementing a strategic business plan focusing on operational process improvements.

- Captured a $30K sale based solely upon reputation for providing top-notch service.

- Secured an average of 25 annual contract renewals through service quality, competitive pricing, and superior service.

Revenue Growth

Formal Education

Bachelor of Business Administration in Management - University Name, City, ST

Your Name

PROGRAM OFFICER FOR EDUCATION

Phone Number • Email Address
Your LinkedIn Profile URL • City, State, & Zip

PROGRAM DEVELOPMENT, MANAGEMENT & OUTREACH EXPERT

STRATEGIC VISIONING • FUNDRAISING • RECRUITMENT — EDUCATION ADVOCACY GROUPS & NON-PROFITS

Forward-thinking, spirited educational activist with a passion for directing cooperative initiatives that advance public education and develop the next generation of leaders. Adept at influencing across cultures, communities, and socio-economic levels. Positioned to leverage recent HR and business experience into a non-profit managerial role.

EXAMPLES OF VALUE & INDUSTRY ACCOMPLISHMENTS

✓ **Non-Profit Strategic Planning & Results** — Highly active in not-for-profit world. Doubled donor base to 600+ and raised $1.85M+ on anniversary campaign that funded 683 grants for 1,037 teachers / 319 schools by devising [Name of Foundation] strategy and enhancing grant funding programs.

✓ **Education & Literacy Advocacy** — Previous career track includes 8-year tenure as high-achieving elementary educator with MA candidacy in Urban Education. Selected out of 600 teachers to educate colleagues statewide via best practices training video; industry-acclaimed state board of education video still in use today.

✓ **Valuable Partnerships & Collaborations** — Ready to leverage long-fostered connections with schools and trust-based relationships within teacher-serving organizations / education-committed affiliates into success.

VALUE OFFERED

Strategic Planning • Program Design / Implementation • Project Management • Change Leadership • Community Outreach • Grant Writing & Fundraising • Compliance • Recruitment • Partnership Building • Team Leadership & Training • HR Best Practices • Business Administration • Marketing Communications • Event Planning

NON-PROFIT & EDUCATION SECTOR EXPERIENCE

EXECUTIVE BOARD MEMBER / GRANT EVALUATOR / REGIONAL COORDINATOR, Small Grant Observation Program
NAME OF NON-PROFIT ORGANIZATION • City, ST • [Date – Date]

Absorbed all areas of operations as board liaison on five strategic committees. **Earned appointment to 3-member executive committee after high-impact year as board member:** revitalized relationships between board and director during critical growth phase; trained and mentored fractured staff on professionalism and conflict resolution.

Influenced formation of strategic planning committee. Aligned programming to needs of public school teachers and students by board-chairing and facilitating three critical focus groups.

- **Strategic Planning Committee** — Propelled fundraising, decision-making, and achievement of elusive organizational goals by redrafting mission and purpose statements, and introducing 3-year growth plan: evaluated grant trends, external education reform movement, and value of programming offered.

- **Program Optimization** —
  - Enhanced effectiveness of Small Grant Observation Program as Regional Coordinator by consulting board on prerequisites for awards. Organized site observation visits to 278 grant-funded schools / classrooms while personally training school observers. Increased funding resources by forging strategic partnerships.
  - Provided 200 teachers with access to new teaching approaches by overhauling grant review and selection process on Study Grant Program, subsequently raising number of study groups to 35.

- **Grant Awards** — Analyzed hundreds of grants and recommended fellowship awards totaling $200K yearly as board member on Fund for Teacher Selection Committee; attained grants which benefited 568 educators.

- **Event Planning & Marketing** — Attracted 400 teachers—1.5x more than previous year—to annual Teacher as Leaders & Learners Workshop by chairing volunteer team that planned and promoted event.

- **Compliance** — Created foundation's first whistleblower policy and introduced internal controls after contracting consulting firm and overseeing audit process as lead on Audit Committee.

CURRICULUM WRITER, COMPANY NAME • City, ST • [Date – Date]

Approached by company owner to upgrade learning standards and practices, and instill higher-order thinking and deeper learning while writing curricula. Consistently met tight deadlines while juggling multiple, complex projects.

- **Curricula Innovation** — Enhanced academic achievement for elementary school pupils by integrating technology and interactive quizzes into lesson plans.
- **Model Primary Curriculum** — Emphasized improvements in student learning experiences through inquiry and project-based approach to curriculum design.

ELEMENTARY SCHOOL TEACHER, SCHOOL NAMES • City, ST / City, ST • [Date – Date]

1st Grade Teacher: School Name [Date – Date] • 2nd Grade Teacher: School Name [Date – Date]
2nd Grade Teacher: School Name [Date – Date] • 1st Grade Teacher: School Name [Date – Date]

Consistently received top performance evaluations. Selected to draft district-wide literacy and math curricula after assisting school and district leadership teams to **enhance school impact.** Co-led quarterly conversations to discuss progress on student performance and school practices. Managed classrooms of up to 34 students with no aide while mentoring three student teachers to full-time roles. Advised on various literacy, math, and school climate committees.

- **Teaching Excellence Recognition** — Handpicked by state board of education out of 600 candidates to present best teaching practices for state training video series.
- **Universal Literacy Standardization** — Aligned student achievement, school practice, and team management with district and state literacy standards as leader of planning team.

HR & BUSINESS MANAGEMENT EXPERIENCE

HUMAN RESOURCES / BUSINESS MANAGER, COMPANY NAME • City, ST • [Date – Date]

Engaged by CFO to **infuse HR discipline and business structure into $3.4M early-stage business.** Installed inaugural employee programs and standard operating procedures (SOPs) to facilitate planned growth. **Cut payroll expenses $20K and compliance issues by half** after debuting best-practice compensation / benefits plans. **Solved high staff attrition** by recruiting and onboarding best-fit talent.

> "[Name] is one of the most dedicated professionals I have worked with in 20 years. She introduced strategies that were both effective and efficient for our growing company. She solved myriad issues...and always exuded strength and confidence. Her determination and culture-building skills are top notch..."—**CFO, Company Name**

EDUCATION, CERTIFICATIONS & TRAINING

Master of Arts (M.A) Program Candidate, Urban Education, University Name • City, ST • [Date – Date]
Bachelor of Arts (B.A.), Licensure, Elementary Education, University Name • City, ST • [Date]

Teaching Licensure K-9 — State and State
Teaching and Technology Certificate, University Name • [Date]
Minnesota Educational Effectiveness Program: Absorbed and implemented strategies to assist schools make research-based improvements, sponsor meetings, form task forces, and set strategic goals.

ADDITIONAL VOLUNTEER WORK

KPPS City Reading Group – Safe Place Job Readiness Program – State Board Member, Foundation Name
State Public High Schools: Tutor/Mentor—3Ms English Language Learner Program; Reading & Writing Program
Portfolio Evaluator for State Public Schools

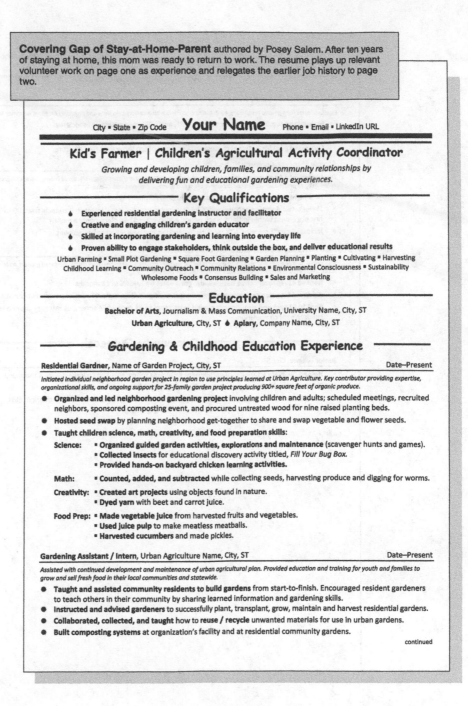

City ▪ State ▪ Zip Code **Your Name** Phone ▪ Email ▪ LinkedIn URL

Kid's Farmer | Children's Agricultural Activity Coordinator

Growing and developing children, families, and community relationships by delivering fun and educational gardening experiences.

Key Qualifications

- **Experienced residential gardening instructor and facilitator**
- **Creative and engaging children's garden educator**
- **Skilled at incorporating gardening and learning into everyday life**
- **Proven ability to engage stakeholders, think outside the box, and deliver educational results**

Urban Farming ▪ Small Plot Gardening ▪ Square Foot Gardening ▪ Garden Planning ▪ Planting ▪ Cultivating ▪ Harvesting
Childhood Learning ▪ Community Outreach ▪ Community Relations ▪ Environmental Consciousness ▪ Sustainability
Wholesome Foods ▪ Consensus Building ▪ Sales and Marketing

Education

Bachelor of Arts, Journalism & Mass Communication, University Name, City, ST
Urban Agriculture, City, ST ▪ **Apiary**, Company Name, City, ST

Gardening & Childhood Education Experience

Residential Gardner, Name of Garden Project, City, ST   Date–Present

Initiated individual neighborhood garden project in region to use principles learned at Urban Agriculture. Key contributor providing expertise, organizational skills, and ongoing support for 25-family garden project producing 900+ square feet of organic produce.

- **Organized and led neighborhood gardening project** involving children and adults; scheduled meetings, recruited neighbors, sponsored composting event, and procured untreated wood for nine raised planting beds.
- **Hosted seed swap** by planning neighborhood get-together to share and swap vegetable and flower seeds.
- **Taught children science, math, creativity, and food preparation skills:**

  Science:
  - **Organized guided garden activities, explorations and maintenance** (scavenger hunts and games).
  - **Collected insects** for educational discovery activity titled, *Fill Your Bug Box.*
  - **Provided hands-on backyard chicken learning activities.**

  Math:
  - **Counted, added, and subtracted** while collecting seeds, harvesting produce and digging for worms.

  Creativity:
  - **Created art projects** using objects found in nature.
  - **Dyed yarn** with beet and carrot juice.

  Food Prep:
  - **Made vegetable juice** from harvested fruits and vegetables.
  - **Used juice pulp** to make meatless meatballs.
  - **Harvested cucumbers** and made pickles.

Gardening Assistant / Intern, Urban Agriculture Name, City, ST   Date–Present

Assisted with continued development and maintenance of urban agricultural plan. Provided education and training for youth and families to grow and sell fresh food in their local communities and statewide.

- **Taught and assisted community residents to build gardens** from start-to-finish. Encouraged resident gardeners to teach others in their community by sharing learned information and gardening skills.
- **Instructed and advised gardeners** to successfully plant, transplant, grow, maintain and harvest residential gardens.
- **Collaborated, collected, and taught** how to reuse / recycle unwanted materials for use in urban gardens.
- **Built composting systems** at organization's facility and at residential community gardens.

continued

―――――――――――――――――――――――― **Additional Experience** ――――――――――――――――――――――――

Sales Associate, Company Name, City, ST   Date–Date

Increased sales for high-end retail store, by assisting customers with accessory selections and providing excellent customer service.

- **Maintained top 5% ranking** for volume, UPT, and ADP among 20 sales associates.
- **Exceeded daily revenue goals by 50%.**
- **Surpassed goal for national contest**; attained one of top three slots for City store.

Account Manager, Company Name, City, ST   Date–Date

Developed prospect list of government and commercial companies in need of IT consultants. Used cold calling, networking, telemarketing, and entertaining to present services to key decision-makers and developed rapport with clients.

- **Held highest interview-to-deal closing ratio** (3:4) companywide.
- **Skyrocketed dormant account 400%** by developing new business, increased contacts from 90 to 374, solidified first placement within initial 4-week period and averaged two placements a month.
- **Increased profit margins 70%** by pursuing and landing new business key account.

Field Marketing Representative, Company Name, City, ST   Date–Date

Maximized sales of office and household products within territory including 16 big-box retail stores. Increased product sales, maximized shelf space, and merchandised for product lines such as ABC, DEF and GHI.

- **Ranked #1 representative nationwide**; grew sales by **1,064%** in 12 months.
- **Achieved 1st place rank and generated triple digit growth** in national permanent marker contest.
- **Shot to #1 spot and simultaneously led sales team to #1 spot** while serving as category captain in national children's toy competition.

―――――――――――――――――――――――――― **Community Outreach** ――――――――――――――――――――――――――

Junior League, City, ST   Date–Present

- **Helped facilitate after-school enrichment programs** for parents and children grades K through 3.
- **Sponsored a child** in program linking disadvantaged children with volunteers.
- **Contributed to school improvement project** by collaborating to paint cafeteria with bright circus theme.

♦ ♦ ♦ ♦ ♦

Phone Number ◆ Street Address ◆ City, State

YOUR NAME

Dependable | Results-Driven | Punctual | Organized

1st TERM CARPENTRY APPRENTICE & GENERAL LABORER
Leveraging physical strength and analytical skills ✦ Contributing to city's economic growth

Determined carpentry apprentice experienced in completing complex projects; including construction of two charity homes in local community.

Exemplary track record of success in safety compliance and team leadership; evidenced by military background. Recognized as a team-player and performer; consistently finishing assigned projects by current employer under budget and ahead of schedule.

A trouble-shooter who effectively and efficiently resolves issues while meeting and achieving challenging goals and objectives. Distinguished military career.

Core Strengths

- Team-Building & Leadership
- Corporate Mission | Vision Fulfillment
- Safety Management & Quality Control
- Staff Training
- Verbal & Listening Skills

- Analytical & Mathematical Skills
- Employee Supervision & Training
- Physical Strength & Stamina
- Attention to Fine Detail
- Maintenance & Support

Technical Skills

- Renovation & Design
- Framing
- Dry walling
- Roofing

- Finishing
- Cabinetry
- Flooring
- Ductwork

- First-Aid & CPR
- Valid Driver's License
- WHIMIS
- Forklift Operator

Performance Highlights

Carpentry Assistant   Date-Date
Company Name – City, State
Privately operated, Company Name specializes in residential renovation and finish carpentry. Worked directly under supervision of owner.

- Renovated basement laundry-room that surpassed customer expectations.
- Assisted in demolition and restoration of bathroom that included installation of a porcelain tile tub / shower surround.
- Continued to gain valuable knowledge and experience with home renovations, which included installing ductwork, insulation and re-siding.

Page 1 of 2

Performance Highlights (continued)

General Laborer Volunteer　　　　　　　　　　　　　　　　　　　Date - Date
Company Name – City, State
XYZ Charity is a non-profit organization working towards a world where everyone has a safe and affordable place to live.

- *Supported the construction of two homes in the City Community.*
- *Acquired and expanded upon growing knowledge of construction and carpentry techniques.*

Previous Employment History

Nightshift Grocery Clerk　　　　　　　　　　　　　　　　　　　Date - Date
Company Name – City, State
Performed stock work in a timely manner; ensured labels and pricing were accurate throughout store.

Store Standard Lead Hand | Backroom Material Handler　　　　　Date - Date
Company Name – City, State
Trained two employees in safe product handling for back storage room and sales floor; ensured policies and procedures for cleaning and maintaining safe environment were always followed.

Lead Hand Painters Assistant | Bridge Assembly　　　　　　　Date - Date
Company Name – City, State
Prepared products for painting and attained forklift certification. Participated in the assembly of bridge components for this highly respected aerospace and defense company.

2nd Lieutenant / Junior Officer　　　　　　　　　　　　　　　Date - Date
Armed Forces – City, State
Promoted from officer cadet to 2nd Lieutenant; recognized for leadership skills with troop members during field training. Demonstrated excellent stamina and physical strength during training.

Education

Social Service Worker Diploma
College of Applied Arts and Technology Name – City, State

Bachelor of Arts, History
University Name – City, State

YOUR NAME

City, ST Zip | Phone | Email Address

TARGET: PUBLIC RELATIONS

✓ **Award-winning communicator** with insider's understanding of news media and passion for promoting non-profit organizations.

✓ **Strong relationship building skills** and ability to connect with leaders throughout a community to achieve organizational objectives.

PROJECT MANAGEMENT ~ COMMUNITY RELATIONS ~ MEDIA RELATIONS ~ WEBSITE CONTENT & SOCIAL MEDIA

PROFESSIONAL EXPERIENCE

WEEKEND ANCHOR & REPORTER – COMPANY A, CITY, ST — DATE TO DATE

WEEKEND ANCHOR & REPORTER – COMPANY B, CITY, ST — DATE TO DATE

Gained well-rounded experience in dual role as a weekend news anchor and reporter. Led newsroom each weekend, managing all facets of newscasts; supervised one reporter and up to 10 production team members while juggling duties of assignment desk editor, producer and solo anchor. **During tenure at Company A, weekend newscast ratings rose from No. 2 to No. 1 for City Name.**

- **Project management:** Managed large projects from planning through execution, like a three-part series on "cold" crime investigations for Company A that resulted in police reopening all the cases. Efficiently balanced daily duties with long-term projects.
- **Relationship skills:** Established strong relationships with numerous leaders throughout government, non-profits, hospitals, law enforcement and other sectors, which resulted in many exclusive stories.
- **Community relations:** Drove Company B's involvement with Nonprofit Name, which helped raise more than $140,000, and spearheaded stories publicizing charitable causes that raised more than $85,000.
- **Website content:** Rewrote stories for web and used content management system to post them on site.
- **Social media:** Posted compelling updates, which contributed Facebook fan growth from 63,000 to 95,000 for Company A; Company B grew from 45,000 to 79,000.
- **Marketing:** Wrote copy for promo spots advertising the evening newscasts on weekends, which contributed to 17% ratings increase for weekend newscasts with Company B.
- **Awards:** Recognized with two awards from the State Press Association: "Best Investigative Reporter" and "Best Reporter, General Assignment."

ASSISTANT PRODUCER – COMPANY NAME, CITY, ST — DATE TO DATE

Selected full-time following successful internship; only one of six interns to be hired in full-time role. Wrote stories for newscasts, gathered information and conducted off-camera interviews.

EDUCATION

B.A., Broadcast Journalism – University Name, City, ST

COMMUNITY INVOLVEMENT

Volunteer – XYZ Nonprofit, Date to Date

YOUR NAME

SENIOR MARKETING EXECUTIVE

City, State ■ Phone Number ■ Email Address

BUSINESS TURNAROUND SPECIALIST

BRAND DISTINCTION | TOYS AND GAMES | CHANNEL MANAGEMENT

Award-winning business strategist recognized by Company Name CEO for encyclopedic knowledge of children's toy sector and ability to transform failing departments into profit centers. Highlights include:

✓ Turned around underperforming multi-million dollar operations and enhanced revenue by over one hundred million per annum.

✓ Drove change initiatives and communicated strategic vision, which inspired Sales and Marketing teams to exceed divisional KPIs by 50%.

✓ Capitalized on unchartered markets and products which drove exponential profits of $130M in five years.

✓ Balanced risk through exhaustive research to avoid all unnecessary losses. Offloaded unprofitable business lines and raised $65M in new capital.

EXECUTIVE SUMMARY

- Strategic Planning
- Integrated Marketing
- Channel Strategies
- International Business
- Profit & Market Growth
- Building Effective Teams
- New Product Evolution
- Change Leadership

PROFESSIONAL EXPERIENCE

TOY MANUFACTURER CHARITY START-UP
DATE — PRESENT

Co-established a charity that designs and manufactures safe, high-quality toys, made from recycled materials, and which provides disadvantaged young adults with job opportunities. Raised five-figure government funding at start-up. Concurrently undertook a career break from ED roles to care for terminally ill family member.

- **Strategic Partnerships:** Accessed outstanding talent pool through affiliations with public and private sector employment agencies; designed learning programs that supported development of each volunteer.
- **Market Growth:** Delivered $35,000 sales in first year; secured agreements with eight national retailers.

COMPANY NAME, CITY, STATE
DATE — DATE

International toy and electronics manufacturer with a turnover of > $6B and 28,000 employees worldwide in 2013.

EXECUTIVE DIRECTOR, PRESCHOOL DIVISION - DATE-DATE

Orchestrated U-turn of declining $750M business, which generated significant and sustainable net revenue growth of 15% in first full year to exceed all targets. Owned P&L across five categories, mobilizing Sales and Marketing team of 75 to implement international expansion plan.

OPERATIONAL EXCELLENCE

- **Transformational Leadership:** Masterminded substantial cultural change; restructured staff and promoted future stars. Inspired team to achieve all stretch targets, which increased sales by over 20% across the board.
- **Continuous Process Improvement:** Streamlined "above and below the line" marketing procedures across Preschool Division, modeled HQ infrastructure to optimize efficiency while improving process quality by 15%.
- **Strategic Execution:** Doubled profit in Baby business in one year from $35M to $70M. Terminated loss-making product lines and sold off distressed segments to four competitors.

MARKETING ACUMEN

- **Product Repositioning:** Created new profit stream through previously under-marketed "Learn Rocket." Firmly embedded product across US, which acquired seven major accounts and produced 22% surge in turnover.
- **Branding Specialist:** Spearheaded launch of "Power Wheels" to toddler toy market in the US from a zero base. Placed product in high profile stores and leveraged triple profit of every Company ABC Preschool line.
- **New Product Development:** Spotted gap in the market and pioneered personalized "New Baby" product, swiftly taking over as market leader, producing 20% increase in revenue in first year.

INTERNATIONAL PROJECT LEADER, CONTINENTAL EXPANSION TEAM, BRAZIL - DATE

STRATEGY MANAGEMENT

- *Leadership:* Selected to head international project. Directed team to redefine flawed distribution model in Central and South America, company's second largest market.
- *Margin Enhancement:* Catapulted annual regional profit levels from 3% to 18%; addressed sales structure, market cultivation, and competitive environment.

COMPANY NAME, CITY, STATE   DATE – DATE

International children's toy manufacturer and wholesaler with a turnover of > $500M and 275 employees.

SENIOR ACCOUNT MANAGER - DATE – DATE

Parachuted in to revitalize failing multinational $35M account. Promoted twice over three years for performance excellence, which maximized wallet share with key customers and nurtured profitable relationships with clients.

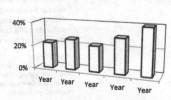

Sales Increase

TACTICAL CUSTOMER APPROACH

- *Client Turnaround:* Transformed inherited negative relations with largest soft toy customer, A-Z. Raised prices to A-Z by 11% in 2004 alone.
- *Relationship Management:* Secured and expanded key account business. Prevented potential loss of VIP client, rejuvenated relationship, and guaranteed continued delivery, equaling 15% of divisional income.

CAMPAIGN HIGHLIGHTS

- *Strategic Planning:* Generated sales increase of 20% to 37% each year in a declining market; developed channel-specific marketing strategies while leading category management projects.
- *International Marketing:* Designed and executed sales campaign for largest marketing project in company's history, "The Smashing Robot" European launch. Effected explosive growth to become best-selling electronic toddler toy in Europe. Specially selected to present campaign strategy to Executive Board.

BRAND MANAGER, INFANT AND TODDLER TOYS - DATE – DATE

Captured 22% of the toddler market from a static 8% legacy start. Initiated entry of new brand, and devised and executed ground-breaking strategy, which included multichannel brand storytelling.

MARKETING CHAMPION

- *Innovative Marketing Campaign:* Originated award-winning "above the line" marketing strategy, which included customer promotions, TV, print and poster campaigns. Won Fox's **"Best New Ad Campaign 2002"** and Marketing Digest's **"Best ATL Strategy 2002."**

PRODUCT EXPERTISE

- *Market Research:* Optimized competitive advantage through in-depth SWOT and market analysis; identified opportunities to expand into new markets; recommendations formed future brand strategy.
- *New Product Launch:* Propelled "Doctor Dolittle" toys into US market via complex marketing mix. Realized exponential gains and $7M first year revenue in a stagnant market.

EDUCATION

University of State, City, ST

Master of Business Administration (MBA)

Bachelor of Arts (BA) in Marketing and Communication with Honors

---

Your Name ■ Phone Number ■ Email Address ■ Page 2 of 2

▪ ▪ ▪ **Your Name**

City, State ▪ Email
Phone ▪ LinkedIn URL

Sales Director | Sales Manager | Recruiter

Dynamic sales director and turnaround expert with track record for propelling sales teams and organizations to new heights.

▪ ▪ ▪ Key Achievements ▪ ▪ ▪

✓ **Ranked #1 in annual sales** out of 77 sales representatives in Northwest region. Repeatedly exceeded sales goals and awarded Recruiter of the Year honors.
✓ **Trained under-producing sales team to earn #1 spot in the region** within three months.
✓ **Achieved 200% in new acquisitions** for territory within six months.
✓ **30+ personal sales awards** and seven personal achievement medals for outstanding performance.

▪ Sales Strategies	▪ Under-producing Markets	▪ Conflict Resolution
▪ New Business Development	▪ Negotiation Strategies	▪ Systems and Processes
▪ Sales Team Management	▪ Strategic Alliances and Partnerships	▪ Operations Management
▪ Training and Development	▪ HR and Performance Management	▪ Profit and Loss Oversight
▪ Challenging Territories	▪ Customer Relationship Management	▪ Customer Savvy

Education

Bachelor of Business Administration, *magna cum laude,* University Name
Marine Corps Recruiter School, City, ST (Sales Training, Lead Generation and Prospecting, Appointment Setting, Qualifying Prospects, Presentations, Handling Objections, Closing Sales, Referral Generation)

Professional Highlights

United States Marine Corps, Master Sergeant (E-8)	Date–Present
**Sales Manager	Business Development	Relationship and Human Resources**	Date–Present

Assigned to solve sales, management, operations, and brand problems. Challenged to increase sales (recruitment), to hit goals, to turn around under-performing recruiting teams, and to improve brand perceptions. Territory included strong competition from each branch of military and regional colleges and universities selling programs to same customers. More than 40% of territory was unreachable or resistant due to negative publicity and brand perceptions.

▪ **Championed change and invigorated stalled growth** by developing and launching **rebranding campaigns** and target-specific sales programs for underdeveloped market segments. **Re-sectored sales region** to better align sales team. **Ignited a higher sales closing ratio** through dynamic training of sales force.
  ▪ **Increased sales 75%** within the first two months.
  ▪ **Catapulted sales team to exceed quarterly sales goal six times** by using special managerial approach.
  ▪ **Achieved 101% sales quota for 19 consecutive months.**
▪ **Identified market trends and accurately forecasted sales results** using strategic sales methodologies.
▪ **Rebranded USMC military image** by creating solutions that increased positive community presence crafted strategic alliances and partnerships to build and grow brand exposure in region.
▪ **Created team environment** by overcoming internal rivalries and insecurities while maintaining competitive momentum; ensured unified team success. **Exceeded profitability goals** by assessing operational needs, decreasing costs, reallocating funds to achieve sales team objectives and goals, and remain under budget.
▪ **Maintained 99% employee retention,** while Eastern Recruiting Region lost 24% due to mismanagement and sales representative burnout.
▪ **Achieved difficult target quota year-after-year** by developing out-of-the-box sales and negotiation strategies and coached sales reps and sales clients to ensure successful fulfillment of rigid sales goal.

"Outstanding management abilities...great initiative and resourcefulness in overcoming obstacles...After leading his first team to sustain victory, Name was selected to assume a larger sales office undergoing personnel and production related deficiencies, he turned it around, transforming the staff into a cohesive and disciplined team of professional sales reps."
Major Name Last Name, United States Marine Corps

▪ ▪ ▪ *more Your Name on following page* ▪ ▪ ▪

Professional Highlights Continued

Sales Team Training and Development

Rejuvenated sales team (recruiters), established sales quotas, and provided training and coaching to achieve individual and organizational goals. Mentored and directed all functions for two sales offices (recruiting stations) and 12 sales representatives. Increased sales while improving selection of candidates recruited to meet higher qualification guidelines. Strategically implemented new training improved sales presentations and trained sales agents to exceed expectations.

- **Produced two sales managers** through modeling, training, development, and leadership skills.
- **Trained and cultivated** new sales representative who achieved Rookie Recruiter of the Year.
- **Delivered unmatched results** by motivating team to take lead for first time in 17 months.
- **Developed a highly targeted prospecting, area canvassing and sales closing approach** that mobilized team to **achieve 103% of contract quota and 140% of final sales goal.**
- **Employed strategies and scripts that persuaded gatekeepers to open doors** and educated and won-over target market influencers (parents, teachers, and friends).
- **Taught life-cycle of the sale and needs-based approach** that increased confidence levels, ability to work independently and resulted in stronger interviews and higher conversion rates. Topics: prospecting, lead generation, prospect qualification, customer-centric presentations, overcoming objections, and closing.
- **Coaching and training** resulted in a savvy master sales team that successfully **met difficult objective of 100% contact** with every high school graduate **in 1,000+ square mile territory.**

> *"Master Sergeant Name's personal commitment to the success of Region Name and Region Name, State offices...the leadership he provided, and his untiring commitment to excellence has been and continues to be directly responsible for the success and stability of City, State...he maintained high prospecting levels and achieved contract and shipping quotas...his performance has exceeded all expectations."* **Major Name Last Name, United States Marine Corps**

Promotional Events

Represented company (USMC) at events, community outreach programs and schools to prospect and close sales.

- **Spearheaded special event campaigns and decreased costs** by booking prospecting / sales events at low cost, high exposure venues; managed radio and print media advertising.
- **Generated attention, engaged audience, and generated sales** using humor, customer-centric needs assessment, and solution-based sales approach.

Human Resource Manager

- **Played key role in 54th Presidential Inauguration** in coordination, participation and movements of 5K Marines during the inaugural ceremony televised worldwide.
- **Recognized for exceptional administrative effort** with first *Navy & Marine Corps NameConference.*
  - **Successfully executed the challenging task** to coordinate the travel, accommodation and transportation arrangements for concurrent arrival of 25 Generals/Admirals and assistants.
  - **Personally commended** for this effort by the Commandant of the Marine Corps (CMC) and his superior, the Chief of Naval Operations (CNO).

Career Snapshot

United States Marine Corps

HR Manager, City, ST	Date–Present
Sales Manager / Recruiting Station Commander, City, ST	Date–Date
HR Manager, City, ST; City, UK; City, ST	Date–Date
Sales Representative / Canvassing Recruiter, City, ST	Date–Date

Company, City, ST (Part-time)	Date–Date

Sales Associate - *Quickly identified the greatest sales needs and utilized selling skill sets that surpassed the sales of 99% of store employees. Consistently developed rapport, store loyalty and repeated business with customers.*

■ ■ ■

Your Name

Phone Number • City, ST • Zip Code
LinkedIn URL • Email

CHIEF OPERATING OFFICER • VP OPERATIONS • GENERAL MANAGER

High-Impact Culinary Executive -- Operations and Design Expert
Driving exponential sales globally, leading to unparalleled profitability

Growth-focused executive and top performer in restaurant sales **exceeding aggressive revenue targets**. Verifiable success transforming enterprises from **financial loss to profitability** in record time with marketing strategies that increase profitability while slashing costs. Verifiable **expertise leading multi-million dollar restaurant designs** and build-outs to unparalleled success under challenging market conditions. Passionate about extraordinary food and quality service proven by continued business from **clients including NBC, Viacom, Morgan Stanley** and *Good Day America*.

BUILDING FLAGSHIP CULINARY BRANDS INTERNATIONALLY GENERATING $288M+ SALES ANNUALLY

- Revenue Growth Strategies
- P&L Accountability
- Quality Management Analytics
- Business Development
- Food and Beverage Management

- Restaurant Design and Build-Outs
- Inventory Management/Controls
- Global Restaurant Launches
- Regulatory Compliance and Controls
- Marketing/Sales/Public Relations

- Team Leadership/Staffing
- Guest/Vendor Relations
- Capital Budgeting/Forecasting
- Operations/Facility Management
- Catering/Banquet Management

NEW YORK CITY | TORONTO | LOS ANGELES | CHICAGO | MONTREAL

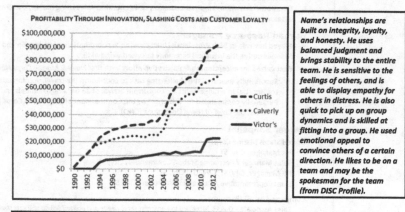

PROFITABILITY THROUGH INNOVATION, SLASHING COSTS AND CUSTOMER LOYALTY

Name's relationships are built on integrity, loyalty, and honesty. He uses balanced judgment and brings stability to the entire team. He is sensitive to the feelings of others, and is able to display empathy for others in distress. He is also quick to pick up on group dynamics and is skilled at fitting into a group. He used emotional appeal to convince others of a certain direction. He likes to be on a team and may be the spokesman for the team (from DISC Profile).

CAREER EXPERIENCE

COMPANY NAME, CITY, ST   DATE–PRESENT

Top, privately held US industry leader in high-end regionally sourced restaurants. Reporting to CEO, directed operations and new restaurant build-outs for flagship brands in New York City, Chicago, Montreal, Toronto, and Los Angeles **generating $288M+ annually. Highest grossing independent restaurant group in the US** with 3,500+ employees and 4,550 seats.

(continued next page)

VICE PRESIDENT OPERATIONS - Date – Present   Los Angeles | Times Square | Upper East Side | NYC

Reported to CEO to lead design, build, and launch a $15M build-out with 850 seats and 27,000^2 ft. ahead of schedule. Accountable for sales, labor, food, and liquor expenditures through a daily reporting structure to head office in focusing on cost of goods sold vs. actual sales.

- **Reduced weekly payroll from $150K to $123.5K while** driving optimal customer service and retention.
- Removed 200 tons of waste from landfill by initiating an environmental management program pilot that was implemented corporate wide **slashing operating costs by $25K** per location.

DIRECTOR OPERATIONS - Date – Date   Times Square | Upper East Side | NYC | Washington DC | Bahamas
ASST. DIRECTOR OPERATIONS - Date – Date   Times Square | Upper West Side | NYC

Reported to CEO and COO as Director of Operations; led successful and profitable operations for nine locations with **accountability for 1,000+ employees and $60M P&L.** *Maintained five locations as Assistant Director of Operations.*

- Designed/launched a 700 seat, 32,000^2 ft. restaurant on time, which created 200+ jobs.
- Designed and launched restaurant in Bahamas, which included developing high-performing team and supervising training process.
- Led marketing and merchandising, menu development, IT infrastructure, POS programming and maintenance, website upgrades, weekly chef/general manager meetings to review P&L, evaluate labor, cost of goods and sales.
- Challenged by CEO to decommission two underperforming restaurants in less than two years; built highly successful new business model and retaining 90% of staff with 185-seat restaurant launch and 110 employees.

GENERAL MANAGER - Date – Date   Times Square | NYC
ASST. GENERAL MANAGER - Date – Date   Times Square | NYC

Reported to COO as General Manager with 278 direct reports for two locations. Spearheaded several high-impact technology solutions as Assistant General Manager, which led to increased efficiency, improved table turnarounds, and expanded profitability.

- **Drove sales by 28%** through website with merchandise, menu offerings and catering options, which recruited numerous high-profile clients such as Company Name, Company Name, and Company Name.
- Spearheaded disaster mitigation and recovery plan, which **reduced insurance premiums by 19%.**
- Dramatically improved efficiency and profitability for table turnovers by initiating **ground-breaking open table reservation and database system to track food, costs, and sales data to appropriate revenue center.**
- **Increased revenues by developing after-hours wine tasting event,** which resulted in a highly profitable catering.

EDUCATION, PROFESSIONAL DEVELOPMENT AND CERTIFICATIONS

- University Name – Marketing | University Name – Electrical Engineering, Architectural Design, and Finance
- Restaurant Management and Restaurant Architectural Design
- MS Project Certification

*"**Name** is a seasoned restaurant professional with great positive energy and people skills that make him an effective corporate manager. He has strong P&L focus and is extremely hands on in his approach. His relentless work ethic and his knowledge of design and construction made his collaboration invaluable in the dozens of restaurants we opened and operated together for many years." Name, CEO, Company Name*

Your Name

City, State | Email Address | Phone Number

Qualified Chef

Hardworking and passionate seasonal Head Chef, with more than 15 years experience across international and offshore food preparation, meal planning, and ordering coordination. | Expertise in all facets of cooking, line management and strategic planning, utilizing a wide range of culinary tastes and styles.

Known to quickly adapt to new teams and challenging environments -- driven to exceed customer expectations while meeting business objectives and targets. | Provide strong supervision and team work through provision of fresh, regionally sourced food, quality monitoring, and team management expertise.

Core Competencies

☐ Food Safety	☐ Exemplary Customer Service	☐ Large Scale	Bulk Cooking
☐ Catered	Corporate Events	☐ Waste Management	☐ Operational Improvements
☐ Inventory Planning	☐ Team Building	Leadership	☐ Fine	Casual Dining
☐ Budget	Cost Management	☐ Complex Dietary Requirements	☐ Cultural Diversity

Career Summary & Highlights

QUALIFIED CHEF

Maintained all aspects of kitchen management across three continents; as Seasonal Chef, during peak tourist season included bistro, a-la carte, buffet style, bulk cooking, and corporate functions.

✓ Regularly reduced food / supply costs more than 25% by streamlining suppliers, implementing new stock control methods, and maintaining 'quality instead of quantity' produce in remote locations.

Highlights:

HEAD CHEF | Company Name, City, ST

Managed all aspects of kitchen service on 182ft Cruise Ship throughout Tropical Islands included all meals, beachfront buffets, large customized corporate charters, and functions for up to 200 diners.

✓ Recruited and trained up to six new catering employees as high turnover of staff, due to long hours (12-16hr per day); efficiently provided quality, nutritious meals for large groups in stipulated time.

✓ Coordinated all menu planning, costings and orders, which included receipt and storage of stock into cool room, ensured temperatures monitored during transfers, and food safety policies / procedures were met.

HEAD CHEF | Company Name, City, ST

✓ Spearheaded restaurant turnaround, from $3M renovation, which involved recruitment of seven new team members, resulted in 700% growth in sittings, and reduced $5K a week loss, breaking even within 2 months.

CHEF | Various Restaurants, Country

✓ Acted as English / Language translator for high-profile business person's various restaurants, presenting new Western / Asian palate experiences.

✓ Quickly attracted international and local customers, which resulted in new and repeat business across tapas style restaurants.

continued

Your Name

Phone Number

Professional History

CASUAL CHEF - Hotel Name, City, ST	Date - Date
CHEF | BARTENDER - Restaurant Name, City, ST	Date - Date
HEAD CHEF - Restaurant Name, City, ST	Date - Date
CHEF | FRONT OF HOUSE - Restaurant Name, City, ST	Date - Date
HEAD CHEF - Bistro Name, City, ST	Date - Date
CHEF - Restaurant Name, City, ST	Date - Date
CHEF - Hotel Name, City, ST	Date - Date
HEAD CHEF - Cruise Ship, Tropical Islands	Date - Date
SOUS CHEF - Lodge Name, City, ST	Date - Date
CHEF DE PARTIE - Restaurant Name, City, ST	Date - Date
SOUS CHEF - Restaurant Name, City, ST	Date - Date
CHEF - Restaurant Name, City, ST	Date - Date
BUFFET CHEF - Hotel Name, City, ST	Date - Date
CHEF - Restaurant Name, City, ST	Date - Date
APPRENTICE CHEF - Hotel, City, ST	Prior to Date

Education & Training

Culinary Arts Degree
University Name

Commercial Cookery Qualification
College Name

Your Name

City, State   Phone Number   Email Address   LinkedIn Profile

SUPPLY CHAIN MANAGER   OPERATIONS DIRECTOR   PROJECT MANAGER

Transformational leader with over 20 years' experience building highly effective teams, bringing order out of chaos, and managing change. Decisive style with a proven record of negotiation and collaboration toward mission success. Bringing strategic planning, customer focus, and communications experience to drive innovation and growth.

LEADERSHIP STRENGTHS

Change Management	Transformational Leadership	Budget Development
Operations Planning	Conflict Resolution	Project Management
Supply Chain Strategies	Department Integration	Process Improvement
Risk Management	Quantitative Assessment	Strategic Planning

CAREER HISTORY

Director of Operations, Department Name   Date – Date
Branch of Service, Base Name, Location or City, State

Transformed moderately performing department into a value-driven organization by aligning operations across Human Resources, Communications, Finance, IT, Logistics, and Contracts. Streamlined finances and increased transparency through consolidated management of 35 accounts, $7M in federal research grants, and mobilizing human potential.

- **Directed transition to Salesforce ERP under 6 months** from concept to implementation by collaborating with department leaders and transition partner, resulting in 11K cases processed annually
- **Distilled core values from 16 down to 4** by leading development of 3-year strategic plan, analyzing streams of input to re-focus values outwardly, manage change, and enable effective vision casting and business planning
- **Reduced expenses by $68K/yr.** by mapping out roles and aligning the right talent for the job, eliminating redundancies and increasing department efficiency by 15%
- **Achieved 3-yr. re-accreditation award** from Commission on Accreditation of Rehabilitation Facilities (CARF) program by leading the team through compliance process, resulting in the highest accreditation award issued

Customer Relationship Manager   Date – Date
Branch of Service, Base Name, Location or City, State

Led active program that generated smooth communications and customer service between headquarters, 27 home-based ships, 78 functional areas of over 15K personnel along with relationships with local businesses and government.

- **Integrated structure of 2 major organizations into 1** using effective change management strategies and business analysis to reduce/eliminate redundancies and saved $1.5M annually
- **Overcame multiple policy and physical barriers to open mass-transit option** through the base by working with area managers, tracking security issues, and determining a value that led to low-cost access for off-base workers
- **Generated 100% readiness posture** for hurricane contingency plans including wide-area step-by-step protection plan and recovery scenarios, conducting cooperative practice with local community to meet readiness criteria

Director of Operations   Date – Date
Branch of Service, Base Name, Location or City, State

Directed a global organization supporting fluid levels of assets and executing strategic planning, supply chain mgmt. and training through creative division of labor to multiply limited resources and accomplish all objectives within budget.

- **Exceeded distribution targets by 40%** for Alaska earthquake recovery drill through complete strategic planning, managing a global supply chain, logistics, and on-site leadership to conclude a 12-month planning cycle

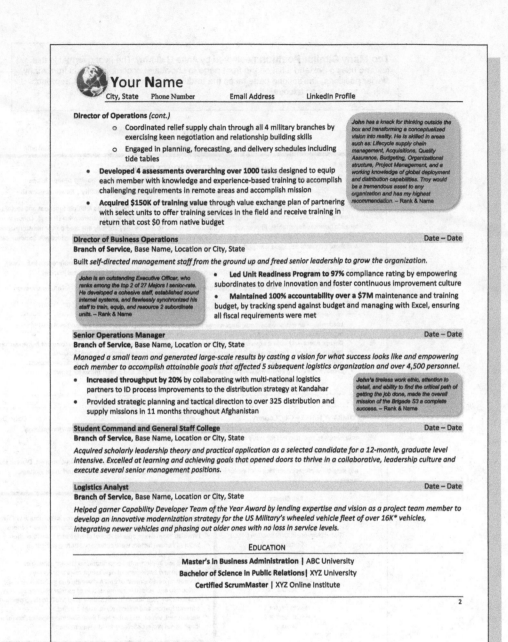

Your Name

City, State   Phone Number   Email Address   LinkedIn Profile

Director of Operations *(cont.)*

- o Coordinated relief supply chain through all 4 military branches by exercising keen negotiation and relationship building skills
- o Engaged in planning, forecasting, and delivery schedules including tide tables
- **Developed 4 assessments overarching over 1000** tasks designed to equip each member with knowledge and experience-based training to accomplish challenging requirements in remote areas and accomplish mission
- **Acquired $150K of training value** through value exchange plan of partnering with select units to offer training services in the field and receive training in return that cost $0 from native budget

> *John has a knack for thinking outside the box and transforming a conceptualized vision into reality. He is skilled in areas such as: Lifecycle supply chain management, Acquisitions, Quality Assurance, Budgeting, Organizational structure, Project Management, and a working knowledge of global deployment and distribution capabilities. Troy would be a tremendous asset to any organization and has my highest recommendation.* – Rank & Name

Director of Business Operations   Date – Date
Branch of Service, Base Name, Location or City, State

Built *self-directed management staff from the ground up and freed senior leadership to grow the organization.*

> *John is an outstanding Executive Officer, who ranks among the top 2 of 27 Majors I senior-rate. He developed a cohesive staff, established sound internal systems, and flawlessly synchronized his staff to train, equip, and resource 2 subordinate units.* – Rank & Name

- **Led Unit Readiness Program to 97%** compliance rating by empowering subordinates to drive innovation and foster continuous improvement culture
- **Maintained 100% accountability over a $7M** maintenance and training budget, by tracking spend against budget and managing with Excel, ensuring all fiscal requirements were met

Senior Operations Manager   Date – Date
Branch of Service, Base Name, Location or City, State

Managed a small team and generated large-scale results by casting a vision for what success looks like and empowering each member to accomplish attainable goals that affected 5 subsequent logistics organization and over 4,500 personnel.

- **Increased throughput by 20%** by collaborating with multi-national logistics partners to ID process improvements to the distribution strategy at Kandahar
- Provided strategic planning and tactical direction to over 325 distribution and supply missions in 11 months throughout Afghanistan

> *John's tireless work ethic, attention to detail, and ability to find the critical path of getting the job done, made the overall mission of the Brigade S3 a complete success.* – Rank & Name

Student Command and General Staff College   Date – Date
Branch of Service, Base Name, Location or City, State

Acquired scholarly leadership theory and practical application as a selected candidate for a 12-month, graduate level intensive. Excelled at learning and achieving goals that opened doors to thrive in a collaborative, leadership culture and execute several senior management positions.

Logistics Analyst   Date – Date
Branch of Service, Base Name, Location or City, State

Helped garner Capability Developer Team of the Year Award by lending expertise and vision as a project team member to develop an innovative modernization strategy for the US Military's wheeled vehicle fleet of over 16K* vehicles, integrating newer vehicles and phasing out older ones with no loss in service levels.

EDUCATION

Master's in Business Administration | ABC University

Bachelor of Science in Public Relations | XYZ University

Certified ScrumMaster | XYZ Online Institute

2

Your Name

City	Phone Number	Email	LinkedIn

EXECUTIVE/PROJECT DIRECTOR

Influencer, catalyst and enabler, solution finder and relationship builder - making change happen

Organizational Transformation | Business Development | Corporate Visibility | Revenue Growth

Recognized for entrepreneurial mindset and significant global experience working across multiple functions and sectors, including FTSE 100 companies. Excel at analyzing business processes and systems and transforming strategic concepts into tangible business deliverables. Proven ability in mentoring teams to ensure they are fully engaged during transformation periods, resulting in higher engagement and improved productivity. Highly collaborative, able to effectively communicate and share concepts and ideas with partners and stakeholders at all levels.

Business mentor and keynote speaker for multinational organizations. Presented at numerous conferences in Europe, USA, Middle East and South-East Asia and published various articles in academic and professional journals.

"I have a passion and skill for helping organizations move from strategic concept to successful implementation."

SIGNATURE SKILLS / STRENGTHS

- ✓ **Leadership** – an inclusive approach; empowering teams to take ownership of work and to grow/develop within the organization. Successfully leading business through periods of development and growth.
- ✓ **Change Agent** – significant experience in effective organizational transformation, always taking account of human factors.
- ✓ **Results Oriented** – focused approach to exploring ways to achieve effective results to benefit business.
- ✓ **Influencer** – adept at working with cross-functional teams and bringing people onboard with ideas or concepts.
- ✓ **Creative** – in finding innovative ways to approach operational challenges, and opportunities for growth.

CAREER HISTORY & VALUE IMPACT

COMPANY NAME – City, Country   Date–Date

Bespoke consultancy supporting organizations across Europe, SE Asia. Focus on organizational transformation of multinational, mid-size, not for profit and governmental organizations.

FOUNDER AND DIRECTOR

Co-created high impact results-oriented solutions focusing on organizational performance and development. Diverse short and long-term projects, working with senior leaders and engaging key stakeholders to advance and meet strategic business needs.

Key Clients	Highlights
Multi-national 1	✓ Created revenue streams for NGO and improved corporate visibility.
Multi-national 2	✓ Built partnerships and collaborations with external organizations.
Global Non-profit Organization (NGO)	✓ Provided expertise in organizational change and transformation.
Company 1	✓ Ensured human factors were considered during periods of
Company 2	organizational transformation.
Household Brand	✓ Created and implemented organizational change strategies.
Academic Institution 1	✓ Improved and implemented new talent review processes.
Academic Institution 2	✓ Advised on development of EMEA diversity and inclusion strategy.
NGO 1	✓ Supported and guided implementation of gender balance strategy.
NGO 2	✓ Trained 250+ consultants in soft skills – used MBTI tools to develop
Health Sector 1	communication, and effectively manage conflict.
Health Sector 2	✓ Researched, wrote, and submitted award winning application for a
Banking	longitudinal project of six-sigma implementation.

continued

KEY PROJECTS - examples

Company Name - EXECUTIVE DIRECTOR – City, Country   Date–Date

Maintained operational responsibility for 29 city networks and their Boards (total of 320, mainly volunteers), 40,000 global community.

➢ Developed and implemented a new strategy which focused on improving operational excellence, governance, financials, and collaborations across city networks.
➢ Pioneered new customer-centric engagement process and built partnerships and collaborations with corporate partners and external organizations including X, Y, government organizations and other NGOs.
➢ Generated several new revenue streams; raised visibility by adding 3 new (Asia, Middle East and one in Europe) networks and launching a new global website customized to every city network.

Company Name - CONSULTANT - various locations   Date–Date

Provided support and facilitation to teams in corporate departments, manufacturing, and consumer groups.

➢ Developed a global health risk assessment to support employees on 12 different health risks.
➢ Provided Senior Vice-President with a full research based / best evidence report on mental health.
➢ Consulted and facilitated multiple sites on management and team resilience program.

Company - CONSULTANT – City, Country   Date–Date

Furnished organizational transformation consultancy services to EMEA Sales Operations Department during period of high growth and organizational pressure.

➢ Moved team into change mindset with strategies to overcome and manage stress; improved communications, working relationships, and communication with other departments.
➢ Assisted department in developing a strong strategy, objectives and branding which was successfully shared with EMEA organization.
➢ Continued growth of the department - financially, head count, and team leads.

Company - CONSULTANT – City, Country   Date–Date

Provided consultation to respond to key challenges inhibiting continued business growth.

➢ Implemented new organizational change strategy that maintained entrepreneurial spirit of company.
➢ Revised and implemented new talent review processes to incorporate key organizational values, which incentivized employees and supported employee development.

EDUCATION & PROFESSIONAL DEVELOPMENT

B.Sc. Psychology
University Name (date–date, incomplete)
M.Sc. Exercise and Health Science (Cum Laude)
University Name (date–date)
Science and Management of Health and Fitness
College Name

Effective Negotiation – Business School Name (date)
Women in Leadership – Business School Name (date)
Appreciative Inquiry – Company Name (date)
Non-Violent Communication – Company Name (date)
Solution Focused Coaching – Company Name (date)

Your Name

City, State, Zip • Phone • Email

Public Policy • Nonprofit • Advocacy Communications

Senior communications / editorial management professional with communications / publishing expertise and hands-on community advocacy and nonprofit experience. Producer of clear and profitable policy-oriented communications for educational, promotional, and advocacy efforts. Expert at leveraging understanding of legislative / political process to inform and develop communication strategies. **Award-winning community advocate.**

Performance Highlights

- Conceptualized, developed, and directed the production of **top-selling digital and print policy-oriented communications products** for leading regulatory-oriented publisher.
- Assisted in **securing funding for local education and neighborhood initiatives** by drafting letters, position statements, and hearing testimony to support community housing development advocacy efforts.
- Contributed to success of publisher's **highest-grossing educational webinar series** by keeping team abreast of regulatory and legislative developments to spur ideas for new revenue-generating webinars.

Competencies

Public Relations | Communications Plans and Strategies | Articles | Position Statements | Testimony Letters | Talking Points | Proposals
Social and Digital Media | Print and Digital Publications | Fact Sheets | Web Content | Scripts and Presentations

Professional Experience

Company Name | City, State | Date of hire to present

Associate Publisher, Date position started—present | Senior Managing Editor: Date to Date | Sr. Editor: Date to Date
Editor: Date to Date | Assistant Editor: Date to Date

Effectively analyzed legislative and regulatory issues and developments which resulted in creation and direct production of best-selling publications and communications products. Promoted through increasingly responsible editorial management positions to oversee publisher's largest (nearly 30 titles) and most profitable ($2 million) line of digital and print publications. Managed contractors, legal experts, and up to 10 editors. Received several bonuses. *Career highlights*:

- Directed, motivated, and retained team through merger and major print-to-digital product transition and **doubled percentage of revenue from digital products** with minimal staff turnover.
- **Expanded HR policy publications and products by more than 30 percent** by developing / launching new titles and updating existing products in response to regulatory changes and compliance requirements.
- **Facilitated creation and launch of company's highest selling employee benefits publications** on health care reform, portability, and privacy regulations.
- **Sharpened marketing messages** by editing direct mail brochures, flyers, email text, telemarketing scripts, and web pages to support launch and growth of subscription-based publications.
- Oversaw development of industry special reports and white papers to assist in lead generation. **Co-edited blog and managed primary Twitter handle** for HR editorial group.

Independent Editorial Company | City, State | Date to present
Wrote, coordinated, and designed annual reports and provided editing services for nonprofit organizations.

Early Career included *nonprofit communications experience* as publications specialist and writer/editor for a health care and an environmental association.

continued

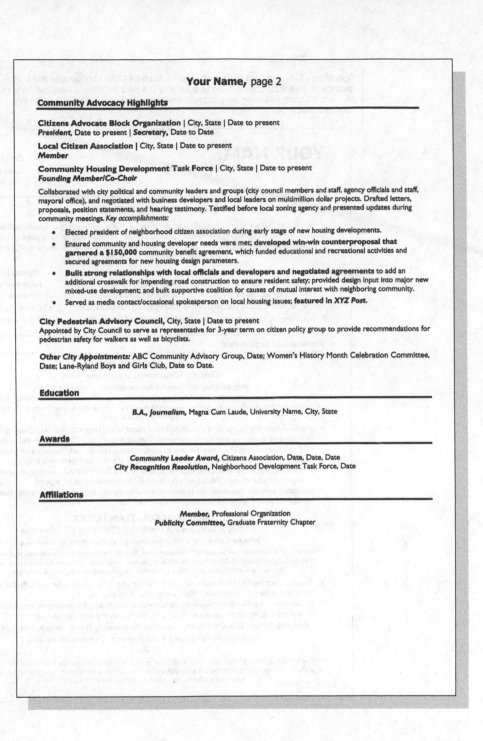

Your Name, page 2

Community Advocacy Highlights

Citizens Advocate Block Organization | City, State | Date to present
President, Date to present | *Secretary,* Date to Date

Local Citizen Association | City, State | Date to present
Member

Community Housing Development Task Force | City, State | Date to present
Founding Member/Co-Chair

Collaborated with city political and community leaders and groups (city council members and staff, agency officials and staff, mayoral office), and negotiated with business developers and local leaders on multimillion dollar projects. Drafted letters, proposals, position statements, and hearing testimony. Testified before local zoning agency and presented updates during community meetings. *Key accomplishments:*

- Elected president of neighborhood citizen association during early stage of new housing developments.
- Ensured community and housing developer needs were met; **developed win-win counterproposal that garnered a $150,000** community benefit agreement, which funded educational and recreational activities and secured agreements for new housing design parameters.
- **Built strong relationships with local officials and developers and negotiated agreements** to add an additional crosswalk for impending road construction to ensure resident safety; provided design input into major new mixed-use development; and built supportive coalition for causes of mutual interest with neighboring community.
- Served as media contact/occasional spokesperson on local housing issues; **featured in *XYZ Post.***

City Pedestrian Advisory Council, City, State | Date to present
Appointed by City Council to serve as representative for 3-year term on citizen policy group to provide recommendations for pedestrian safety for walkers as well as bicyclists.

Other City Appointments: ABC Community Advisory Group, Date; Women's History Month Celebration Committee, Date; Lane-Ryland Boys and Girls Club, Date to Date.

Education

B.A., *Journalism,* Magna Cum Laude, University Name, City, State

Awards

Community Leader Award, Citizens Association, Date, Date, Date
City Recognition Resolution, Neighborhood Development Task Force, Date

Affiliations

Member, Professional Organization
Publicity Committee, Graduate Fraternity Chapter

YOUR NAME

City | State, Zip Code
LinkedIn URL | Email
Phone Number

Boilermaker | First Class Welder

Boilermaker Welder specialist, confidently direct teams of 30+ craftspeople across shipbuilding, mining, marine, and construction projects. | Infuse career-wise depth of experience on fixed plant processing systems through to structural steel welding and design modifications. | Continually produce quality x-ray standard weld tests across a range of technical positions.

- » Shipbuilding and Upgrades
- » Plan Modifications
- » Quality Assurance
- » MMAW & FCAW Welding
- » Drawing Interpretation

- » Heavy Industrial Maintenance
- » Marine Vessels and Structures
- » Confined Space Work
- » Ordering and Procurement
- » Stainless Steel Fabrication

- » Working at Heights
- » Fabrication and Fit-outs
- » Workflow Scheduling
- » Critical Lift Coordination
- » Risk Analysis

Professional Experience

LEADING HAND BOILERMAKER
Company | Department, City ST | Date - Date

Ship Building » Structural Reinforcement » Team Leadership

Company was awarded $450 million contract to upgrade eight frigates, with anti-ship missile defense (ASMD) capability
» Delivered welding and fabrication work scope, with high-quality workmanship to meet stringent deadlines within two dry-docking ship facilities.

- » Acknowledged and subsequently promoted for leadership and organizational skills; became Company's first and only female Leading Hand, confidently managed teams of 3-30 employees within three months.
  - ✓ Promoted from initial boilermaker role to Leading Hand, coordinated 10 workers on Vessel Name's structural strengthening and installation of 90 tonne of lead into ballast tanks project.
  - ✓ Managed Vessel B and Vessel C frigates' Supplementary Defect List (SDL) work scope across team of six highly skilled craftsmen, liaising with Commonwealth representative for sign-off.
- » Facilitated daily pre-start meetings, undertook risk assessments, and created Job Hazard Analysis (JHAs) in addition to writing hot works and confined space permits.

BOILERMAKER - TEAM LEADER
Company A, Company B & Company C | City & City ST | Date - Date

Structural Welding » Mine Processing Repairs » Plant Maintenance

Provided high-level support, as part of FIFO shutdown crew, through installation, modification and maintenance of fixed plant and equipment across Company, Company and Company mine sites. » Successfully adapted to numerous site projects with limited pre-planning coordination and multiple changes to work scope.

- » Acted as team leader of four craftsmen, closely liaised with different site supervisors, field operators and other contractors on projects; met 100% safety procedural targets.
  - ✓ Completed shutdown maintenance and removals across fixed plant equipment, which included cone and jaw crusher repairs, reclaimer shutdowns, and conveyor pulley change-outs at:

Company Name - Site A, Site B, Site C and Site D | Company Name - Area A, Area B and Area C

Company Name - Project A and Project B | Company Name - Site E

» » »

"Name has the ability to deliver - she's a 'set and forget' worker, a rarity in the industry. Put her in charge of a work crew on a client's maintenance task, and she has the ability to deliver. The job is done exactly how you want it, normally under time and budget." ~ AB - Mechanical Supervisor | Company B, Site E

Professional Experience (cont)

BOILERMAKER - TEAM LEADER
Company A, Company B & Company C | City & City ST | Date - Date (cont)

» Reduced allocated time frame for maintenance projects via assessment of job needs; planned tools and a work methodology which involved correlation of job records and handover note completion.
- ✓ Carried out vibrating grizzly change-outs and rock ledge repairs, reclaimer bucket wheel change-outs, apron feeder change-outs, as well as primary feed chute reconstruction projects.
- ✓ Assisted crane operator for heavy lifts, plus other methodologies as Dogman / Rigger, to remove and install pulleys, gearboxes, idlers, crushers, reclaimer buckets, and other faulty equipment.

» Delivered on stringent compliance across OHS paperwork in relation to permits (hot works, confined spaces, work at heights - fall arrest and harness), lock-out procedures, JHAs, and sentry duties.

» » »

"I'd just like to extend a big thank you for all the support you provided... It was a great outcome for the facility, getting back up and running at least 36hrs prior than we'd previously planned through your support and action." ~ AB - Maintenance Superintendent | Company, Site A

BOILERMAKER | WELDER
Company | Department, City ST | Date - Date

Workshop Fabrication » SMAW & FCAW Welding » Structural Steel

Stepped into workshop covering all aspects of fabrication for fixed plant equipment and structural steel works. » Solidified workmanship across internal workshop extension and client projects, focusing on exceeding contract deadlines.

» Fabricated bucket wheels for iron ore reclaimers, which included preparation and completion of new builds, with a team-focused approach of 'getting all jobs out on time' across busy 12,000m² workshop.

» Efficiently completed FCAW welding in all positions (6G) to both job specifications and industry, company and stringent quality assurance standards.
- ✓ Saved 15% downtime by operating EWP and forklift on high safety-risk structural work, which further involved setting up drop zones and barricades through to improving JHAs and safety paperwork.

» Assisted with slinging of loads for crane operators, performed overhead crane usage, and identified workflow process improvements from initial build through to final inspection.

» » »

"... very personable, resourceful and highly knowledgeable in everything related to marine fabrication and welding... maintained the highest standards in quality workmanship, safety, design modifications and team leadership." ~ AB - Manager | Company C, Area A

Education & Training

Engineering Tradesperson | Fabrication	OHS High Risk Certification
Boiler-making - Metal Construction, 1st Class Welding	Construction Industry White Card
Basic Rigging | RB	Elevated Work Platform | EWP
Forklift Operations | LF	Dogman | DG
Working at Heights	Confined Space

YOUR NAME

City, State | Phone Number | Email Address

SALES | SERVICE | LOGISTICS | INVENTORY
Delivering excellence in service, sales and support

Multi skilled professional offering a unique blend of skills in service, operations management, logistics, inventory and fleet management, with a stable and successful employment record with a leading agribusiness firm.

Talented communicator, adept at building rapport with people at all levels, sharing knowledge and supporting operations across all areas. Strong work ethic, with a flexible and adaptable approach, as evidenced from length of service and variety of roles held with Company Name.

Collaborative and cooperative team player, happy to contribute at multiple levels to meet objectives. **Highly suited to an organization seeking a multi-disciplined professional with a broad range of sales, service and inventory skills.**

" ... loves people, helping others and his work ... completes every task with a smile and nothing is ever too much trouble ... any organization would be lucky to have his services ..." P. Whitmore, 2017

KEY SKILLS

- Warehousing & Stores
- Logistics
- Inventory Management
- SAP Specialist (Inventory)
- Fleet Coordination
- Supplier/Customer Relations
- Sales Enquiries & Quotes
- Training & Development
- OH&S

CAREER HIGHLIGHTS

Enjoyed a long and successful career with Company Name, demonstrating superior loyalty and commitment, progressing through sales, operations and logistics roles based on performance. Contributions included:

Adaptability: Demonstrated a highly flexible and adaptable manner; grew and developed with company through multiple internal / external mergers and acquisitions.

Sales & Service: Supported improvements to sales and productivity as Sales and Operations Manager. Directed strong customer service culture based on solutions sales approach.

Logistics & Fleet Management: Stepped up to manage fleet requirements for >30 business units and logistics for >22 business units nationally.

SAP: Played a key role as part of project team rolling out a new computer system nationally, which included program specification, system testing, staff training, implementation, and ongoing support as a subject matter expert.

Inventory Control: Spearheaded rapid improvements to inventory management and reporting through introduction of single master file, together with a suite of reports for management.

" ... the most team-focused person I've ever worked with ... simply a joy to collaborate with ... forever grateful for the skills and knowledge you shared ... I credit you with my career advancement ..." J. Anderson, 2017

continued

CAREER HISTORY

AAA CO. PTY LTD   **1990 – 2017**

Agribusiness with operations across rural merchandise, livestock, fertilizer and grain, seed and stock feed, risk, finance, and insurance.

Positions included: Sales Supervisor | Fleet & Logistics Controller | Operations Manager

Attained progressive tenure working across all areas of operations, which included sales and service, logistics and fleet management, and operations. Facilitated and contributed to improvements across business through new systems, technologies, training programs, and management approaches that enhanced inventory control, service standards, and productivity.

- **Customer Service:** Developed strong working relationships with clients and staff, which built sustained relationships that fostered loyalty and satisfaction.

- **Fleet:** Coordinated fleet of vehicles, which included monitoring and modifying leases, processing accident claims, repairs and registrations, as well as toll and infringement notices.

- **Sales Administration:** Provided a professional point of contact for suppliers and customers; accurately placed orders and supplied quotes.

- **Inventory:** Managed end of month reporting for approximately 300,000 inventory items. Provided one-on-one training to warehouse and inventory personnel following implementation of new SAP system.

- **OH&S:** Ensured all staff were aware of workplace safety policy and procedures, conducted routine fire drills, and attended bi-monthly OHS Policy Committee meetings, communicating updates and changes to staff.

- **Sales, Service & Operations:** Drove operations and supervised, led, and motivated sales personnel, which resulted in delivery of high-level service to wide-ranging agricultural clients.

> *"… loyal, reliable and dedicated are just three words I would use to describe you … thank you for your outstanding contributions to our business …" E. Gibson, 2017*

EARLIER CAREER SUMMARY

WESTERN RETAIL GROUP

Leading retail group with a national network of >200 stores.

Positions included: Retail Sales, Stores & Warehousing

Worked on a casual basis, initially in sales / customer service and progressed to a store's / warehouse role; accurately received and dispatched stock.

- **Customer Service:** Delivered high levels of customer service through rapport building and active listening to find solutions to client needs.

- **Warehousing:** Managed movement of stock within the warehouse, ensuring efficiency and safety during all dispatch and stock movement activities.

- **Product Knowledge:** Built a strong working knowledge of products, supporting sales and service enquires.

Chapter 18

Award-Winning Creative Marketing Resumes

re you ready to cash in on all the possible bells and whistles to create your next winning resume? Then take the time to browse through this chapter, where I have included award-winning creative resumes from the Career Directors International competition, Toast of the Resume Industry Awards (TORIs).

The TORIs are the professional resume-writing industry's best of the best, recognizing top resume writers from around the world in the single longest-running annual resume competition (2000 to the present).

WARNING

These examples represent individual people and their unique experiences; they are provided only as an example of what is possible in a resume. Please consider them as roadmaps, not rules, when creating your next resume.

TIP

The resumes in this chapter are meant to be networking resumes. They will not survive ATS or other keyword resume scans. Be sure to always include a scannable copy of your resume along with a highly formatted one to ensure that you are covering your bases.

Jacob Matthews

555-555-5555 | jmatthews@email.com | linkedin.com/in/name

Chief Financial Officer—Banking & Financial Services

Operationally Savvy Finance Expert ✧ Growth & Turnaround Titan ✧ Prescient Provocateur

Exceptionally strong leader who is recognized—above, below, and laterally—for conventional finance and accounting expertise coupled with rare commercial and operational intellect. Empathetic CXO partner who creates cross-functional alliances to rebuild the balance sheets, turning perennially underperforming banks into growth engines. Spot-on predictor of market shifts, enabling prioritization of strategic initiatives.

Banking Leadership Highlights

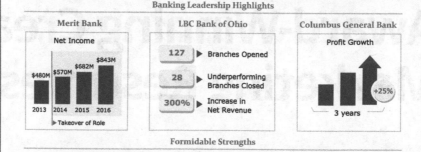

Merit Bank	LBC Bank of Ohio	Columbus General Bank
Net Income: $480M (2013), $570M (2014), $682M (2015), $843M (2016). Takeover of Role	127 Branches Opened; 28 Underperforming Branches Closed; 300% Increase in Net Revenue	Profit Growth: +25% in 3 years

Formidable Strengths

M&A Strategy | General Accounting & Control Functions | Risk Mitigation | Profit Maximization
Regulatory Compliance | Financial Planning & Analysis | Change Management | Team Building & Leadership
High-Growth Strategies | Performance Management | Cross-Functional Collaboration | IT Transformations

Professional Experience

MERIT BANK | Los Angeles, CA | Regional financial services company | 10K employees | $82B AUM
Chief Financial Officer (2014–Present)
Turned a sluggish bank into a newsworthy growth story and compelling investment case, delivering a 75% increase in net income, from $480M to $843M.

Protected P&L while galvanizing a growth-oriented team of 6 direct reports. Championed a strong M&A defense and uncovered growth opportunities to quickly reinvigorate stagnating revenue and profit.

Drove M&A Success ... Unlocked Synergies ... Curtailed Risk ... Tipped the Revenue Scale

✧ Orchestrated the fusing of two independent banks into a single organization and quickly identified segments with the most growth potential to prioritize efforts. Eliminated overlaps in branches, kiosks, and ATMs to maximize synergies.
✧ Identified yawning product gaps and drove a nimble acquisition strategy to fill them. Acquisitions included a digital banking platform and a card payment processor that attracted new corporate accounts and contributed to double-digit market share improvement.
✧ Restored vitality to asset quality metrics through staunch derisking efforts, propelling organization from worst-performer status to one of the best in 1 year.
✧ Recognized lucrative fee and cross-selling opportunities that delivered 15% in top-line growth.

> *"We hired Matthews for his reputation of taking the helm during severe storms and charting the course to a more profitable tomorrow. He has absolutely delivered." — Lee Edwards, CEO, Merit Bank*

LBC Bank of Ohio | Columbus, OH | Regional bank | 6K employees | $40B AUM
Chief Financial Officer (2007–2014)
Liberated struggling bank from near-bankrupt, minor-player status to #2 in the state.

Fine-tuned the P&L machine, embracing the challenge of driving volume and capturing market share while creating a culture of risk mitigation and collaboration among 5 direct and 23 indirect reports.

Exceeded Growth Expectations ... Eclipsed the Competition ... Evangelized a Cultural Shift

✧ Led an aggressive profitable growth agenda, opening 127 new branches in highly strategic locations, — catapulting total assets and net revenue threefold—while closing 28 poorly performing branches.
✧ Launched products that were a first for the region, including a sustainable investing category. Promoted vigorous cross-selling strategies and revamped fee structure, generating revenues that pushed the institution to #2 in the state in just 12 months.
✧ Built a risk-aware team and launched IT infrastructure that revealed daily risk exposure.

> *"Jacob radiates positivity but is well aware of challenges looming over the horizon. Better still, he knows just what to do about them." — David Jacobson, CEO, LBC Bank of Ohio*

Columbus General Bank | Columbus, OH | Bank ranking 4th in the state | 5K employees | $9B AUM
Finance Director (2004–2007) **Senior Finance Analyst** (2002–2004) **Finance Analyst** (2000–2002)
From entry level analyst to running a tight P&L for a 136-branch bank in just 5 years.

Recognized through quick promotion for collaborative spirit, business improvement ideas, and ability to invigorate performance. Inspired team of 8 direct and 30 indirect reports. Stretched a budget of $300M.

Launched New Infrastructure ... Expanded Footprint ... Unleashed Profit Potential

✧ Built a solid finance area from scratch and then crafted and executed the general financial strategy of the organization to drive the growth agenda and guarantee shareholder value.
✧ Inaugurated 108 profitable new branches after conducting careful due diligence, building reach and presence from 28 branches to 136.
✧ Combed segments, products, and overall operations for revenue-generating and profit-maximizing opportunities, thrusting the bottom line up 25%.

> *"Matthews is a fast-rising star. He's truly unstoppable." — Geoffrey Martin, COO, Columbus General Bank*

Education

Master's in Bank Management ✧ Ohio State University ✧ 2008

Certified Public Accountant (CPA) ✧ 2006

Bachelor of Science, Business & Finance ✧ Columbus State University (Ohio) ✧ 1999

CERSEI HARRINGTON

SENIOR FINANCIAL ACCOUNTANT

Rise to a challenge, unfazed by setbacks, motivated by what holds the world together.

"My passion for finding solutions, exposing errors and helping a business flourish, makes me work harder, learn more, practice longer, lead more effectively, and smile more. It keeps me at work hours after everyone else has left, and inspires me to help colleagues excel."

Contact

✉ cerseiharrington12@email.com 📱 843-555-5543 in Linkedin.com/in/cerseiharrington

Experience

Specialist Accountant, Port of Beaumont, TX   2012–Present

"Every day brings a new challenge, and with every task, a new skill. Investigative work is complex—sometimes requiring extensive research to simply understand the task."

Report to: Commercial General Manager. **Company:** Fifth largest port in the US, with $78.5M in total trade. **Budget:** FY14 approval budget of $62M

Hitting the ground running without handover, job instructions or manuals, set the scene for this challenging, complex and satisfying engagement that represents a 'cut above' to the traditional accounting role. Maintaining 100% accuracy is critical to ensure the Port of Beaumont maintains financial stability.

Role Overview: Manage the capital budget from conception to completion across all business units—ensuring capital expenditures are linked to the 50-year Master Plan, five-year outlook and corporate plan. On appointment, the focus of the role was to contribute to the company's transition from individual pricing to a central port services agreement with a pricing structure that helped maintain revenue neutrality.

- **Process Standardization, Role Definition, Risk Containment:** Prevented the departure of key employees by creating a 40-page manual detailing methods for sustaining consistency and accuracy, and curbing risk through financial modeling.

- **Test and Learn Function:** Responded to lack of internal documentation by creating a document recording the goods handling framework and pricing models. Comprehensive document detailed mechanics, input needs, component details and calculations, and timetables.

- **Mastered Complex Financial Modeling:** Reverse-engineered the methodology used to model terminal infrastructure costs. Investigated government documentation, disseminated data to derive patterns in asset values, and reviewed frameworks to fill gaps.

- **Trends, Improvement Recommendations, Presentations:** Delivered and presented reports to senior management that identified inaccuracies, revealed improvement opportunities and recommended implementation plans. Adapted complex information to relate to each audience's needs—de-cluttering duplicated or complex content for ease of understanding.

- **Handpicked for Additional Business Improvement Tasks:** Rewrote end-of-month financial Board report to reallocate revenues; assumed control of local area spend reporting, capital program changes, vessel charges, project accounting, pay reviews, and commissioning audits.

Strengths

Accounting System Design

Budget Preparation and Development

Data Analysis and Interpretation

Asset Management

Financial Audits

Fixed Asset Analysis and Security

Financial Report Generation

Cost Accounting

Testimonial

"Cersei's attention to detail and inquisitive nature means she is often given the task of trouble-shooting. If there is a solution, she will be sure to find it."
—Fred Smith, Management Accountant, XCEE Corporation

Technology

- Microsoft Office
- Microsoft Windows
- MS Access
- MS Project
- CSSP
- JD Edwards
- Navision

Experience Narrative

Asset Accountant, Port of Beaumont, TX   (2010–2012)

Reported to: Finance Manager. **Budget:** Entire Capital Expenditure Budget: FY10 approval budget of $45M and cash flow of $36M; FY11 Approval Budget of $125M with cash flow of $92M; FY12 approval budget of $195M with cash flow of $116M.

Improved deteriorating interdepartmental communications over a long-term issue where the fixed asset register—unlinked to the property management module—had introduced a point-of-failure in updating properties. Reconciled two systems with a land-use plan, and launched a new form for departmental communication and input.

- **Curtailed Project Budget Blowouts:** Amended accounting software to permit projects to block and warn the project owner when reaching 80%, 90% and 100% of approved project costs. Initiative curtailed potential for project costs to overrun and cemented formal process to acquire additional funding and Board approvals.
- **WIP Improvements:** Transformed fixed assets register from a WIP high of $36M to just $830K.
- **Relationship Management:** Eliminated an 'us and them' environment that had soured relationships with project owners, asset holders and company departments. Placed 'improving relationships' high on the agenda—an initiative that delivered an unparalleled level of trust across the management team and project coordinators, and as a valuable bi-product, improved accuracy and quick responses to requests.

Cost Accountant, Port of Beaumont, TX   (2007–2010)

Monitored, analysed and reported on internal costs of operational expenditure, transitioned information to external organisations and government departments, and worked with management team to deliver accurate forecasts to deadline.

- **Reduced Coding Corrections by 90%:** Identified inaccuracies stemming from initial transactions. Arranged monthly departmental meetings to discuss costs, budgets, dimension combinations and general ledger accounts, and over time became a trusted advisor on cost allocations. Supported efforts through software modifications that prevented specific scenarios and general ledger transfers.
- **Efficiency Improvements:** Cut processing time sending fiscal information submissions through TRIDATA (a web-based program) from five days to a few hours. Composed a report with a personally created spreadsheet tool that combined general ledger accounts and maps, and sent a text file to TRIDATA.
- **Accuracy Improvements/Productivity Improvements:** Transformed the performance of a non-accounting qualified team struggling to understand the impact of regular cost reviews. Maintained constant contact with employees overseeing budgets, and resolved issues on-the-spot. Upon handover of the role, end-of-month accruals were minimal, accuracy had improved, and staff awareness of actual costs had elevated. Manual reversing journal entries became a task of the past—reducing the time allocated to month-end processing.

Commercial Supervisor, Port of Beaumont, TX   (2005–2007)

"As the Commercial Supervisor on the expansion project, I was commended by management for the quality and consistency of my performance, and meeting and exceeding GPC's expectations"

- **Workflow Management:** Implemented an efficient workflow system that targeted important KPIs.
- **Led by Example:** Trained, supervised staff, and mentored team members—delivering a unified and performance-driven team. Result: backlogs were reduced, and for the first time in some time, KPIs began to be achieved.

Prior Experience

Contracts Administrator, CHD Contracting (2005)
Project Scheduler/Contracts Administrator, AboveGround Services (2003–2005)

Education and Training

Post Graduate Business (Accounting), University of Texas, Arlington
Bachelor of Technology, University of Texas, Arlington

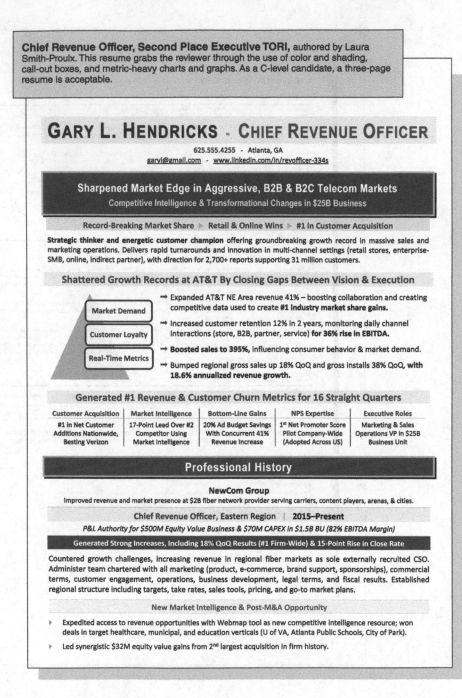

GARY L. HENDRICKS - CHIEF REVENUE OFFICER

625.555.4255 · Atlanta, GA
garyl@gmail.com · www.linkedin.com/in/revofficer-334s

Sharpened Market Edge in Aggressive, B2B & B2C Telecom Markets
Competitive Intelligence & Transformational Changes in $25B Business

Record-Breaking Market Share ▷ **Retail & Online Wins** ▷ **#1 in Customer Acquisition**

Strategic thinker and energetic customer champion offering groundbreaking growth record in massive sales and marketing operations. Delivers rapid turnarounds and innovation in multi-channel settings (retail stores, enterprise-SMB, online, indirect partner), with direction for 2,700+ reports supporting 31 million customers.

Shattered Growth Records at AT&T By Closing Gaps Between Vision & Execution

Market Demand

Customer Loyalty

Real-Time Metrics

→ Expanded AT&T NE Area revenue 41% – boosting collaboration and creating competitive data used to create **#1 industry market share gains.**

→ Increased customer retention 12% in 2 years, monitoring daily channel interactions (store, B2B, partner, service) **for 36% rise in EBITDA.**

→ **Boosted sales to 395%,** influencing consumer behavior & market demand.

→ Bumped regional gross sales up 18% QoQ and gross installs 38% QoQ, **with 18.6% annualized revenue growth.**

Generated #1 Revenue & Customer Churn Metrics for 16 Straight Quarters

Customer Acquisition	Market Intelligence	Bottom-Line Gains	NPS Expertise	Executive Roles
#1 in Net Customer Additions Nationwide, Besting Verizon	17-Point Lead Over #2 Competitor Using Market Intelligence	20% Ad Budget Savings With Concurrent 41% Revenue Increase	1st Net Promoter Score Pilot Company-Wide (Adopted Across US)	Marketing & Sales Operations VP in $25B Business Unit

Professional History

NewCom Group
Improved revenue and market presence at $2B fiber network provider serving carriers, content players, arenas, & cities.

Chief Revenue Officer, Eastern Region | **2015–Present**
P&L Authority for $500M Equity Value Business & $70M CAPEX in $1.5B BU (82% EBITDA Margin)

Generated Strong Increases, Including 18% QoQ Results (#1 Firm-Wide) & 15-Point Rise in Close Rate

Countered growth challenges, increasing revenue in regional fiber markets as sole externally recruited CSO. Administer team chartered with all marketing (product, e-commerce, brand support, sponsorships), commercial terms, customer engagement, operations, business development, legal terms, and fiscal results. Established regional structure including targets, take rates, sales tools, pricing, and go-to market plans.

New Market Intelligence & Post-M&A Opportunity

▸ Expedited access to revenue opportunities with Webmap tool as new competitive intelligence resource; won deals in target healthcare, municipal, and education verticals (U of VA, Atlanta Public Schools, City of Park).

▸ Led synergistic $32M equity value gains from 2nd largest acquisition in firm history.

AT&T

Ignited revenue growth via impact to business sales, retail, marketing, and partner relations at #1 US telecom provider.

SVP Marketing & Sales Operations (CMO), Northeast Area | **2011–2015**

Direction for 300-Member Team & $25M Budget (Indirect Authority for $500M Total Spend) in $25B Business Unit
Supporting 31+ Million Customers in 11 States, Plus 8 Product Lines, Partners, & CRM

Led AT&T in Total Revenue / Customer Churn for 16 Quarters: 17% Growth & 48% EBITDA Margin

Reinvigorated Marketing and Sales Operations, rebuilding collaboration with regional, HQ, and cross-functional groups; increased efficiency, cut rework, and improved results against KPIs. Led agent negotiations, sales incentives, training, and marketing, plus systems-network conversions. Sponsored millions in CAPEX store budget.

Performance Across Stores, High-Opportunity Markets, & B2B Settings

▸ Grew revenue 41%, with 17% rise in customer acquisition, from restructuring and focus on risk-taking, partner alliances, and innovation. Eliminated redundancies with flat management structure.
　→ Supplied real-time metrics (adopted in 2,000 US stores).

▸ Increased sales 20% from New Store Design changes; cut costs with distribution channel transitions.

> **Achievements Snapshot**
> ▪ 125%+ of Goal: New Accts & Strategic Products
> ▪ Yearly Increases in Net Promoter Scores
> ▪ Salesforce Deployment With No Sales Interruptions
> ▪ First New Store Design Launch Company-Wide

▸ Rolled out collateral touting ROI (network coverage, speed, service); shared learnings across B2B sales. Identified lucrative growth markets.

▸ Delivered 22% YoY increase from competition, displacing contenders in high opportunity markets.

"Passionate about winning – with integrity – I look at all angles to fully understand the opportunity."

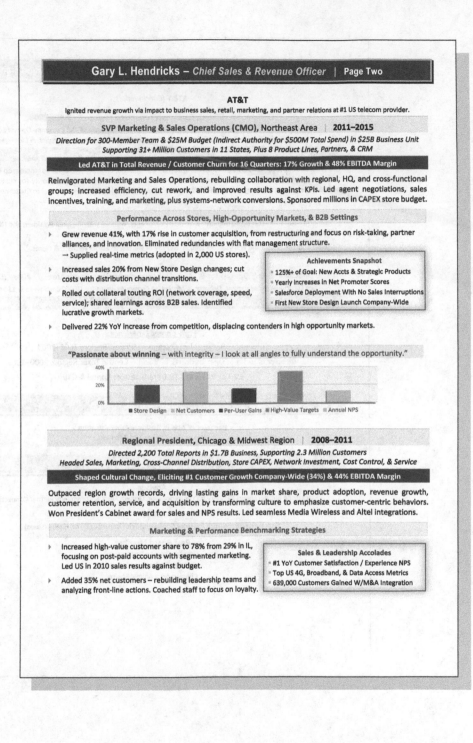

■ Store Design　■ Net Customers　■ Per-User Gains　■ High-Value Targets　■ Annual NPS

Regional President, Chicago & Midwest Region | **2008–2011**

Directed 2,200 Total Reports in $1.7B Business, Supporting 2.3 Million Customers
Headed Sales, Marketing, Cross-Channel Distribution, Store CAPEX, Network Investment, Cost Control, & Service

Shaped Cultural Change, Eliciting #1 Customer Growth Company-Wide (34%) & 44% EBITDA Margin

Outpaced region growth records, driving lasting gains in market share, product adoption, revenue growth, customer retention, service, and acquisition by transforming culture to emphasize customer-centric behaviors. Won President's Cabinet award for sales and NPS results. Led seamless Media Wireless and Altel integrations.

Marketing & Performance Benchmarking Strategies

▸ Increased high-value customer share to 78% from 29% in IL, focusing on post-paid accounts with segmented marketing. Led US in 2010 sales results against budget.

> **Sales & Leadership Accolades**
> ▪ #1 YoY Customer Satisfaction / Experience NPS
> ▪ Top US 4G, Broadband, & Data Access Metrics
> ▪ 639,000 Customers Gained W/M&A Integration

▸ Added 35% net customers – rebuilding leadership teams and analyzing front-line actions. Coached staff to focus on loyalty.

AT&T *(Continued...)*

Director Retail Sales, Carolina & Tennessee Region | 2007–2008

Supervised 1,500 Employees Supporting 2 Million Customers Throughout 158 Company-Owned Sites
Administered Store Portfolio & Capital Allocation for New Site Selections, Retrofits, & Closings

Attained #1 Rankings in Net Customer Additions, Rate Plan Generation, & Other Sales Metrics

Led team to next-level success against existing Top #3–#5 rankings, creating strategies for increased momentum and implementing Net Promoter Scores key to improved team effort; held broad authority for customer-facing and revenue growth challenges in retail SMB channel. Conveyed real-time metrics pivotal to Customer Additions.

First-Time NPS Use Across The Company, With Results From New Sales Tool

‣ Launched Net Promoter Score initiative with District Manager, working with Regional President and HQ for retail store deployment. Built training program.

‣ Built frontline headcount analysis tool (still in use) key to staffing forecasts across 158 stores.

Director Training Operations & Marketing Communications, South Area | 2003–2007

Led Curriculum Development, Delivery, & Marketing Communications for 10,000 Employees in 11 States

Built 1st Combined Structure Adopted Firm-Wide; Reached #4 in Training Magazine Top 125 Organizations

Early Career Experience:

Director of Retail Sales, Chicago / Midwest Region, 2001–2003

Director of Indirect Distribution & B2B Sales, Central Texas Region, 2000–2001

Earlier Roles at AT&T Predecessors Contel & GTE

Education

Bachelor of Arts in Business Administration
University of Wisconsin, Madison

Professional Affiliations

Advisor
Blackstone Entrepreneurs Network (CO Entrepreneur, Growth Firm, & Community Partner Connections)

Ninja
QuarterHealth (Startup Advisory Conferring With Impact CEOs on Health Issues)

Past Board Member
Greater Chicago Partnership
Chicago Technology Center
Chicago Area Animal Shelter

JESSE SMITH, MD, FACEP

123 Main Street | Cincinnati, OH 45230 | 513.555.5555 | jessesmith@notmail.com | www.linkedin.com/in/JesseXSmith

Formidable Executive & Board Leadership
Big-Picture Thinking · Strategic Growth Initiatives · World-Class Patient Care

Grew Organization to $1.5B+ | Achieved 28% Annual Growth | Led National Team of 1,700+ | Partnered 3,500+ Physicians

Industry juggernaut and thought leader with an unmatched track record of positioning physician networks for explosive growth. Nationally respected winner of many prestigious awards. Transformed CEP USA into one of the largest physician management companies in the country. Extensive success in executive physician leadership and motivation. Expert in leading large physician groups across multiple specialties while devising top-level strategies that enhance hospital market share, performance, and revenue across the entire hospital ecosystem. Known for guiding hospital-based physicians to improve collaboration, patient satisfaction, and quality of care. History of adopting clinical practices that help hospitals minimize future CMS financial penalties.

Notable Strengths

- Billion-Dollar Growth
- Legislative Regulatory Advocacy
- Industry & Trend Analysis
- Emerging Technologies
- Crisis Management

- Professional & Trade Associations
- Consensus & Coalition Building
- Long-Term Business Planning
- Population Health Management
- Client Engagement & Retention

- Diversity Management
- Physician Practices
- Board Leadership
- Marketing Strategies
- C-Suite Relations

Career Narrative

CEP USA, Nationwide Locations, Cincinnati, OH

The 5th largest comprehensive physician management company in the United States, partnering 3,500 physicians and providers within 100+ unique hospitals to improve patient care in multiple practice specialties.

6.2 Million
Patients Treated Annually

2100 — Physician Partners
950 — PAs & NPs
1500 — Scribes

OVER 180 — Practice Locations

President / Chief Executive Officer (CEO), 1999 to Present
Chairman of the Board, 2005 to Present

Scope of Executive Leadership: Generate and leverage detailed analysis to provide a balanced rationale and broad range of options for the Board of Directors. Provide informed perspective on healthcare trends and ensure seamless integration of medical care and appropriate admissions for acute care patients. Lead and motivate enterprise executives to peak performance levels while driving success of 1,700+ indirect reports.

Exceptional Growth and Service: Expand the enterprise into new markets and diversify service lines. Identify and capitalize on new ways to create value for hospital clients, surpass the competition, and win client loyalty. Ensure enterprise's success by helping hospitals and healthcare systems succeed in their respective markets and realize their vision/mission for the communities they serve. Maintain remarkably high client retention rate and leverage glowing client testimonials to drive new business success.

National Industry Events: Oversee planning of 90+ meetings each year, bringing 1,200+ providers, support staff, and hospital clients together from 200+ hospitals across the country to provide educational opportunities and recognize exemplary performance achievements. Act as Master of Ceremonies for annual partnership meeting and host award dinners with 1,600+ attendees.

Positioned $86 million enterprise to achieve $1.5+ billion in total revenue; maintained consistent 14% annual growth throughout tenure, realizing yearly increases of up to 28%.

Organizational Growth:

- **Led organization to boost enterprise revenue 10-fold over a 15-year period,** despite decades of stiff competition from larger public/private equity-owned physician management companies.

- **Expanded practice locations from 36 to 178** between 1999 and 2015 by building a robust business development pipeline and employing high-impact marketing communication strategies. Ensured steady growth for new and existing stores.

- **Brought annual patient visits from 930,000 in a Ohio-only physician practice to 6.2+ million across 15 states** between 1999 and 2015. Achieved initial enterprise strategic goal of doubling revenue and amount of total patients seen 2 years early.

- **Built relationships with key clients** such as Pride Health, Plenner Health, Tenet, HCA, Ascension, Providence Health, Norwegien Health, Advocate Health, Adventist Health, and Methodist Health initiatives.

- **Developed 180+ new physician practices** with a variety of non-profit, faith-based, and public/investor-owned hospital clients.

- **Enabled an affiliated Risk Retention Group (RRG) to achieve $80 million in assets** and receive an A+ rating by PIAA. Collaborated with RRG to develop innovative capital source to address capital requirements for growth.

- **Successfully implemented the strategic vision to adopt enterprise IT processes** and installed first Chief Information Officer. Provided enterprise direction for multiple IT infrastructure upgrades and revamped public/private websites, which get millions of page views annually. Added numerous enterprise software programs across enterprise such as Salesforce, Qlikview, Ingenious Med, and Lawson.

- **Spearheaded Acute Care Continuum enterprise strategy,** helping hospital clients integrate clinical care for hospital-based physician practices (HBP) and patients with acute conditions as defined by CMS across transitions of care.

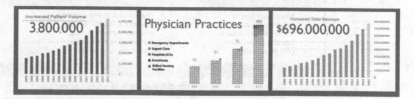

"The institution of emergency medicine would not be what it is today without his unparalleled contributions. His work has transcended clinical operations to the establishment of financial paradigms that hospitals and emergency departments use to treat millions of patients a year." — *Sandra Brenner, MD, CEO, Belleview Hospital*

Enhanced Performance & Efficiencies:

- **Significantly improved Board efficiency and strategic planning processes** by introducing policy governance approach, calendar agenda, and electronic data packets. Empowered Board and enterprise management with tools to better communicate with 4,000+ individual providers while streamlining processes.

- **Informed clients, built brand awareness, and developed internal thought leaders** by creating newsletter and blog. Served as Executive Editor; generated engaging copy and recruited additional content providers.

- **Created state-of-the-art Web portal** that connects 7,000+ individuals in the enterprise.

Communications & Issue Resolution:

- **Steered critical legislative and regulatory decisions** to influence policy at state/national levels; served on various PACs.

- **Served as expert executive witness,** representing enterprise in many complex legal matters.

Served as Staff Physician in the Emergency Department at Hamilton County Hospital Medical Center for 35+ years.
Worked as Director of Cincinnati Avenue Urgent Care Center for 2 years.

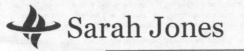

Sarah Jones

Austin, Texas
512 111 1111
sarahjones@e-mail.com
LinkedIn Profile

CHIEF EXECUTIVE OFFICER

Phenomenal Revenue Growth │ Business Rescue & Turnaround │ Industry Leader

"Jones is a phenom with a midas touch. Just having her name associated with your company is enough to boost the share price by 10 points." – USA Business Review (2015)

Multitalented business leader with a glistening track record of success in generating revenue, slashing costs, and optimizing production on a global scale. Effective, efficient, energetic, and enigmatic business guru with the expertise needed to secure #1 leader status in all core markets.

Track Record of Excellence

→ *Catapulted Winning Eleven Energy into #1 Market Position with 35% Revenue Growth* ←
→ *Personally Negotiated Exclusive Contract with Saudi Aramco for $1 Billion Offshore Project* ←
→ *Revitalized & Revived Enigma Energy Inc. to become #1 High-Growth Small Cap Firm in USA* ←

Areas of Expertise

- Inspirational Leadership
- Strategic & Tactical Planning
- Human Resource Management
- Performance Management

- Corporate Turnaround & Development
- Organizational Growth & Development
- Environmental Strategy Formulation
- Joint Venture Partnership Negotiation

- Revenue Generation
- Contract Negotiations
- Mergers & Acquisitions
- Regulatory Compliance

By the Numbers

➡ Reversed slow earnings growth by cultivating strong demand for high-margin products which **boosted revenues by $3B** prompting the company to lift its dividend. Delivered consistent top and bottom line growth by **increasing revenues by a CAGR of 35% through to 2014.**

➡ Commissioned an extensive analysis of all core operating areas and identified opportunities to streamline processes, increase efficiency, and boost productivity. **Reduced overall operating costs by 18% while maintaining profitability and increasing marketing spend.**

Revenue in Billions

(bar chart showing values for 2010, 2011, 2012, 2013, with y-axis 0 to 60)
■ Core Products - Total Sales
■ Services - Total Sales

CAREER HISTORY: A WINNING LEGACY

WINNING ELEVEN ENERGY INC., Austin, Texas (2006 to Present)

Winning Eleven Energy Inc. is a $50B publicly traded integrated energy company strategically focused on developing one of the world's largest petroleum resource basins. The company has 3,000 employees worldwide.

Chief Executive Officer

Unanimously chosen by the board of directors to provide unimpeachable leadership to a once proud energy powerhouse left reeling by an 'at-fault' environmental catastrophe and loss of multiple lucrative contracts. Forged an iron-clad grip on existing legal challenges, personally re-negotiated and rescued $1B in development contracts, and successfully re-branded the company as a paragon of environmentalism.

Actions & Results:

- **Invigorating Leadership:** Sounded the clarion call for all employees to stand up and play their part in helping return the company to glory after the damaging E-1 Environmental Disaster. **Developed a world-class environmental strategy designed to exceed all federal requirements. Completed the company's redemption by securing the world's first-ever 'Energy Friends of the Environment' award.**

- **Profit Increase & Cost Reduction:** Generated significant profit increases despite challenging economic conditions and overseas operations being burdened with uncertainty surrounding regional security. **Closed a $2B strategic acquisition and boosted sales of plastics, polymers, and resins by $800M.**

- **Long-Term Security:** Liberated $2B in cash by disposing of faltering product lines and subsidiary companies, and rapidly adjusted to oil market collapse by shifting focus to low-cost conventional vertical plays with best-in-industry assets. **Currently positioned for phenomenal revenue growth upon market reversal.**

ENIGMA ENERGY INC., Houston, Texas (2000 to 2005)

Enigma Energy Inc. is a $35B publicly traded oil & gas company with interests in USA, Canada, Saudi Arabia, Kazakhstan, Iraq, and Nigeria. The company has 1,900 employees worldwide.

Chief Executive Officer

Hand-picked by the board of directors to revive the declining fortunes of a major multi-national energy company suffering from an overzealous M&A strategy, stagnant profitability, and a moderate rise in operating costs. **Championed a complete review of the senior leadership team, implemented stringent performance metrics, and increased revenues by $12B over 5 years.**

Actions & Results:

- **Common Sense:** Initiated a major review of core operations and identified multiple areas for improvement. **Sold several non-core producing assets, reduced non-essential headcount, and saved $6B over 4 years.**

Cost Reduction in Billions

- **Business Acumen:** Cultivated productive and profitable joint venture partnerships with a key ally in Canada which provided access to one of the largest petroleum resource basins on earth. **Increased profitability by 23%.**

- **Industry Innovation:** Leveraged new technological advancements in 4D seismology, distillation, and isomerization to improve exploration, drilling, production, processing, and distribution activities.

FORMULA OIL & GAS INC., Houston, Texas (1995 to 2000)

Formula Oil & Gas Inc. is a $15B publicly traded oil & gas company with operations in USA, Saudi Arabia, Kazakhstan, Iraq, and Russia. The company has 800 employees worldwide.

Chief Executive Officer

Recruited by the CEO to capitalize on winning market conditions and ensure attainment of a pre-determined fiscal and operational strategies designed to position the company as a serious player on the global stage. **Immediately crafted a plan to enter key international markets and diversify the product portfolio which delivered a remarkable $15B growth over a 5-year period. Increased stock price by 65%.**

Actions & Results:

- **Ingenuity**: Led the charge into uncharted international territory by forging mutually beneficial joint venture partnerships with established industry leaders. **Offered critical operational expertise and succeeded in closing $6B worth of contracts in the Middle East.**

- **Leadership**: Assembled talented teams of experienced industry professionals to add credibility to a burgeoning international market presence. **Reduced operating costs by 22%.**

- **Change Management**: Introduced the first comprehensive **health & safety program for the oil & gas industry in North America**. Skillfully managed and overcame all change-related resistance.

- **Enterprise & Daring**: Led a whirlwind M&A program which resulted in the acquisition of 7 of the most promising junior energy companies on the continent. Cultivated new acquisitions to maturity and **generated an additional $4B in revenues as a direct result of the program.**

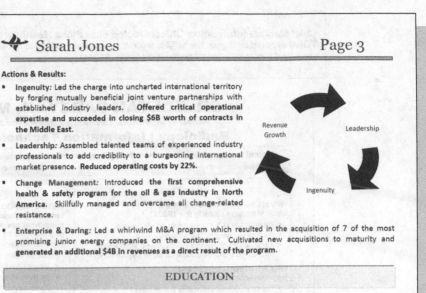

EDUCATION

Master of Business Administration – Baylor University, Waco, Texas

Bachelor of Commerce – Baylor University, Waco, Texas

AFFILIATIONS

President, Local Chapter (2004 to Present) – US & Canada Oil & Gas Professionals

President, Local Chapter (Since 2000) – Association of Women in Energy

COMMUNITY INVOLVEMENT

Mentor (Since 2008) – Graduate Leadership Program, Texas Board of Trade

Founder & Director (2008 to Present) – Female Energy Professionals Support & Mentorship Program

DR. ZOLTÁN PARZYAN, MD

Pioneer of Informatics, TeleMedicine, and Medical IT

Radiology | Information Technology

Medical Doctor | Consultant | Health-App Creator | ACA-Compliance Expert | Inventor

Tallahassee, FL 34238 / Tel: (404) 503-4842 / Email: zoltanp@gmail.com / LinkedIN Profile

CHALLENGE	SOLUTION
Why are so many of the USA's top medical centers stuck in the 1980s? - Patients are still entering info on clipboards - Waiting too long to see a doctor - Admin staff still using FAX machines. Misplacing records. Not coordinating with other departments **Why are so many healthcare transformations faltering?** - Transformations inevitably fail without buy-in by the doctors - But doctors detest taking orders from the business side – MBAs and IT people	Call the "IT DOCTOR" – the technologist and mobile-health consultant who solved all of these problems for 14 of the USA's top medical centers, including: - Florida State University MC - Jersey City MC - Hartford Hospital - University of Pittsburgh MC - Cornell Weill, NYC - Columbia Presbyterian, NYC - Women's Hospital, Boston

PROFESSIONAL EXPERIENCE

Medical informatics and IT standards: Dicom, ICD10, PACS, SOX, HIPAA • Big data • Medical & business analytics • Data warehouse • Proposal writing • Cloud computing • Enterprise architecture • Program management • P&L• R&D

FLORIDA STATE UNIVERSITY, MED CENTER, Tallahassee, FL   Aug 2014–Present
The region's largest health services system / Research leader in health management and medical informatics.
Chief Medical Information Officer (CMIO)

> Transformed FSUMC's back office from paper and Excel worksheets to 100% digital. Advised FSUMC on implementation and meaningful use of inpatient EPIC Systems, EMR (McKeson), ambulatory EHR (AthenaHealth, Allscripts), PACS, and Sentri7.

- Established system-wide governance of electronic medical records (EMR), which resulted in enthusiastic representation from all clinical areas and medical specialties.
- Implemented universal Computerized Physician Order Entry (CPOE). Increased CPOE compliance from 40% to 90% over three months.
- Reduced cost-of-care and improved patient safety by implementing clinical-decision support tools, evidence-based protocols, robust analytics, and training.
- Set up population-health analytics for the Gulf Cost Health Partners Accountable Care Organization (ACO), for example, physician scorecards and group practice (GPRO) data reporting.

UNIVERSITY OF PITTSBURGH (UOP), Pittsburgh, PA   JUL 2000–JUL 2014
The region's largest health services provider / A national leader in health mgmt and informatics education and research.

> SUMMARY: Initially attended UOP as a scholarship student in the Department of Health Management and Informatics. As a board-certified radiologist, collaborated with UOP's radiology department on emerging trends in telemedicine, which led to 13-year affiliation with UOP.

SENIOR RESEARCH INFORMATICIAN (2012–2013): Hired by UOP Medical Dean as first member of the newly created Institute of Translational and Clinical Sciences (ITCS), which accelerates medical discovery "from lab bench to patient bedside" – managed by UOP but includes experts from all areas of the UOP campus, such as engineering, business, medicine, and journalism.

- **INFRASTRUCTURE**: Created the digital "plumbing" for data acquisition, sharing, and processing. Consolidated EXCEL worksheets into new data-management system running on a centralized server.

- **REDCAP**: Investigated various DMS solutions. After an exhaustive search, selected and implemented REDCAP (a DMS created by Vanderbilt University).

- **LIGHT SQUARED PROJECT**: Co-led a 6-person team – IT, nursing, medical records, quality – which implemented LIGHT SQUARED, part of a $12M CMS innovation award.

  ✓ Built the health-analytics platform, including data warehouse. Directed consulting projects for external clients – such as PA Dept of Health – that generated $250K annual recurring revenue.

  ✓ Provided analytics support for multiple research projects, including: statistics (multivariate regression, GAM) and data mining (clustering, decision trees, association rules).

> **INVENTED A DIABETES MONITORING SYSTEM**
>
> At UOP, solved a longstanding problem posed by children and teens who resist injecting themselves with insulin.
>
> - Invented a glucose monitor with small wireless transceiver that reports each patient's status to a central database.
>
> - If the person does not self medicate, the system sends reminders (and escalate warnings to parents when needed).

UOP RESEARCH FELLOWSHIP – POSTDOCTORAL FELLOW – MEDICAL INFORMATICS (2009–2012): Recognized by National Library of Medicine (NLM) – awarded a fellowship for pioneering work in health management and informatics. Published 23 peer-reviewed articles.
Researched image exchanges, digital pathology, data mining, and natural-language processing.

CLINICAL INSTRUCTOR MEDICAL INFORMATICS (2004–2009): Promoted into a newly created position. Created an informatics curriculum for radiology residents. Replaced the existing PAC system (3-year project).

- **Pre-Implementation**: The existing PAC system had slowed down – overloaded with too many users and too much traffic – and could not scale up. Led comprehensive redesign of back-office processes.

- **Vendor Selection**: Led exhaustive evaluation of possible vendors and selected GE's next-gen system.

SOFTWARE SUPPORT EXPERT (2000–2004): While studying at UOP for an MS in Informatics, proposed a digital imaging system – similar idea to the "Medinet" system I built for 20 hospitals in Budapest (1997). UOP balked at the high investment, but accepted an outsourced-turnkey solution provided by GE Medical Systems – the very first contract for an application service provider (ASP) – and an early version of cloud computing.

- **GE PROJECT MANAGER, INITIAL PHASE**: Led a five- person informatics team. Co-designed and implemented the USA's first cloud-based PACS – picture archiving and communication system – long before emergence of the term "cloud computing."

- **Achieved Key Goal ("Film to Filmless")**: Generated $438K per year in labor productivity by re-designing workflows and automating the image-routing process for 60-person radiology staff. Saved $1.1M in capital spend (CAPEX), increased patient safety, and created free time for physicians.

TEACHING | RESEARCH GRANTS | MEDINET PROJECT

ZOLTAN HERCZY SCHOOL OF MEDICINE, Budapest, HU (1994–1999), Ass't Professor of Med Informatics.

- **MEDINET**: Conceived original idea for Hungary's first Medical Metro Network – high-speed wireless, wide area medical network – used to exchange medical images (the first of its kind in East Europe). Wrote a proposal that won a $0.5 million award from the World Bank.

- **INFORMATICS CURRICULUM**: Developed first nationally recognized Health Informatics program medical students. Provided classroom lectures and seminars to medical students, residents, and faculty.

EDUCATION

Postdoctoral Fellowship, Medical Informatics, US NATIONAL LIBRARY OF MEDICINE, 2009–2012

M.S. in Health Management and Informatics, UNIVERSITY OF PITTSBURGH, Pittsburgh, PA, 2003
Full scholarship from Cap Gemini Ernst & Young – awarded to the top student in a class of 55

Doctor of Medicine (MD), ZOLTAN HERCZY, UNIVERSITY OF MEDICINE, Budapest, Hungary, 1993

MEDICAL PRACTICE

Resident Physician, Radiology, FUNDENI GENERAL HOSPITAL, Budapest, Hungary, 1994-1999
Family Physician, THEODOR BURGHELE GENERAL HOSPITAL, Budapest, Hungary, 1993-1994

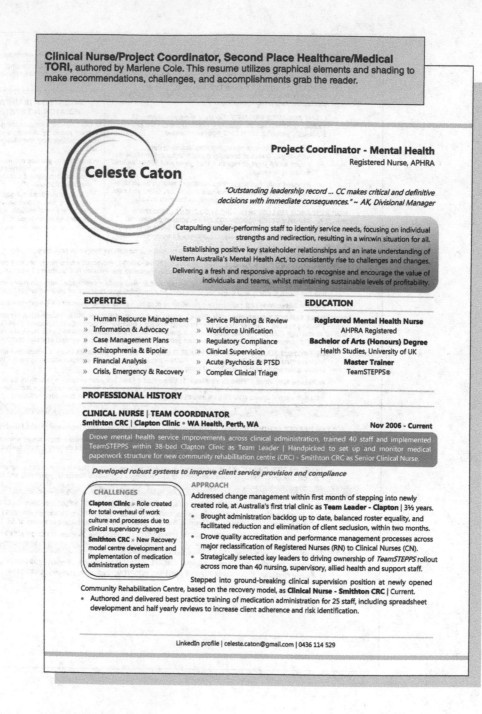

Clinical Nurse/Project Coordinator, Second Place Healthcare/Medical TORI, authored by Marlene Cole. This resume utilizes graphical elements and shading to make recommendations, challenges, and accomplishments grab the reader.

Project Coordinator - Mental Health
Registered Nurse, APHRA

Celeste Caton

"Outstanding leadership record ... CC makes critical and definitive decisions with immediate consequences." ~ AK, Divisional Manager

Catapulting under-performing staff to identify service needs, focusing on individual strengths and redirection, resulting in a win:win situation for all.

Establishing positive key stakeholder relationships and an inate understanding of Western Australia's Mental Health Act, to consistently rise to challenges and changes.

Delivering a fresh and responsive approach to recognise and encourage the value of individuals and teams, whilst maintaining sustainable levels of profitability.

EXPERTISE

» Human Resource Management
» Information & Advocacy
» Case Management Plans
» Schizophrenia & Bipolar
» Financial Analysis
» Crisis, Emergency & Recovery

» Service Planning & Review
» Workforce Unification
» Regulatory Compliance
» Clinical Supervision
» Acute Psychosis & PTSD
» Complex Clinical Triage

EDUCATION

Registered Mental Health Nurse
AHPRA Registered
Bachelor of Arts (Honours) Degree
Health Studies, University of UK
Master Trainer
TeamSTEPPS®

PROFESSIONAL HISTORY

CLINICAL NURSE | TEAM COORDINATOR
Smithton CRC | Clapton Clinic ● WA Health, Perth, WA   **Nov 2006 - Current**

Drove mental health service improvements across clinical administration, trained 40 staff and implemented TeamSTEPPS within 38-bed Clapton Clinic as Team Leader | Handpicked to set up and monitor medical paperwork structure for new community rehabilitation centre (CRC) - Smithton CRC as Senior Clinical Nurse.

Developed robust systems to improve client service provision and compliance

CHALLENGES

Clapton Clinic » Role created for total overhaul of work culture and processes due to clinical supervisory changes

Smithton CRC » New Recovery model centre development and implementation of medication administration system

APPROACH

Addressed change management within first month of stepping into newly created role, at Australia's first trial clinic as **Team Leader - Clapton** | 3½ years.

- Brought administration backlog up to date, balanced roster equality, and facilitated reduction and elimination of client seclusion, within two months.
- Drove quality accreditation and performance management processes across major reclassification of Registered Nurses (RN) to Clinical Nurses (CN).
- Strategically selected key leaders to driving ownership of *TeamSTEPPS* rollout across more than 40 nursing, supervisory, allied health and support staff.

Stepped into ground-breaking clinical supervision position at newly opened Community Rehabilitation Centre, based on the recovery model, as **Clinical Nurse - Smithton CRC** | Current.

- Authored and delivered best practice training of medication administration for 25 staff, including spreadsheet development and half yearly reviews to increase client adherence and risk identification.

LinkedIn profile | celeste.caton@gmail.com | 0436 114 529

Celeste Caton

EMPLOYMENT HISTORY cont...

WARD MANAGER
Bensham Centre • Newcastle Healthcare Trust (NHT), Newcastle UK 2006 - 2008

> Brought onboard to turnaround operational and workforce management as budgetary blowouts and employee relations issues were at an all-time low | Channelled exceptional strengths in HR management, conflict resolution and team dynamics to systematically address best clinical outcomes, staff morale and patient safety.

Implemented cost saving strategies and identified processes to manage poor compliance

Overhauled operations and enhanced workforce utilisation, successfully reining in $1.3 million budget by 25%, across day hospital, inpatient unit and community services - all under one roof.

- Maximised service quality, and reduced spending by one third, within two months through intensive business plan review and outsourcing of agency and service provider contracts.
- Swiftly dealt with theft, bullying and patient abuse via instantaneous audits, performance management, risk assessments and patient surveys.
- Addressed escalation in staff tension and anxiety through extensive training in *'Control and Restraint of Patients'* to assist in de-escalation.
- Managed high-level recruitment, 24 hour roster planning and fatigue management to ensure all staff, patient and visitor safety met.

"Celeste's unique capacity to quickly and expertly gain people's confidence is through her innate personality, which is the key to her success."
DS - HR Officer NHT

CHARGE NURSE | ACTING TEAM LEADER
Bassetlaw Hospital • Carlton & Ward B2, Nottinghamshire UK 2004 - 2006

> Recruited as trouble-shooter, shifting team dynamics, through an innate ability to gain confidence and instigate real behavioural changes within work teams | Driving factor in training and compliance monitoring throughout sweeping changes to Mental Health Act and improvement to clinical practices.

Fostered a culture of service, support and guidance to advance client outcomes

CHALLENGES

Carlton Clinic » Major absenteeism of 50% across every shift roster, due to continuous issues with stress, bullying and lack of training

Ward B2 » Removal of client seclusion rooms, and no safety systems in place caused major staff anxieties

APPROACH

Worked against hostile staff, and challenges within 25-bed acute mental health inpatient setting for in-crisis clients. Shifted team dynamics within 10 months, driving increased process consistency and priorities as **Team Leader - Carlton**.

- Created a non-judgemental space and built trust across individual and group meetings for 35 staff members, within first six weeks.
- Implemented mentorship program and utilised team leadership for education focus to improve absenteeism by 70% within three months.

Established new systems and spear-headed UK's first trial to discontinue client seclusion, as **Charge Nurse** within **Ward B2** (29-bed inpatient ward).

- Launched four-week transitional lead-in involving strategy meetings, client contracts, medication regime changes, and police response procedures.

Leadership: Clinical Supervision | Diploma of Human Resources | Teach and Assess in a Clinical Practice | Auditing Tool Management | Mentorship/Preceptorship in a Clinical Practice | Appraisal, Performance Management and Conflict Resolution

Clinical: Post-traumatic Stress Disorder (PTSD) | Care Programme Approach-Discharge Planning | Suicidal & Parasuicidal Behaviours | Psychosocial Interventions | Electroconvulsive Therapy (ECT) Treatment | Wound Care Management | OH&S Infection Control | Working with Adult Survivors of Childhood Sexual Abuse Scene | ED Psychiatric Liaison | First On Scene

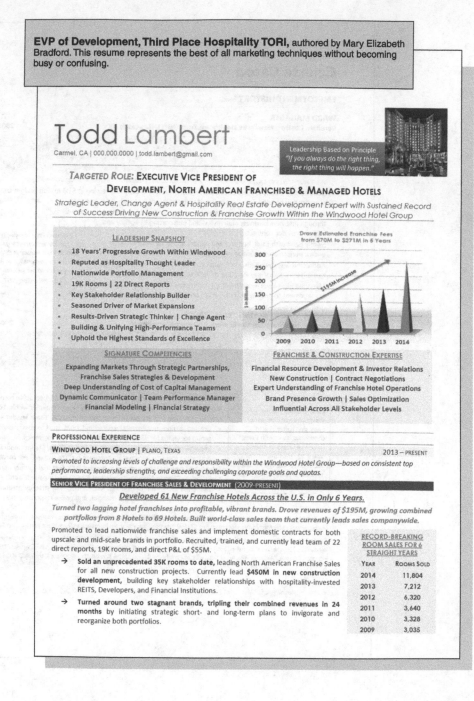

Todd Lambert

Carmel, CA | 000.000.0000 | todd.lambert@gmail.com

Leadership Based on Principle
"If you always do the right thing, the right thing will happen."

TARGETED ROLE: EXECUTIVE VICE PRESIDENT OF DEVELOPMENT, NORTH AMERICAN FRANCHISED & MANAGED HOTELS

Strategic Leader, Change Agent & Hospitality Real Estate Development Expert with Sustained Record of Success Driving New Construction & Franchise Growth Within the Windwood Hotel Group

LEADERSHIP SNAPSHOT

- 18 Years' Progressive Growth Within Windwood
- Reputed as Hospitality Thought Leader
- Nationwide Portfolio Management
- 19K Rooms | 22 Direct Reports
- Key Stakeholder Relationship Builder
- Seasoned Driver of Market Expansions
- Results-Driven Strategic Thinker | Change Agent
- Building & Unifying High-Performance Teams
- Uphold the Highest Standards of Excellence

Drove Estimated Franchise Fees from $70M to $271M in 5 Years

$195M Increase

SIGNATURE COMPETENCIES

Expanding Markets Through Strategic Partnerships,
Franchise Sales Strategies & Development
Deep Understanding of Cost of Capital Management
Dynamic Communicator | Team Performance Manager
Financial Modeling | Financial Strategy

FRANCHISE & CONSTRUCTION EXPERTISE

Financial Resource Development & Investor Relations
New Construction | Contract Negotiations
Expert Understanding of Franchise Hotel Operations
Brand Presence Growth | Sales Optimization
Influential Across All Stakeholder Levels

PROFESSIONAL EXPERIENCE

WINDWOOD HOTEL GROUP | PLANO, TEXAS   2013 – PRESENT

Promoted to increasing levels of challenge and responsibility within the Windwood Hotel Group—based on consistent top performance, leadership strengths, and exceeding challenging corporate goals and quotas.

SENIOR VICE PRESIDENT OF FRANCHISE SALES & DEVELOPMENT (2009-PRESENT)

Developed 61 New Franchise Hotels Across the U.S. in Only 6 Years.

Turned two lagging hotel franchises into profitable, vibrant brands. Drove revenues of $195M, growing combined portfolios from 8 Hotels to 69 Hotels. Built world-class sales team that currently leads sales companywide.

Promoted to lead nationwide franchise sales and implement domestic contracts for both upscale and mid-scale brands in portfolio. Recruited, trained, and currently lead team of 22 direct reports, 19K rooms, and direct P&L of $55M.

→ **Sold an unprecedented 35K rooms to date,** leading North American Franchise Sales for all new construction projects. Currently lead **$450M in new construction development,** building key stakeholder relationships with hospitality-invested REITS, Developers, and Financial Institutions.

→ **Turned around two stagnant brands, tripling their combined revenues in 24 months** by initiating strategic short- and long-term plans to invigorate and reorganize both portfolios.

RECORD-BREAKING ROOM SALES FOR 6 STRAIGHT YEARS	
YEAR	ROOMS SOLD
2014	11,804
2013	7,212
2012	6,320
2011	3,640
2010	3,328
2009	3,035

- → **Create strategic development plans** to leverage brand proposition and rapidly expand franchised and managed assets into key markets nationwide.
- → **Recruited, trained, and currently lead the top-performing U.S. Franchise Sales Team in the company,** amassing more wins and awards than any other team by a wide margin. Team is additionally reputed for expert-level strategies in high-stakes commercial real estate negotiations.

VICE PRESIDENT OF NEW CONSTRUCTION FRANCHISE SALES (2006-2009)

Drove New Hotel Construction To Unprecedented Levels.

Led the construction and development of 64 new Windwood Hotels, totaling 6,800+ rooms.

Promoted into key leadership position and challenged to spearhead massive effort to double development and construction of new hotel franchises nationwide. Recruited, trained, and led team of 12 direct reports and managed $1B consisting of 3 portfolios.

- → **Achieved 100% increase in new hotel development and construction in 3 years.** Grew portfolio from $500M to $1B.
- → **Developed a nationwide market expansion plan** and feasibility study that became the company model for accuracy in calculation of profitability, project costs, and cash-on-cash returns.
- → **Trained and mentored team to proficiency** in feasibility, project development, construction costs, financial modeling, depreciation analysis, and site selection.

REGIONAL VICE PRESIDENT OF FRANCHISE SALES & DEVELOPMENT (2002-2006)

Awarded Regional Vice President of the Year for 2 Consecutive Years.

Turned around underperforming team of 6—taking them to #2 nationwide in just 6 months, and then to #1 nationwide YOY for 2 years. Team consistently exceeded all sales quotas.

Promoted to lead franchise sales across 5 states and within 6 months, took team from last place to second place nationwide for most rooms sold. Achieved multiple awards for consistent, record-breaking sales results.

- → **Won Regional Vice President Sales Award** by an unprecedented 30% landslide over all regions nationwide.
- → **Groomed and mentored one of the highest-performing sales teams in USA.** Exceptional performance of team members included 70% of team winning National Sales Awards by a 40% lead.
- → **Drove 25% of all rooms sold total franchise fees collected nationwide** within a 5-state region.

EARLY ROLES: DIRECTOR OF FRANCHISE SALES & DEVELOPMENT (2000-2002) | FRANCHISE SALES EXECUTIVE (1999)

Awarded #1 Salesperson of the Year: 2001 and 2002.

#1 Sales Director in two Mid-year Incentive Categories. Awarded Rookie of the Year in 1999.

COMMUNITY INVOLVEMENT & BOARD APPOINTMENTS

Board Member, Texas Hotel and Restaurant Association, 2013-present

ACADEMIC CREDENTIALS & CERTIFICATIONS

Bachelor of Science, University of Texas, Austin, TX

Leadership Training: Leading Your Organization, The Leadership Experience at NYU, Diversity and Inclusion Leadership, Respect in the Workplace and Sexual Harassment Supervisor Responsibilities.

Todd Lambert | 000.000.0000 | resume, page two

COLM O'DONOVAN
087.123.4567 | colm@corkseatours.ie

AWARD-WINNING SEA SAFARI CAPTAIN & TOUR GUIDE

Businessman and adventurer who connects with tourists and locals alike to explore the stunning coastline of Ireland. Progressive thinker who considers fuel efficiencies, environmental implications, and safety requirements while maintaining a love of the water and zest for life.

Winner of the 2017 Future Achiever Award from the Irish Marine Industry Board (IMIB).

Shortlisted for the 2017 Marine Tourism & Leisure Operator of the Year from the IMIB.

Maintains a 5* rating on TripAdvisor.com and ranks among the 'Top 10 Things to Do in County Cork.'

CAREER SNAPSHOT

CORK SEA TOURS
Owner & Operator

Launched a sea safari business in County Cork, which became the premier tour company in the south of Ireland. Turned a profit after 6 months on the water. Led more than 150 sea safaris with 100% safety rating.

SPIKE ISLAND ADVENTURES
Boat Operator

Partnered with established adventure center to provide water transportation from Crosshaven to Spike Island Adventures. Brought >1,600 passengers safely across the harbor while also providing an entertaining atmosphere aboard the boat.

CORK HARBOR WATER TAXI
Lead Water Taxi Operator

Transported >1,000 riders in <6 months across Cork Harbor to Cobh and other small ports around the County Cork coastline. Enabled the company to maintain operation during the winter months.

CROSSHAVEN BOATS
Boat Builder

Built high-performing boats from the ground up solely from experience gained through apprenticeship and observation. Performed above and beyond owner's expectations and was gifted a €30,000 boat as a token of gratitude for hard work.

MYRTLEVILLE BOAT REPAIR
Boat Repairman

Hired to paint boats and quickly became an apprentice for the lead boat repairman. Continued to grow passion for the water by gaining extensive knowledge and experience in repairing and maintaining top-of-the-line vessels.

QUALIFICATIONS & EDUCATION

QUALIFICATIONS ACHIEVED: Powerboat Level 1 & 2, Advanced Powerboat Certificate, Instructor's Certificate
All certifications were achieved by the age of 18.

EDUCATION GAINED: Bachelor of Arts in Business Administration from Cork Institute of Technology, 2003
Graduated at the top of the class and served as Class Speaker.
Maintained a 3.8 GPA while also playing Goalkeeper for Institute's Hurling Team.

PROFESSIONAL & LIFE EXPERIENCES

CHIEF TOUR GUIDE & OWNER/OPERATOR | Cork Sea Tours, Cork City, Co. Cork   2014 – Present
Created tourism company to share extensive knowledge and pride of the Cork Harbor and coastline.

> *"Colm is a star. His tour is by far the best thing we did in Ireland! 5* all across the board! Thanks, Colm!"*
> *– Jenny M, TripAdvisor Review*

- Operated at full capacity for summer months meaning more than 1,500 passengers experienced time on the water, often for the first time.
- Built relationships with local fishermen and business owners to collaborate on services, such as organizing BBQs and spotting wildlife to ensure the best experiences possible.
- Maintained safety standards above the national requirements, including SOPs, extensive First Aid kits, and two anchors on each boat.

BOAT OPERATOR | Spike Island Adventures, Spike Island, Co. Cork   2013 – Present
Partnered with adventure center to transport participants from Crosshaven to Spike Island.

> *"Colm's customer service is the first thing our clients experience – and his is top-notch."*
> *– Padraig O'Caoimh, Owner of Spike Island Adventures*

- Provided an additional selling point to the adventure center by providing short coastline tours as part of the center's all-inclusive package.
- Safely transported >1,600 passengers from Crosshaven to Spike Island Adventures.

LEAD WATER TAXI OPERATOR | Cork Harbor Water Taxi, Crosshaven, Co. Cork   2011 – 2013
Operated a 10-passenger water taxi from Crosshaven to Cobh year round.

> *"Our best operator. Full stop." – Thomas Murphy, Co-Founder of Cork Harbor Water Taxi*

- Worked with business owners to grow service 100% by marketing to both locals and tour groups.
- Brought >1,000 passengers across the harbor, navigating around shipping vessels and cruise ships.

CANCER SURVIVOR | Cork City, Co. Cork   2010 – 2011
Diagnosed with a high-grade, stage 4 form of Non-Hodgkin's Lymphoma in the esophagus and discovered it had spread to several vital organs.

> *"I'm not a quitter and the love of the water and the desire to get back on my boat is what got me through." – Colm O'Donovan*

- Remained in the hospital for >2 months; received chemo every 21 days for 6 months.
- Dramatically turned a corner and reached complete remission from cancer after 9-month battle.

BOAT BUILDER | Crosshaven Boats, Crosshaven, Co. Cork   2006 – 2010
Gained reputation of being a perfectionist when building boats, from every screw being tightened to the last stroke of paint being applied perfectly.

> *"One of the best boat builders we've ever had ... such as solid man." – Fergus Delaney, Owner of Crosshaven Boats*

- Built a €75,000 vessel to the owner's specifications, including size, hardware, and design. Owner commented that 'the boat not only ran perfectly, but she feels like an extension of myself.'
- Received a €30,000 boat as a token of gratitude from owners of company for devotion and dedication to work and the craftsmanship put into every build.

EARLY CAREER EXPERIENCE | Boat Repairman, Myrtleville Boat Repair, 2004 – 2006

LIFE PHILOSOPHY

"I know it's cheesy, but it's true – Life really is too short to not be doing something you love. I've been through the ringer in my life and I fought to survive. That life-altering battle just made it more clear to me that I want to spend my life on the water and my deepest desire is for others to experience that love as well. That's what I'm doing with all my work in Cork – to allow people to appreciate the freedom and serenity of the water, wildlife, and coastline of Ireland.'

MARK TURNER

Dallas, TX ▪ 214-222-2222 ▪ mark.turner@gmail.com ▪ LinkedIn Profile

INFORMATION TECHNOLOGY LEADER

Spearheading Strategies and Harnessing Technologies
to Align Business Needs and Raise Organizational Performance

Business-Centric IT Leadership ▸▸ Technology Innovation ▸▸ ROI-Focused Projects ▸▸ Business & IT Transformation

Visionary technical leader, offering diverse accomplishments and experience in information technology across various industries. Reputation for transcending business needs, building stronger teams, and optimizing capabilities. Gifted at bridging the gap between business and technology to realize essential integration.

LEADERSHIP PROFICIENCIES

Infrastructure Management ~ Technology Optimization ~ Cost-Saving Initiatives ~ Revenue Growth ~ Emerging Technologies ~ Vendor Relations & Negotiations ~ IT Security & Compliance ~ Strategic Roadmaps ~ Enterprise Integration ~ Budgeting & Cost Control ~ Operational Efficiency ~ Staff Leadership ~ Change Management

CAREER HIGHLIGHTS:

→ **Positively challenged executive management** to gain greater insight and appreciation for IT. Executed 5-year rolling strategy, restructured department, and expanded staff 60%.

→ **Elevated operational performance** through technology upgrades which reduced data center size 50%, boosted virtualization 40%, improved network capacity 10X, and achieved 130% ROI over 3 years.

→ **Produced substantial increase in IT security.** Safeguarded assets, secured corporate buy-in, and increased compliance with 3-year, $4.5M IT security strategy.

→ **Developed strategies that transformed several corporate cultures.** Led system consolidation of $18B multi-energy group. Presented with leadership award for outstanding achievement.

> "Mark *has a **deep understanding** of IT processes, systems, and solutions and is **very effective at leading teams of** people to deliver them.*
>
> – President, BizTech Ltd.

CAREER CHRONOLOGY and ACHIEVEMENTS

BizTech Ltd. – Dallas, TX | 2009 – Present

DIRECTOR of INFORMATION TECHNOLOGY

Tasked with transforming IT into a strategic business partner, collaborating closely with CFO and executive management. Promote technology utilization and efficiency and introduce roadmaps, governance standards, and best practices. Direct a team of 50 to ensure goal attainment across 85 operating locations. Drive $14M budget execution for infrastructure, security, enterprise systems, and IT support.

DIRECTOR of INFORMATION TECHNOLOGY continued...

Aligned IT with Business. Utilized strategic roadmaps to prioritize, align, and integrate information technology throughout the business, strengthening the quality and efficiency of IT services.

→ Employed defined programs for infrastructure, enterprise systems, system integration, and operational support to escalate department growth **50% over 5 years.**

→ Implemented best practices and executed first 5-year strategic plan. Turned around morale and raised labor efficiencies **66%** in just 2 years.

Enhanced Security. Constructed security team and instituted IT security best practices and initiatives that drastically reduced corporate risk.

→ Achieved Sarbanes-Oxley Act (SOX) and Dallas Privacy Act compliance for the first time.

→ Designed strategy to move **85 locations** off legacy data network. Upgraded infrastructure and built disaster recovery site to improve reliability, security, and redundancy with **98% uptime.**

Upgraded Technologies / Reduced Costs. Championed multiple technology upgrades, improvements, and sustainability strategies to better support business needs and lower costs.

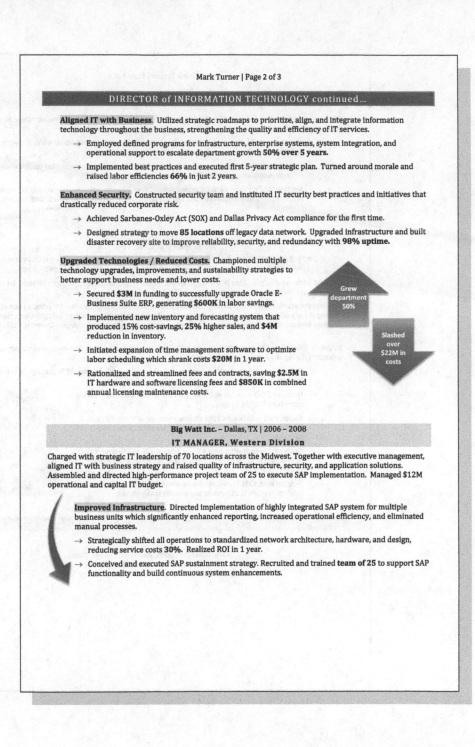

→ Secured **$3M** in funding to successfully upgrade Oracle E-Business Suite ERP, generating **$600K** in labor savings.

→ Implemented new inventory and forecasting system that produced 15% cost-savings, **25%** higher sales, and **$4M** reduction in inventory.

→ Initiated expansion of time management software to optimize labor scheduling which shrank costs **$20M** in 1 year.

→ Rationalized and streamlined fees and contracts, saving **$2.5M** in IT hardware and software licensing fees and **$850K** in combined annual licensing maintenance costs.

Grew department 50%

Slashed over $22M in costs

Big Watt Inc. – Dallas, TX | 2006 – 2008

IT MANAGER, Western Division

Charged with strategic IT leadership of 70 locations across the Midwest. Together with executive management, aligned IT with business strategy and raised quality of infrastructure, security, and application solutions. Assembled and directed high-performance project team of 25 to execute SAP implementation. Managed $12M operational and capital IT budget.

Improved Infrastructure. Directed implementation of highly integrated SAP system for multiple business units which significantly enhanced reporting, increased operational efficiency, and eliminated manual processes.

→ Strategically shifted all operations to standardized network architecture, hardware, and design, reducing service costs **30%.** Realized ROI in 1 year.

→ Conceived and executed SAP sustainment strategy. Recruited and trained **team of 25** to support SAP functionality and build continuous system enhancements.

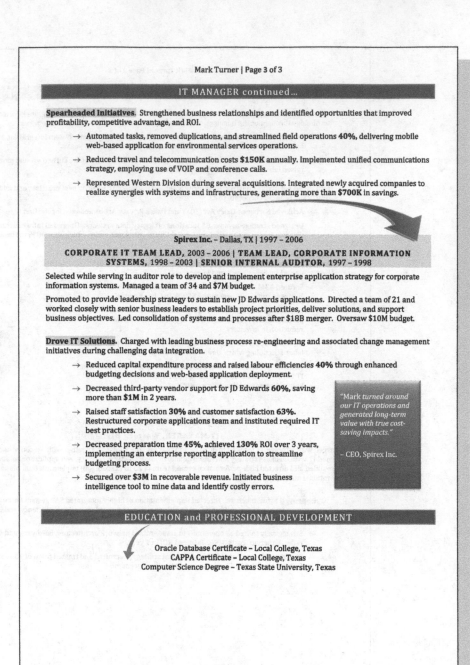

IT MANAGER continued...

Spearheaded Initiatives. Strengthened business relationships and identified opportunities that improved profitability, competitive advantage, and ROI.

→ Automated tasks, removed duplications, and streamlined field operations **40%**, delivering mobile web-based application for environmental services operations.

→ Reduced travel and telecommunication costs **$150K** annually. Implemented unified communications strategy, employing use of VOIP and conference calls.

→ Represented Western Division during several acquisitions. Integrated newly acquired companies to realize synergies with systems and infrastructures, generating more than **$700K** in savings.

Spirex Inc. – Dallas, TX | 1997 – 2006

CORPORATE IT TEAM LEAD, 2003 – 2006 | **TEAM LEAD, CORPORATE INFORMATION SYSTEMS**, 1998 – 2003 | **SENIOR INTERNAL AUDITOR**, 1997 – 1998

Selected while serving in auditor role to develop and implement enterprise application strategy for corporate information systems. Managed a team of 34 and $7M budget.

Promoted to provide leadership strategy to sustain new JD Edwards applications. Directed a team of 21 and worked closely with senior business leaders to establish project priorities, deliver solutions, and support business objectives. Led consolidation of systems and processes after $18B merger. Oversaw $10M budget.

Drove IT Solutions. Charged with leading business process re-engineering and associated change management initiatives during challenging data integration.

→ Reduced capital expenditure process and raised labour efficiencies **40%** through enhanced budgeting decisions and web-based application deployment.

→ Decreased third-party vendor support for JD Edwards **60%**, saving more than **$1M** in 2 years.

→ Raised staff satisfaction **30%** and customer satisfaction **63%**. Restructured corporate applications team and instituted required IT best practices.

→ Decreased preparation time **45%**, achieved **130%** ROI over 3 years, implementing an enterprise reporting application to streamline budgeting process.

→ Secured over **$3M** in recoverable revenue. Initiated business intelligence tool to mine data and identify costly errors.

"Mark turned around our IT operations and generated long-term value with true cost-saving impacts."

– CEO, Spirex Inc.

EDUCATION and PROFESSIONAL DEVELOPMENT

Oracle Database Certificate – Local College, Texas
CAPPA Certificate – Local College, Texas
Computer Science Degree – Texas State University, Texas

Henry Moss
INFORMATION TECHNOLOGY EXECUTIVE

✉ 211 Oak Road • Portland, OR 97201
☎ 541-289-9990 • 📧 henry.moss@gmail.com
www.linkedin.com/in/henrymoss

Enterprise-Level IT Infrastructure Management

Project Management Office Leadership

Big Data, BI, Cloud , ITIL, Agile Methodologies

☑ Align IT with organizational goals while elevating IT efficiencies, mitigating risk, improving system stability and integrity, building customer trust, and contributing to corporate revenues and bottom line.

☑ Excel at creating governance models, methodologies, and KPI processes to prioritize projects for on-time, on-budget delivery.

BUSINESS STRATEGY EXPERTISE

➱ Architecture Builds	➱ Technology Governance	➱ PMO & ITIL Implementation
➱ Cloud Strategy & Planning	➱ Program/Product Management	➱ Vendor Sourcing/Management
➱ Network & Data Security	➱ Project Management	➱ P&L/Budgeting/Forecasting
➱ Application Management	➱ IT Outsourcing	➱ Talent Sourcing & Management

PROFESSIONAL EXPERIENCE

DIRECTOR OF IT SOLUTIONS | 2010 to Present
TechServe Inc. | Portland, OR (*provider of contracted services for corporations and businesses*)

Recruited to design, roll out, and manage the enterprise-level IT infrastructure and governance plans to support organizational goals and implement scalable sophisticated IT project and program solutions for Fortune 100 clients. Budget: $5.3M Staff: 12

➲ *Achieved $1M in savings, stabilized compromised systems, and reversed customer attrition by redesigning entire IT infrastructure and aligning with client expectations and business goals.*

Success Stories Snapshot
☑ Customer Satisfaction ↑60%
☑ SLAs ↑50%
☑ System Availability ↑28%

❏ Within first 2 weeks in position, eliminated network and systems security issues and implemented reliable and secure technologies from routers, switches and firewalls to operating systems and hardwares.

❏ Retired multiple antiquated and disparate systems and replaced with ERP and industry-specific solutions from pay-per-use cloud-based vendors. Attained $600K in upfront savings by centralizing service desks and introducing work-flow automation systems with improved KPIs.

- Added $720K annually in new revenues by introducing RedPrarie's WMS solution for Fortune 500 client.

- Contributed to a 60% improvement in customer satisfaction in just 120 days and 20% increase in account sales by implementing QA customer and employee surveys.

- Improved SLAs by 50% by implementing Yardi, EFMS, and SaaS to manage KPIs across several businesses.

❏ Increased efficiencies in payroll and billing by 400%, saved half a million dollars, and eliminated 8 months in development time by integrating IBM Lotus Notes and Java applications into ERP system.

❏ Eliminated close to 80% of rework by creating formalized SDLC and process optimization. New procedures mitigated risk, improved resource allocation, and streamlined processes.

❏ Captured three quarters of a million dollars in savings and increased system availability from 78% to 99.99% by renegotiating and managing vendor contracts and improving SLAs.

❏ Improved risk mitigation measures 100% and elevated project quality by developing a project risk assessment process and establishing company's inaugural PMO to systematize approach to IT governance.

PROGRAM MANAGER | 2007 to 2010

Joy Juice | Portland, OR *(organic juice manufacturer)*

Created and implemented a viable PMO organizational structure to support Joy Juice North American operations and conducted customer needs analysis and risk assessment for various application integrations using EDI, MS, SQL, JBoss, Websphere, Lotus Notes, XML, and others. Budget: $1M; Staff: 5

Success Stories Snapshot
- ☑ Service Delivery Costs ↓18%
- ☑ Infrastructure Costs ↓15%
- ☑ Design Phase Timeline ↓28%

- ❏ Improved client satisfaction by 50% and cut service delivery costs by 18% by implementing ITIL framework and leveraging business and technology efficiencies through PMO best practices.
- ❏ Trimmed infrastructure costs by 15% by launching project/program management initiatives for IBM Domino Messaging implementations and integrations with Unified Messaging and Rite Fax solutions.
- ❏ Reduced project design phase timeline by 28% by formalizing processes for collecting IT business requirements.

ENGAGEMENT & DELIVERY MANAGER | 2004 to 2007

TechSpace | Portland, OR *(provider of high-tech products and support for aerospace industry)*

Oversaw day-to-day leadership of 70+ team including time, cost, resource, and subcontractor management for $12M in application development and QA/testing practice. P&L: $12M; Staff: 72

- ❏ Added 25% in project sales by sourcing/mentoring talent for QA and software engineering teams.
- ❏ Boosted on-time delivery rate by 80%+ using Critical Chain Project Management and Theory of Constraints.
- ❏ Supported a 20%+ growth in business by engaging in pre-sales and business development activities and overseeing prototype presentations for various technology implementations.
- ❏ Grew revenues by $12M by leading offshore CMM 5 process implementation with iterative methodology.

IT MANAGER/SYSTEMS ANALYST | 1999 to 2001

PharmaLink | Portland, OR *(integrated pharmaceutical company)*

Hired as Systems Analyst and quickly promoted to manager level responsible for building efficiencies and cost savings into the IT process. P&L: $2M; Staff: 7

- ❏ Captured $300K annual savings in development costs and saved hundreds of hours in development time by introducing a customized product-based groupware application and integrating SAP and Lotus Notes.
- ❏ Improved business process efficiencies by 100% and cut approval transaction times by 57% by designing and developing workflow applications.
- ❏ Acted as sole developer, corporate intranet/extranet; used Lotus Script, VBScript, and Java.

TECHNICAL EXCELLENCE

Platforms:	Windows (all versions), UNIX (AIX, LINUX, Sun), Dell 2950/R710, IBM 365, NetApp FAS3000
Languages:	C, Java, VBScript, Lotus Script, HTML, CSS, JavaScript, XML, SQL, PL/SQL
Databases:	Domino (all versions), Sybase, SQL Server 2005, Oracle 10g, DB2
ERP/CRM:	JD Edwards Enterprise One, SAP R/3, SFDC, knowledge of MS Dynamic NAV
Software:	Crystal Reports, VSS, Jenkins, WebSphere, JBoss, Lotus Notes, Exchange, Google Docs, IBM Rational DOORS, HP QTP, QC, HP LoadRunner, Selenium, Office 365, WMS, Yardi, Questback, MS Azure, MS Project Server 2007, MS Project, Visio, SharePoint
Methodologies:	PMBOK, PRINCE2, CMMI, SQA, TQM, Six Sigma, ITIL, Agile/Scrum, SOX

EDUCATION, CERTIFICATIONS & PROFESSIONAL AFFILIATIONS

MS, Project Planning & Management, Portland State University, Portland, OR, 2001
BS, Engineering, University of Oregon, Eugene, OR, 1999

RAYMOND HYNES

(321) 456-7890 • rhynes_@mail.com • LinkedIn

ACCOUNTING AND FINANCE ASSISTANT

Rookie of the Year, ready to enter the corporate world to maximize the knowledge acquired during college years combined with enriching experience gained in associations and internships.

VALUED ADDED:

- **Sharp analytical skills:** Identified an error in billing calculations successfully halting a 4% historical discrepancy in miscellaneous expenses.
- **Customer service champion:** Intervened in a client dispute and suggested changes to the original agreement retaining the second most important account.
- **Skilled writer in English and Spanish:** Translated and proofread multiple business documents avoiding external service fees.

"Raymond is an innate leader. I see him growing into supervisory positions within a short period, not only for his intelligence but for his charisma and high work ethic." – HR Manager, FA Accountants

KNOWLEDGE AREAS

Account Analysis	A/P & A/R Processing	Financial Reporting
Bank Reconciliations	Inventory Systems	Payroll & Bookkeeping

VALUE-FILLED INTERNSHIP EXPERIENCE

FA ACCOUNTANTS, SPRINGFIELD, MA   2016 – 2017

INTERN
Oversaw accounting and administrative functions at a CPA firm with a portfolio of 120+ clients across several industries including insurance, healthcare and manufacturing with up to $100M in revenue, each with varying legal requirements and business dynamics.

- Collaborated in a project to implement an inventory system for a major local distributor which achieved 99% accuracy and 25% reduction in warehouse space.
- Updated the accounting books for five recently acquired accounts, automated functions by implementing Peachtree and trained 45 associates.
- Created several spreadsheets to measure auditor productivity and track engagements which resulted in 15% reduction in non-billable hours.
- Selected for the internship with four other students out of a pool of 80: received the Rookie of the Year Award and several cash prizes.

LEADERSHIP HIGHLIGHTS

DELTA KAPPA EPSILON FRATERNITY, BOARD MEMBER   2014 – 2016

- Coordinated social and philanthropic events leading a 10-member committee; executed 80 events with a $12K budget, establishing a fraternity record.
- Addressed an outstanding debt of $20K; strengthened collection efforts with other colleagues and implemented strict expense control, reducing overall debt by 90%.
- Designed an 8-week educational program on mission, duties and responsibilities that impacted 26 new fraternity members.

EDUCATIONAL BACKGROUND

IVY LEAGUE UNIVERSITY, BOSTON, MA   DEC. 2016

BACHELOR OF BUSINESS ADMINISTRATION, MAJOR IN ACCOUNTING (GPA: 3.90)

Business and Data Analyst, First Place New Graduate TORI, authored by Eve Ruth. This resume takes non-traditional data and showcases it in an ascending pyramid along with use of color, shading, and call-out boxes.

ANTHONY HOLMES

512-555-5555 • tonyholmes@isp.net • Austin, Texas • LinkedIn URL

BUSINESS & DATA ANALYST

Building a better business through analytics

Relentless in defining the optimal strategy and most efficient approach to **data collection, analysis, and reporting** to steer organizational growth and transformation. Exceptionally well versed in business and technology—supported by intellectual curiosity and a razor-sharp focus on exposing, understanding, and seizing opportunities in marketing and customer care.

Driving profits, increasing productivity, and solving real-world business problems

Acquired proficiency and firsthand experience through advanced education (MBA and MS in Marketing Research) and engagements with **Google, Firestarter Ad, and the City of San Antonio.** Learned to tackle business challenges by asking the right questions:

- How should we utilize data to increase productivity, cut costs, and overcome critical business obstacles?
- How can we leverage qualitative and quantitative information to understand customers and shape our marketing programs?
- What is the fastest, most synergistic way to integrate data collection with our overall business strategy?
- How do we bridge the gap between technology and business to accelerate projects and deliver clear, actionable insights?

MBA
MS, Marketing Research
Consulting Experience
Google, City of San Antonio & Others
Broad-Based Perspective
Scientific Experimentation, Military Leadership & Technology

AREAS OF EMPHASIS

- **Data Strategy, Planning & Execution**
- **Qualitative & Quantitative Research Design**
- **Data Interpretation, Utilization & Monetization**
- **Big Data & Digital Analytics Implementation**
- **Business & Technology Alignment & Collaboration**
- **Data-Driven Business & Marketing Management**

EXPERIENCE HIGHLIGHTS

GOOGLE | 2016 to Present
Market Research Consultant

Identified an opportunity to target and capture an untapped market segment (50M U.S. businesses with <20 employees). **Pitched the idea—and landed this consulting engagement with Google,** earning credit as part of the capstone project for MS degree in Marketing Research.

- Recognized that **small businesses need data analysis** to uncover hidden opportunities and skyrocket performance.
- Created custom-designed market survey to pinpoint client needs and ascertain the best marketing approach to promote **simple, accessible analytic software** to small businesses.

FIRESTARTER AD | 2015
Market Research Consultant

Pioneered and directed a customized research project to provide **data analysis for strategic planning and decision support.** Evaluated a broad, multi-tiered market of customers (businesses) and their clients (consumers) through qualitative and quantitative research and analysis. Generated highly detailed and precise reports.

Market Research Consultant, *continued...*

→ Performed data analysis to evaluate a pivot in the company's operating model and plan a successful response to intense competition in the digital and creative marketplace.

→ Executed the two-phase study, interpreted data, and **translated findings into meaningful insights** and concise, well-considered recommendations for short- and long-range business planning.

CITY OF SAN ANTONIO | 2014 to 2015
Commercial Strategy Intern

Enhanced data visualization, utilization, and reporting for marketing and real estate teams. Queried, cleaned, and analyzed large data sets and demonstrated the value of analytics, which compelled the city to establish a new position and recruit a seasoned Data Analyst.

→ Designed business intelligence tools that **changed the way the organization reviewed, interpreted, and reported data.**

→ Built an interactive dashboard to compile and track metrics in real time.

> "Anthony created powerful data tools that impact our bottom line. He also changed the way we hire interns. Until we met him, we didn't realize that real innovators were out there."
>
> *Marketing Director, City of San Antonio*

UNITED STATES ARMY | 2008 to 2013
Data Systems Specialist

Earned promotions and transitioned to different roles and responsibilities during progressive military career. Coached and managed teams to develop **databases and advanced digital data systems** for seamlessly, uninterrupted communications. Planned and executed 170+ specialized operations in challenging, unpredictable settings.

→ **Quickly learned and mastered new skills**—including advanced technology systems and basic Arabic language (served as translator for two years).

→ Trained and energized teams to transform two vital functions from "fail" to "pass" with 100% score.

HEWLETT PACKARD RESEARCH | 2004 to 2008
Research Technician

Conducted meticulous research in laboratory environment. Documented plans, processes, and findings, and prepared comprehensive reports. Performed in-depth data analysis in accordance with scientific research protocols.

→ Devised independent research to discover an infrared security dye for future product development.

→ **Reduced costs, increased efficiency, and decreased environmental impact 90%** by formulating a new award-winning process for recycling laboratory solvents.

EDUCATIONAL BACKGROUND

University of Texas at Austin – School of Business
MS in Marketing Research – 2016
MBA in Technology and Innovation Management – 2015

Rutgers University
Bachelor of Science in Chemistry – 2004

Select Training & Certifications:
R Statistical Language ▪ Data Manipulation in R with dplyr ▪ Data Visualization in R with ggvis
edX Verified Certificates in Data Science & Machine Learning ▪ Statistical Thinking for Data Science & Analytics ▪ Machine Learning for Data Science & Analytics ▪ Analyzing & Visualizing Data with Power BI ▪ Python for Data Science ▪ Introductory Python Programming

NOAH HUDSON

MUSIC AND FILM SCORING GRADUATE

STAMFORD, CT | ☎ 610-883-7923 | ✉ noah.hudson@yahoo.com | www.linkedin.com/in/noahhudson/

♪ **Music and Film Scoring major with exceptional academic pedigree** from Ivy League school; combines hands-on experience within the music, theater, TV and film arenas with passion for commerce and business development.

♪ **Built profitable entertainment company from scratch,** maintained 3.9 GPA and simultaneously undertook high profile film and music internships.

♪ **Outstanding technical proficiency in scoring software;** rapid learner and teacher of new technology.

EDUCATION

Bachelor of Music, Film Scoring, *Yale School of Music, 2012 – 16*

Classes: Film Scoring Practicum | Dramatic Scoring | Entertainment Law | Music Business Management | Orchestral Mock-up & Production

➥ Straight 'A' grades on multi disciplinary projects; forged fruitful partnerships with Music Production majors; wrote music for voice-overs, sound effects and theater.

➥ Ranked on Dean's List every semester.

PROFESSIONAL EXPERIENCE

Founder & CEO, Music Nation Entertainment

New Haven, CT, 2013 - current

Business Growth | World class Clients | Award Winning Entrepreneur

Launched entertainment agency that provides talent management and in-house video and audio production. Created and presented business plan to industry professionals; developed network to orchestrate meetings and obtained $20K seed capital.

➥ Generated exponential revenue growth; on track to realize $90K turnover in 2016 with 30% profit margin.

➥ Secured top industry clients, including William, Saatchi & Saatchi and Syco Entertainment.

➥ Enhanced brand image through publicity and joint ventures; initiated strategic partnerships with prominent breweries and night club chains.

➥ Won Young Achiever's Award, Start-up of the Year, 2014.

HIGHLIGHTS

♪ Yale Music Scholarship, 2012

♪ Young Conductor of the Year, 2014

♪ Young Musician of the Year, 2015

♪ Performed on Broadway, 2013

♪ Grade 8 Cello & Classical Guitar

MUSICAL SCOPE

NOAH HUDSON

Intern, Cat's Paw Music, New Haven, CT, Spring 2016

Business Turnaround | Technical Expertise | Music Client Network Growth

Headhunted by CEO for specialist technical proficiencies. Enhanced client experience from studio support to post-production edit; simultaneously carved out strong affiliations across Connecticut's music sector.

- Assigned increasingly wider remit by CEO, including oversight of flagship, revenue-heavy clients.
- Revamped production processes to attain 100% go live status by 9am, supplanting tardiness and underperformance.
  - ▲ Boosted studio profit margin by 18%.
  - ▲ Enabled composers, including John Luther Adams, to accomplish daily objectives in challenging timeframes.

Intern, Film & Music Productions, Stamford, CT, Summer 2015

Reduced Lost Studio Time | Enhanced Client Management | Minimized Risk

Transformed caliber of disjointed studio support to seamless client care for renowned composers and music producers, including Stephen Sondheim.

- Slashed legacy loss of paid studio hours; spearheaded new catering system and implemented pre-recording studio maintenance checks.
- Mitigated business risk; strengthened client documentation processes, including upgrading of NDAs.

VOLUNTARY EXPERIENCE

Concert Manager, Yale School of Music, New Haven, CT, 2012 – 15

Brainstormed Initiatives | Increased YSM Following | Engaged Students

Headed recording and release of first EP available to purchase via iTunes for non-Yale audience. Oversaw YSM studio; optimized student / customer experience through refining internal systems and processes.

- Proposed iPad use as studio sign-in tool; enabled automatic database management and easier tracking of studio use.
- Ensured all 114 band members experienced a personal recording session despite lengthy waiting lists; coached junior team members to overcome challenges, and encouraged top performance.

ACHIEVEMENTS

Theater: Handpicked from >5000 cellist applicants to perform in special production of Andrew Lloyd Webber's Cats on Broadway.

TV: Selected as one of three from 400 students to produce music for television commercial; aligned theme to brand vision through close client collaboration and delivered compelling music score.

Music: Advanced cello and classical guitar skills; specializes in jazz music. Active band member in Yale Concert Band and Yale Symphony Orchestra.

Radio: Grew loyal campus audience to >1000 weekly, as DJ on Yale Campus Radio.

ACCOLADES

"Noah is one of those rare student employees who comes along every once in a blue moon, and when they do, you don't want them to leave. One of my all-time favorites."

Maria Sanchez-Pearson
Manager, Cat's Paw

"Interns with talent like this are hard to find. Noah made a genuine difference to our studio's efficiency."

Miles Fisher
Senior Client Manager,
Film & Music Productions

TECHNICAL EXPERTISE

- ♪ Digital Performer
- ♪ Logic Pro Tools
- ♪ Kontakt 5
- ♪ Finale PrintMusic
- ♪ Cubase 7.5
- ♪ Forte Home

CHARITY

- ♪ Pioneered Yale Symphony Orchestra Outreach Program, 2015, which promoted classical music to young people.
- ♪ Event-managed one-time performance that raised >$15K in ticket sales alone.

Chief Commercial Officer, First Place Sales TORI, authored by Sandra Ingemansen. This resume offers color, checkmark-style bullets, graphics, graphs, and bold accomplishment metrics to make content more memorable.

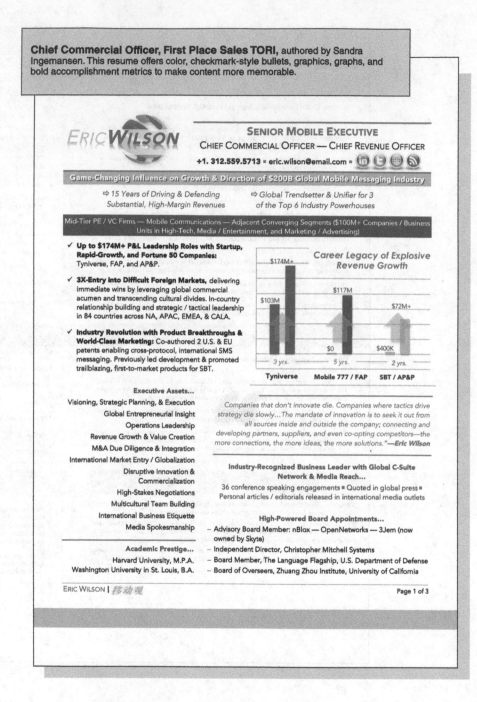

ERIC WILSON

SENIOR MOBILE EXECUTIVE
CHIEF COMMERCIAL OFFICER — CHIEF REVENUE OFFICER

+1. 312.559.5713 ▪ eric.wilson@email.com ▪

Game-Changing Influence on Growth & Direction of $200B Global Mobile Messaging Industry

⇨ 15 Years of Driving & Defending Substantial, High-Margin Revenues ⇨ Global Trendsetter & Unifier for 3 of the Top 6 Industry Powerhouses

Mid-Tier PE / VC Firms — Mobile Communications — Adjacent Converging Segments ($100M+ Companies / Business Units in High-Tech, Media / Entertainment, and Marketing / Advertising)

✓ **Up to $174M+ P&L Leadership Roles with Startup, Rapid-Growth, and Fortune 50 Companies:** Tyniverse, FAP, and AP&P.

✓ **3X-Entry into Difficult Foreign Markets,** delivering immediate wins by leveraging global commercial acumen and transcending cultural divides. In-country relationship building and strategic / tactical leadership in 84 countries across NA, APAC, EMEA, & CALA.

✓ **Industry Revolution with Product Breakthroughs & World-Class Marketing:** Co-authored 2 U.S. & EU patents enabling cross-protocol, international SMS messaging. Previously led development & promoted trailblazing, first-to-market products for SBT.

Career Legacy of Explosive Revenue Growth

$174M+
$103M
$117M
$72M+
$0
$400K
3 yrs.   5 yrs.   2 yrs.
Tyniverse   Mobile 777 / FAP   SBT / AP&P

Executive Assets...

Visioning, Strategic Planning, & Execution
Global Entrepreneurial Insight
Operations Leadership
Revenue Growth & Value Creation
M&A Due Diligence & Integration
International Market Entry / Globalization
Disruptive Innovation & Commercialization
High-Stakes Negotiations
Multicultural Team Building
International Business Etiquette
Media Spokesmanship

Companies that don't innovate die. Companies where tactics drive strategy die slowly...The mandate of innovation is to seek it out from all sources inside and outside the company; connecting and developing partners, suppliers, and even co-opting competitors—the more connections, the more ideas, the more solutions."—Eric Wilson

Industry-Recognized Business Leader with Global C-Suite Network & Media Reach...

36 conference speaking engagements ▪ Quoted in global press ▪ Personal articles / editorials released in international media outlets

High-Powered Board Appointments...

– Advisory Board Member: nBlox — OpenNetworks — 3Jem (now owned by Skyte)

– Independent Director, Christopher Mitchell Systems

– Board Member, The Language Flagship, U.S. Department of Defense

– Board of Overseers, Zhuang Zhou Institute, University of California

Academic Prestige...

Harvard University, M.P.A.
Washington University in St. Louis, B.A.

ERIC WILSON | 移动观

Page 1 of 3

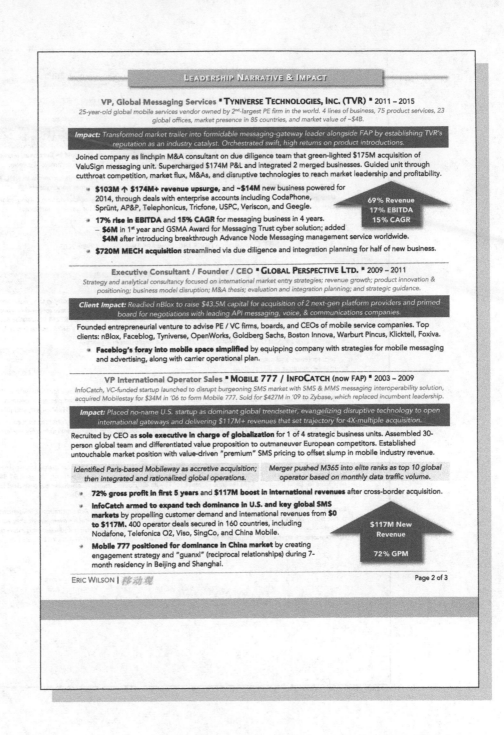

VP, Global Messaging Services ▪ TYNIVERSE TECHNOLOGIES, INC. (TVR) ▪ 2011 – 2015

25-year-old global mobile services vendor owned by 2nd-largest PE firm in the world. 4 lines of business, 75 product services, 23 global offices, market presence in 85 countries, and market value of ~$4B.

Impact: *Transformed market trailer into formidable messaging-gateway leader alongside FAP by establishing TVR's reputation as an industry catalyst. Orchestrated swift, high returns on product introductions.*

Joined company as linchpin M&A consultant on due diligence team that green-lighted $175M acquisition of ValuSign messaging unit. Supercharged $174M P&L and integrated 2 merged businesses. Guided unit through cutthroat competition, market flux, M&As, and disruptive technologies to reach market leadership and profitability.

- **$103M ↑ $174M+ revenue upsurge**, and ~$14M new business powered for 2014, through deals with enterprise accounts including CodaPhone, Sprünt, AP&P, Telephonicus, Tricfone, USPC, Veriscon, and Geegle.
- **17% rise in EBITDA** and **15% CAGR** for messaging business in 4 years.
  - **$6M** in 1st year and GSMA Award for Messaging Trust cyber solution; added **$4M** after introducing breakthrough Advance Node Messaging management service worldwide.
- **$720M MECH acquisition** streamlined via due diligence and integration planning for half of new business.

69% Revenue
17% EBITDA
15% CAGR

Executive Consultant / Founder / CEO ▪ GLOBAL PERSPECTIVE LTD. ▪ 2009 – 2011

Strategy and analytical consultancy focused on international market entry strategies; revenue growth; product innovation & positioning; business model disruption; M&A thesis; evaluation and integration planning; and strategic guidance.

Client Impact: *Readied nBlox to raise $43.5M capital for acquisition of 2 next-gen platform providers and primed board for negotiations with leading API messaging, voice, & communications companies.*

Founded entrepreneurial venture to advise PE / VC firms, boards, and CEOs of mobile service companies. Top clients: nBlox, Faceblog, Tyniverse, OpenWorks, Goldberg Sachs, Boston Innova, Warburt Pincus, Klicktell, Foxiva.

- **Faceblog's foray into mobile space simplified** by equipping company with strategies for mobile messaging and advertising, along with carrier operational plan.

VP International Operator Sales ▪ MOBILE 777 / INFOCATCH (now FAP) ▪ 2003 – 2009

InfoCatch, VC-funded startup launched to disrupt burgeoning SMS market with SMS & MMS messaging interoperability solution, acquired Mobilestay for $34M in '06 to form Mobile 777. Sold for $427M in '09 to Zybase, which replaced incumbent leadership.

Impact: *Placed no-name U.S. startup as dominant global trendsetter, evangelizing disruptive technology to open international gateways and delivering $117M+ revenues that set trajectory for 4X-multiple acquisition.*

Recruited by CEO as **sole executive in charge of globalization** for 1 of 4 strategic business units. Assembled 30-person global team and differentiated value proposition to outmaneuver European competitors. Established untouchable market position with value-driven "premium" SMS pricing to offset slump in mobile industry revenue.

Identified Paris-based Mobileway as accretive acquisition; then integrated and rationalized global operations.	*Merger pushed M365 into elite ranks as top 10 global operator based on monthly data traffic volume.*

- **72% gross profit in first 5 years** and **$117M boost in international revenues** after cross-border acquisition.
- **InfoCatch armed to expand tech dominance in U.S. and key global SMS markets** by propelling customer demand and international revenues from **$0 to $117M.** 400 operator deals secured in 160 countries, including Nodafone, Telefonica O2, Viso, SingCo, and China Mobile.
- **Mobile 777 positioned for dominance in China market** by creating engagement strategy and "guanxi" (reciprocal relationships) during 7-month residency in Beijing and Shanghai.

$117M New Revenue
72% GPM

ERIC WILSON | 移动飞

Director, International Sales ▪ UTANGO, INC. (now division of REALCONNECTIONS) ▪ 2002 – 2003

$26.9M VC-backed wireless media & entertainment services startup. Early-stage business results and technology prompted future acquisition by MoreThan in '04 and $350M buyout by RealConnections 2 years later.

Impact: Positioned risky upstart for future growth, market leadership in mobile entertainment services, and ensuing acquisition after shifting business paradigm from pure enterprise business to include consumer-aggregated content.

Sought out by founders and **restructured Utango business model after gaining foothold in European market.** Launched offices in London and Brussels, adapting scope and sales process to European commercial culture.

- **$1.3M SMS licensing deal cut with Ericskon**—plus content distribution agreements secured with **NHL, PGA Tour,** and **Cannefour of France**—by carving out sports and fast-moving consumer goods niches.
- **Utango recognized as pioneer among M2M wireless service providers** by co-developing cutting-edge technology that increased operating efficiencies and profit-earning potential for gaming machines.

International Services Director — Product Development Director — Business Development Director

SBT COMMUNICATIONS INC. (now AP&P WIRELESS) ▪ 1998 – 2003

SBT, a Fortune 50 company, underwent a period of massive organic and acquisitive growth during '90s. Formed joint venture with BellNorth Corp. in 2002 to form Cingle Wireless, 2ⁿᵈ-largest wireless carrier.

Impact: Expanded global reach and product offerings, skyrocketed international roaming revenues, and catalyzed seamless post-merger integration (PMI) as fast-growing Fortune 50 erupted far beyond $1B EBITDA.

Ignited meteoric revenue spike by driving relationships, market development, and connectivity in U.S., Asia, and Europe. Diversified portfolio to 15 groundbreaking products. Assumed high-visibility corporate role and convinced incoming CEO to pursue international roaming as flagship service. Concluded tenure with **$72M P&L authority,** providing mobile industry thought leadership on 65-member integration team after SBT's $62B USAtech acquisition.

- International Services Director: **$400K ↑ $72M revenue explosion in 2 years**— $36M during first 8 months—by scaling business, introducing geographic segmentation, and negotiating carrier-to-carrier agreements with 125 mobile operators in 30 countries.

  17,900% Revenue

- Product Development Director: **$15M revenue upswing** by launching and promoting 3 value-added voice applications—including innovative Wildfire technology for Northwest Bell—thereby turning this SBT subsidiary into 1ˢᵗ U.S. wireless carrier to offer voice-activated personal communications. Spearheaded development of $15M joint corporate strategic investment between SBT, Microsift, and IBN.

- Business Development Director: **$100K sales surge in 3 months** and quick path to global brand recognition after introducing handset rental solution targeting gaming, hospitality, and international airline channels.

— Early Career Successes —

As Managing Director of **LODESTAR CONSULTING**, capitalized on earlier marketing and campaign management experience to raise brand recognition, reputation, and value for corporate and political clients. *Impact:* **$1.8M** in new sales for Land Rambler; **$1M** revenue increase for Toyuta distributor; **multimillion-dollar partner deal** for Skyhansa; and **125% higher constituency awareness** for renowned European politician.

Earned 2 Presidential Senior Executive Appointments (G.H.W. Bush & Reagan Administrations), influencing public policy on international trade, government finance, and economic and high-tech development after excelling as Technology Trade Association Congressional Lobbyist. Began career conceiving and executing marketing communications strategy on congressional and presidential campaigns as Legislative Aide to U.S. Senator.

ERIC WILSON | 移动观   Page 3 of 3

Senior Technology Sales Manager, First Place Sales TORI, authored by Cheryl Lynch Simpson. This resume strikes a balance between the clean use of white space and big pops of color and charts to make content and results prominent.

denise reynolds

SENIOR TECHNOLOGY SALES MANAGER

ACHIEVED 16 STRAIGHT YEARS OF DOUBLE-DIGIT YOY SALES

LEADERSHIP STYLE:
- Drove unprecedented triple-percentage sales gains, catapulting US sales from 28% to 76% of HP's business. Fueled above-and-beyond team performance by harnessing talent and empowering emerging leaders.

BEST-IN-CLASS MARKETING:
- Capitalized on new marketing initiatives to catalyze +12% profits, +13% market share, and +24% consumer awareness.
- Pioneered social blogging outreach recognized by *Computing Magazine* for boosting brand visibility 53%.

SALES & MARKETING RESULTS:
- Strengthened cash flow by slashing advertising budget $143M (44%) and lowering company inventory 52%.
- Restructured divisional field structure to trim headcount 23%; lowered promotional spending from $212M.

OUT-PACED SALES GOALS UP TO 130%			
YEAR	TARGET	SALES	% TO PLAN
2014	$184M	$214M	130%
2013	$172M	$201M	128%
2012	$156M	$198M	125%
2011	$76M	$97M	123%
2010	$58M	$69M	120%
2009	$22M	$27M	118%

CORE COMPETENCIES:
- ATTAINING BREAKTHROUGH SALES
- DOMINATING RETAIL CHANNELS
- MAXIMIZING VERTICAL SALES
- SUSTAINING MARKET SHARE
- TURNING AROUND PROFITABILITY
- REBUILDING SALES TEAMS
- OVER-PRODUCING REVENUE TARGETS
- INCREASING DIGITAL LEADS
- REVAMPING SALES COMP PLANS

SENIOR SALES LEADERSHIP EXPERIENCE

HEWLETT PACKARD
NORTH AMERICAN VP OF SALES [2009 – Present]   1997 – Present

Promoted to reverse declining national sales growth, rebuild product development, and regain market dominance. Direct $46M divisional P&L with 325 staff, 300 agency personnel, and 4.2K US channel partners. Lead $27M in domestic advertising.

TURNED AROUND US SALES:
- Halted hemorrhaging sales, regained growth, and pushed revenue from $28M to $46M. Revamped national sales team and compensation strategies around rebranded products.
- Improved printer revenue 28% ($21M) by deepening brand-level margins. Cut costs $14M and decreased spending 19%.

$21M SINGLE-YEAR SALES GAIN

REVITALIZED PRODUCT DEVELOPMENT:
- Championed "test and learn" strategy to reinvigorate innovation, restructured talent development, and revamped product line leadership. Streamlined new product rollout cycle from 18 to 3 months.
- Transformed product positioning through realignment of brands with profit targets. Consolidated 12 product lines to 3 and rewrote web marketing playbook while strengthening channel partner training and product knowledge.

AUSTIN, TX • 490.528.7033 • DREYNOLDS7@GMAIL.COM

SENIOR SALES LEADERSHIP EXPERIENCE CONTINUED

RECAPTURED MARKET DOMINANCE:

- Propelled market share from 7.2% to 20.2%, the largest netbook industry boost, employing aggressive advertising benchmarked against key competitor strengths.
- Fueled 3-place industry ranking rise from #5 to #2 in 2 years by earning #1 Consumer Reports product accolades.

DIVISION GM [2006 – 2008]

Tapped to spearhead market share recapture initiative for a division producing 55% of sales revenue and contribution margin for HP's US business. Directed a team of 227 and 1.4K matrixed personnel with $38M P&L accountability.

DOMINATED RETAIL SALES MARKET:

- Guided retail sales up 98% over 2007 by designing and steering a 3-phase marketing blitz for the all-new LaserJet brand.

CAPTURED CONSUMER SOCIAL MEDIA FEEDBACK:

- Upgraded market positioning for new product launches, integrating social media into consumer research. Increased social media participation >74%.

YOY GROWTH	2006	2007	2008
>100%			
>75%			
>50%			
>25%			
<25%			

NORTHEAST REGIONAL GM [2003 – 2005]

Positioned region for next-level sales performance, strategizing and leading organizational realignment impacting 373 employees and 1.7K channel partners in 14 states. Enhanced marketing and incentives; managed $26M P&L.

SALES & PARTNER TURN-AROUNDS:

- Surpassed sales contribution margin $70M above forecast. Gained 1.5 market share points in ultra-competitive market.
- Reorganized field sales force into 4-region structure while boosting pre-owned sales from 73% to 141% – the highest level industry-wide.

SET NEW INDUSTRY SALES BENCHMARK

VP OF SALES – HP PRINTERS [2000 – 2003]

Produced the highest US annual sales in 53 years and propelled profit margin 32%. Drove national sales operations, from partner management and distribution to sales training and incentives with a 278-member team and a $17M P&L.

NORTHEAST REGIONAL SALES MANAGER [1997 – 2000]

Improved partner development 34% in 28 Northeastern markets.

ADDITIONAL HP EXPERIENCE: Promoted rapidly through 7 territory and district management promotions spanning sales and business development in NJ, OH, MI, IL, and NY.

EDUCATIONAL CREDENTIALS

Executive Development Program • WHARTON SCHOOL OF BUSINESS
MBA in Sales & Marketing • COLUMBIA UNIVERSITY
BA in Economics with a Minor in Business Administration • UNIVERSITY OF SOUTHERN CALIFORNIA

AUSTIN, TX • 490.528.7033 • DREYNOLDS7@GMAIL.COM

MICHAEL SWANSON

YIELDING HIGH-GROWTH BY CREATING FIRST-RATE CUSTOMER EXPERIENCES

VISION, ACCOUNTABILITY, CONSISTENCY, FOCUS, TENACITY

1208 PINEVIEW STREET • 123-989-9070 • MICHAELS@MSN.COM • LINKEDIN: IN/MICHAELSWANSON

CONSULTATIVE SALES & BUSINESS EXECUTIVE

ENVISIONING solutions and driving them to reality, EMBRACING Challenges, SOLVING Complex Business Issues

Optimizing market potential, consistently yielding high revenue growth through complete immersion as a customer ambassador, creating <u>customer experiences</u> that differentiate businesses, delivering, <u>every time</u>.

100% SERVICE EXCELLENCE ▶ Across the USA, Italy, Mexico, Korea, Canada, and the Caribbean ◀

360-degree view of sales cycle refined through a 20+ year career driving sales and account growth. Captured high-growth in highly competitive markets through impeccable services to discerning customers as a master of sincere relationship building. Dissolved sales barriers with the courage to evaluate market entry from a fresh perspective. High-performance under pressure.

SALES & MARKETING	EXECUTIVE LEADERSHIP	BUSINESS GROWTH
Market Analysis & Assessment	Cross-Cultural Awareness Intercultural	Global Business Expansion
New Product Launches	C-Level Networking	Revenue & Profit Growth
Direct Sales Presentations	Executive-Level Negotiations	New Territory Expansion

HIGHLIGHTS OF GROWTH STRATEGY

SUPERIOR SALES CYCLE MANAGEMENT DELIVERING MARKET SHARE GROWTH, TERRITORY EXPANSION, AND EXPONENTIAL HYPER GROWTH

- ▶ Harnessing the power of relationships for business success, developing and delivering holistic and responsive solutions beyond customers' original request. Rationalized sales channels aligned with market potential – growing market share by 30%.
- ▶ Converted low-performing technology sales teams into business-aligned and solutions-focused partners, capturing 25 new accounts.

LOU & SUE SURFACES	STARX	JOHN MOE CORP	LOU & SUE SURFACES	EARL & PAUL
>$15M	>$10M	>116%	>105%	>110%
2015 gross profit growth through new segmentation	Overcome barriers in enterprise sales	Delivered account growth in 3D engineering software	Quartz / solid surface manufacturer	Positioned as #1 commercial fabricators in tristate

PROFESSIONAL EXPERIENCE & ACHIEVEMENTS

Regional Account Manager, LOU & SUE SURFACES. Hoover, Alabama (previous tenure: 2008 to 2011) 2014 to Present

Re-engaged owing to previous stellar reputation with company as a high-growth, solutions-focused sales strategist. Tasked with expanding gross profit margins. Propelled sales, living up to reputation and surpassed sales targets:

2016 vs .2015	Distributor #1	Distributor #2	Distributor #3	Distributor #4
	>92%	>74%	>23%	4%

Revived stagnant sales, optimizing profitability through organic sales growth strategy. Mounted deep expertise in complete sales cycle management from canvassing through qualifying to relationship management. Positioned corporation to capitalize on sales pipelines for the long-term by solidifying alliance with distributors, building loyalty to the brand, and solidifying customer base.

> Sales Leadership Mantra
> Our customers' success is my success. It is a win, win!

- Key in exploiting potential opportunities by creating a new sales segment (distribution), realizing enduring revenue generation and broadening Lou & Sue Surfaces' national reach.

- Touted and epitomized excellence in customer service through a multi-faced sales approach: problem solving, anticipating customer's needs, and aligning solutions with market potential—often directing customer toward far-sighted solutions.

- Regarded as a mentor, credible leader, and company stable. Altruistic leadership style has trickled to employees and customers, creating a synergistic and service-oriented environment.

Account Executive, STARX Technologies, Charlotte, NC   2013 to 2014

Assumed the role of rain maker and delivered a 20% percent growth in the Charlotte territory,
despite first time in enterprise solutions/software sales

Repaired company's reputation in the Charlotte market owing to poor management of relationships and subpar service. Turnaround floundering sales performance by a 10% reversal within a few months. Strengthened diluted brand, established market presence quickly, tapping into background in service sales as a strategy designer and executioner.

- Powered an increase in software sales, closing 25 new accounts ranging from $15K to $55K each, creating a new high-performing territory for the company.
- Recognized as a master relationship builder and networker after poaching a coveted $20K account away from a major competitor, securing critical business for a new program launch.
- Launched client-focused business plans and territory development roadmaps, claiming a strategic partner role and converting contacts into sales dollars through persistency—amounting to an overall 20% growth.

Regional Sales Manager | Regional Sales Representative, LOU & SUE SURFACES, Alabama   2008 to 2011
Quartz / solid surface manufacturer. A subsidiary of LOMO Group, South Korea ($31B), with a plant in Canada and sales offices in the US

Presented and delivered on a 90-day business plan, realizing unprecedented sales growth of 105% sales growth for Tuft in Canada
and 35% in the Southeast. Drove a 50% growth for Bunex across the Southeast

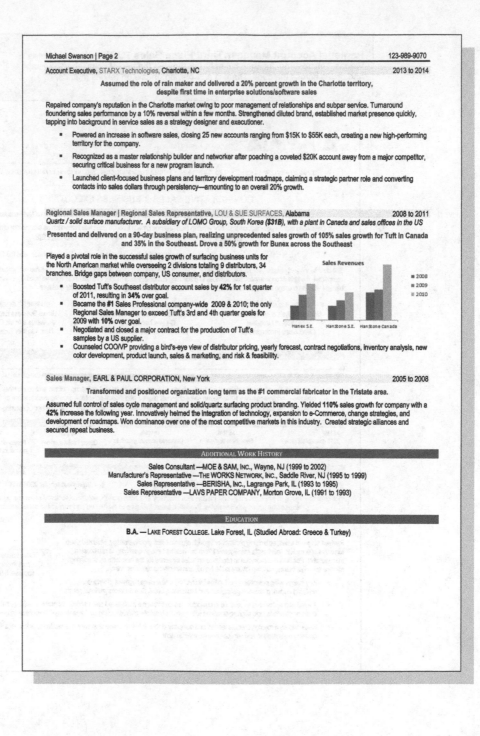

Played a pivotal role in the successful sales growth of surfacing business units for the North American market while overseeing 2 divisions totaling 9 distributors, 34 branches. Bridge gaps between company, US consumer, and distributors.

- Boosted Tuft's Southeast distributor account sales by **42%** for 1st quarter of 2011, resulting in **34%** over goal.
- Became the **#1** Sales Professional company-wide 2009 & 2010; the only Regional Sales Manager to exceed Tuft's 3rd and 4th quarter goals for 2009 with **10%** over goal.
- Negotiated and closed a major contract for the production of Tuft's samples by a US supplier.
- Counseled COO/VP providing a bird's-eye view of distributor pricing, yearly forecast, contract negotiations, inventory analysis, new color development, product launch, sales & marketing, and risk & feasibility.

Sales Manager, EARL & PAUL CORPORATION, New York   2005 to 2008

Transformed and positioned organization long term as the #1 commercial fabricator in the Tristate area.

Assumed full control of sales cycle management and solid/quartz surfacing product branding. Yielded **110%** sales growth for company with a **42%** increase the following year. Innovatively helmed the integration of technology, expansion to e-Commerce, change strategies, and development of roadmaps. Won dominance over one of the most competitive markets in this industry. Created strategic alliances and secured repeat business.

ADDITIONAL WORK HISTORY

Sales Consultant —MOE & SAM, INC., Wayne, NJ (1999 to 2002)
Manufacturer's Representative —THE WORKS NETWORK, INC., Saddle River, NJ (1995 to 1999)
Sales Representative —BERISHA, INC., Lagrange Park, IL (1993 to 1995)
Sales Representative —LAVS PAPER COMPANY, Morton Grove, IL (1991 to 1993)

EDUCATION

B.A. — LAKE FOREST COLLEGE, Lake Forest, IL (Studied Abroad: Greece & Turkey)

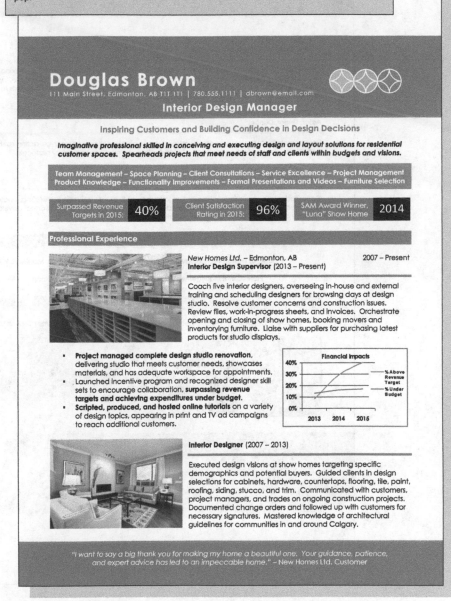

Douglas Brown

111 Main Street, Edmonton, AB T1T 1T1 | 780.555.1111 | dbrown@email.com

Interior Design Manager

Inspiring Customers and Building Confidence in Design Decisions

Imaginative professional skilled in conceiving and executing design and layout solutions for residential customer spaces. Spearheads projects that meet needs of staff and clients within budgets and visions.

Team Management – Space Planning – Client Consultations – Service Excellence – Project Management
Product Knowledge – Functionality Improvements – Formal Presentations and Videos – Furniture Selection

| Surpassed Revenue Targets in 2015: | 40% | Client Satisfaction Rating in 2015: | 96% | SAM Award Winner, "Luna" Show Home | 2014 |

Professional Experience

New Homes Ltd. – Edmonton, AB   2007 – Present
Interior Design Supervisor (2013 – Present)

Coach five interior designers, overseeing in-house and external training and scheduling designers for browsing days at design studio. Resolve customer concerns and construction issues. Review files, work-in-progress sheets, and invoices. Orchestrate opening and closing of show homes, booking movers and inventorying furniture. Liaise with suppliers for purchasing latest products for studio displays.

- **Project managed complete design studio renovation,** delivering studio that meets customer needs, showcases materials, and has adequate workspace for appointments.
- Launched incentive program and recognized designer skill sets to encourage collaboration, **surpassing revenue targets and achieving expenditures under budget.**
- **Scripted, produced, and hosted online tutorials** on a variety of design topics, appearing in print and TV ad campaigns to reach additional customers.

Financial Impacts

% Above Revenue Target
% Under Budget

2013   2014   2015

Interior Designer (2007 – 2013)

Executed design visions at show homes targeting specific demographics and potential buyers. Guided clients in design selections for cabinets, hardware, countertops, flooring, tile, paint, roofing, siding, stucco, and trim. Communicated with customers, project managers, and trades on ongoing construction projects. Documented change orders and followed up with customers for necessary signatures. Mastered knowledge of architectural guidelines for communities in and around Calgary.

"I want to say a big thank you for making my home a beautiful one. Your guidance, patience, and expert advice has led to an impeccable home." – New Homes Ltd. Customer

Custom Flooring Solutions Inc. – Edmonton, AB   2002 – 2006
Interior Designer, Sales Representative

Consulted with customers and builders, taking site measurements and take-offs for all flooring. Collaborated on residential and commercial design projects involving carpet, resilient, tile, laminate, and hardwood floors. Inspected locations and provided quotations, presenting sample boards to clients. Designed showroom and graphics, and merchandised.

Self-Employed, Royal Cruise Lines – Vancouver, BC and Montreal, PQ   1996 – 2002
Actor, Singer, Dancer

Performed in local productions and headlined shows on international cruise ships, acting as show manager and dance captain for two contracts. Assisted with guest relations and safety protocols.

Johnson Manufacturing Ltd. – Edmonton, AB   1992 – 1996
Interior Designer

Optimized space planning for office system layouts involving CAD operations, detailing, and material and finish specifications. Designed and prepared trade show booths. Liaised with product development team, conveying customer needs. Selected materials for new projects.

Education and Professional Development

Interior Design Technology Diploma – Montreal Technical Institute, Montreal, PQ

Professional Management Certificate – University of Alberta, Edmonton, AB

Technical Skills

Microsoft Office Suite (Word, Excel, Outlook) | Homefront Profit Builder | Arris | Teklynk Labelview

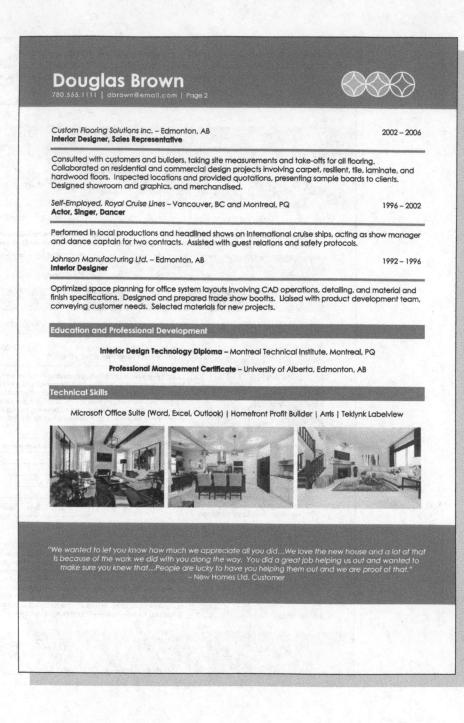

"We wanted to let you know how much we appreciate all you did…We love the new house and a lot of that is because of the work we did with you along the way. You did a great job helping us out and wanted to make sure you knew that…People are lucky to have you helping them out and we are proof of that."
– New Homes Ltd. Customer

FARHAN ABDURAHMAN   EXECUTIVE LUMINARY & INNOVATION EVANGELIST

Willing to Relocate ▪ farhana@mac.com ▪ +971.55.555.5555 ▪ linkedin.com/in/farhana

Influencer: Unrelenting in Achieving Daunting Business Goals with Integrity and an Empowered Team

Proactive, numbers-focused strategist with 15-year history of finding the fastest route from failure to turnaround and from launch to profitability. Heavy hitting negotiator who builds long-term, trust-based relationships with partners. Dedicated to building shareholder value by transforming ideas into profitable products and services that change the world.

- **Bring multinational best practices** learned through leadership at global airlines and in partnership with Global 2000, regional, and government organizations across technology, courier, agricultural, medical/pharma, NGO, retail, and consumer goods industries.

- **Translate between country and company cultures.** Offer broad view of leadership formed while working with global supply chains, turnarounds, and business development. Completed in-person business operations in **20+** countries across MENA, Asia, Russian Federation, CIS, and Europe.

- **Speed innovation** by anticipating market needs, developing industry-changing offerings, and implementing internal processes that enable the best use of corporate mindshare.

- **Lead teams that create value,** drawing on experience heading groups as large as 100+. Mentored several entry-level and mid-level hires into effective leaders.

Business Planning
Turnarounds
Supply Chain
Startups
Strategic Partnerships
Cash Management
P&L Management
Debt Restructuring
Risk Management
Product Development
Talent Development
Channel Management
Marketing
Deal Structuring
Pricing Strategies
Sales Leadership

Executive Contributions

ROYAL JORDANIAN AIRLINES, Amman, Jordan; June 2012 to Present
Low-cost airlines with 91 scheduled destinations in MENA, Indian Subcontinent, Central Asia, and Europe.

HEAD OF CARGO—RAPID GROWTH • TURNAROUND • PRODUCT & SITE LAUNCHES • TEAM DEVELOPMENT

Recruited by CEO to assume executive leadership of existing and new cargo markets. Major goals were end-to-end automation of operations, sales and profit growth, and increased market penetration. Territories include UAE, Morocco, and Egypt. Also lead business development of ground handling contracts. 8 direct, 400 indirect reports.

Quickly Realized Double-Digit Profit and Sales Growth in Challenging Circumstances

- **Delivered 158% of projected 2012 profit, despite taking charge for only half the fiscal year.** Redesigned pricing structure, hedging against market changes by ensuring wholesale prices were fixed and fluctuations were absorbed by retail partners.

- **Realized 20% YOY sales growth in 2013, despite 25% reduction in capacity.** Designed and added new high-value offerings, including Valuable Cargo, Diplomatic Mail, Postal Cargo, and Fresh Produce.

- **Set stage for 20% YOY growth in 2014.**

- **Improved cash position 40M AED, transforming exposure into a cash surplus** by securing bank guarantees and renegotiating contracts with 45 partners.

- **Grew existing ground handling and supply chain contracts and added supply chain contracts with iconic companies,** many on the Global 2000 list.

20% YOY (P) Sales Growth 2014
20% YOY Sales Growth 2013
158% Projected Profit 2012
Despite 25% 2013 Capacity Cut & Only 6 Months' 2012 Tenure

Set Stage for Future Growth via Country Turnaround, New Launches, and Lean Operations

- **Turned around Morocco hub from 20% decline to thriving business that hit all 2014 targets,** using new high-value service offerings and lean operations to counteract European crisis impacting the market.

- **Launched profitable Egypt hub, growing 10X YOY despite decreased capacity.** Also launched successful RAK, UAE hubs.

- **Improved efficiency and improved business intelligence by digitizing manual processes.** Defined functional refinements to SaaS (software-as-a-service) solution and negotiated pricing at <10% of market rate.

GULF AIR GSC, Kingdom of Bahrain; April 2011 to May 2012
Principal flag carrier of Kingdom of Bahrain. Airline serves 38 destinations in 23 countries across MENA, Asia, and Europe.

RCM: Gulf, Middle-East, & Africa—**CHANGE MANAGEMENT • COMPLIANCE • HIGH STAKES NEGOTIATIONS**

Recruited to realize profitability goals that had eluded Gulf Air due to union and other pressures stemming from government ownership and strong competitors. Assumed executive accountability for cargo business. Served as face of company for ground handlers, DGCA authorities, Ministry of Tourism & Transport, OAL, Ministry of Civil Aviation, and immigration authorities. 8 direct, 100 indirect reports.

Realized Triple-Digit Sales & Profit Growth with New Products and Shift in Sales Culture

- **Realized profitability in cargo within 3 months, growing volume 1,200%, from 100 to 1,300 tons per month.**
- **Expanded gross revenues 150% and boosted net profit 110% over 2010.** Revived latent offerings and added new premium services, including Trucking (plus specialized Saudi-Bahrain route), Courier, Post Mail, Valuable Cargo, Gold Bullion, Currency, Express, and others.
- **Attracted clients by developing premium cargo facility that became marketing focal point.** Worked with airport to enable quick access for cargo clients. Built cohesive culture by implementing and attending weekly team lunches.
- **Landed major global accounts,** transitioning sales team from "presentation" to consultative sales approach. Personally coached sales executives, attended sales calls, and negotiated high-value deals.

> 1200%
> Cargo Volume Growth
> 150%
> Revenue Growth
> 110%
> Net Profit Growth

More than Doubled Profits by Streamlining Operations & Strengthening Fiscal Controls

- **Improved quality while reducing staff 78%.** Worked with labour unions, soliciting their input on changes. Negotiated transfer of many displaced workers onto partner teams. Centralized 4 offices into 2. Introduced delivery timelines.
- **Boosted sales and lowered overhead with new business model.** Allowed partners to sell products as distributors and redesigned commission structure, negotiating favourable terms despite partners' initial resistance and adding new distributors and trade partners.
- **Empowered team members by having everyone contribute business plans.** Developed particularly talented resource to lead business development.
- **Ensured strict financial compliance** by implementing transparent processes and tools.

SAUDIA, Jeddah, KSA; August 2010 to March 2011
Premium airline with 120+ destinations in MENA, Indian Subcontinent, Central Asia, and Europe. 10 KSA destinations.

COUNTRY MANAGER—**KPI BOOST • 24/7 CALL CENTRE OPS • REGULATORY COMPLIANCE & NEGOTIATIONS**

Recruited in the wake of inconsistent profitability, oversaw existing passenger and nascent cargo business for 176 monthly flights. Liaised with several government agencies and labour groups. 5 direct, 48 indirect reports.

Brought Consistent Profitability, Improved Cash Position, and Laid Out Path to Doubling of Service Area

- **Achieved profitability at all stations within 2 months of assuming leadership.** Lowered operations costs by ensuring strict GSA financial compliance. Increased market penetration and overall sales by improving distribution channels. Centralized operations for KSA into 24/7 operations and sales centre.
- **Maximized resources by negotiating bilateral agreements for all Air Arabia subsidiaries with 2 major industry groups.** Initiated growth with business plans—accepted by global leaders—to add 6 new KSA destinations.
- **Slashed regulatory fines 62%, from 16M SR to 6M SR.** Networked and negotiated with regulators.
- **Launched Cargo Services and Air Arabia Holidays brands, paving the way for continued growth.**
- **Broke KPI records, including 85% seat occupation at all 4 stations and 99% on-time performance.**

SENIOR EXECUTIVE: COUNTRY MANAGER ▪ BUSINESS HEAD   farhana@mac.com ▪ +971.55.555.5555

AIR ARABIA PJSC, Sri Lanka, Maldives, & South India; April 2007 to August 2010
Premium airline with 120+ destinations in MENA, Indian Subcontinent, Central Asia, and Europe. 10 KSA destinations.

COUNTRY MANAGER—TALENT DEVELOPMENT • LEAN OPERATIONS • MARKET PENETRATION • NEW LOBs

Recruited to close Sri Lankan business in the wake of civil unrest and fiscal loss. Instead, made it profitable, overseeing 98 monthly flights and a network of 110+ retail agents. Headed cargo project in India and Sri Lanka, building dedicated cargo team that is still in place at HQ. Steered media and sales teams in effective digital campaigns. 4 direct, 22 indirect reports.

Elevated "Unsalvageable" Market to Profitable Business Line amid Civil Unrest

- **Recognized potential in market. Planned and implemented turnaround instead of closure.** Cut office space 66%, hired young workers who'd been forced by war to drop out of college, and reduced business hours.

- **Radically increased market penetration from 1 agent to 110+, winning "Best Turnaround."** Exceeded revenue targets 34%, 62%, and 19%, respectively, in 2007, 2008, and 2009.

- **Fostered loyalty and quality in employees by providing performance bonuses.** Enhanced work environment, providing personal Internet access and entertainment. Some entry-level mentees are now industry leaders.

- **Developed new products and launched Air Arabia Holidays brand.**

- **Collaborated to reduce 55,200 USD in handling costs and prevent credit card fraud.**

119%
Sales Target 2009

162%
Sales Target 2008

134%
Sales Target 2007

Turnaround following corporate plans to close business.

BRITISH AIRWAYS WORLD CARGO, Mumbai, India; 2005 to 2006
Flag carrier of the UK, with 183 destinations worldwide.
Account Manager, Central India—Managed key accounts, PR, and customer service within cargo organization. Oversaw 42-member telesales rep group. Led sales training programs as well as sales operations for high-priority and high-touch cargo offerings. Built employee recognition programs, collaborated on call centre restructuring, and implemented quality tools that are still in place. **Key contributor to reaching 126% of sales target—1.9M USD vs. 1.5M USD.**

EMIRATES AIRLINE, Mumbai, India; 2003 to 2005
Largest airline in the Middle East, with flights to 133+ cities in 74 countries.
Passenger Sales & Service Agent, Central India—Accountable for operations of passenger sales and service agents, including telesales and field sales teams for packaged tours, business, and leisure travel. **Introduced key programs and processes, many of which are still in place and/or have become industry best practice.** These include Performance Matters QA program, business planning and goal setting for sales agents, dedicated refunds team, dedicated interline team, and dedicated ad hoc inquiries team.

JET AIRWAYS INDIA PRIVATE LIMITED, Mumbai, India; 1999 to 2003
Major Indian airline serving 76 destinations worldwide.
Corporate Sales Executive—Hired to manage corporate sales business cycle, including prospecting, strategic alliances, selling, and account management. Executed integrated marketing campaigns incorporating sponsorships, trade shows, and multimedia advertising. Key accounts included Essar Group, KPMG, TATA Motors, Canadian Consulate, British Deputy High Commission, WPP Group, Johnson & Johnson, Lowe, Novartis, Merck, Glaxo SmithKline, Siemens, TCS, ICICI Prudential, and Maersk.

Early Leadership

Jet Airways:
Independently conceived and executed project to create fare structure that would appeal to the middle class traveler. Personally performed in-field market research.

Results:

- **200% Sales Growth in 18 Months**

- **First low-cost air fare in India—Apex and Check Fares.**

Academic Qualifications and Professional Development

Bachelor of Arts in Business, University of Chennai, Chennai, India; 1999

Foundation in Travel and Tourism Diploma, International Air Transport Association, Geneva, Switzerland; 1998
International Cargo Agents Diploma, International Air Transport Association, Geneva, Switzerland; 1997

Corporate Training: Customer Service and Pricing Training at Jet Airways and Emirates Aviation College, respectively

5

The Part of Tens

Chapter **19**

Ten Ways to Improve Your Resume

Think your resume could sparkle with a few tweaks? Feeling like you've busted your chops and still are on the outside looking in? Close but no cigar? Here are ten easy fixes to power up your resume to OnTarget status.

Match Your Resume to the Job

To dart past job software filters, a resume must closely meet the requirements in the job description. If you know what company recruiters are looking for, make sure you put it in the top quarter of your resume. If instead you're posting your resume in databanks, research the career field for typical requirements and include those that apply to you. Maintain your focus on including target keywords and then providing support with your experience.

Use Bulleted Style for Easy Reading

Using one- or two-liners opens up your resume with white space, making it more appealing to read. Professional advertising copywriters know that big blocks of text suffocate readers. Let your words breathe! Remember, less is more with wording and page content.

Discover Art of Lost Articles

Although using articles — *a, an,* and *the* — in your resume isn't *wrong,* they also aren't common. Delete them for a crisper and snappier end result. Recruiters and employers expect to read resumes in compact phrases, not fully developed sentences. The first person *I* is another word that your resume doesn't need. Look at the following examples:

With Articles	Without Articles
I reported to the plant manager of the largest manufacturer of silicone-based waxes and polishes.	Reported to plant manager of largest manufacturer of silicone-based waxes and polishes.
I worked as the only administrative person on a large construction site.	Worked as only administrative person on large construction site.

Sell, Don't Tell

Forget sticking to the old naming-your-previous-responsibilities routine. Merely listing "Responsible for XYZ" doesn't assure the prospective employer that you met your responsibility or that the result of your efforts was worth the money someone paid you. Plus, this kind of generic overview won't make you stand out from all the other qualified applicants.

By contrast, read over your resume and make sure you have answered that pesky "So what?" question, which is lying in ambush for each bit of information you mention. Try to imagine what's running through a prospective employer's mind when you relate that you were responsible for XYZ: *So what? Who cares? What's in it for me?* Anticipate those questions and answer them by including the challenge you faced, the actions you took, and the results you attained. (Chapter 9 discusses this advice in more detail.)

Show Off Your Assets

Employers are wild about snaring the cream of the crop. If you have a high rank in any significant group (graduation, sales, attendance record, performance ratings), make sure that fact appears prominently on your resume. Use dollar amounts, percentages, rankings, awards, and honors to make it clear.

Make Sure Your Words Play Well Together

Old wisdom: Use a lot of action verbs to perk up reading interest in resumes. *Later wisdom:* Cash in some of the action verbs for nouns, the keywords that ward off anonymity in sleeping resume databases. *New wisdom:* Use both nouns and verbs. See Chapter 10 for more about all this wisdom.

Reach Out with Strength

Highlight the qualifications and past job activities that speak to the kind of job you want and the skills you want to use. If, for instance, you want to transition from military training to civilian training, remain riveted to your training skills without diluting your message by mentioning your ability to keyboard 80 words per minute.

Don't muddle your resume's message with minor skills or skills you no longer want to use or need for the position for which you are applying; stay on message and ruthlessly delete what doesn't qualify you for your target job.

Trash a Wimpy Objective

Imagine an actor striding onto a stage, stopping, and then standing there like a log, addressing the audience: "I came to find out what you can do for me."

Not exactly a curtain raiser — any more than beginning your resume with simply awful objective statements like: "Seeking a chance for advancement," or "where my skills will be utilized."

Retire trite messages such as this one: "To obtain a responsible job with challenging and rewarding duties." Does someone out there really want an irresponsible position? One that's dull and unrewarding?

Cross out these generic meanderings and go for a straightforward objective header statement that parrots back to the employer the job for which you're applying. If your target position is Project Manager, then your objective header can be "Project Manager – PMP Certified."

Don't be afraid to take it one step further and use the exact title the company lists. That way, they will know the resume is written just for them.

Deliver the Right Document

If it just isn't clear from the job advertisement what file format of resume is desired by the HR department, go ahead and ask. But when you can't reach someone and don't know the answer, cover your bases. Submit a resume saved in a .doc format (typically created in the preferred MS Word) along with one formatted in ASCII (plain text). (See Chapter 4 for more about the ASCII format.)

Erase the Leave-Outs

Eliminate clutter by removing useless information that doesn't support the reasons why you're a qualified candidate. Here's a short list of the worst offenders:

>> The title word, "Objective." It's understood that the top line under your contact info will be your job target.

>> "References available on request." Listing the references on your resume is even worse.

>> Your Social Security number or driver's license number.

>> The date your resume was prepared.

>> Your company's telephone number.

>> Your high school or grammar school.

>> Dates you spent involved in college extracurricular activities.

>> Dates you were involved with professional or civic organizations, unless you're using them to fill in gaps or add heft to your claims.

>> Names of (human) past employers; put these on your reference sheet with contact information.

>> Most jobs older than 10 to 15 years ago to avoid showing your age or over qualifications.

>> Any content that doesn't qualify you for the position or emphasizes that your heart and skills lie elsewhere (jobs, volunteer work, affiliations, education).

>> Activities not related to your job target that could be considered inflammatory or might cause discrimination, such as religious or political affiliation, age, race, and dangerous sports.

Chapter **20**

Ten Ways to Increase the Odds of Landing a Job

Although the Internet makes uncovering a gold mine of job possibilities easier than ever, your mission is to separate the gold from the sand in finding the right opportunities for you. This chapter aims to help you get your resume to the right eyes for the right jobs without fumbling around and wasting time.

Send Your Resume in the Right Tech Form

The job search process is now primarily digitized, producing a variety of devices and websites where your online resume can be marketed.

The big question savvy job seekers are asking right now is which form they should use to send resumes to a specific online location, such as a job board. Read the instructions on each website, of course, but you have the following three options:

» The **full-design resume,** when used as an online document, conveys a visual message as well as information expressed only in typographic text. Graphical design elements vary — the most popular are lines, white space, bullets, columns, graphs, symbols, and colors (see Chapters 11 and 12 for more on these design elements). The advantage: Human eyes find full-design resumes far more inviting to read than plain-text resumes. This is the one you always want to use when the system accepts full-designs such as MS Word or PDF.

>> The **plain-text resume** is an online document constructed without formatting in plain-text file format. You can use any character that's on your keyboard, including dashes, asterisks and plus signs, capital letters, and white space. But you can't use bullets, boldface, or underlined text. (For more on plain text, see Chapter 4.) This resume isn't attractive visually and should be used only when the system requires it.

>> The **hyperlinked** (or *linked*) resume is an online document that anyone can access easily by moving from one website to another. When used for resume transmission, you store a full-design resume on a website, and then, within a plain-text resume, embed a link that connects to it. This option is rarely provided for online job applications but might be used in networking when connecting someone to your online resume.

WEB HOSTING SITES

As part of your job search, consider finding an online home to park your full-design resume — either your personal website or a free or fee web hosting site. Plenty of websites enable you to post a full-design resume.

Some sites operate as paid hosting services and charge a low monthly rate (under $10 a month) for small personal websites you can use to host the link to your full-design resume and your professional portfolio, if you wish.

Others are free, but read the fine print.

Still other sites are free and mean it, but understandably encourage you to eventually upgrade to a modestly priced paid membership — such as Yola (www.yola.com), a service that gets rave reviews from experts and users alike.

When you need a hosting site for a multimedia resume, remember to choose one — such as VisualCV (www.visualcv.com) — that can accommodate images, charts, references, awards, and more.

Don't Chase Every Job

Are you part of the resume mob, applying for anything and everything that doesn't crawl? Two words: Stop it! From this moment on, let loose your online resume only when you have serious qualifications (such as you have four of the four "must have" qualifications in the job posting). What's in a selective distribution policy for you? Plenty:

» You don't waste your time, leaving more of it to thoughtfully respond to job postings for which your prospects are realistically bright.

» Your hopes aren't dashed for something that's not going to happen, causing you to suffer the black-hole blues.

» You don't blemish your image with recruiters, one of whom may someday shepherd you to a terrific job. Recruiters, whose income depends upon finding "perfect" candidates for specific positions, are likely to be annoyed if you send them generic resumes over and over.

As a swamped recruiter said: "When I'm looking for a chief financial officer and an industrial engineer applies, why should I spend time I don't have to personally respond?" He has a point.

Hit the Bull's-Eye with Your Resume

Most generic resumes are now goners (as I discuss in Chapter 9). Make it easy for employers to consider you for a specific job by matching your resume to the job description for each job you target.

If you submit your resume without knowing the particulars of an open job, you probably won't organize your information to match. Use the exact words the job description calls for. If the job says you must have "more than three years of experience," say precisely that; don't assume the applicant tracking system (ATS) software will figure it out from the dates. Never try to impress by overstating what you offer, exceeding the job requirements; if the job posting calls for five years' experience, for example, say you have five years' experience; don't say you have 22 years' experience. When you appear overqualified for a job, you will likely not get an interview because the company believes you are applying for anything and are not likely to stay in the position when the right fit for your experience becomes available.

In customizing your online resume, pay special attention to the requirements section (qualifications required) of the posting. Tailor and submit a different resume for each position you qualify for within the same company.

TIP

Give your database-dwelling resume new life every three days. Refreshing your resume is especially important on general job boards. Recruiters scour them all day long and rarely look back more than two days. Make a minor revision, such as deleting an insignificant word, typing it back in, and saving the change. This simple action lifts your resume to the top of the pile again.

WARNING

Never expect a passively posted resume to help you find a job. Footwork and networking are needed to get your great OnTarget resume into the right hands. (See Chapters 2 and 4 for more on this topic.)

Move Fast, Follow Guidelines

When you're hotly pursuing a job opening, timing is destiny. Jobs are flying off the shelves in today's economy. Back in the day, you may have been smart to wait a couple weeks to make your move after the first wave of candidates had passed through the resume pile. Not anymore. Those who apply first have an advantage: As soon as a prospective employer finds several promising people, interviewing begins.

REMEMBER

Pay attention to the date a position is posted because listings more than a few days old may already be filled. You can still apply, of course, but don't be surprised if you don't hear back because the job is no longer available.

Follow directions given in the job posting, even the tiresome tasks of cutting and pasting job applications and answering questionnaires.

TIP

You may be able to save time filling out online job applications with an automatic form filler. Most automatic form fillers are free or offer free trials. Plus, some search engines such as Chrome save much of your standard contact information, allowing you to select it and automatically paste it.

Neutralize Chilling Information

Use your email to skirt two knock-out punches that can cause a screener to fly over your resume:

>> **Location:** Employers resist the expense of relocation unless your talent is unavailable in their locale. Tell a true version of a story like this: Suppose you're in Montana and the job is in Atlanta. Say in your email that you went to school in the South (or vacationed there), love it, and, at your own expense, hope to return as soon as possible. You can also rent a post office box so you can receive mail locally and provide a local address.

>> **Money:** A job posting asks for your salary history or salary requirements; you fear you're a little rich for the company's budget but that as soon as they appreciate the value you bring, it won't be a problem. Say in your email that you look forward to disclosing the personal information at a job interview and ask whether you should bring copies of your W-2 forms. Don't be afraid to say that the salary is negotiable. For some people, quality of life trumps the salary amount.

Additionally, consider the cost of living where the job is posted. I had a client in New England who applied for a job on in a city in Florida with a dramatically lower cost of living. He put together a chart to show what his higher New England salary translated to in lower-cost Florida, and was a shoe-in.

Using enough of the right keywords on your resume gooses an ATS to rank you as a higher and better match for a specific job, putting you in the running for the interview list. (For more on ATS and other online screening potential employers use, see Chapter 4.)

Go Directly to the Hiring Manager

When your resume is stuck in a black hole, send another copy to the hiring manager — the decider. But how do you find the name? A quick-and-simple search is adequate for most jobs. At small companies, the decision-maker may be the head of your function; at larger companies, the decider may be a few notches down from the vice president of your function. Other easy-button tips include:

>> Call the company and ask.

>> Research the company's website, which usually displays leadership bios and main phone numbers; decode the formula for the decider's email address by looking at the company's press releases.

>> Try a web search for the company name plus the decider's function or likely title.

>> Research using LinkedIn, which can be a powerful and easy way to track down your target. If you need an email address after you identify someone, try Zoom Info (www.zoominfo.com).

- » Reach out to your networks on social media, such as Twitter, Facebook, and LinkedIn. Send word to all your connections that you're interested in the job and ask whether they can name that name.

- » Consider using fee services to reach hiring managers. LinkedIn offers both free accounts and fee accounts. Among the paid variety are premium accounts, which enable you to send messages straight to hiring managers and recruiters who aren't in your network.

- » If you're a college student or graduate, your alumni office or career center may provide alumni contacts at companies you're targeting.

- » Don't neglect local chapters of your industry's professional association for great networking, connections, and identifying your target. The inside lane is where success happens most.

Find an Inside Advocate

Assuming your uncle doesn't own the company where you want to work, your number-one best way to get hired is to find a valued company employee who is willing to act as a conduit to the hiring manager. Harried and hurried hiring managers may decide the best way to hire good people is to consider those recommended by satisfactory employees on the theory that birds of a feather flock together.

Your next best move: Find an inside advocate who can deliver your resume to the company's HR recruiters and say a few encouraging words about you.

For more than a decade, CareerXRoads recruiting consultants Mark Mehler and Gerry Crispin annually surveyed large, highly competitive, high-profile corporations on their sources of hire. Excluding inside promotions and transfers, the sourcing study always reveals that referrals win out, numbering more than a quarter of all external hires. More recent surveys from SilkRoad mimic the same findings.

When you're on the outside looking in and have exhausted all your resources, turn to social media and professional organizations, asking (or tweeting), "Who do you know who works at [fill in the blank]?"

Keep on Keepin' On

When you don't hear a word back, it may not be your fault. Your resume may have been lost in a black hole. Here are a few things that could have sent your resume into the employer's abyss:

>> The job was cancelled or frozen, denied budget approval, or never existed outside the hiring manager's wish list.

>> A job listing may have been contracted for 30 days, but the job was filled on day five and the recruiter simply forgot to take down the listing.

>> The job was a high-turnover gig and posted even when there was no immediate opening because managers like to have replacements standing by.

>> An employee in the job was on the firing line but received a last-minute reprieve. Unfortunately, no one told you.

>> Worst of all, a job may have been locked up for a friend or internal candidate but posted to prove the employer abides by equal opportunity employment practices.

Find It on Company Websites

Thousands of companies big and small have career sections on their websites. They don't necessarily advertise all their openings on pay-to-post job boards, meaning you may discover hidden jobs by reviewing company sites.

As you scan a company site, back up to its home page and click to press releases, annual reports, about us, and relevant general areas for any edge you can use to enhance your application when you move to the careers area.

TIP

Susan P. Joyce, the talent behind Job-Hunt.org, reminds you: "In addition to visiting the employer's website to see what the company does, check it out on Yahoo! Finance, BusinessWire, Hoovers, and similar digital compilers of information to discover the latest news about the employer and the employer's industry."

REMEMBER

When you reach the careers area and begin submitting your resume in earnest, remember to pay close attention to each requirement of the position and customize your resume to show that your qualifications are a bull's-eye for those requirements. (For more on resume customization, check out Chapter 9.)

Pay attention to specific instructions on each company's site, and don't be surprised if you're asked to take online pre-employment tests or respond to screening questions.

Use Job Boards with Caution

How many job boards are there in the world? The count is elastic from year to year, but estimates place the number operating globally as high as 50,000 and growing. Job boards have become the dominant information source for identifiable open jobs. Even newspapers, in addition to printed pages, now post their help-wanted ads online in job-board style.

But, here's the downside to all that information:

>> You and every other job seeker in the world know about job boards and are accessing them.

>> Job boards can suck up your time and make you feel like you're being productive when in reality you're only being busy.

>> Companies still prefer to hire candidates who were referred to them, even for their jobs posted online.

This combination can be a recipe for disaster as you push all your job search efforts into applying online for jobs. Those resumes then end up in a black hole. With a single job easily receiving more than 1,000 applicants, even very qualified candidates can slip through the cracks. And that number is conservative for companies such as Google, which regularly receives 20,000 resumes each week and has had record weeks where 70,000 resumes were received!

TIP

Use job boards as a springboard to identify companies who are hiring and to determine which ones are worth pursuing. While it can't hurt to submit your resume, avoid waiting and instead get active using other methods in this chapter to reach the decision-maker.

If you decide to go the job-board route, strategize with these:

>> Job search aggregator sites scour the Internet for job openings and list them all in one place. The top five are Indeed (www.indeed.com), SimplyHired (www.simplyhired.com), CareerJet (www.careerjet.com), LinkedIn Jobs (www.linkedin.com/jobs), and JobRobot (www.jobrobot.com).

>> CareerCast (www.careercast.com) is a job portal containing 1,001 job boards powered by Adicio in the United States and Canada. When you're trying to decide which jobs mesh with your talents, interests, and qualifications, check out the site's annual free *Jobs Rated Report* at www.careercast.com/jobs-rated.

WARNING

Some job seekers post anonymous resumes online to maintain their privacy and stay out of trouble with their current employer. An anonymous resume is stripped of the subject's name and contact information, and generic descriptions are substituted for company names in the experience section. Anonymous resumes are distributed by job sites or third-party employment services, but employers often consider them to be a waste of time and won't accept them. I recommend you think twice before deciding that this is your best approach.

Chapter **21**

Ten Tips for Choosing Professional Resume Help

I n addition to reading this book, how do you best come up with a resume that ushers you into prime interviewing territory? Should you hire a professional resume writer or go it alone?

There's plenty to be said in favor of hiring a professional writer, who not only is an expert in classic marketing principals but also is tuned into the brave new world of job search — from swirling social media to racing-ahead technology.

Professionally crafted resumes not only boost your confidence but actually make money for you by shortening your job search — for example, when you're searching for a $50,000-a-year job, each week of unemployment costs you about $950 in lost pay. By working with a certified professional, you can dramatically reduce the time you spend unemployed.

REMEMBER

Organize your own material to present to the professional writer just as you organize your taxes to hand over to an accountant. Organizing your information primes your mind for job interviews. But don't be intimidated because a qualified professional will guide you toward what is needed.

In an age of personalization — personal financial advisers, personal trainers, personal career coaches — why not a personal resume pro? I have witnessed dramatic, life-changing results produced by the efforts of talented professional resume writers. Prime candidates who could benefit from using a resume service are first-time resume writers, people in a competitive professional or managerial job market, people with a checkerboard history, people who haven't thought about resumes in years, people who are shy and have trouble selling themselves, and anyone who takes what they do for granted. Frankly, if resume writing isn't your full-time job, you could benefit by working with a professional resume writer. Follow the tips in this chapter to avoid hacks and select a resume pro wisely. (And for a list of recommended resume services, flip to the appendix.)

Choose a Resume Writing Service, Not a Clerical Service

Clerical services are word processors and typists. If all you needed were someone to format what you have already written, then this would be it.

But most people need much more: identifying keywords for your target position; describing your unique selling proposition (USP) and bottom line value; capitalizing on the challenges you faced, actions you took, and results you attained; determining how to overcome little glitches such as layoffs and job gaps; ensuring your resume content is Applicant Tracking System (ATS) compatible; and even figuring out how to make volunteer leadership relevant.

All these factors require someone who specializes in resume writing — not in typing. Truly talented resume professionals make it their business to know what it takes to sell you to the various audiences who will review your resume. They take over the otherwise daunting tasks of uniquely positioning your experience and expertise for your target and making sure your resume puts you in a positive and authentic light that checks all the right boxes.

Zero in on Certified Professionals

Chances are if you request a resume writer referral from friends and colleagues, you'll be met with quizzical looks. One reason that professional resume writers can provide a gold standard in job seeker marketing is because they are still a hidden gem for many.

Despite the lack of recognition, professional resume writing is a serious industry with training, certification, and continuing education requirements. Find a resume writer who holds a certification from a reputable organization that requires continuing education and champions adherence to new trends. These qualifications are critical to making your investment worthwhile.

The best organization today is Career Directors International (CDI), which offers a variety of resume certifications. Each certification requires writing at the highest standards and maintaining continuing education units. When you visit its website, you can find a job seekers portal called Find a Career Pro (www.careerdirectors.com/find-a-career-professional/), which allows you to search for a resume writer and/or career coach to assist you. Here you can also find instructions on how to carefully select your service provider.

Full disclosure: I personally founded CDI after 20 years of success as a resume writer and career coach. My accolades included numerous resume-writing and job-placement awards, publication in more than 15 resume compendiums, resume expert for 54 national professional associations, and a documented success rate of clients landing new and better positions in just a few months. Fourteen years ago I recognized the need to create a resource for resume writers where the focus was on what works today and how can we prepare for tomorrow's changes. Today I work with resume writers, not job seekers, to ensure that CDI meets its goals through its training, certifications, industry surveys, resume competitions, and educational resources for career professionals. That way, the tools offered to job seekers and the skills of our member writers remain top notch.

WARNING

Not all resume writers or the certifications they earn are created equal. Be careful not to be drawn in by slick resume writer websites that promise a lot but give you no idea whom you'll be working with or what qualifications they currently hold.

Further, just because a writer says she's certified, do your homework. Visit the granting agency's website to make sure the person you're considering working with is listed. Then, check to see whether that organization is keeping up with resume trends. Some key examples include that they: require continuing education to maintain the credential, are pioneering trends in the industry by publishing reports, and are maintaining a value-added job seeker blog or related educational resource that shows their modern approach. At the very least, you want someone with continuing education requirements, not someone who earned a certification 20 years ago and has not stayed up-to-date.

Request a Free Initial Consultation

Request a free, brief consultation, which will be handled in person, on the phone, or by online video chat. Speak not to the boss or a sales representative, but to the writer. The same firm can have good and poor writers.

Expect an initial consultation to involve many questions about you — your prior career and current goals — and how the resume writer can help. If you have specific challenges or concerns, voice them. If the resume writer doesn't know how to answer them, you should probably keep looking.

Trust your intuition. Do you feel comfortable with the individual after he or she has shown knowledge about your industry and handling your challenges? Do the writer's resume samples look like the ones in Part 4, giving you confidence that the writer is on point with current trends? If your answers are "yes" and that individual has a verifiable certification with continuing education requirements, chances are you have found a good match.

REMEMBER

A consultation is not a DIY conversation where you are told step by step what is wrong with your resume and how to change it. This session is exploratory in nature to determine what you need and how the writer can help.

Evaluate the Writer's Resume Samples

In this book, I share a variety of professional resume samples with you (Chapters 15 through 18 are chock full of 'em!). You are now an educated job seeker who knows what to look for in a resume professional. When shopping around on websites, look for resume samples and expect them to be this good. If you find samples that use weak words, tell but don't sell, are mostly empty or far too full of content, and aren't playing up keywords, challenges, actions, and results — run!

Expect the samples to give you a strong indication of what a resume writer's work looks like today. If there are no samples, then you have no way of identifying that writer's level of talent. While someone could be an excellent resume writer, not having work samples is cause for a deeper look or a second thought. You need someone who can walk the talk, and samples are another way to gauge that effectively.

Ask for References

Some resume writers have hard-hitting testimonials that include all or partial elements of a client's name and even the jobs they landed. But others serve up fluff. In either case, you're going by what the resume professional lists on his or her website. Just as you probably wouldn't invest a chunk of change in something you bought online without first reading all the online reviews posted by third parties, neither should you jump to buy resume-writing services from someone based on what you see on the writer's website.

You can check LinkedIn and even Facebook to see whether they have third-party recommendations (search by company name and writer's name). Those recommendations should indicate tangible results (such as how quickly interviews and jobs were landed), not simply how much better a resume looked or how much more confident the candidate felt.

You can also ask for references to contact. Most resume writers can give you a short list of satisfied clients who have agreed to act as a reference.

REMEMBER

Don't expect more than a handful of references to contact. Most job seekers wish to remain anonymous, so a short reference list is common, no matter how talented the resume professional.

Watch Out for an Overuse of Forms

Although many professional resume writers have you fill out a detailed form at some point in the process, a form is rarely the best or only way for someone to gather all the needed information to write your resume. The resume professional should interview you either before or after you fill out the form to make sure all your unique experiences, strengths, and accomplishments have been uncovered.

Identify Generalists and Specialists

In resume writing, you may run into generalists and specialists. For instance, if your career is in information technology, then you want to make certain that the professional you select has knowledge and experience working with people in your field. Occasionally, you'll find someone who has worked in your profession and is now a resume writer, but it is more the exception than the rule. Typically, a specialist is simply someone who prefers to work with job seekers in certain niche professions.

Conversely, don't be afraid of generalists. Generalists with all the right bells and whistles (such as awards, certifications, concrete testimonials, and even degrees in technical writing) are also skilled at extracting information, performing any necessary research, identifying keywords, and marketing you on paper through both powerful wording and dynamic layout. Experienced generalists will have worked with job seekers in multiple fields and at multiple levels, which gives them flexibility and adaptability to meet any challenges.

REMEMBER

A resume professional doesn't have to specialize in your field to be able to provide you with the expertise you need. Be sure to ask whether the professional has experience in your field, look for samples on his website that show a familiarity, and watch what he says to gain a sense of his comfort zone with your field. Many professionals are adept at interviewing and researching, so they do not need to specialize in order to provide you with superior service.

Look for a Fair Price

Prices vary by locale and depend on a number of factors, but expect to pay between $300 and $1,500 for most resumes. Executive resumes often range between $750 and $3,000. You pay the most in these situations:

» **Heavy time investment:** The professional must spend many hours to document your value, such as when you're changing careers.

» **Killer job market:** Hoards of people want the job you want, and the professional has the expertise to make you stand out from the crowd.

» **Challenging problem:** When you have a background of job hopping, employment gaps, and other kinds of issues discussed in Chapter 14, the professional has to have the expertise to present your qualifications in a favorable light.

» **Customizing resumes:** If you're using a two-page resume, for example, you can probably pay for a core resume and customize only the first page for each different job, retaining the second page across your search. You pay extra for a few customizations of your core resume. For more on core resumes, visit Chapter 8.

» **Document packages:** Many job seekers now understand that cover letters, online profiles, accomplishment sheets, follow-up letters, and other career marketing documents are the nuts and bolts of a 21st-century job search and turn to professional resume writers for assistance with a comprehensive solution. (For more details about these documents, check out the book *Job Search Letters For Dummies* [Wiley] by Joyce Lain Kennedy.)

Take Aim

Customize! For maximum impact, you need to target each resume you send out to a specific employer or career field. Look for a resume professional who understands this concept. You need a resume that has "you" written all over it — *your* theme, *your* focus, and *your* measurable achievements — all matched to a career field you want. Skip over those who sell the same cookie-cutter resume over and over or ask you to choose the template you like most.

TIP

Avoid resume pros who offer assembly-line presentations, virtually indistin-guishable from thousands of others created by the service. Ignore resume pros who plug your information into a fill-in-the-blanks standard form, garnished with prefab statements.

Know That a Cheap Resume Is No Bargain

Appreciate the hidden costs of a poor resume: A hack job can cost you good job interviews and thus good jobs.

When the finished product is in your hands, you should be able to say:

» This is an OnTarget resume. It shows that my qualifications are a great match for the job I want.

» This resume suggests that I offer the employer a good return on investment by showing how I stand out from equally qualified applicants and how I can make or save the company more money than I cost.

» I like reading my resume; it won't put the recruiter to sleep.

Chapter **22**

Your Ten-Point Resume Checklist

Before going public with your resume, read through it a final time with the following checklist in mind. Give yourself 10 points for each item only when your resume meets that OnTarget standard. If you don't get a score of 100, go back and try again.

Qualifications

You've customized your resume by matching your qualifications (skills, education, accomplishments, and so on) with the specific requirements of a job, or by matching your qualifications with the expected qualifications in a career field. (Chapter 9 discusses the customizing requirement and why it's so important.)

Image and Focus

You don't say the equivalent of, "I thought you might have an opening I could fill," but state what you want to do for an employer and why you're the most qualified to do it. You consider your resume's overall impression — its look and feel. Your resume has a unifying theme: You present yourself as focused, not merely desperate to accept any job. (Refresh your recall of focus in Chapter 9 and of image in Chapter 11.)

Format and Style

You select the best format for your situation. For example, *reverse chronological* when staying in the same field, or *chrono-functional* or *hybrid* when changing fields. (Chapter 6 covers formats.)

RESUME POWER

In this age of constant change and information — when a seemingly endless stream of platforms for communication engulfs us — resumes endure.

Despite this constant change, resumes remain the most important personal power tool in job-finding because the medium can be converted to meet the needs of any platform, whether e-reader, social media profile, web portfolio, or good old stamp-and-envelope printed resume in the mail.

The resume — regardless of its final form — conveys what is needed to sell you and shows employers that your qualifications meet their requirements.

Regardless of what you might hear or read, the resume isn't going away anytime soon. If you want to get hired, you have to adapt to ongoing changes in how information is compiled and delivered, and sell yourself, your experience, and your accomplishments in some resume-style document or profile.

Employers want your message to put them in a comfort zone where they're assured that you'll make more money for them, deliver greater benefits to them, or save them more time and treasure than it costs to hire you.

That's the strategic message you must deliver in each resume. Anything less is a dangerous roll of the dice. Get OnTarget with your resume and your job search strategy, and the job you desire won't be far off.

Accomplishments and Skills

You directly relate your skills to the skills and competencies needed for the job. You cite at least one accomplishment for each skill or competency. You measure any claim you can by using numbers, percentages, or dollar amounts. (Turn to Chapter 8 for measurement tips.) You highlight results, not just a list of duties and responsibilities. Always use the CAR formula: state the *challenge* you faced, relay the *action* you took, and show your *results*.

Language and Expressions

You make the most of your word choices. You use adequate keywords (nouns) to make your resume searchable by software. You use action verbs to put vitality in your resume for human eyes. You eliminate words that don't directly support your bid for the job you want, as well as such meaningless words and phrases as "References available." You use industry jargon where appropriate, but you translate acronyms, technical jargon, or military lingo into easy-to-understand English. (Chapter 10 reviews word usage.)

Content and Omissions

Your content supports your goal. You create a funnel effect in your resume by starting with the objective header statement, moving into the summary, supporting this with keywords, and proving it all with experience. That is, you draw the prospective employers down into your resume by grabbing and keeping their interest.

You list education before experience only if you're a new graduate with virtually no experience, or if your target job is related more to education and training than experience. You don't list personal information that isn't related to the job you seek, such as marital status, number of children, or height. (For a refresher on content, see Chapter 7.)

Length and Common Sense

You use a length that makes sense for the amount of information you're presenting. Even though today's resumes are shorter and crisper (because most are crafted for digital distribution), certain guidelines remain. You limit your resume to one page if you are lightly experienced, two pages if you are extremely experienced, and three pages only if you are an executive or consultant. Additionally, your resume can stretch even longer when it's a professional resume or a curriculum vitae.

TIP

When you find you have an unusually long list of supporting information, such as articles you have published, presentations you have given, or relevant training you have completed, it's acceptable to have a third-page addendum. Set it up with your contact information at the top just like your resume and title it *Addendum* in the same font size as the headers on your resume. Now you have an interchangeable third page that you can provide as it's relevant.

REMEMBER

Don't jam-pack a jumble of text on one page, making your resume way too difficult to read and way too easy to ignore. Instead, spend some extra time to reword what you have to say and pare down to what matters most to get you the job interview.

Social Media and Other New Things

You tailored a message showing your value to an employer. Consider this criterion when you offer your resume on LinkedIn, Facebook, Twitter, other social media sites, or on teeny-weeny mobile screens. Although seasoned workplace veterans come across as with it and youthful by using the new tools, the fact that you're up-to-date alone isn't enough to get you hired. (If you didn't use one of the new platforms to convey your resume, count this criterion as a free throw and give yourself 10 points by doing so now.)

Sticky Points and Sugarcoating

You thoughtfully handle all problem areas, such as grouping or removing irrelevant, long-ago, part-time, and temporary jobs. You account for all the gaps in the time frame of your resume. You scour your resume for possible hidden negatives and eliminate them as described in Chapter 14.

Proofreading and More Proofreading

Your resume contains no typos, no grammar disasters — no errors of any kind. You not only use your computer's spell checker, but you double- and triple-check your resume. You ask others to carefully read it. Typos are hot buttons to many employers — two goofs and you're gone.

Appendix

Directory of Resume Writers

Many professional resume writers contributed samples and information to this book in the form of resume samples (Chapters 15–18), ATS resumes (Chapter 4), LinkedIn profile samples and advice (Chapter 2), step-by-step creative resume strategies (Chapter 12), and military resume instructions (Chapter 13).

If you're stumped on how to proceed with your resume or feeling stuck on getting started, you may want to contact one of the professionals listed in this appendix to help you put your resume together.

This appendix includes each contributor's contact information. If an arrow (↑) appears by the author's name, it means that person has earned a resume writing certification from Career Directors International (CDI). If a star (*) appears, he or she has won a resume-writing award from CDI. If a pound sign (#) appears, it means the individual's work should be in here but I could only include so many resumes, no matter how fantastic they are!

Niya Allen-Vatel
Career Global
Bronx, New York
Phone: (888) 507-8247
Email: info@careerglobal.co
https://careerglobal.co/

Meg Applegate
Hinge Resume Collaborative
Indianapolis, Indiana
Phone: (317) 643-4802
Email: hingeresume@gmail.com
www.hingeresume.com

Kimberly Robb Baker *
This Little Brand
Chicago, Illinois
Phone: (312) 566-8387
Email: kim@thislittlebrand.com
http://thislittlebrand.com/

Susan Barens
Golden Ratio Ltd.
Fort Mill, South Carolina
Phone: (440) 610-4361
Email: helpmeachieve@golden
ratiocoaching.com
www.goldenratiocoaching.com

Jacqui Barrett-Poindexter ↑
Career Trend
Lake Texoma, Texas
Phone: (903) 523-5952
Email: jacqui@careertrend.net
www.careertrend.net

Karen Bartell ↑
Best-In-Class Resumes
Massapequa Park, New York
Phone: (631) 704-3220
Email: karen@bestclassresumes.com
www.bestclassresumes.com

Laurie Berenson ↑
Sterling Career Concepts, LLC
Franklin Lakes, New Jersey
Phone: (201) 573-8282
Email: laurie@sterlingcareer
concepts.com
www.SterlingCareerConcepts.com

Brenda Bernstein ↑ *
The Essay Expert, LLC
New York, New York
Phone: 718-390-6696
Email: BrendaB@TheEssayExpert.com
www.TheEssayExpert.com

Skye Berry-Burke ↑*
Skye Is The Limit Resume and Career
Solutions
Ontario, Canada
Phone: (705) 206-9988
Email: info@skyeisthelimit.ca
www.skyeisthelimit.ca

Mary Elizabeth Bradford ↑*
Global C-Suite Resume Writer
Phone: (830) 331-9398
Email: maryelizabeth@maryelizabeth
bradford.com
www.maryelizabethbradford.com/

Bridget (Weide) Brooks
Resume Writers' Digest /
BeAResumeWriter.com
Omaha, Nebraska
Phone: (402) 393-4600
Email: bb@bearesumewriter.com
www.bearesumewriter.com

Phaedra Brotherton
Resumes and Career Strategies
Arlington, Virginia
Phone: (703) 920-5322
Email: info@resumesandcareer
strategies.com
www.resumesandcareerstrategies.
com/

Donald Burns *
Executive Promotions, LLC
New York, New York
Phone: (917) 519-0487
Email: donaldburns1@gmail.com
www.ExecutivePromotionsLLC.com

Erin Cambier
Superior Resume & Career Services
Sioux Falls, South Dakota
Phone: (605) 275-3736
Email: erin@superiorresume.com
www.superiorresume.com

Maria Caraballo ↑*
Career Branding Inc.
Juncos, Puerto Rico
Phone: (787) 955-5704
Email: maria@cbincpr.com
http://careerbrandinginc.com/

Paula Christensen
Strategic Career Coaches
Green Bay, Wisconsin
Phone: (920) 264-0806
Email: paula@strategiccareer
coaches.com
www.strategiccareercoaches.com/

Marlene Cole ↑*
Pilbara Resumes / New Generation
Careers
South Australia, Australia
Phone: +61 4 3412 2659
Email: marlene@newgencareers.com
www.newgencareers.com

Sarah Cronin ↑
Sarah Cronin Consulting
Queensland, Australia
Phone: +61 7 5525 7587
Email: info@sarahcronin.com.au
www.sarahcronin.com.au

Darlene M. Dassy ↑*
Dynamic Resume Solutions
Sinking Spring, Pennsylvania
Phone: (610) 678-0147
Email: darlene@dynamicresume
solutions.com
www.dynamicresumesolutions.com

Jeri Hird Dutcher *
Workwrite
Moorhead, Minnesota
Phone: (218) 791-4045
Email: Jerihd@gmail.com
www.WorkwriteResumes.com

Ken Docherty ↑*
Docherty Career Management, Inc.
British Columbia, Canada
Email: ken@dochertycareer
management.com
www.DochertyCareerManagement.com

Kelly Donovan
Kelly Donovan & Associates
Lake Elsinore, California
Phone: (909) 235-6383
Email: kelly@kellydonovan.com
www.kellydonovan.com

Matthew Dupee
Rad4Career
Vero Beach, Florida
Phone: (772) 217-9639
Email: mjdupee@outlook.com
www.rad4career.com/

Maureen Farmer ↑
Word Right Career and HR Consulting Inc.
Nova Scotia, Canada
Phone: (902) 466-6661
Email: maureen@wordrightcareer.com
https.wordrightcareer.com

Jennifer Fishberg
Career Karma Resume Development &
Career Services
Highland Park, New Jersey
Phone: (732) 421-2554
Email: info@careerkarma.net
www.careerkarma.net

Cliff Flamer *
BrightSide Resumes
California, United States
Phone: (510) 444-1724
Email: info@brightsideresumes.com
https://brightsideresumes.com/

Anne Galloway ↑
power-to-change
Noord Holland, Netherlands
Phone: 31615561377
Email: anne@power-to-change.eu
http://www.power-to-change.eu/

Louise Garver ↑
Career Directions Intl, LLC
Beavercreek, Ohio
Phone: (937) 429-1332
Email: louise@careerdirections
llc.com
https://careerdirectionsllc.com/

Jill R. Grindle
Pinnacle Resumes, LLC
Bourne, Massachusetts
Phone: (774) 302-4229
Email: jill@pinnacleresumes.com
www.pinnacleresumes.com

Susan Guarneri ↑*
Guarneri Associates
Rhinelander, Wisconsin
Phone: (715) 362-9120
Email: Susan@AssessmentGoddess.com
www.AssessmentGoddess.com

Tiffany Hardy ↑*
Top1Resumes
Phoenix, Arizona
Phone: (480) 848-6268
Email: tiffanyhardy@top1resumes.com
https://www.top1resumes.com

Laura Hartnell ↑
Laura Hartnell Career Transition Services
Ontario, Canada
Phone: (519) 420-8447
Email: laura@laurahartnell.ca
https://www.laurahartnell.ca/

Gayle Howard ↑*
Top Margin Executive Resumes
Melbourne, Australia
Phone: +613 9690 9499
Email: getinterviews@topmargin.com
www.topmargin.com

Sandra Ingemansen ↑*
Resume Strategies
Chicago, Illinois
Phone: (312) 212-3761
Email: sandra@resume-strategies.com
www.resume-strategies.com

Billie P. Jordan ↑
Advantage Resumes & Career Services
Maysville, North Carolina
Phone: (910) 743-3641
Email: bjordan1@ec.rr.com
www.AdvantageResumes4you.com

Gillian Kelly ↑*
Outplacement Australia
Brisbane, Australia
Email: info@outplacementaustralia.com.au
www.outplacementaustralia.com.au

Erin Kennedy ↑*
Professional Resume Services, Inc.
Lapeer, Michigan
Phone: (877) 970-7767
Email: erin@professionalresume
services.com
www.professionalresume
services.com

Peter Lavelle
Rez Builder Resume and Job Service
Stillwater, Minnesota
Phone: (651) 769-4246
Email: peter@rez-builder.com
www.rez-builder.com/

Michelle Lopez ↑*
Brand YOU Studio
Western Australia, Australia
Phone: +61 8 9274 1257
Email: michelle@brandyoustudio.
com.au
www.brandyoustudio.com.au

Natalie MacLellan ↑
Best Foot Forward
Ontario, Canada
Phone: (855) 422-8494
Email: natalie@bestfootforward.co
https://www.bestfootforward.co

Victoria McLean *
City CV
London, England
Phone: +44 207 100 6656
Email: victoria@citycv.co.uk
www.citycv.co.uk

Jennifer Miller ↑*
Professional Edge Resumes
Alberta, Canada
Phone: (403) 860-1381
Email: info@professionaledge
resumes.com
http://professionaledgeresumes.
com/

Judith Monaco
Monaco Writing & Consulting Services, LLC
Savannah, Georgia
Phone: (912) 999-6279
Email: judithmonaco@comcast.net
www.monacowriting.com/

Zakiyyah Mussallihullah
Andy Thomas Careers Now
Laurel, Maryland
Phone: (704) 280-8420
Email: zakiyyah@andythomas
careersnow.com
http://andythomascareersnow.com/

Sari Neudorf
SDN Consulting
St. Louis, Missouri
Phone: (314) 283-6976
Email: sari@sdnconsulting.biz
http://www.sdconsulting.biz/

Tyrone Norwood ↑
Norwood Consulting Group
Birmingham, Michigan
Phone: (248) 905-1624
Email: info@norwoodconsulting.org
www.norwoodconsulting.org

Lisa G. Parker ↑
Parker-CPRW
Claxton, Georgia
Phone: (888) 601-0595
Email: msparker@parkercprw.com
https://parkercprw.com/

Marie Plett *
Aspirations Career Services, Inc.
Cincinnati, Ohio
Phone: 317-600-7727
Email: marie.plett@gmail.com
http://www.aspirationsresume.com/

Rachel Vander Pol *
RVP Career Services
San Diego, California
Phone: (760) 270-0275
Email: rachel@rvpcareerservices.com
www.rvpcareerservices.com/

Barb Poole ↑*
Hire Imaging LLC
Lafayette, COPhone: (320) 253-0975
Email: barb@hireimaging.com
www.hireimaging.com

Audrey Prenzel ↑*
Audrey Prenzel Career Transition Services
Ontario, Canada
Phone: (613) 391-7029
Email: audrey@audreyprenzel.com
www.audreyprenzel.com

Annette Richmond ↑
career-intelligence Resume Writing &
Career Services
Norwalk, Connecticut
Phone: (203) 807-4360
Email: annette@careerintelligene
resumewriting.com
http://careerintelligence
resumewriting.com/

Michelle A. Riklan *
Riklan Resources
Marlboro, New Jersey
Phone: (800) 540-3609
Email: michelle@riklanresources.com
www.riklanresources.com

Eve Ruth ↑*
Compelling Resumes
Seattle, Washington
Email: info@compellingresumes.com
www.compellingresumes.com/

Barbara Safani ↑*
Career Solvers
New York, New York
Phone: (347) 480-1827
Email: info@careersolvers.com
https://www.careersolvers.com/

Posey Salem ↑
Radiant Resume Career Services
Pittsburgh, Pennsylvania
Phone: (412) 628-8104
Email: ARadiantResume@gmail.com
www.RadiantResumeServices.com

Robin Schlinger ↑*
Robin's Resumes
Atlanta, Georgia
Phone: (404) 875-2688
Email: robin@robinresumes.com
https://robinresumes.com

Cheryl Lynch Simpson ↑*
Executive Resume Rescue
Westerville, Ohio
Phone: (614) 891-9043
Email: info@executiveresume
rescue.com
http://executiveresumerescue.com/

Laura Smith-Proulx *
An Expert Resume
Arvada, Colorado
Phone: (303) 364-4411
Email: laura@anexpertresume.com
http://anexpertresume.com/

Michelle Swanson ↑
Edwardsville, Illinois
Phone: (618) 741-0454
Email: michelle@michelleswanson.com
www.michelleswanson.com

Denise Taylor
Amazing People
Tewkesbury, United Kingdom
Phone: +44 0 7931 303367
Email: denise@amazingpeople.co.uk
www.amazingpeople.co.uk

Adrienne Tom ↑*
Career Impressions
Alberta, Canada
Phone: (888) 781-3056
Email: adrienne@career
impressions.ca
www.CareerImpressions.ca

Rosa Vargas ↑*
Career Steering
Orlando, Florida
Phone: (321) 704-7209
Email: rosamrw@gmail.com
https://careersteering.com/

Kara Varner ↑
A Platinum Resume
Colorado Springs, Colorado
Phone: (719) 200-4200
Email: aplatinumresume@yahoo.com
www.aplatinumresume.com

Jeanette Walton ↑
Walton's Words
Victoria, Australia
Phone: +61 414 787 924
Email: jeanette@waltonswords.com.au
www.waltonswords.com.au

Natalie Winzer ↑
iHire, LLC
Frederick, Maryland
Phone: (877) 798-4854 x 322
Email: natalie.winzer@ihire.com
www.ihire.com

Lucie Yeomans
Agave Communications LLC/Your
Career Ally
San Tan Valley, Arizona
Phone: (480) 235-2354
Email: lucie@yourcareerally.com
www.yourcareerally.com

Index

by experience and age, 271–305

by industry and career field, 231–270

job descriptions, 139

necessity of, 133–134

one-size-fits-all resume, 134–136

for special circumstances, 307–349

using, 10

using crossover language, 139–142

persuasion, wow words for, 148

phone number, 95

photos, for social media profiles, 25

pigeonholed, 24

Pinterest, 56

Pipl (website), 65

plain-text resumes, 44–47, 404

planning case studies, 54

Plett, Marie (resume writer), 180, 184, 359–360, 429

poison words, 160–161

Pol, Rachel Vander (resume writer), 370–371, 429

political correctness, 198

Poole, Barb (resume writer), 429

portfolios, 90–91

posting

about growth experiences, 71

kudos on social media, 70

tips, 33

power summary. *See* summary section (resume)

pre-employment screening, 52

Prenzel, Audrey (resume writer), 429

prescreening, 52

presentation exercises, 54

presentations

compiling, 124

gathering, 116

President/CEO, creative resume example for, 359–360

printed resumes, 175–176

privacy, resume blasting services and, 57–58

Privacy Rights Clearinghouse (website), 111

Professional Experience, as a recommended header, 48

professional help, 413–419

Program Manager of Non-Profit, OnTarget resume for, 256–257

programs (conference), finding keywords in, 159

projects, gathering data on, 116

promotions, announcing, 70

pronouns, first-person, 161

proofreading, on resume checklist, 424

Property Manager, OnTarget resume for, 267–268

publications

compiling, 124

gathering, 116

purchasing domain names, 14

Q

qualifications, on resume checklist, 421

R

Radiologic Technologist, OnTarget resume for, 236

Really Simple Syndication (RSS), 38–39, 56–57

recommendations, gathering, 116

recruiters

contingency, 59–60

facilitating (*See* keywords)

overexposure to, 58–59

retained, 59–60

reference refresher, generic resumes for, 137

references

asking for from resume writers, 417

providing, 113

'References available upon request,' 160

Regional Account Manager, creative resume example for, 387–388

Registered Nurse, OnTarget resume for, 241–242

reliability, as a strength for seasoned workers, 195

Remember icon, 3

Repetitive Positions in News Anchor Role, OnTarget resume for, 331

Repetitive Positions in Wellsite Management, OnTarget resume for, 314–315

research field, wow words for, 151–152